Dear Jones,

I'm not saying good-Bye because I'll definitely be calling you and hopefully we'll get together for a few evening at the theatre or something.

I use this book quite a lot in my work, hope you find it useful in yours. It's a reminder of our Shakespeare days together.

On A more serious note, your ways and work have touched us all here and I know our loss will be Kennedy's gain.

My Best to you on your new venture.

Love,
Marion
June, 1991

Onstage and Offstage Worlds in Shakespeare's Plays

Onstage and Offstage Worlds in Shakespeare's Plays

Anthony Brennan

R

Routledge
London and New York

First published 1989
by Routledge
11 New Fetter Lane, London EC4P 4EE
29 West 35th Street, New York, NY 10001

Typeset by Mayhew Typesetting, Bristol
Printed in Great Britain
by T.J. Press (Padstow) Ltd, Padstow, Cornwall

British Library Cataloguing in Publication Data

Brennan, Anthony, *1938—*
Onstage and Offstage worlds in Shakespeare's plays
1. Drama in English. Shakespeare, William, 1564–1616 – Critical studies
I. Title
822.3'3
ISBN 0-415-00774-7

Library of Congress Cataloging in Publication Data

Brennan, Anthony.
Onstage/offstage worlds in Shakespeare's plays.
Includes index.
1. Shakespeare, William, 1564–1616 — Technique.
2. Reporters and reporting in literature. 3. Messengers in literature.
4. Battles in literature. 5. Offstage action (Drama) I. Title.
PR2997.R4B7 1989   822.3'3   88-32528
ISBN 0-415-00774-7

Contents

Contents

Preface

This study is a development of some of the ideas I touched on in an earlier book, *Shakespeare's Dramatic Structures*. Here, as there, I am indebted to a long line of critics who have centred their interest on the architectonic aspect of the plays. Among the many writers who have influenced my work are Stephen Booth, Nevil Coghill, H. T. Price, Bernard Beckerman, David Bevington, Muriel Bradbrook, Alan Dessen, Madeleine Doran, Andrew Gurr, Alfred Harbage, Joan Hartwig, James Hirsh, Jean Howard, Michael Goldman, Granville-Barker, Emrys Jones, Maynard Mack, William Matchett, Philip McGuire, Frank Kermode, Marco Mincoff, Norman Rabkin, Mark Rose, and J. L. Styan. There are inevitably many others who have helped to shape my approach over the years. I have not concentrated in this study on the specific technical effects Shakespeare uses to give evidence of his offstage world. That skill has already been thoroughly documented by Francis Ann Shirley in *Shakespeare's Use of Off-Stage Sounds*. I owe a particular debt of gratitude to Francis Berry's book *The Shakespeare Inset*. I have not adopted Berry's categories nor focused on the 'inset' passages he examines, but I acknowledge his insightful and pioneering work in looking at some of the techniques I am analysing here.

The meanings of many of the scenes and characters with which I am dealing have been analysed by critics and I am not proposing radical departures from many of their accounts. What I do hope I am contributing is some information about how these familiar effects are created by an exploration of the techniques that Shakespeare regularly developed to shape the responses of an audience. I am pursuing the details of how Shakespeare structures his scenes, the artistic choices he makes, and how he distributes his material between onstage and offstage events. Critics often complain testily about such an approach because the emphasis on the plotting and logistics of the plays may seem to undervalue the fact that they are made with words. I am willing to yield to no one in my admiration for Shakespeare's poetic skills, but there is certainly no shortage of analyses which elucidate their extraordinary power. I am concerned here with the techniques which ensure that those aspects of Shakespeare's art achieve their maximum effect. They have their effect to some degree because of the ordering of the scenes and the way the characters are developed by alternations between what we see and what we hear about them. It does not seem to me that we can ignore such skills because they have not appeared so often and so well-developed in drama that they can be taken as routine aspects of play-making.

I have used the text of the Pelican Shakespeare, and the statistical data presented are specific to it. I am aware, of course, that in the Quartos and the Folio text some of the details I am analysing, entrances and exits, stage directions, are missing and have been added by later editors. Modern editions still vary in length depending on what elements from the various texts of Shakespeare's day are admitted. The material I am using is, for the most part, standard in modern editions. Line-counts vary from one edition to another, especially because of the way the prose in the plays is set up. My arguments are concerned particularly with proportions, and those figures are, I believe, broadly representative of many editions. I should point out, however, that the figures I have presented vary even from those given in a table of data from the Complete Pelican Shakespeare. The table is riddled with errors which may result from the work of several researchers operating on different basic principles, some of them perhaps, in computing the length of a role, counting each half-line as a full line and some counting it, as I do, only as a half-line. Less accessible to explanation are the occasions when the scenes or the total lines in a play are incorrectly counted. The figures I present are as accurate as mind-numbing checking and rechecking can make them. I persisted because it is a basic assumption of my approach that one of the chief means the playwright uses in shaping the responses of an audience is the control of the proportions of the various elements he weaves together. It is simply one way of registering what this study focuses on – the mingled yarn of the plays.

My introduction to theatre began with the 300 or so productions I attended, in my teenage years, of a local weekly repertory company in England. My interest in the offstage world began to develop as I tried to envisage what it was like in the wings when the nine-member company, augmented by a few local 'hired men', mounted with the use of extensive doubling their bi-annual productions of a Shakespeare play. My curiosity about the offstage chaos of costume changes was assuaged a little by a field report of a schoolmate of mine performing the Player-Queen in their production of *Hamlet*. Tom Stoppard's curiosity about the offstage life of the characters at Elsinore led him, of course, to produce a full-length play about them. My own interest in the offstage life of the characters, as opposed to that of the actors, developed when, aged 17, I performed the role of Macbeth. Stumbling back from the offstage chamber where I had left Duncan's 'silver skin laced with his golden blood', I felt a little of the strange power of evoking for an audience the horror of a climactic action it had not directly witnessed. A few years later, at the ripe age of 23, I attempted to present the role of the 69-year-old Krapp in Beckett's play and had to cope with its Chinese-box structure of offstage worlds. In his annual birthday message Krapp is recording events which have occurred mostly outside the room in which the audience observes him. When he plays back the tape of the 39-year-old Krapp (who incidentally also refers to the jabberings on the tape of his 27-year-old self) the audience has to track back 30 (and 42) years to this same room, which is one recession into the offstage, when the original recording was made. The actor of Krapp must make the audience travel in imagination outside the room through the various incidents being recalled in memory, such as the tryst in the punt to which he obsessively returns, in the regress to other selves in other places. Much of the onstage action the audience observes is mine – the banana routine, the excursions into the shadows for drink, the working of the tape machine which sparks irritated imprecations in response to his past selves. Krapp onstage is merely the residue of the dwindling offstage life the audience must create in imagination. My interest in such worlds has continued in acting and directing drama among university groups. When one is trying to elicit a response from an audience, it is useful to consider some of the issues I am dealing with here in order to decode the techniques behind the dynamic structure of a play. Directors search within the rhythms of the play to find those clues which seem to tell them how each scene must be put onstage to work most effectively.

Anyone who has ever acted knows the excitement of coming from the offstage world into the gaze of the audience. Acting is a difficult and elusive art, a constant battle to sustain convincing life. A good playwright helps in that task not only in providing good parts to play onstage but also in reinforcing the illusion by offering details of the offstage world into which his characters periodically disappear. As I have indicated I owe a debt to the many scholars who have analysed Shakespeare's techniques before me. My primary debt, as always, is to those actors and directors, and particularly to those of the Stratford Festival Company in Ontario and the Royal Shakespeare Company who have, over several decades, spurred my interest in the way the plays are made, in their practice of using all of the resources Shakespeare gives them. I would like to record my gratitude to the Social Sciences and Humanities Research Council of Canada for the grant which allowed me to undertake much of this research.

Introduction

In this study I wish to examine some of the ways in which Shakespeare worked around what might seem to later ages to have been limitations in his theatre, and exploited them to his own advantage. He wrote complex plays, often with multi-layered plots, which contain dozens of characters and which violate the classical unities, and he did so with a small acting company performing on a bare thrust stage. That stage, compared even with theatres developing in his own age, had only unsophisticated technical facilities. Productions in later periods often developed staging techniques to make up for the deficiencies they perceived in Shakespeare's own theatre. Massive costuming budgets could be used to provide historically accurate dress, castles or forests could appear from the flies, complex sound and lighting systems could give us a dazzling experience of the storm Lear endures on the heath, large regiments of actors could be deployed to give the audience the sense of a truly regal court or the turmoil of battle. Such attempts to give Shakespeare the advantages of big budgets and large companies often provide considerable losses along with the gains they seek to supply. The addition of extensive scenery, a large company of actors, and elaborate stage business in 'fleshing out' a Shakespeare play may add considerably to its running time. This may result in over-extending the patience of the audience and can be compensated for only by cutting the text, which may be a mild slimming exercise for the play but occasionally amounts to something like the amputation of a limb. We can decide from production to production whether what Shakespeare in Sonnet 64 calls 'such interchange of state', in which we experience 'increasing store with loss and loss with store', is really worth it. What seems to me unarguable, however, is that such expansion and excision often hides from view the structural skill of the plays. Shakespeare organized his plays to suit the resources available to him, stretching them to the limits perhaps, making virtues of his necessities, and often proving that less is more. It has gradually been realized in this century that we can capture the flow and rhythm of his plays and have a chance at uncovering the richness of their structures if we take into consideration the circumstances of the thrust stage and the company for which they were written. This study is an attempt to define some of the ways Shakespeare made a virtue of his necessities.

This idea is, in itself, quite a common one in Shakespeare. Shakespeare's sonnets embroider the idea richly as they ingeniously exercise the mind in the images of gain and loss: the secondary gains which come as compensation for separation from the loved one, the constancy and wisdom of age which can tolerate the careless changeableness of youth, the power of verse to triumph over mortality, the expulsion of despair at all one's misfortunes by focusing on the singular blessing of one's friendship. Duke Senior makes a similar point when he indicates to his followers that they have been able to make gains in the countryside for the loss of their court:

> Sweet are the uses of adversity
> Which, like the toad, ugly and venomous,
> Wears yet a precious jewel in his head;
> And this our life, exempt from public haunt,
> Finds tongues in trees, books in the running brooks,
> Sermons in stones, and good in everything.
>
> (*As You Like It*, II. i. 12–17)

Amiens, in reply, congratulates his lord because he is able to 'translate the stubbornness of fortune/Into so quiet and so sweet a style' (II. i. 19–20), which is an apt description also of what Shakespeare is doing in exploiting the nature of his theatre. Lear says on the storm-stricken heath 'The art of our necessities is strange,/And can make vile things precious' (III. ii. 70–1), when he accepts the shelter of a hovel. He has begun to recognize his sophistication and will soon try to undress to acknowledge his kinship with animals. This is a considerable development from the view of the nature of necessity which Lear formulated when his daughters, cutting down his hundred knights, reach the bottom line as Regan asks 'What need one?' (II. iv. 258):

> O reason not the need! Our basest beggars
> Are in the poorest things superfluous.
> Allow not nature more than nature needs,
> Man's life is cheap as beast's. Thou art a lady:
> If only to go warm were gorgeous,
> Why, nature needs not what thou gorgeous wear'st,
> Which scarcely keeps thee warm.
>
> (II. iv. 259–65)

Here, in endorsing the idea that people pursue other needs besides the basics which sustain life, and distinguish themselves from animals by their attachment to the superfluous, he seems to have little idea of what man can do without. The daughters have a need to cut down his entourage to make Lear a dependant and to take uncontested authority in the kingdom. Lear needs the knights as a symbolic assertion that he still retains 'The name, and all th' addition to a king' (I. i. 136).

Shakespeare's plays constantly indicate the differing needs individuals have from their own particular perspectives and how their needs change along with their circumstances at different points in the play. This same variation in need and in the use of resources to supply that need is true not only of the characters in the play but also of Shakespeare's method of writing it. The needs of the audience and Shakespeare's own artistic needs, and the solutions he applies to them, vary from scene to scene and from play to play. I will examine specific methods whereby Shakespeare makes of what would seem to be a confining limitation an expansive advantage and adds a latent necessity to an apparent necessity in his structural strategies.

My focus here is on the handling of the relationship between the onstage world and the offstage world, between the world that Shakespeare shows us and the one he tells us about. Often, because of the complex strands of his plots and the crowded details of the interactions between many characters, Shakespeare has not only to report events that cannot easily be staged but also to choose from his sources which events to make the active substance of his scenes, which events to transmit by incidental report, which events to omit altogether, and what characters and actions to add to make up for deficiencies he perceived in his sources. In undertaking this tailoring of material Shakespeare had to keep practical considerations in mind. There are characters who disappear from his plays for lengthy intervals, and we may often ascribe this to his juggling of a limited number of actors to perform a variety of roles. In noting that the plays involved considerable doubling for several actors we can view this as either a limitation in the development of character and plot, the practical necessities of a company's size impeding the free flow of an artistic imagination, or we can see it as compelling Shakespeare to ingenuities in his structures which can provide incidental benefits for an audience. We can see the attempt to produce battle scenes with a mere handful of actors as comically and pitiably inadequate, or we can see the battles in all their variety as an exercise in theatrical legerdemain and ingenuity. We can recognize that many roles in Shakespeare's plays, and especially the major roles in the tragedies, are so large and so exhausting that an actor may well need a period offstage to husband resources for the extraordinary emotional demands such roles make. In supplying such a need Shakespeare must avoid an awkward hiatus in the momentum of the play and may reap additional advantages in a shrewd development of events in the absence of the hero. In tracing the workings of this on/off switch from the simplest examples of reported events within a scene to the large structural organizations involved in battles or in keeping an audience abreast of the actions of an absent hero for many scenes, I wish to indicate how

Shakespeare, in pursuing the virtues of necessity, far from bending to the limitations of his theatre, strove to extract unexpected gains from them. Shakespeare does not give the impression of being cabined, cribbed, confined, bound in, but rather seems to work with the resources of his theatre 'like a creature native and indued unto that element'.

This is nowhere clearer than on an occasion when he seems to be complaining about the limitations of his theatre as in the words of Chorus in *Henry V*: 'But pardon, gentles all,/The flat unraised spirits that hath dared/On this unworthy scaffold to bring forth/So great an object' (Prologue, 8–11). Chorus proposes, by provoking our imaginations, to provide a supplement to the inadequate resources of the stage. Yet Chorus, far from being a necessity, is rather a thing superfluous when we consider that Shakespeare had already written eight history plays without resorting to such a formal narrative device. Shakespeare had hitherto provided the elements we find in Chorus – vivid pictorial imagery, national fervour for war, channel crossings, preparations for battle, victory celebrations – within the natural flow of scenes instead of in separate prologues to each phase of action. Far from abridging events Chorus often elaborates them or presents incomplete and misleading accounts of what the audience is to see in actions to which he serves as formal presenter. He certainly provides rhythmic pauses and contributes to the atmosphere of the play but, as I shall show in a later chapter, he is serving a deeper structural function in the play in the complex presentation of war as well as, and at times in spite of, the simple functions he purports to be fulfilling.

My exploration of the way in which Shakespeare creates a complex and fruitful relationship between his onstage and offstage worlds is connected in several ways to the work Francis Berry undertook in his study *The Shakespeare Inset*. Berry was interested primarily in how narrative 'intrusions' are handled in specific speeches, presenting reports of action that the audience is not allowed to see onstage. He deals with the foregrounding of offstage action in passages such as Ophelia's report of Hamlet's appearance to her ungartered, Gertrude's account of Ophelia's drowning, Mistress Quickly's report of Falstaff's death, Enobarbus' speech about the meeting on the Cydnus. He indicates how we are often watching a character who makes an appeal to our mind's eye to create pictures of events experienced elsewhere, moving us from the here-and-now to the there-and-then. Berry defines different uses for narrative intrusions such as the interior-plot-required inset, the expository inset, the song inset, the voluntary inset, and indicates a range and variety in their usage. I recognize the value of these categories, but I am attempting here to deal not only with such single speeches but with a whole range of reporting, with the transmission of offstage events to the audience, with the whole relationship between offstage and onstage which is handled by Shakespeare with a richly ingenious variety of techniques. Berry treated these speeches as recurring elements of specific devices. I am endeavouring to indicate how central to an understanding of the structure of Shakespeare's plays the handling of offstage and onstage events is, and how thoroughly this permeates the dramatist's strategies for shaping the responses of an audience.

Many modern critical approaches are based on the assumption that a writer does not really know what he is doing, or that what is of central interest are ideas and attitudes which can be extracted from his work which he endeavoured to conceal or of which he was not completely aware. I am quite willing to grant that a writer may not be conscious of all the effects of his work, but I do regard the creative process to be, to a considerable degree, a highly organized endeavour to achieve specific effects. A writer shapes his work, solving problems as they arise and unfolding, with practised craftsmanship, strategies which work in concert, to compel the attention of his audience. It is, no doubt, useful to reveal those matters which a writer does not seem to be deliberately aiming at but which a clever critic can unfold. It is my view, however, that we have not yet done nearly enough work, in the analysis of drama, in examining the methods which writers consciously employ to work on an audience. Vast amounts of the criticism of Shakespeare's dramas, in the past and continuing in the present, take little account of the fact that they are skilfully designed to work on an audience watching and listening in a theatre. We cannot begin to understand the structural design of plays without continually bearing that in mind.

Drama is quite different from other forms of literature in that, as it is a performed art, the writer is intimately aware of his effects being achieved in collaboration with others. A dramatist is reinforced for calculating his effects, for knowing what works and what does not, and for devising strategies which produce clear responses. Novelists and poets cannot have such direct reinforcement, even in live readings, for their works are not usually designed solely or primarily for recitation and for reception by a group. They become aware of the response of critics and readers, but that, whether official or unofficial, in print or by personal communication, is not of the same order as an audience's response in a theatre to drama. Drama is a group experience and shapes a group response. We are certainly free to have an individual response to a drama, but the effect of a play on us is considerably shaped by the fact that we are responding among others. An audience is able to affect a performance, as any actor can testify. A good audience can make the actors sharper and more concentrated in their efforts to articulate clearly the director's sense of the author's intent. The dramatist who attends the theatre, as we may assume Shakespeare did, on a daily basis, can learn from audiences which structures and strategies produce the desired effect and which do not, can calculate whether passages which fail are the fault of the actors or the writing. It is often possible for the writer to suggest ways of reshaping a production or to take the opportunity to rewrite his material to produce more successfully the effect at which he originally aimed. It is the feedback of information in the terms the author intended to provoke – tears, tension, laughter, sympathy for a character or the lack of it, applause – which encourages the author to strive for specific effects and to learn the techniques by which they are achieved.

It is often said that the teaching of drama is difficult because it is frequently presented as a reading experience which misses out its central performative aspect. The consideration of performances in specific productions, which may vary over a huge range in interpretation, is an essential part of the evaluation of drama. I also believe that a major concern ought to be a careful examination of how the texts are constructed for performance. A dramatist constantly makes choices about how best to present his story. He must decide how many characters are required, how often each character appears onstage, which characters share extended conversations and which do not, which scenes to present to an audience and which to withhold, what varying levels of awareness the characters have about the events in which they are engaged, how much of a character's inner motivations or secret thoughts to reveal to an audience and when to disclose them, what ordering of events and juxtaposition of plots most effectively compels the attention of the audience. These matters are the basic syntax of the dramatic structure. In examining a text we can see how a dramatist handles these elements which have to be taken into consideration in *any* performance of a play. Scripts are constantly supplying information about how they are to be realized in performance not only in the stage directions but in the manner in which they are constructed, in the choices the dramatist has made and the emphases evident in the rhythm and organization of his story. We can confirm our sense of the writer's choices by the consistency of the techniques he uses within a play and from play to play. We can see the flexibility of his practice in the way techniques are varied and adapted to the differing needs of individual plays.

Selection and ordering of material is important in all forms of literature. The dramatist, however, because of the performance aspect of his work, is responding to circumstances which supply him with certain advantages and constraints. His work is designed to be received not only among a group but also as a more or less continuous experience within a finite period of time. A novelist must accept the fact that his work may be read straight through or may be absorbed piecemeal over days or weeks in a variety of places and in competition with all sorts of other activities undertaken by the reader. There may be various distractions during a theatre performance, and the viewer is always free to leave, but the dramatist can generally count on the fact that his audience has its attention focused on the stage. It will, if he is skilled, patiently attend for two or three hours the unfolding in a continuous manner, or with only those intervals he or the director have designated, the full effect of his story. This is why what a dramatist learns through feedback from an audience is so important. So much of his art depends on his ability to compel attention and to use the limited time available to him to maximum advantage. He has to judge every choice he makes with a shrewd awareness of proportion. The more he shows of one plot or character, the less he can show of another. If he develops some scenes at great length he will have to find ways of telescoping other elements of the story important to his general design. Some of the narratives in verse and prose and the chronicle histories on which Shakespeare's plays are based go on for many thousands of lines or are spread over hundreds of pages and are not shaped by any constraints of time or space equivalent to the two-hour traffic of the stage. Shakespeare digests them, often reducing many pages of narrative to a brief incident or a report. On the other hand, he may choose to make a minor character mentioned in passing a major figure in his drama, as he does with Enobarbus, referred to in only a couple of sentences by Plutarch. In the limited time available to him the dramatist must make everything count and shape each detail of his material so that it serves several purposes at once, latent and more complex ones as well as the obvious and straightforward ones.

The manipulation of the interrelationship between events onstage and those offstage is fundamental to the drama of all periods. The messenger delivering his report, as in the account of Oedipus blinding himself offstage, is a principal structural device in Greek drama. We can recognize the potency of the offstage world if we recall the remarkable and mysterious effect of that strange sound of the string snapping and the sound of axes chopping away at the conclusion of *The Cherry Orchard*. We register also the impact on a play of characters who never appear onstage at all, who may in fact be dead but who have had a crucial shaping effect on the characters we do see onstage. All we ever see of General Gabler in Ibsen's *Hedda Gabler* are the pistols his daughter uses, but we are constantly aware of how his imposing character has affected Hedda. In a similar sense, we are aware of the shadow of Macgregor, who never appears in Pinter's *The Homecoming* but nevertheless looms over Max and his family. In Beckett's *Waiting for Godot* we have a play largely structured around the routines in killing time in anticipation of the occasion when that mysterious and potent figure, Godot, will come from offstage into the presence of Vladimir and Estragon onstage. Even though a boy brings reports of Godot in that offstage world we, like the tramps, can never be certain of his existence because he never does come onstage. He is an example at an extreme limit and is one of many of Beckett's jokes on the nature of theatre conventions and of the power of an offstage character who may govern an action though he may not, in fact, exist.

The potency of the offstage is often confirmed as a fundamental principle of art. Breughel's painting *The Fall of Icarus*, about which Auden wrote so well, does not keep its purported subject entirely offstage but it certainly moves it towards the wings by foregrounding all kinds of other activities we are induced into observing first. We sometimes find that the reactions of people to an unseen event may be more effective than a direct experience of it. This is true occasionally, though perhaps not often enough, in film. In a climactic moment in David Lean's *Dr. Zhivago* we see the advance of the militia with swords drawn on defenceless protesters in a snow-laden street. It is obvious that a massacre is about to occur, but the camera pans away from the action and up to Omar Sharif's character, Zhivago, observing the gathering confrontation from the balcony. Though we hear sounds of the carnage we see nothing of it, but focus instead on the flinching in Zhivago's eyes as he registers the bloodshed. The camera then pans back to the corpse-strewn street after the cavalry has departed. Here, as so often in Shakespeare's art, reactions take up as much time or more than the actions which inspired them.

The technique of determining the relation between onstage and offstage events is central to the organization of dramatic rhythm in a play. A dramatist has to meet a variety of needs in shaping his work. He usually has to keep a plot in motion, organizing a story-line which unfolds through a series of actions. He also has to create a world of detail, of atmosphere in which these actions take place and characters who can engage our interest sufficiently to make us pursue a plot to its outcome. A writer is usually doing many of these things at the same time. But plays vary constantly in the way emphasis is placed on these different elements.

It is a commonplace of criticism that some of Shakespeare's early history plays are crammed with enough plot-details that might, later in his career, have provided him with material for several plays. He does not always devote as much detail to individualizing his characters as he was to do in some of the later history plays. It would be false to argue, however, that there is a general progression in Shakespeare's career towards structuring plots around ever more richly individualized characters. In the final romances we have a vivid sense of artifice in which controlling devices of plot often set a limit to the amount of space devoted to the detailed rounding-out of characters. The different forms of drama mix these elements in different proportions in supplying the needs of an audience. In farce we often get flat, two-dimensional characters with little development who may become mechanisms tied to a rapidly paced plot crammed with events. The same is often true in melodrama, where roundness of character may be subordinated to suspenseful plotting. In comedy and tragedy there may be an increased focus on character and a sustained effort to provide a range of details which gives a fuller picture of a particular comic or tragic world.

It is impossible, of course, in practice to separate out in any simple manner elements of plot from those of character, because they are so deeply interdependent. But critics often base dissatisfaction with a play on the sense that a balance between the elements has not been effectively maintained. It is often suggested that, in *Romeo and Juliet*, the mechanism of the plot with its series of accidents dooming the lovers in the second half of the play, diminishes the tragic force built up earlier in the play. After the intriguing psychological complexity of the first half of *Measure for Measure* some critics feel that, when the Duke begins to manipulate matters with bed-tricks and substituted heads, the mechanism of plot becomes too dominant, making it more difficult for the audience to accept the changes the characters are required to make. If we compare *The Comedy of Errors* with *Twelfth Night*, as stories about twins, we can see how much more dominant plot-interest is in the earlier play with its heavy reliance on the mechanism of farce. The pairs of twins in the earlier play are differentiated only to the point where they can make the buffoonery of mistaken identity the more enjoyable. The characters in *Twelfth Night* are much more richly rounded and interest us beyond the functions they serve in the complex plotting of confused identity. The way these elements are related to each other varies from form to form, from play to play, and at different times within one play. In *Hamlet* and *Othello* the audience's interest is compelled by the secret intrigues at the heart of the play, and the characters are revealed by the ways they are enmeshed in this complex plotting. That is not the case to the same degree in *Macbeth* and *King Lear*.

There are plays, of course, in which these complementary forces are treated in quite a radical way. Chekhov's characters are for the most part very well rounded. It would not be true to say that this is achieved at the expense of plot. Although the characters may change we have a pervasive sense of stasis or merely glacial progress because the plot is often composed of mundane details of quotidian events. The characters, burdened by emptiness and an awareness of the futility of their actions, often seem disconnected from a meaningful flow of events. In Beckett's plays we have a frontal assault on the very integrity of play-making techniques such as plotting and the construction of character. The pitifully trivial events and actions tacked together as a plot are a parodic reflection on the idea of life as a story of linear progress. Beckett's circular plots present us with characters who seem to be getting nowhere save closer to the grave. The characters are often elusive. We are teased with fragments of realistic detail that we can never form into a coherent picture, and it is difficult ever to get a fully rounded picture of them because we are constantly made aware of their theatricality. We cannot trust reports about offstage action because our faith that there is a world elsewhere continuous with the world we see on stage is constantly undermined. I would be willing to argue that Shakespeare, in structuring the tedium and emptiness of plot-events in *Troilus and Cressida*, very effectively anticipated the sense of stasis that we associate with Chekhov. In the way that he empties the main plot of Lear on the heath of any significant sequence of events, and focuses on the varying moods of Lear's mind and the mad games he plays in unfolding his nihilistic, philosophical musings, Shakespeare was working on techniques in which Beckett came to specialize. But Shakespeare's methods are not habitually at these extremes. The way plot and character are developed depends to a very significant extent on the way he manipulates the relationship between the onstage and offstage worlds.

In many of Shakespeare's plays there are elisions in reports of offstage activity which are simply the conventional mechanics of the dramatic structure. I will note a few examples of these so as to better indicate by contrast how the techniques in which I am primarily interested are not so straightforward. Characters may be brought together who are required to unfold news or plots of which the audience is already fully aware, and so scenes often conclude with a promise of such unfolding of information to be accomplished offstage in preparation for further developments when they next appear before us. Of scores of examples one can point to the way Iago promises, in *Othello*, to give the unhappy Roderigo 'further reason' for 'knocking out' Cassio's brains at the conclusion of IV. ii. Though Roderigo has been a little more resistant to being exploited than hitherto we know that he is pliable enough to bend to Iago's scheme. We have seen it before (II. i) and scarcely need to have the play held up while we witness it again. The whole sequence in *All's Well That Ends Well* where Helena informs Diana and the Widow of her situation is handled in a series of onstage/offstage alternations. In III. v Helena first meets them and hears of Bertram's attempts to seduce Diana. She goes off with them to propose some precepts to the virgin Diana. At their return in III. vii it is clear that Helena has unfolded her story to the widow and proposes herself as substitute for Diana in the bed-trick. They go offstage to work out the details and logistics. There is no need to detain an audience with the specifics of a conventional situation at this stage because Diana, having been informed of the arrangements, can reveal them onstage to Bertram, as she does in IV. ii. The bed-trick, of course, takes place offstage, and we hear of it as merely one of the sixteen businesses Bertram has despatched when he cockily reports on his busy evening to his friends in IV. iii. His feckless attitude to the parcel of dispatch conducted, as he thinks with the silent Diana, offstage receives its just reward when Parolles volubly reveals himself as someone Bertram did not truly know either and characterizes him as foolish, idle, lascivious, and a whale to virginity.

The business of keeping off the stage a tracking of events and unfolding of plots that the audience, though not all of the characters, are fully aware of, is frequently operative at the conclusion of the play. Most of the plays do not leave characters totally unenlightened about the course of events in which they have participated, but there are several in which there are enough loose ends that some leisure will be required offstage to unravel what has happened. The Abbess in *The Comedy of Errors* promises a full account of the long history of the separation of the twins and parents from her own point of view which Shakespeare wisely does not inflict on audience members who heard an extended account of it from Egeon at the outset. Orsino in *Twelfth Night* promises some further exploration of errant details of the story to be undertaken offstage, as do Leontes in *The Winter's Tale*, Prospero in *The Tempest*, and the King of France in *All's Well That Ends Well*. Horatio in *Hamlet*, it can be argued, has to survive the slaughter since he is the only person who could unfold the details to Fortinbras and the amazed court of the carnage that has invaded the stage – and a very long evening it promises to be offstage, which he previews in a concise, general survey anticipating that detailed report (V. ii. 368–75). Malcolm in *Macbeth* (V. viii. 60–73) gives a brief survey of what will have to be done, when time is available, to repair Scotland's fortunes. Duke Vincentio in *Measure for Measure* will need more time than the play will allow to recover Isabella from her commitment to convent life and so proposes to pursue the issue of marriage with her offstage.

These are very clear examples of the straightforward mechanics of play-making. I am concerned in this study with examples of offstage/onstage switches that are more complex. Many of them are not dictated by the straightforward need for dramatic economy. Given Shakespeare's frequently practised skill of elision, they draw attention because they may at times seem to be superfluous and to duplicate material, though on closer examination we can see that they are required for other purposes. We have to acknowledge from the outset that Shakespeare's application of the relation between the world offstage and the world onstage is more often not merely shaped by necessity but is also a matter of artistic choice. It could be argued that the report Enobarbus makes of the first meeting of Antony and Cleopatra on the Cydnus could only have been avoided with the financial resources, technical equipment, and the on-location shooting of the film-crews of a later age. This, however, neglects the fact that this sumptuously detailed evocation of the event may be as vivid in the imagination as anything a movie camera could present to us. The impact of an event may be created to a large degree precisely by denying an audience a direct experience of it.

Normally we might assume that we would put our principal trust in the evidence registered by our eyes. Shakespeare's handling of reports reveals to us the complexity and ambiguity of the truth. We might tend to think that accounts of offstage events may be less trustworthy than those of events we have witnessed. Frequently we accept accounts of offstage action with little question. Cassius, at the battle of Philippi asks Titinius 'Are those my tents where I perceive the fire?' (V. iii. 13) and receives an affirmative answer. Titinius is sent offstage to make sure of what is happening, and his journey is reported by Pindarus from 'higher on that hill' to Cassius below. As with the fire in the tents, it is obviously much easier to report such details of battle as offstage action than to undertake the difficult task of presenting such events onstage. Pindarus reports what he sees and assumes that Titinius is captured by the enemy. This immediately becomes a turning-point in the battle, for it leads to the suicide of Cassius. Events onstage are not so much determined by an offstage event but by a misinterpretation of an offstage event. The question that Messala asks when the dead Cassius is discovered could be asked of many reports in Shakespeare: 'O hateful Error, Melancholy's child,/Why dost thou show to the apt thoughts of men/The things that are not?' (V. iii. 67–9). What men make of what they see offstage may result, without any deliberate intent, in erroneous reports. We can often see how seemingly factual reports – of events we have witnessed onstage, to those characters who did not experience them – can be untrustworthy because they contain the inbuilt bias of the observer who misreports them for his own purposes, a situation we find in many of Iago's reports to Othello.

One of the most telling moments in all of Shakespeare, which points to the care we must take in dealing with the offstage world and the dangers in trusting the evidence of our eyes, occurs in Edgar's account to his father of what he 'sees' from the top of the cliffs at Dover (IV. vi. 11–24). Here we have a report of a scene that would normally be offstage. Because Gloucester is blind Edgar can conjure up onstage the dizzying pictorial images of what he sees when he looks down the cliffs. We are simultaneously aware that we are looking at two characters who are standing on a flat stage where there are certainly no cliffs, even though we also know that the blind Gloucester believes that he is standing at the edge of what is not there. The description, however, does not apply only to what we can see in physical terms but also to the pictures that it evokes in the mind's eye. We are induced to 'see' the figure gathering samphire from his perilous perch half-way down the cliffs. We see the fishermen far beneath on the beach who seem to be no bigger than mice. We see the surge of surf over the pebbles of the beach, and its murmuring sound is evoked even though we are assured that we are so high up that we cannot hear it. The scene vividly described in 14 lines is so compelling that we may feel, as Edgar claims for himself, a sensation of vertigo. In other words, we see what Gloucester cannot see, we see what is offstage even when it is claimed to be onstage and when it flatly contradicts the evidence of our eyes. Reports can imaginatively transport us from 'here' to 'there', and because of the power of poetry they can also transport us from 'here' to another 'here', making by an alchemical process gold out of dross, scenery which never has to be accounted for in a production budget.

Shakespeare can make us see what is not to be seen, what is offstage, but he can also show us how a character can make others see what has never happened, or can describe what has happened in a way that makes it clear he has seen or sees things in different ways from the audience and other characters. When we observe Macbeth reacting in horror to the hallucination of the dagger we have no doubt whatsoever that his feverish imagination allows him to see it, although we can see no dagger at all. When Macbeth starts in horror at the Ghost of Banquo, or when Hamlet, in Gertrude's bedroom observes his father's spirit we, like these central figures, can see the Ghost as well. We can also believe that the other characters onstage cannot see the apparitions to which their attention is directed. What is onstage to us is non-existent and believed by the other characters to be merely the result of imaginative 'ecstasy' in the minds of the heroes. We realise, too, that the accumulation in report of persuasive detail may still misrepresent an event. In *Cymbeline* Iachimo's story to Posthumus of his despoiling of Imogen's honour is based on a good deal of evidence about the furnishings of her bedroom and about intimate details of her body, as well as on the presentation of the bracelet which Iachimo claims to have received as a gift. The report is certainly a vivid account of Iachimo's experience in that room save that, as only we know from witnessing his visit, it omits the one crucial detail that Imogen, far from being an active partner during his visit, was asleep. In other reports we can see that they may be shaped to have one effect and yet produce an entirely unexpected reaction; for instance, the report Cleopatra sends through Mardian of her death is intended to deflect Antony's fury but produces his suicide.

The audience is able to observe all the varying effects of the reports and how they may sustain or misrepresent the truth because its members are privileged and empowered with the kind of comprehensive knowledge that is denied to the characters. Although audience members cannot come to a situation entirely free from their own biases, their objectivity, relative to those onstage is always of a higher order. Shakespeare provides commentators and observers within many of his plays who pride themselves on their own rational, objective evaluations of the world around them – Faulconbridge, Friar Laurence, Thersites, Apemantus, Lear's Fool, Enobarbus, to mention only the most obvious – and the audience is encouraged to see the limitations in their objectivity, how they submit to the folly they have diagnosed in others and are drawn into the tragic worlds of which they thought themselves to be merely observers. As an audience we come to many scenes in the plays in which we have foreknowledge and greater insight than any of those who are to participate in the action, and that compels our attention not merely to what happens but to how things happen. Because the characters are situated at different levels in the hierarchy of awareness we see how they shape their actions by disguise and plotting to achieve a certain response in others. They may achieve their aims or have them backfire as they fall victim to those with greater knowledge of what is going on than themselves.

As members of an audience we accept a power given to us which is beyond anything we experience in our own lives. Instead of the blinkered viewpoint caused by a personal involvement in an event, consisting of egocentric reaction, confused guesswork, and speculation about what lies behind the actions of others, we are, as audience, given information, foreknowledge, and insight. We accept it at the price of the loss of a power we often have in life – the power to interrupt and to try to shape an outcome that we desire.

That is the final paradox of the dramatic structure. We share all the information of offstage events that some of the characters hear about, we see all of the onstage events as an unfolding related sequence which none of the characters fully share, and we do so because, although the action occurs in our midst and the actors may speak to us directly in private, we are always firmly offstage. We cannot supply the characters with what they have missed, with the information that would save their lives. We are given the privilege of total access, of being here, there, and everywhere, of being peeping Toms and eavesdroppers. Shakespeare even confirms our special status in such roles when he gives us the advantage of those who think they have the privilege of inside information in catching others out in unguarded moments. Othello, as a peeping Tom, finally thinks he is getting a look behind the mask of the man who is cuckolding him (IV. i) though the audience knows that Iago is creating for Othello a Cassio who does not exist. Benedick and Beatrice, as eavesdroppers, hear and accept versions of each other as pining lovers, which the audience knows to be invented by their friends, but which in some sense anticipate and create their eventual roles as marriage-partners. In contracting to witness people acting out of ignorance, we have to accept our incapacity to act on our omniscience.

We are, of course, always aware that those onstage floundering in confusion and stumbling towards death are only actors and in no real danger. We may feel some sense of shame at the indignity and degradation we are obliged to witness, but we do not usually feel guilt about our refusal or incapacity to interfere as we might do in real events outside the theatre. But knowing that we are watching actors does not diminish our capacity to feel apprehension, admiration, anguish, joy, pain, and a sense of loss in response to the experience of the characters.

There is no doubt that Shakespeare often abridges his stories by employing reports of action offstage. It is useful to remember that because of the flexible conventions of his theatre we can see that he often chooses to do so rather than being obliged to do so. He was not inhibited by any need to adhere to the dramatic unities. His plays could elide and eliminate time, making a continuous story out of events picked out from decades, or could run to a detailed schedule of days. He could present actions in a sequence of scenes from locales all over one town, all over England, or move back and forth from England to France, Egypt to Rome, from interior to exterior, from natural to supernatural at will, and from one plot to another. Equally clearly he did not think an episodic mosaic of events made out of many of these elements would be too difficult for his audience to follow. The epic structure of a play like *Antony and Cleopatra* indicates the freedom he enjoyed in shaping his material. In such circumstances it is obvious that the reporting of events that occur on and off the stage will be a frequent and necessary strategy. When a character such as a Messenger enters, the news he brings from elsewhere may be a significant development in the plot. Our interest is not usually focused on the messenger himself, for he serves only a simple functional purpose. Yet Shakespeare, occasionally, was capable of extracting great dramatic significance and definable character out of such nameless servants, as with the two remarkable scenes with the unfortunate fellow who brings news to Cleopatra of Antony's marriage to Octavia. The scene does not present any information that the audience does not already know. We have witnessed the events in Rome, a world to which Cleopatra was offstage, so these sequences are entirely devoted to her reactions to the news. Shakespeare needs to keep Cleopatra before the audience's eyes, and this is a telling and vivid way of revealing and developing her character. In fact her part in the plot during Antony's sojourn in Rome is not composed of any significant actions; rather, it is entirely shaped in her reactions to his absence and it may, at first blush, seem wasteful of precious stage time in bringing characters abreast of events the audience has already witnessed. But there is often a different economy in stage time as reactions are unfolded, and characters can be rounded out not only by the way they deliver news but in the way they receive it.

Plays are not composed simply of characters enmeshed in sequences of action performed in the presence of an audience. They are a complex weave of actions and reactions, of events that we see and events we hear about performed offstage, and of the differing reactions of characters to events they have acted in on and off the stage. An action which occupies only a handful of lines may generate reactions which occupy many hundreds of lines. Reports and the reactions they provoke are vividly recurrent opportunities of presenting the audience with differing versions of the truth and the conflicting viewpoints that are at the very heart of Shakespeare's method of dramatization.

It is possible to register the complexity of the relation between report and reaction in a scene such as III. ii. in *Richard II*. Richard has been effectively offstage in Ireland while Bolingbroke has made powerful inroads in his kingdom. He has hopes of confronting successfully the challenge which Bolingbroke poses. But he is not in possession of crucial pieces of information which the audience has accumulated in previous scenes. The scene on the coast of Wales is structured around a sequence of reports which add virtually nothing to the first-hand experience of events we have but which, cumulatively, lead to a situation wherein Richard is bereft of most of the friends, allies, and supporting armies he has been counting on to defeat Bolingbroke. The focus of the scene is not especially on the way the reports are delivered but rather on Richard's reactions to them as he rides an emotional roller-coaster between hope and despair caused by the alternating encouragement of his friends and the disastrous news from his messengers. The substance of the scene is Richard's experience of the loss of power. In terms of plot all that happens is that Richard finds out what we already know;

however, as the scene unfolds we are brought into a long, intimate experience of Richard playing the role of king and his growing awareness that even as player of king his days are numbered. The scene is structured around the reports built into a recurring cycle of highs and lows. The reports provide a variety of information as first Salisbury and then Scroop deliver them. Together they contribute 50 lines to the scene (64–74, 91–2, 104–20, 128, 135–43, 194–203). The events on which these reports are based have already been presented onstage in 150 lines (II. iii. 81 – III. i. 35). To the 50 lines of report to Richard in III. ii. Shakespeare adds 168 lines which detail Richard's reaction to his situation and to the news which darkens and then seals his fate. Richard's reactions thus take over three times as many lines to unfold as the reports themselves.

Some of Shakespeare's most potent dramatic sequences involve a lengthy build-up in anticipation of, as well as reaction to, an event that is never presented onstage at all. We can observe the variety in Shakespeare's practice by noting the different ways in which he handles the sequence of deaths in *Macbeth*. In terms of stage time Macbeth's killing of Duncan in his bedchamber, just out of sight of the audience, occupies 13 lines at the beginning of II. ii, from the exit after his soliloquy in the previous scene until he returns, dazed with horror at his action, to his wife. The preparation for the murder undertaken in those 13 lines begins in the first scene of the play, develops during Macbeth's meeting with the witches (I. iii), becomes the central focus of the two major characters from I. v until Macbeth has 'done the deed', and continues to be the cause of reaction in all of the other characters until III. i when Macbeth turns his attention to Banquo. This sequence occupies almost 800 lines and close to 40 per cent of the whole play, and the vast majority of it is in preparation for and reaction to a climactic event which happens offstage in only 13 of those lines.

Banquo, on the other hand, is killed onstage, but again the proportions are interesting. In III. iii it takes only 19 lines for the murderers to dispatch him. Shakespeare has devoted III. i. 11–142 (132) and III. ii (56) to working up the murderers to the act and to keeping Lady Macbeth in ignorance of any detailed knowledge of her husband's intentions. In III. iv he devotes 23 lines (10–32) to the First Murderer's report of the event the audience has already witnessed, and the remaining 112 lines of the scene (33–144) to the consequences of that action – the Ghost of Banquo haunting Macbeth at the banquet. So the death onstage which occupies 19 lines is given 188 lines of preparation and 135 lines of consequences arising from it.

The choice Shakespeare makes in presenting the deaths of the Macduff family may have been partly shaped by the number of actors, especially child actors, available to him. Most of IV. ii is occupied by fearful reflections of the dangers resulting from Macbeth's tyrannous sway. The slaughter itself occupies only 6 lines and presents, in fact, only one death onstage. When the slaughter is reported by Ross to Macduff and Malcolm in IV. iii. 159–240 it is apparent that it involved many deaths, the entire household 'Wife, children, servants, all/That could be found' (211–12). It seems probable that several children were killed from the number of times the despairing Macduff enquires 'My children too?' (211), 'All my pretty ones?/Did you say all? O hell-kite! All?/What, all my pretty chickens and their dam/At one fell swoop?' (216–19). Shakespeare transmits the horrifying impact of this slaughter by showing the stabbing of the only child we have seen. The boy is onstage for the 84 lines of IV. ii and is allowed an interaction with his mother for 35 lines (29–63), and in that space we have a swift sketch of an innocent, pert, witty, shrewd, insightful, and brave child whose life is snuffed out ruthlessly only a moment or so after we have come to know him, delight in him, fear for him. Shakespeare knows that he does not have to show us all of the brutal savagery that is reported later. The sacrifice onstage of the young boy who has endeared himself to us serves as a sufficient prelude to all the deaths that occur offstage when the murderers go raging through the castle. Shakespeare thus often shows us only part of an action so effectively that he can justify a need to keep much of it offstage.

The death of Lady Macbeth is not shown onstage. News of it is brought in report to Macbeth, and yet this seems exactly right from a number of perspectives. Macbeth and his wife have been drifting apart for a long time in the play. They last appear together onstage at the end of III. iv. when the play has still 919 lines, or almost half its length, to run. As they drift in isolation in their own separate nightmares we would not expect to see Macbeth in concerned attendance at his wife's death-bed. Though he inquires about her health of the doctor in V. iii he is so preoccupied with his own plans and beset with anxiety that he can give only fragmentary and distracted attention to things outside his own fate. This isolation is emphasized precisely by not having any onstage interaction between the two principal characters. But if it would not be to Shakespeare's purpose to have such a scene why did he not show Lady Macbeth killing herself? The answer is that he has eliminated the need to do so by the stunning impact of the sleep-walking scene (V. i). We need to know of Lady Macbeth's fate after Macbeth leaves her behind, and we need to see her onstage. By exhibiting her mad, haunted torment in V. i Shakespeare shows us all that we need to see. We are so shocked by the change in her since we last saw her in III. iv that we can recognize her approaching death implicit in the scene. An exchange with the doctor and a report of her death not only serves the purpose of dramatic economy; it avoids any interruption in the focus on Macbeth's isolation and serves as a key example of his alienation. He reflects distractedly on her death as one more example of the meaningless nullity of life that is wearing him down. The keeping of an event offstage increases the impact of what we see onstage.

In many of the analyses which follow I have outlined the plot-details of a scene, even at the cost of some repetition, in order to articulate clearly the structural designs with which I am dealing and to show how carefully scenes are built up, segment by segment. I have also drawn up a variety of tables to indicate the weighing of various contrasting elements within and between plots or to outline how component parts of battle actions are sewn together. One of the assumptions on which these analyses are based is that a writer's intentions can be elicited not only from the choices he has made but also from the way those choices are reflected in the proportions of the plays. A playwright has a limited amount of time in which to achieve his effect on an audience and, if he is skilled, he will make sure that all of the time available to him counts. How much time he devotes to one plot rather than another is significant; how long a character is onstage and how many of the play's lines he speaks inevitably shapes our responses; how much the interaction of certain characters is developed while that of others is kept to a minimum supplies component details of the writer's strategy. These elements are very directly affected by the presence and absence of characters and the way onstage and offstage events are integrated. I have included, therefore, a good deal of statistical evidence about the plays based on line-counts. I am aware, of course, that editions of Shakespeare vary not only in terms of substantive text but also in the way the text is set out on the page and especially in the way prose is lineated. The line-counts I have used are from the individual editions of the Pelican texts, and it may be considered folly on my part to go to such trouble to produce numbers that are not applicable to other editions. My principal concern here, however, is not so much with the line-counts, (though I have endeavoured to be as accurate as possible) as with the proportions of the plays involved, expressed in percentage form, and these proportions are broadly applicable to many modern editions of Shakespeare. These statistics often confirm with more precision general impressions which we may gather by other means, but they also underline the way that Shakespeare's dramas are a mosaic of elements organized in particular proportions to work on an audience.

The evidence shows that the proportions recur often enough to confirm an intuitive sense of balance in Shakespeare as he applies the same techniques again and again and adapts them to the varying needs of his individual plays. It is clear that numbers of lines cannot easily be computed as exact equivalents or constant units in the evenly paced running-time of a play. Stage-directions not registered in a line-count signal action which may take up a considerable amount of our attention in certain parts of the play. The lines do, however, serve as the most consistent way of approximating a play's length and the most useful method of expressing the proportions of its varying actions from which we can elicit signals of the dramatist's intentions. If we use the weighting of the proportions of the plots, as well as the stage life of the characters and the nature of their interactions, we can begin to see how these constitutive elements are shaped to dovetail together to elicit specific responses.

It can be argued that in tracing the methods Shakespeare uses to shape the way people absorb his dramas I am imposing a uniformity of response which does not exist in a theatre, covering over diversity with an imaginary group psychology. A writer is certainly aware of diversity in his audience, may count on it and deliberately exploit it. Given that Shakespeare's plays are so skilfully devoted to the display of the relativity and multiplicity of viewpoints among his characters it is hardly likely that he underrated this diversity among members of his audience. The effects I am writing about here, however, are broadly based responses and experiences which members of an audience are likely to share. Writers, directors and actors, in deciding how to create or relax tension, how to elicit sympathy for or resistance to a character generally work on the audience as a homogeneous group or as multiples – ideally of an alert and responsive individual. Techniques are developed to try to create an atmosphere which grips the whole audience collectively. If there exist common biases and reflex reactions which might inhibit the successful unfolding of a plot and its characters, then care must be taken to get around or suppress the reactions which might injure the writer's ultimate intent. Drama builds up certain expectations in an audience and can achieve its effects by fulfilling them or frustrating them. A dramatist can deny us sequences we have been led to expect, supply us with news we need to know, and make us aware of the comic or tragic consequences which arise from the fact that many of the characters do not share our knowledge. We are constantly being invited to look ahead and await, with pleasure or sadness, events which may confuse the characters or confirm the doom we fear for them. Our slenderly held hopes for a happy outcome may be crushed in a stunning manner, as in *King Lear*, and we can examine how carefully we are set up for the full impact of the shock. Drama is organized with a varying degree of tension playing on its audience with something like the skill an angler uses in reeling in a fish, and I examine here some of the most widespread and skilfully applied techniques which contribute to this variation in tension.

This study is developed in two parts. I will examine initially the way reports are used in Shakespeare to relate the offstage and onstage worlds, building from simple examples within individual scenes in various plays to related sequences of reports which can be evaluated as part of broader strategies effecting the structure of a whole play. I devote a separate chapter to the variety of ways in which Shakespeare develops specific strategies for interrelating offstage and onstage during the absence of characters from the stage. I look at lengthy absences of relatively minor characters, the specific effects of some briefer stage absences, and the effect of the hiatus which occurs in the onstage lives of many of the tragic heroes. I devote a chapter also to the ways in which Shakespeare co-ordinates a variety of elements in his battles combining physical combat, diplomacy, and speeches of defiance onstage with reports of brave deeds and skirmishes offstage. In Part 2 I examine the ways in which several, or all, of these strategies work in individual plays, and what combined effect the prominent employment of them has in shaping the effect of the plays. In all cases I am concerned to indicate why Shakespeare chose to handle matters as he does rather than in other ways available in the sources or in the speculative alternative methods which can be imaginatively constructed. I am striving to underline an outstanding mark of his art – the ability to make a virtue of his necessities and to hit several birds with one stone.

Part 1

1

'Such news as you never heard of': The functions of reporting in Shakespeare's plays

Biondello rushes on in *The Taming of the Shrew* promising such news as you never heard of and proceeds to describe Petruchio's bizarre attire and the decrepit horse which brings him to his wedding. Such reports about the world offstage are constantly threaded through all of Shakespeare's plays, for the stage not only displays actions but is also a sort of newsroom where accounts of actions far and near are delivered. Shakespeare used reports of offstage action to solve a variety of problems: to unfold expository narrative, to abridge events, to provide, by the means of straightforward dramatic economy, some pace to a plot as it builds up a sense of anticipation in the audience. Reports can be of events which have occurred nearby and just out of our sight, or of events miles away and in another country. They can describe action which could not have been easily represented on the stage, or action on the stage which must be transmitted to other characters who were not present but must be kept abreast of the action. I will look briefly at reports which serve the fairly obvious function of providing dramatic economy. It will quickly become apparent that many reports can serve a number of purposes simultaneously. I will eventually examine how a sequence of reports can serve complex structural functions in the organization of a whole scene and of an entire play.

It is important to recognize at the outset the flexibility of Shakespeare's practice, and I can do so initially by glancing briefly at a few reports which do not serve what would appear to be the most obvious and straightforward function. Very many reports are useful as elisions which serve to put the audience or the characters quickly into the picture by helping in the necessary task of stitching the action together. A report, however, may quite deliberately do the opposite by delaying matters, providing a superfluity of detail, or producing confusion rather than clarification. They may not be simply stitches in the plot but may become part of the fabric of the plot. A notable example of deliberate over-elaboration is the report of Polonius to Claudius and Gertrude about the letter Hamlet has sent to Ophelia, and about the way he has advised his daughter to allow the prince no access to her, which he believes is an explanation of Hamlet's mysterious antic disposition. It is useful to remember that the report Polonius gives is, in part, based on another report of an action offstage in which Ophelia has described Hamlet's distracted visitation to her while she was sewing in her closet (II. i. 77–100). The conclusions to which Polonius has come are not entirely based on first-hand experience, but he shapes his report to support his own interpretation of Hamlet's behaviour even though that interpretation is wrong. Though we cannot be entirely certain it seems likely that Hamlet's visit to Ophelia and the construction of his letter are deliberately designed to produce this report so that Claudius will be led away from rather than towards the truth. The pertinent information which Polonius is required to give could be transmitted in a few lines. Shakespeare, however, exploits the opportunity to develop more fully the character of Polonius as something of a self-important wind-bag, proud of his own sense of decorum, his own devious political methods, and the shrewdness of his insight. He uses the occasion to demonstrate his sense of loyalty and to prove his indispensability. In a play in which everything happens by circuitously indirect methods Shakespeare decides not to transmit the information swiftly but to allow 74 lines (II. ii. 86–159) to this attempt by Polonius to prove that his version of the puzzling matter of Hamlet's strange behaviour is the correct one. We will find in many reports that Shakespeare deliberately avoids supplying us with information in the manner demanded by Gertrude of Polonius, who is, perhaps, temperament-ally incapable of complying with her request for 'More matter with less art'.

I have seen productions of other plays in which a Polonius-like solution has been supplied by a director to make a sustained narrative more acceptable to an audience. At the opening of *The Comedy of Errors* Egeon has to deliver one of the most sustained slabs of exposition in Shakespeare. He supplies an account of the twenty-three-year history of events which has split up his family, brought him to Ephesus, and made him a condemned captive of Solinus. Though his narrative is a reasonably tight account of a complex story it is extremely long (I. i. 31–139), and in these 109 lines the Duke interrupts only twice for a total of 5 lines. This is one of the few straight-forward accounts in a play which, as I shall indicate later, is full of reports which lead to confusion rather than clarity. On a number of occasions I have seen Egeon presented as a windbag who stops and starts but threatens, to the alarm of his auditors, to babble on forever. This provides a good deal of comic business to get the audience through the exposition. There is no indica-tion in the text that Egeon is a tedious bore, and it is not a clear function of the report so to reveal him, though a director may choose to make it one. As I will show, however, there are expository reports in Shakespeare which are designed to reveal character at least as much as to transmit information.

One of the most extreme examples of the failure to transmit information in a straightforward manner occurs in II. i of *Measure for Measure*, where an extensive series of confusing meanders unfolds (41–181) as Elbow strives to reveal what offence his wife has suffered from Pompey. Because of digressions, red herrings, malapropisms, and an irrepressible weakness for irrelevance, Elbow manages, with the aid of Pompey and Froth and the probing questions of Angelo and then Escalus, to reveal virtually nothing in 141 lines. Elbow brings in 'two notorious benefactors' who are 'void of all profanation in the world' but, despite his sense of outrage at some injury done to his wife, we never discover what it is. We are sidetracked into dishes of stewed prunes, Master Froth cracking the stones of the prunes he has eaten, the death of Master Froth's father, the pleasure Master Froth takes in sitting in the Bunch of Grapes, and so forth. The offstage events that have brought Froth and Pompey before the law are impenetrable to all inquiry. This invented sequence which Shakespeare adds to his source story produces a deliberately confusing eddy in the flow of plot. It serves, however, a number of purposes in addition to its pleasure as a comic incident. It introduces the audience to Pompey and provides the first taste of Vienna's seething underworld which has been spawned during Vincentio's lax, neglectful rule. It provides one of the several examples in the play of the law in operation and the problems with which it must cope. In the contrast of the reaction of two judges to Elbow it shows us Angelo's impatience with fools he considers beneath contempt. He sweeps offstage deputing Escalus to investigate the case and hoping that he will 'find good cause to whip them all' (130). Escalus exhibits a much more genial response to the obtuse and incompetent Elbow. We are given some sense of the potential tedium of the processes of the law and of the incapacity of some of those who administer it. Elbow, in his stupidity, conceals a crime and makes prosecution of it impossible, but he is rather less reprehensible than the mighty Angelo who will quite deliberately try to do the same thing. The 'trial' sequence with Elbow, in showing us how difficult it may be to find out what the nature of a crime is, a central problem for justice, sounds one of the major themes in the play. Angelo goes to great lengths to conceal his crimes but eventually discovers that he is quite wrong about some of the offences he believes himself to have committed. When the Duke, in the final scene, patiently uncovers to his surprised citizens the complex events in which they have, without fully understanding them, been involved, we can look back to the scene with Elbow, Froth, and Pompey and realise that the confusion, the incapacity to uncover what has happened, the exposure of a figure who lacks the capacity to be an adequate officer of the law, the suspension of sentence, is an amusingly ironical anticipation of the web of complications in which Angelo entangles himself.

The Two Gentlemen of Verona

It is possible to delineate in an early play like *The Two Gentlemen of Verona*

Shakespeare's use of reports of offstage action in the most basic and uncomplicated form and in ways that begin to point to greater complexity. Early in the play there are several instances of references to offstage action which broach the unfolding of the plot. In I. i. 94ff. Proteus inquires of Speed news about the delivery of his letter to Julia, but we cannot take the sequence as an elision intended to produce dramatic economy. The repetitive demands of Proteus, and Speed's word-play embroidering them, (94–7, 107–11, 122–31, 135–7), give us the sense of Proteus going round in circles so that the reference to offstage action becomes a pretext for extended punning. At I. ii. 34–40 we have Julia's reception of the letter and her enquiry of Lucetta as to where it came from. No detail of offstage action is required here since the focus is to be on the comedy of Julia's anguished dealings with the letter, which Shakespeare is able to elaborate for over 100 lines (34–140). In I. iii. 1–16 Panthino reports an offstage conversation with Antonio's brother about his views on the education of Proteus and his conviction that the young man should be sent abroad to have his manners polished. The picture here of action offstage is not substantial but is presented simply as an elision to provide impetus to the action onstage.

In II. iii. 1–30 we have a complex use of relating offstage to onstage when, in Launce's first comic routine, we have a report of his farewell to his family and a re-enactment of it as he uses shoes, hat, staff, etc. to supply the various roles. This speech can scarcely be said to be an economy in terms of plot. It tells us nothing about characters offstage who will become significant to the plot. It provides us with no information that is essential to the plot. This sequence, and indeed all the other sequences involving Launce, could be cut without affecting the story-line of the play. It can be argued, however, that though this speech is 30 lines long, it is an example of dramatic economy not in terms of plot but in terms of the varying moods and tones of the play. The issues of love and loyalty are refracted through varying prisms of plot at different levels, the most basic of which is the relationship of Launce and his dog, Crab. The main function of this speech is to provide Launce with a comic routine, which works like an 'establishing shot' in the cinema, in 'placing' him for the audience. It is not so much the offstage action in report that is amusing but Launce's hilarious and confused attempts to dramatize it for us with his clothing and possessions. The sequence serves as a comic parody because of the way it contrasts with the emotional farewell of Julia and Proteus in the previous scene, and it throws the dramatic posturing of lovers into perspective by having Launce feature his dog as the cold, heartless mistress of the courtly-love code.

In Launce's second routine (IV. iv. 1–36) we have another report of offstage action in which he and Crab have featured and which is related to the central theme of loyalty and disloyalty. We have seen Proteus betraying his vows of friendship with Valentine and his vows of love to Julia, fecklessly sacrificing others rather than himself because he possesses no tenacity in faith, a sequence I will turn to for other reasons in a later chapter on stage absence. By contrast, Launce goes to extreme lengths to protect his dog. When Crab fouls the floor in Silvia's chamber Launce takes the blame on himself and accepts a beating. He claims that he has taken the punishment of the stocks in the past for accepting blame for the puddings his dog has stolen, and stood in the pillory for the geese he has killed. Such loyalty stands in vivid and comic contrast to the fickle behaviour of Proteus. Launce has even been willing to offer Crab as a present from Proteus to Silvia, though his master, typically oblivious of his sacrifice, berates him for it. In return for this sacrifice Proteus decides to employ Sebastian (Julia in disguise) to replace Launce as his intermediary to Silvia. The explicit connection between the two plots is made by an echo. Launce asks after the beating he has sustained for his dog, 'How many masters would do this for his servant?' (IV. iv. 27–8), and Julia asks, when Proteus has employed her to carry the very ring she gave him on their earlier parting as a gift to Silvia, 'How many women would do such a message?' (IV. iv. 88). Both Launce and Julia are loyal to those who ought to be faithful in service to them but are instead churlishly indifferent. Proteus and Crab have a good deal in common. Launce's farewell to his family and the embarrassment his dog has caused him could conceivably have been presented as onstage action though it would have taken up more time and more actors than Shakespeare would wish to spend on such matters. We can see the essential economy of squeezing more comedy out of the situation by relating them as offstage events which require only one actor and one dog onstage. The comedy arises from the cascade of detail Launce pours out, his confusion, his active assertions and demonstrations of loyalty, his appeals to the audience, his implicit appeals to the dog, the vivid accounts of the distress and punishment he has suffered – all juxtaposed to the still, unmoved, impassive behaviour of the dog. It allows Launce not simply to present one example of the relationship but a thumb-nail sketch of the history of their association which is an unrequited love-affair. The audience is situated as a kind of jury to whom Launce unfolds the account of his humiliations, pleading with us to accept him as one who has done all that could be expected to deserve recognition.

A complex relation between onstage and offstage is established at IV. iv. 156–70 when Julia, in the role of Sebastian, recalls for Silvia how he/she once played in Madame Julia's gown in a feast at Pentecost. We cannot be certain that this is a recall of an authentic offstage event, but it connects very effectively with Julia's present situation and the role-playing she is undertaking. The levels of enactment nest like Chinese boxes to underline the complexity of disguise. The Elizabethan audience is watching a boy actor playing the role of Julia, who has put on the disguise of Sebastian, who claims that he once wore the clothes of Julia and looked very much like her, as he played the role of Ariadne in a pageant. Silvia believes she is watching onstage a servant recalling an offstage event that demonstrates sympathy for

Julia absent offstage. The audience knows that it is watching Julia recalling, at a series of removes in offstage action, the role of forlorn and abandoned mistress. It may be that Julia did once observe a servant dressed in her clothes undertake a moving performance as Ariadne. Now dressed as a servant she has even more reason to be moved by the role of abandoned lover because it is one she has inherited in real life. Onstage we see a permutation and extension of overlaying levels of acting reported as offstage action, a situation Shakespeare enjoyed enough to repeat in a variation of it when Viola, in *Twelfth Night*, in the role of Cesario, expresses the patience of her forlorn 'sister' to Orsino (II. iv. 106–21).

The Tempest

Ariel, in a conversation with Prospero (I. ii. 196–237), delivers a report of the shipwreck which is part of a complex and unusual interweaving of offstage and onstage action. The opening of *The Tempest*, in the manner of many romances, is relatively artless and crude in the way it handles some aspects of exposition. Shakespeare has to accomplish a number of tasks at the outset of this play. He has to bring a number of European courtiers into contact with Prospero and his daughter marooned on their island. He must explain how Prospero comes to be there and has to give an account of his career and the injuries he has received. This amount of information could not easily be delivered in a prologue or by Prospero in soliloquy. Miranda, the only inhabitant of the island to whom it can be reasonably given, is supposed to have been kept in ignorance about her origins during the twelve years of her sojourn on the island, which allows Prospero to unfold his story to her, thus supplying the audience with the requisite information. It is also important to demonstrate Prospero's unusual powers and to split up the European party in different parts of the island so that the various plots can, under the magical control of Prospero, operate in contrast.

Shakespeare has a significant problem here in that, to launch the action swiftly, he has a great deal of exposition to unload, and one of the central sequences is an event which almost invariably in his earlier career would have been presented in report as an offstage action. Shakespeare, however, may have taken advantage of opportunities presented by an indoor theatre to solve some of his problems and to present onstage the effective and arresting action of a shipwreck. If Shakespeare had considered it impossible to present the shipwreck onstage, an alternative, though less vivid, way of handling the situation might have been used. Prospero could have been presented onstage as a command-centre with Ariel rushing on and off to report on the successful completion of his various tasks, as he undertook the shipwreck. This is, in effect, what Ariel does in the report I have cited above, although Shakespeare, having given us a shipwreck, can accelerate matters by having Ariel report on the actions he has completed during the time Prospero has

28

been unfolding the account of his life to Miranda. But if Shakespeare had chosen to present the shipwreck as offstage action he would have encountered disadvantages that were avoided by the daring step of opening the play with it. We would not then have the advantage of being directly introduced to the European courtiers and their servants, nor would we have a vivid experience of Prospero's power. Shakespeare would not have been able to present the audience directly with the image of chaos and disorder, a microcosm of mankind as a ship of fools arguing about the problems of leadership, which becomes one of the central issues of the play. The shipwreck becomes an important 'establishing shot' as an image of fractious division in society which relates backwards to Prospero's history and forwards to many of the scenes we will experience in the play. It seems to me probable that Shakespeare chose to stage some of the shipwreck not simply because it would provide a spectacular opening but because, aware of all the exposition he had to unfold, he needed such an arresting opening. Without the ship-wreck we would have to confront 300 and more lines at second hand about a number of characters we have not yet seen onstage. Instead, by I. ii. 236 – some 300 lines into the play – we have witnessed an exciting action, we have seen onstage all the significant characters save Caliban, Stephano, and Trinculo, though the butler and clown could be presented in I. i. as wandering around in terror amid the shipwreck.

In terms of direct exposition I. ii is one of the most heavily loaded scenes in all of Shakespeare for, strictly speaking, it is composed of nothing else. Miranda's questions, Ariel's demands for liberty, and Caliban's cursing are there simply to provide occasion for further exposition. As we digest these chunks of information about events in the distant past, or about the action which Ariel reports he has just completed offstage, we can see more and more why Shakespeare needed to present some of the shipwreck onstage. Ariel's report is a tidy, economical way of completing the action we witnessed in the first scene, as he describes his performance as a stage manager in dispersing the survivors in a variety of groups about the island (I. ii. 219–24). This allows Shakespeare to set up his scenic structure whereby Ferdinand is separated from the rest of the court party, and Stephano and Trinculo can operate independently of their masters, while the mariners remain charmed in sleep under the ship's hatches until the conclusion of the play. Shakespeare decided to unload all of his exposition in one continuous sequence. Prospero delivers most of it, with some aid from Ariel and, towards the end of the scene, with some information from Caliban and, according to the Folio, with help from Miranda (351–62). In the 374 lines of I. ii we get virtually all of the information about the past that is to be given in the play. From this point onwards we follow the various groups of characters as Prospero manipulates them. It would have been possible to postpone the accounts of Prospero's ascendancy over Ariel and Caliban, servant and son to the witch Sycorax, to later scenes. Shakespeare chooses to complete the account of Prospero's experiences before his exile, immediately after it, and since coming to the island. By the end of I. ii we know that though power was stripped from him in Milan he now has complete power over the three figures with him on the island and over nature itself which has delivered his enemies from Europe into his hands. Though Ariel is impatient to gain his freedom and Caliban to take back the island, we are assured, by the end of I. ii, that there is no serious doubt about whether Prospero will prevail. Prospero will create tension in order to educate those who are subject to his power, and he will experience a struggle within himself as he contemplates relinquishing his revenge and his superhuman powers to rejoin his fellows as an ordinary mortal.

The shipwreck at the opening provides us with an exciting visual experience and may be an anticipatory compensation for the considerable slice of exposition we are called upon to swallow in the following scene. It also ultimately gives a sense of Prospero's power. We are caught up in what seems to be a life-threatening real situation. We find in Ariel's report in I. ii, which completes that action, that neither the voyagers nor the ship have come to any harm because the storm is, in a sense, the first example of Prospero's theatrical skills on display. Thus a dominant technique of the play, that things are not at all what they seem, is introduced. By mingling his onstage and offstage action judiciously Shakespeare establishes Prospero as the unchallengeable source of information in the play and the controlling agent of all the action that we see and of all other action we hear about in report.

The Comedy of Errors

One of the problems a playwright must resolve in order to maintain a compelling momentum and sustain a dramatic economy that avoids wearying repetition for the audience is how to deal with the recounting of onstage events to characters who did not witness them but need to be informed about them. One of Shakespeare's ingenious solutions is to make a play out of the confusion which arises when one character confidently recounts to another an event he is sure he shared only to find that the other has no memory of it whatsoever. The technique of *The Comedy of Errors* rests principally on a virtuoso manipulation of onstage/offstage experiences in which only the audience knows that the incidents recounted are being reported to the wrong twin. Each of the four characters believes himself to be dealing with the increasingly erratic and incomprehensible behaviour of one other character when he is in fact held responsible for and the victim of the actions and experiences of three others.

After Egeon unfolds to the Duke the story of his life and the separations that have occurred between the various members of the family (I. i. 36–139), many of the subsequent reportage sequences are of events the audience has witnessed onstage. This recall of onstage events is quite extensive.

II. i. 44–74	(31)	IV. iii. 12–36	(25)	V. i. 18–26	(9)
II. ii. 7–19	(13)	IV. iii. 76–86	(11)	V. i. 136–58	(23)
II. ii. 153–66	(14)	IV. iv. 8–17	(10)	V. i. 204–48	(45)
IV. i. 22–66	(45)	IV. iv. 62–75	(14)	V. i. 255–65	(11)
IV. i. 85–99	(15)	IV. iv. 79–88	(10)	V. i. 274–80	(7)
IV. ii. 1–16	(16)	IV. iv. 92–7	(6)	V. i. 370–90	(21)
IV. ii. 31–51	(21)				

This makes a total of 347 lines. We can add to these a number of reports which relate to events that occur offstage but which add to the confusion.

I. ii. 44–52	(9)	IV. iii. 1–11	(11)	IV. iv. 134–7	(4)
I. ii. 55–7	(3)	IV. iii. 40–2	(3)	V. i. 62–7	(6)
III. i. 6–18	(13)	IV. iii. 63–5	(3)	V. i. 169–83	(15)
III. ii. 81–144	(64)	IV. iii. 72–3	(2)	V. i. 249–52	(4)

This makes a total of 137 lines. Half of these lines are taken up by the Syracusan Dromio's comic account in III. ii of his entanglement with Nell, the bloated kitchen-wench in the house of Antipholus of Ephesus. Shakespeare works and reworks a series of confusions until various characters are driven almost to madness and to fears that they are possessed by witchcraft. The ingenuity lies in the way most of the other characters are drawn into the confusion. Besides Egeon, who is momentarily drawn into the mare's nest in Act V, only Duke Solinus and Emilia manage to remain relatively uninvolved in the errors. Chaotic confusion is maintained by the way that everyone who stumbles into any one of the twins adds his variant version to what we have seen.

In this kind of structure we can see that a repetition of events witnessed by the audience may not undermine the pursuit of dramatic economy. Drama is not concerned simply with plot and the presentation of a sequence of novel events. It may be based on showing how differently characters experience, perceive, and react to the same events and the consequences of their different levels of understanding. In a structure such as *The Comedy of Errors* all of the play's effects depend on the fact that we are never in confusion whereas the characters, until just under 100 lines from the end, are never in anything but confusion. Shakespeare was aware how, out of a few actions, a whole plot, punctuated with reports, could be spun out for five acts. This, at 1756 lines, is the shortest of Shakespeare's plays, and 484 lines (27.6 per cent) are devoted to report of action on and offstage within the play's time-span. If we include Egeon's account of his history at the outset (I. i. 36–139) and Emilia's conclusion of it at the end (V. i. 348–56), then the lines devoted to reporting in various forms total 597 (34 per cent). Shakespeare never again goes quite to this extreme but he was to use for the rest of his career an ever-increasing complexity of versions of events induced by the deceptive nature of appearances as a basis in his method of dramatization. Shakespeare is not violating dramatic economy or eking out his plot by this extended sequence of confusing reports. This rehashing of events is the substance of the play in which plot and character are fused whereby the irascible Antipholus of Ephesus is driven to the point of violence and Antipholus of Syracuse to fears that he is a victim of sorcery which drives him to seek sanctuary in the Priory. Shakespeare extracts much more comedy than is available in the source play by doubling the number of twins, which makes the reports and repetitions an ever-expanding source of fertile confusions. The skill lies in revolving the four characters on and offstage so that no one of the twins meets his brother, nor does any situation arise in which three of the four are onstage together. The play moves forward and yet constantly looks backwards compounding old errors with new ones in a structure that has pace, balance, and conciseness.

King Lear

We can begin to see the complexity of the relationship between a report and the facts in the account the disguised Kent gives to Lear of the circumstances which have brought him into disfavour and punishment in the stocks (II. iv. 26–44). Kent here condenses events which occurred offstage in his initial reception at Regan's house somewhere between his departure from Lear (I. v. 6) and Cornwall and Regan's entry (II. i. 86) and the events which the audience witnesses onstage (II. ii. 1–147). In that sequence we observed the 'fiery' duke in mounting exasperation dealing with a mere messenger who cares nothing for his authority nor fears the wrath he is arousing. Cornwall finds him beating the steward of Goneril, an ally already vexed by Lear's servants. When called upon to explain his violence Kent falls repeatedly to verbal abuse of Oswald (49–51, 53–5, 59–62, 67–79). When cautioned to behave more decorously Kent roundly answers that 'anger hath a privilege' (65). Kent is so insistent in expressing his spleen that Cornwall questions his sanity (80). When asked why he has assaulted Oswald so violently Kent, with stubborn wilfulness, answers off-handedly that he doesn't like his face and goes on capriciously to indicate that he is not much impressed with the faces of any of his interrogators (84–90). Cornwall believes him to be a figure who, having been praised for his bluntness, uses it as a cover for his misdeeds (90–9). Kent replies by contemptuously aping the kind of servility Cornwall seems to want but indicates that he cannot keep up such base flattery whatever punishment he is threatened with (100–8).

When he fails to gain any explanation from Kent, Cornwall addresses himself to Oswald and receives a brief account of the altercations we have observed (I. iv. 42–87, II. ii. 1–39). Oswald's report (110–19) though brief is coherent and fairly accurate save for the fact that it conceals the way in which, on Goneril's instruction, he provoked Lear into striking him by refusing to acknowledge his authority. But it must strike Cornwall as a breath of clarity, a round unvarnished tale, compared to the irritating lack of compliance he has met with from Kent in a sequence that has already lasted 70 lines (40–109) without yielding any satisfaction. Kent will not even condescend to dispute Oswald's account and so is threatened with the stocks. His crowning piece of impudence is to tell Cornwall that his threats of punishment are useless because he is too old and set in his ways to learn and that as servant to the King he is not subject to the authority of Cornwall. Far from feeling that he has behaved disrespectfully to Cornwall he indicates that the Duke is himself at fault and ought to behave more decorously instead of threatening to punish a servant of the King (122–7).

Kent's report to Lear of the events which led him to the stocks (II. iv. 37–44) is brief and more remarkable for what it omits than what it includes. He details his argument with Oswald but reduces the uproar and cross examination which it occasioned – 95 lines of acrimonious debate (II. ii. 40–134) – to one sentence: 'Your son and daughter found this trespass worth/The shame which here it suffers' (II. iv. 43–4). Kent, asked to explain how he could have deserved the indignity of being placed in the stocks, thus devotes 16½ lines (26–42) to a correct outline of a sequence of events that brought him to a confrontation with Cornwall and Regan, but then gives no detail at all of that confrontation which led to the punishment he records in the final 2 lines of his account. Kent is not shaped as the kind of character who would deliberately lie or consciously suppress the truth in order to excuse himself for the trouble he has brought on his own and Lear's heads. He does acknowledge some folly on his own part in causing an uproar by his instinctive fury in challenging Oswald (41). However, in the characteristic juxtapositions of the play, he would obviously prefer to be a fool who has enough of a sense of honour not to act in the manner of those knaves who are guided, like Oswald, by a cautious self-interest that is cowardly.

In registering the considerable editorial elision in this report, of which Kent is probably unconscious, the audience can see how one sequence of events can lead to such radically varied interpretations. What the audience perceived in Kent's behaviour is a short-tempered, headstrong figure as determined in ignoring the new disposition of power and in making himself vulnerable to it as Lear himself was at Goneril's, and will be again in the ensuing confrontation with his daughters in Gloucester's castle. Kent certainly ought to know that those in authority do not relish being treated with disrespect by underlings. It is because he spoke with such an open lack of restraint to Lear in the first scene that he was banished and went into his disguise. Lear will have to be taught again the lesson he failed to learn at Goneril's hands in I. iv, and Kent is taught again by Cornwall the lesson he failed to learn from Lear. Kent fails to learn the lesson because he does not believe that Cornwall deserves the respect he demands. In some sense we can see that he gets into trouble because, even though he is in the role of a servant, he is still driven by the kind of brusque, stubborn off-hand aristocratic hauteur that is the essence of the Earl of Kent. He does not pass over the altercation with Cornwall because he wishes to suppress the truth or mislead Lear about what happened; he does it because it is of no importance to him, and because, convinced as he is that he bears Lear's authority and that he had done nothing wrong, it is not worth mentioning. He cannot, in other words, make any imaginative effort to see how his behaviour must have looked from the perspective of Cornwall and Regan. The audience, of course, can do so and is forced to do so by the radical editing of Kent's report. We are not obliged to sympathize with Cornwall and Regan but we can see why they act as they do. Cornwall and Regan have received reports from Goneril of the riotous behaviour of the hundred knights that have brought disorder to her household. They have moved to Gloucester's to avoid an anarchic upsetting of their own home. Kent's behaviour confirms their worst fears. Just as Goneril was determined in instructing her servants to put on weary negligence because she 'would breed from hence occasions' (I. iii. 24) to bring matters to a head, so Cornwall puts Kent in the stocks as a demonstrations of the authority Lear is not yet aware he has yielded.

Lear does not ask for any further explanations when he has heard Kent's report. A full account would not, in fact, lead Lear to the conclusion that Kent was asking for the punishment he received. He interprets the situation, as Cornwall intended, as a direct challenge to his authority. For Lear, as for Kent, an inquiry into or an understanding of exactly what happened is lost behind the conviction that is should never have happened at all. The Fool can see which way the wind sits and which way the wild geese fly, and that helps to underline how Lear and Kent cannot see what is happening around them and how their own behaviour is helping to shape the punishment they will receive. That point is emphasized in the way this sequence concludes. The Gentleman has listened to Kent's account and looks down on him trapped in the stocks without being able to make a connection between the two. If Kent has given a full account then his punishment makes no sense at all. He suspects, what the audience knows, that there must be more to the matter than Kent reveals, and so asks 'Made you no more offense that what you speak of' (59). Kent does not have to reconsider for he resolutely replies 'None' (60). Kent does not recognize what he has done, and his version of events does not coincide with the scene the audience has witnessed. Limited, and wilfully so, to his own viewpoint he refuses to recognize how he has antagonized Lear's enemies. Like others who try to help Lear, he manages, with the best of intentions, to make things worse.

The Taming of the Shrew

In *The Taming of the Shrew* there are three notable passages devoted to reports of offstage action, III. ii. 42–67, 154–77 and IV. i. 58–73, although the first of these, Biondello's account of Petruchio's clothing, is more of a description in anticipation of the appearance of a character. This report might seem to be a redundancy since the character appears on stage only 15 lines after the vivid description in concluded. Though it might seem to be useful principally as detailed notes to the costume designer it is, in fact, an important element in the rhythm of the scene. We have already experienced the eccentricity of Petruchio's behaviour in his calculated treatment of Kate in II. i. But this is a mild prologue to the fantastic behaviour he exhibits on his wedding day. What characterizes his manner, apart from his physical roughness and his peremptory speech, is the helter-skelter, break-neck pace of his actions, in which he will brook no opposition. The two speeches of report are a key element in the pacing of the action as we can see if we break the scene into its various, constituent segments.

(a) 1–29 (29) The assembled wedding guests apprehensively wait for Petruchio who is late. Baptista worries about the shame it brings on his family. Kate, vexed and humiliated by such negligent treatment, berates her father for so foolishly exposing her to scorn and leaves the stage in tears.

(b) 30–82 (53) Biondello brings news that Petruchio is on the way and gives, in appalling detail (42–67), a description of his master's inappropriate dress, of the decrepit horse on which he rides, and of Grumio's eccentric attire.

(c) 83–123 (51) Petruchio greets the bewildered guests as though everything is proceeding according to acceptable standards of decorum, but, when it is suggested he improve his appearance, he rejects all offers of help and hurries off to greet his bride. The guests exit to the ceremony.

(d) 124–44 (21) Tranio and Lucentio remain behind discussing a plan to produce a bogus Vincentio to assure Baptista of the financial settlement that has been promised for the marriage of Bianca.

(e) 145–79 (35) Gremio enters from the ceremony and reports the details of Petruchio's violent and boorish behaviour at the wedding.

(f) 180–235 (56) Petruchio and Kate return with the wedding guests, and the groom announces that he and his bride must depart before the feast. He rejects all pleas to remain, including Kate's. She endeavours to dig in her heels by refusing to leave, but Petruchio will not bend to her resistance. Suddenly pretending he is beset with thieves who would steal his property, Kate, he feigns to leap to her defence with his sword and drags her off.

(g) 236–248 (13) The abandoned guests shake their heads in amazement at what they have seen but determine to proceed with a feast with Bianca and Lucentio as stand-ins for the absent bride and groom.

In terms of structure the various segments, in both manner and matter, are related to each other.

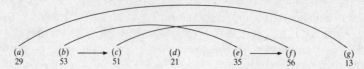

In terms of the pacing and rhythm of the scene there is a careful variation which focuses attention on the two most active and climactic segments (c) and (f) which are prepared for by the reports in (b) and (e).

(a) 29 A slow opening, as guests wait to see if the wedding for which they are assembled will take place.

(b) 53 Matters begin to gather momentum in the cascade of detail contained in Biondello's report.

(c) 51 The momentum drives into high gear in Petruchio's urgent inquiries for Kate and his peremptory dismissal of all complaints about his style of dress.

(d) 21 The pace relaxes briefly as sub-plot matters are dealt with.

(e) 35 The pace hastens again in Gremio's report of the whirlwind wedding.

(f) 56 It moves back into high gear when Petruchio refuses to modify his plans, draws his sword, and whirls Kate offstage.

(g) 13 The pace relaxes again in a coda of a commentary of reactions from the bewildered guests.

The reports embedded in this scene are a little odd in that, as I have noted, Biondello's might seem superfluous and Gremio's is of an action that could have been presented onstage to provide a comic climax to the scene. We can learn something about the nature of dramatic economy if we can determine why these artistic choices were made. Economy may be achieved in many ways and cannot be judged simply in terms of the number of lines or amount of stage time but must be interpreted as a way of doing things which provides maximum impact. The reports are strands in a total scenic structure and provide prefatory build-up for the segments (c) and (f) where Petruchio is onstage and causes everyone to gape in disbelief. We frequently find in Shakespeare that less is more, or that a varied method of presentation is better than too much of a good thing. In the remainder of the play there are a number of scenes which will exhibit Petruchio's unpredictable and intemperate behaviour towards Kate. These sequences have to be spaced out to avoid tiring the audience by repetition and to avoid alienating the audience irretrievably from Petruchio as a cruel tyrant. Petruchio is involved not only in reforming Kate but in calling into question the values of Paduan society in its concern with surface rather than essence and in its preoccupation with money and decorum. All of the other characters in the devious manœuvrings of the sub-plot are so busy deceiving themselves and each other that they are completely unprepared for the shock of the last scene. The audience follows Petruchio's plan step by step and can recognize in it a more fruitful concern with achieving an understanding with Kate, albeit at the cost of surprising and violent tactics, than any of the other characters are capable of achieving with each other. We are not surprised by the concluding scene not only because we have experienced each phase of Kate's transformation but because Petruchio's behaviour is implicitly a criticism of the superficial values he finds around him, nowhere more vividly made evident than in this wedding scene. He rejects all demands that he dress in a more decorous manner, behave in more seemly ways, or conform to any of the conventional norms before, during, and after his marriage.

Petruchio is onstage in the 248 lines of this scene for 93 of them and he speaks 59½ of them. But in fact 222 lines of the scene are devoted to descriptions of him, demonstrations by him, and reactions to him. Only the 21 lines of segment (d) 124–44, and 5 lines of segment (g), 244–8, are concerned with other matters. His dealings in the scene are as much with the wedding guests as with Kate herself. She leaves the stage in tears at line 26 and does not return until line 180, although Gremio's report on the wedding (154–77) does make reference to her amazement. Kate is onstage in the scene for 82 lines (only 56 of them with Petruchio) and speaks 28½ lines, only 10½ of them to Petruchio. Only 7½ of Petruchio's 59½ lines in the scene are addressed directly to her. After rejecting the values of this society Petruchio drags Kate off into isolation, into the unsocial world of his home, away from the world that has produced a Kate who is not 'conformable as other household Kates' (II. i. 280), where he can conduct his harsh experiment in deprivation without any interference. What defines Petruchio, therefore, is not only his own wild behaviour but the reception by others of his behaviour. This is a society that has found great difficulty in dealing with or accepting Kate, and, to solve the problem, it yields her up to a man who behaves very much like a marauding brigand. It is important that he browbeats not only Kate but everyone else, for it makes her more vulnerable and more liable to change, marooned, as she soon is, in Petruchio's household with no allies and with only tyrannized servants for companions. She finds in him an image of her own hitherto tyrannical, unpredictable behaviour. This scene of her wedding day, therefore, exhibits Petruchio in a variety of eccentric ways and indicates how little he cares for any censure of his manner, so that she gets a complete picture of the man she is stuck with as she is torn away from the security of a world she has dominated and so completely undervalued.

If we turn now to the reports themselves we can consider what they contribute to the structure of the scene. Biondello's account can not be judged superfluous as a preface to Petruchio's appearance onstage. I have observed in a number of productions a Petruchio who enters with a padded, puppet-horse, matching Biondello's description, attached around his waist, and it is possible that such a device could have been used in Shakespeare's theatre. I would argue, however, that a designer should not be allowed such licence because a major proportion of Biondello's report, and its most extravagant and absurd details, are of the horse which does not appear onstage. The report breaks into three sections: (*a*) on Petruchio's appearance 42–7 (5½); (*b*) on the horse and its harness 47–60 (13½); (*c*) on Grumio's appearance (62–7) (6). The horse as the centre-piece of the report is so decrepit a ruin that it works much better if left entirely to the imagination. Petruchio's dress is outrageous enough, but a horse is a possession which, even more than a modern automobile, signals in itself and in its elaborately ornamental fittings conspicuous consumption and the status of its owner. Biondello describes a beast that rivals Rosinante as a parody of what, by societal standards, is fitting to the occasion. On Petruchio himself we are given six pieces of information about his dress, and each piece is embroidered with further defining detail which makes what is, in the first place, inappropriate an even deeper affront to decorum – 'a pair of boots that have been candle-cases, one buckled, another laced' (43–5). About the horse we have details of the saddle, then twelve details of the diseases from which it suffers and various aspects of its physical debility, to which are added a description of three more pieces of the harnessing in their tatty, crudely mended condition. The bravura description concludes with details of four incongruous elements of Grumio's attire fadged together into another image of monstrosity. It is not only the overkill of detail which makes Biondello's account comic, it is the long, unfolding sequences of clauses which demands a breathtaking speed of delivery, a cascade of bad news in one relentlessly extended sentence 19 lines long, which is then interrupted by a question and concluded in another sentence 6 lines long. The description thus introduces not only the grotesque but a rising pace in an advancing tidal wave of detail which builds to Petruchio's entrance.

We have to consider whether this does not diminish the shock value of Petruchio's entrance when, like a comic version of Caius Marcius at Corioles, he endeavours to strike Padua 'like a planet'. It is doubtful whether any designer could make a costume that we could absorb in its particularized detail to induce jaw-dropping amazement as effectively without the aid of Biondello's speech. And if we refuse to pile Pelion on Ossa and do not bring a stuffed bombast horse on stage, then the offensive centre-piece of the description works tellingly on the imagination of the audience. Biondello's description, as a kind of advertisement for coming attractions, helps to focus our attention on the dress so we can savour each detail quickly. We can laugh at the speech and then at the dress itself as well as at the stunned reactions of the guests to Petruchio's appearance. It is a fundamental rule of comedy that though outrageous behaviour may be amusing in itself it is much more effective when set in context, and what makes it funny is the reactions of other people to it. Biondello's report, therefore, prepares us for a shock and ensures that we are alert enough to focus on how it affects those onstage. It allows us to observe how Petruchio has calculated his behaviour to breach

one level of decorum after another. We can see that this is not simply
unpredictably wilful behaviour but that there is method in his madness as he
resists all efforts to shift him from his course. This is the more effective in
that Kate is not onstage to absorb the initial shock. She has left before
Biondello's report and only reappears after the ceremony in a shell-shocked
state.

Following Petruchio's first transit in this scene across an amazed Paduan
society, we have a slight break from the main drive of the scene as Tranio
and Lucentio plot how to gull Baptista. Throughout the play those involved
in devious and guileful deceptions to win Bianca are frequently seen, as here,
congratulating themselves on their subtlety and wit. Whether involved in
bargaining, exchanging clothes, performing roles, or passing off imposters to
fool Minola, they are engaged in a world of surface appearances rather than
in essential characteristics. No one seems to grasp Bianca's real nature, save
Hortensio who tires of the chase, until the final scene when she, as much as
Kate, surprises every one. So the secretive, behind-the-back plotting that we
find in the central segment of III. ii. is, characteristically, in contrast with
the frontal assault we find in Petruchio, in the surrounding segments, as he
pursues his own aims.

In Gremio's report of events in the church (154–77) we hear, as offstage
action, a sequence that could have been presented onstage as the climax to
the day's events. Shakespeare chooses instead to present the aborted wedding
feast as his climax, and we can see why. The wedding is made very amusing
in report, and Kate is described as being too stunned and bewildered to
object. Petruchio is being presented in the scene as an irresistible tide, piling
one outrage on another. The report of his appearance was bad enough, his
actual appearance confirmed what scarcely seemed credible. Could things get
worse still? Gremio's report of the ceremony proves that they could. It gives
an account of a physically violent Petruchio who challenges any bystander to
oppose him, who cuffs the priest to the ground, swaggers and drinks healths
like a pirate, and insults the sexton by throwing wine dregs on him for no
very clear reason. The emphasis in this vivid report is on the priest's
behaviour and on the sexton's appearance. The violence is applied mainly to
those around Kate, to bystanders and his own servants, throughout the play,
so that she may be intimidated more by his general manner rather than by
the direct application of physical abuse to herself. The violence done to her
at the ceremony is confined to the clamorous smack of a kiss which echoes
through the church. These events though comic were enough, Gremio
reports, to drive him from the church 'for very shame' (176).

Shakespeare probably already has most of his available actors onstage in
this scene, so it could be argued that to put the wedding ceremony onstage
we would have needed all of his company, or in terms of Gremio's account,
at least actors to play the priest and the sexton. Shakespeare will require an

actor to play Curtis in the next scene and eventually several others to play Petruchio's terrified servants, very likely from those who perform the Induction. But it seems likely that Shakespeare chose not to stage the church ceremony not because of practical limitations but for sound artistic reasons. Gremio's account, in its use of reported speech and precision of detail, is the next best thing to being there. Again, we may assume that because Petruchio will be featured in a number of tyrannical postures Shakespeare wants to avoid a long string of scenes in which Kate is humiliated and the audience induced into impatience with Petruchio's cruelty. The report allows for a build-up of anticipation, for a picture pieced together in a crescendo of eccentricity until Petruchio comes bouncing back onstage. For a moment we might believe that matters could not get any worse. But the scene is designed to keep unfolding a series of surprises for the guests, for Kate, and for the audience who are all asking 'what will Petruchio do next and how far will he go?' The report also extends Kate's absence from the stage so that when she returns after all these indignities she must be in a state of amazement which induces a volcanic explosiveness of suppressed fury.

We have to guess at Kate's amazement, for she has been absent for a crucial 153 lines of the scene (27–179). She did not have the advantage of a forewarning about Petruchio's appearance in Biondello's report, nor did she witness Petruchio's entrance and his peremptory refusal to spruce himself up. He must have swept her directly into the ceremony without leaving her time to catch her breath. It is her absence from the stage which stores up dramatic energy for the climax of the scene in segment (f). She has had no chance to express her outrage to him about his tardiness, about his appearance, nor to register her fury at the wedding. We hear from Gremio only that, at the wedding, she 'trembled and shook' (163) and of the kiss that echoed through the church. So what reactions we see and hear from her are all held in reserve until after Petruchio's *fait accompli*. We can see how each segment, and particularly the reports, fit into a sequence which has a rhythm that almost directs itself onstage because it builds so steadily to a climax. This is because we are not only compelled to wonder what Petruchio will do next, but we are shaped by a carefully maintained tension as to how Kate will react to it all. She has already had a battle of wits with Petruchio, has slapped him, and, in most productions, been involved in some rough-and-tumble (II. i). Petruchio has been able to browbeat others, swept aside objections by Baptista and Tranio, terrorized the priest, and insulted the sexton. The audience is, however, waiting throughout for the other shoe to drop, for what we might call the main bout on the fight-card.

Shakespeare builds up carefully to the confrontation we have been awaiting since the outset of the scene. Faced with Petruchio's declaration that he will leave the feast Baptista objects, then Tranio entreats and is refused, Gremio does the same, and then Kate entreats and seems to win, only to find that he is content to have her entreat but not to stay. To her second request, 'Now if you love me, stay', he says, 'Grumio, my horse!' (200), forcing Kate's hand. She has, perhaps, momentarily spoken in a placating manner, but now at last she makes the stand which the audience has been expecting and which Petruchio has quite deliberately provoked. Gremio exactly echoes the audience's sense of the inevitability of the clash when, as the stand-off is established, he says 'Ay, marry, sir, now it begins to work' (214). Kate seems momentarily to have the advantage when Petruchio appears to accede to her command that the feast go forward (215–22). We may suppose those onstage are nodding knowingly that Kate, the local champion and terror incarnate, would not be easily put down when Petruchio, in a sudden, astonishing, violent manœuvre wins the match by a technical knockout. He makes his most extreme statement of his absolute ownership of her as a chattel (225–9), treats her as a moody child, feigns a romantically heroic defence of her against the thieves who would steal her, and, like a pirate, sweeps up his booty and departs before any further objections can be made. In nine out of ten modern productions he hoists her over his shoulder and carries her off as she beats furiously on his back. The reports are strategic devices for achieving this climax. Instead of having Petruchio before us throughout, Shakespeare presents his raiding expedition in stages.

The sequence of entrances and exits induces continuous movement and agitation. If we allow for 2 attendants we can register the commotion simply by adding up the entrances and exits. There are 8 people who come on at the outset of the scene; 2 depart at line 26 (Kate and Bianca); Biondello enters at line 29; Petruchio and Grumio enter at line 82 (there are now 9 actors on stage) and they exit at line 119; Biondello, Baptista, Gremio, and the attendants exit (123), leaving only Tranio and Lucentio onstage. They are joined by Gremio (144) and then all the rest of the wedding party including Hortensio. There are now (if we include 2 attendants) 11 onstage, and they all remain until Petruchio, Kate, and Grumio depart (235), and the rest exit at the conclusion of the scene. In this 235-line scene there are 20 entrances and 20 exits; 8 of the 12 actors involved in the scene make 2 entrances and exits each. Biondello and Hortensio make 1 entrance and exit apiece, as do Tranio and Lucentio, the only two characters to remain onstage throughout the scene. We can see clearly here how Shakespeare can generate energy and pace by the on/off switch of characters, and how the choice of what to show onstage and what to keep offstage can be orchestrated effectively to compel the audience's attention. Kate, who has frequently been described as a devil, appears to have been plucked from a world in which she did not fit, and in which she appeared to be indecorous and mad, to live in a wild, anarchic, unconventional world where she will be treated to the lack of respect she has hitherto exhibited to others, in which, as Bianca sees it, 'being mad herself, she's madly mated' (240).

When we look at the source play, *The Taming of a Shrew*, we can see that Shakespeare may have picked up some hints for this scene, but the strategy in building the scene and in making reports of offstage action support onstage events to sustain a rising tension is entirely his own. Biondello's report on Petruchio's appearance is an addition by Shakespeare. In the source play Ferando enters 'baselie attired' unannounced. He has a reasonable and practical explanation of his dress when he indicates that he expects such brawling with Kate after the marriage that he has donned poor clothes that can be torn without any loss. This defensive posture is less stunning and enigmatic than the behaviour Petruchio exhibits. When others try to persuade Ferando to dress properly for the wedding he is far more open about his intentions than Petruchio is. In the source play Kate comes on to confront Ferando before the wedding and to scold him for his base attire, a diffusion of the tension before the post-wedding confrontation that Shakespeare does not permit. Ferando, again in defensive posture, promises Kate expensive and exotic clothes. As in Shakespeare, the source play has the marriage take place offstage, but the interim is filled by Polidore's boy and Sander talking inconsequentially about the wedding feast they anticipate. Gremio's report of the amazing scene in the church, which builds up anticipation of coming battle, appears to be entirely Shakespeare's invention. In Shakespeare, when the wedding guests and the married couple return, there is a phased sequence of appeals to Petruchio not to whisk his wife away before the wedding feast, building up to Kate's appeal and eventual last-ditch stand. In the source play Kate declares immediately that Ferando can leave but that she intends to stay to enjoy the feast. Shakespeare builds towards the showdown step by step in a rising tension which comes to a climax in Petruchio's 'defence' of his wife with drawn sword. There is no such rhythm in the source play. Ferando simply insists that they depart, explaining that on this day he is in charge whereas 'to morrow thou shalt rule,/And I will doo whatever thou commandes' (Bullough, *Narrative and Dramatic Sources of Shakespeare*, vol. 1, p. 88, Scene viii. II. 94–5). Throughout the sequence Ferando seems uncertain whether he can maintain his authority, and the guests are half inclined, after the couple leaves, to believe that Kate will triumph in the end. Shakespeare develops the sequence as an explosive *coup de théâtre* engineered by Petruchio. The reports of offstage action are launching-pads which give Petruchio great momentum each time he comes onstage, so that Kate has to absorb a sequence of shocks as she finds that her life seems to be turning into a walk across a minefield.

Shakespeare has not yet exhausted the advantages to be gained in providing reports of offstage action in this minefield. In the next scene (IV. i) we have more news of Kate's 'education'. Grumio enters, chilled and discomforted, and is allowed almost 50 lines to establish the misery he has suffered on the dreadful journey from Padua to Petruchio's home. There are several glances at it (1–3, 17–22, 32–3, 46–50) before we get a detailed account (58–73). We are able to anticipate from Grumio's numbed and bespattered condition and from his report that Kate must be in an even worse plight. This journey with horses rolling in mud could not have been presented onstage, but Grumio's account of it, like Biondello's report, sets up the audience so that we will not only have to observe carefully Kate's bedraggled dress when she enters but can do so in the knowledge of the epic series of catastrophes that have produced her crestfallen condition. This report, after an initial interruption by Curtis, is unfolded in one 11-line sentence, clause by clause, piling one humiliating hardship on top of another. She has not only fallen under her horse in the mud but has been left by Petruchio who, instead of rescuing her, beat Grumio for allowing the accident to happen. This report appears to be entirely Shakespeare's invention. Ferando and Kate, in the source play, arrive after a brief 20 line summary by Sander to the other servants which describes his master's attire and his leaving of the wedding feast but contains no details of the journey.

Grumio's report with its sequence of clauses extending from 'how', which occurs twelve times in 11 lines, is a litany of cumulative disaster. When Petruchio enters (104) some 31 lines later we find him still in a foul, impatient temper and not at all subdued by the sequence of accidents. He demands attention, barks at his servants and cuffs them, sings and issues orders as though nothing untoward had happened to unsettle his determination to play the attentive host. The sequence is the more effective in that Shakespeare keeps Kate silent after her entrance. Again he is working on the principle that bizarre antics can be amusing in themselves but the comedy is increased if we focus on the amazement of those responding to them. After she enters Kate observes her husband's erratic behaviour for 37 lines without saying a word, though Petruchio addresses her, in apparently tender concern amid all his other orders and his physical abuse of his servants, on five separate occasions. The wild oscillation from violence to everyone else and gentleness to her clearly bewilders Kate. She is onstage (she leaves at line 165) for 62 lines and yet speaks only 3 of them. This is evidence enough of her dispirited condition, mounting perhaps to terror, especially when we note that 1 of her lines is to deflect Petruchio from abusing a servant and the other 2 are attempts to calm her husband's agitation. The principal device in producing this muted Kate and making her behaviour explicable to the audience is Grumio's report of her wretched journey. Events offstage are an economical way of preparing for behaviour onstage.

There is one key detail in Grumio's account which is crucial not only to her subsequent entry but to her long-term development in the play. When Grumio says 'how she waded through the dirt to pluck him off me; how he swore, how she prayed, that never prayed before' (68–70), we have the first in a sequence of significant details which build up, scene by scene, to indicate that Kate is beginning to lose her egocentric wilfulness as she becomes capable of pitying others. This is the first step on her journey from isolation outside community back into it. This sequence of details allows the actress to signal to the audience a gradual process of change so that we are prepared for her emergence as a transformed figure in the final scene, though everyone in Padua is stunned by it. The next step, as I have noted above, occurs later in this scene (IV. i. 140) when Kate tries to stem the tide of Petruchio's anger by excusing the servant he strikes, 'Patience, I pray you, it was a fault unwilling', and a further step occurs when she tries to calm him down (IV. i. 155–6). At IV. iii. 7–8 she admits to Grumio that she has been spoiled at her father's house, 'But I, who never knew how to entreat/ Nor never needed that I should entreat,' though she is now willing to beg him for food. Soon she begs Petruchio for food (IV. iii. 44) and, while no doubt grimacing impatiently, is induced to give thanks for it (IV. iii. 47). Kate's recognition of what Petruchio is up to is erratic and full of angry relapses, but we do see her slowly understanding that she is a victim of a purposeful game rather than of a mad husband. She more fully understands that in IV. v when, instead of resisting his capricious demands, she submits to them, acknowledges the game, (18–22), and then goes him one better by mockingly aping his arbitrary madness in her address to Vincentio, (36–40), as a 'Young budding virgin'. All of her steps on this journey are different ways of recognizing needs external to her own, of becoming conscious of her own behaviour rather than being a victim of it, and of using it to advantage when occasion requires. Grumio's report of her behaviour in the mud is a turning-point in her life. It may be that, in the face of Petruchio's tempestuous nature, she is feeling the need of solidarity or an eventual ally, but in protecting another from an injustice she can forget her own misery. When Kate prays, having never prayed before, she is asking for external aid, but she is acknowledging for the first time that the temper she has hitherto tyrannically used to get her own way is of no avail. This instance of pliability at last opens the door to another way of life.

The three reports I have examined in *The Taming of the Shrew* only add up altogether to about 70 lines and yet they are crucial to the initial stages of the taming process. Everyone has asserted that Kate is unmanageable, and we have seen her to be sharp of tongue and capable of violence in tying up Bianca and striking her, in framing Hortensio's head with a lute, and in striking Petruchio (II. i). If Petruchio is to take this fortress of ill-temper it will have to be by storm, a swift move that stuns her so that she can never recover her balance to go back on the offensive. The reports are accounts of Petruchio's devastating offensive strategy which establishes a breakthrough. Kate tries some recovery tactics within these scenes and in subsequent scenes, but we see her, in effect, back-pedalling, moving steadily away from her role as Kate the Shrew.

The use of a report of offstage action to set up the onstage appearance of a bedraggled figure, which we find early in Shakespeare's career, in Grumio's account of Kate's suffering, is a device he never outgrew. He produced an effective variation on it in Falstaff's humiliation in *The Merry Wives of Windsor*. In III. iii we witness the fat knight scrambling in desperation into the buck-basket to hide among the filthy linen that is to be sent to Datchet Mead. We cannot witness the ducking onstage, and we do not need a report from a second-hand witness. Instead, Shakespeare presents us with the stowaway himself, bedraggled and furious, as he reports with horror his undignified experiences in the Thames (III. v. 3–20). Witnessing the slapstick action would no doubt be amusing, but it is infinitely more amusing to witness it through reaction as the chastened Falstaff, in shuddering terror, recalls his brush with death. The comedy is based on the visual contrast of this soaking heap with the confident peacock who had strutted in so confidently to undertake the wooing of Mistress Ford (III. iii. 35–74).

Shakespeare returned to this device again at the end of his career. In *The Tempest* Ariel's reports of his offstage activities is one of the key elements in telescoping the action. His account of the tricks he has played on Stephano, Trinculo, and Caliban (IV. i. 171–84) is presented in vivid pictorial terms as we are taken from 'here' to 'there' to experience the discomfort of the drunks. Though the steeping in the 'filthy mantled pool' would have been impossible to stage, much of their humiliation could have been presented directly to the audience. Ariel has been onstage up to his invisible tricks in II. i, III. ii, and III. iii. Puck in *A Midsummer Night's Dream* was able to conduct an extensive amount of mischief onstage. But we do not need any more evidence of Ariel's skills onstage. After the spectacular presentations of the banquet and the masque the teasing of the drunks might have been an anti-climax. Shakespeare economizes here by picking on a detail, the soaking of the drunks, as the key element in their humiliation which will set up the audience for their undignified entrance a few lines later. Ariel's speech is full of details that appeal to the eyes, ears and, finally, in the thorny plants, to the sense of touch. The bedraggled figures of Stephano and Trinculo are in need of new clothes and so are attracted to the 'glistering apparel' spread out for them on the line. Their sense of priorities is 'so distorted that even Caliban can see that their whole enterprise of taking over the island is being sacrificed to the acquisition of some gaudy robes – 'trash' as Caliban calls them.

Henry IV, Part 1

With this play I wish to look at two scenes to indicate the widely different uses to which Shakespeare could put reports. In one sequence in I. iii we appear to be dealing with expository information of an offstage event. This kind of report is not a major focus of my interest because it usually serves a function of providing straightforward economy which requires little analysis. Such reports provide a framework and grounding which help the audience to understand the action with which the play opens. Shakespeare, however, can also use such narrative accounts to serve a more complex function in unfolding a character as he does here. I will then turn to a sequence in the play in which a great range of different types of reports, serving several different functions, are used in organizing the structure of one of the most complex scenes in Shakespeare.

The first speech Hotspur delivers in *Henry IV, Part 1* (I. iii. 26–69) is an example of an opportunity provided for an actor to create an immediate and strong definition of character. This expository report might at first seem over-elaborate and tangential to the business at hand. Hotspur gives extensive detail to an encounter that has taken place before the starting-point of the action of the play. We have been informed by the king of the prisoners Hotspur has taken at the battle of Holmedon and of his refusal to yield them up (I. i. 70–5, 91–5), so his report serves as an explanation and excuse for his recalcitrance. In the 41 lines of the speech 14 lines are directly related to the king on the matter of failing to yield up the prisoners (29, 46–53, 65–9). The remaining 27 lines are given to two sections (30–45, 53–64) of Hotspur's vivid and contemptuous description of the exquisite and fastidious courtierly manners of the king's emissary who made the demand for the prisoners. This account of an offstage event is one of the most precise descriptions of a character Shakespeare ever wrote and the more remarkable in that it is of someone who never appears onstage. Yet it is, of course, a very effective piece of dramatic economy because it so vividly characterizes Hotspur in his furious reaction to this 'certain lord'. This clean-shaven, perfumed, snuff-taking, smooth-talking, diplomatic courier, with his disdain for the vulgarity and noise of battle and his choice prescription, amidst a field of corpses, of 'parmacity for an inward bruise', is the polar opposite of the engaged, workmanlike warrior, Hotspur, smarting from the wounds he has received in the service of his king. The implication to be taken is that any man who trusts such a 'popingay' does not appreciate who his true servants are, which is the burden of the Percies' complaints in this and subsequent scenes.

It is not merely the content of the speech but the manner of its delivery which gives us the full flavour of Hotspur. With such an impressive launching of his role an actor is required, with the traits and habits of thought developed here, only to fill in further detail. In this speech we see him vividly reliving the encounter as he takes us from 'here' to 'there' and, once there, is carried away by his fury as he describes the exhibition of affected manners which irked him. He makes an effort to return to the main issue after his first furious onslaught but is carried away again as he recalls and piles up examples of the behaviour of his effete interlocutor. The sequence juxtaposes a man whose very element is the battlefield with one who is an alien there. It thus helps indirectly to set up the opposition between Hotspur, the soldier, and Hal, already adverted to by Henry IV in I. i, as the playboy prince seen by the audience (I. ii), who is not serving in the king's cause.

We have experienced Hal, in his soliloquy (I. ii. 183–205), as a wily operator with long-term goals determined to keep his own council. We see Hotspur as a blunt-speaker who has great difficulty in hiding his real nature. This sequence, in a sense, also points the way to the battle of Shrewsbury where Henry IV, with his many counterfeits abroad, is not entirely at home on the battlefield and where we will find Falstaff's discretion and disdain for fighting juxtaposed to Hotspur's valour.

In the report Hotspur's tongue runs away with him, and he proceeds to deliver another report of battle (I. iii. 94–112) in his defence of Mortimer as a loyal servant of the king. The Hotspur, who can barely rein his temper in his first speech, quickly becomes, by the end of this scene, the skittish, unbridled colt almost beyond the control of his kinsmen, Northumberland and Worcester. He finds 'this king of smiles' (245), who gained his crown with the aid of the Percies with 'a candy deal of courtesy' as a 'fawning greyhound' (249–50), very much like the emissary he scorned at Holmedon. He is a man not easily comfortable with the 'half-faced fellowship' (208) the scheming Worcester proposes. From this first speech we can see why Hal will come to parody him as a figure 'that kills me some six or seven dozen Scots at a breakfast, washes his hands, and says to his wife, "Fie upon this quiet life! I want work"' (II. iv. 98–100). Here is the man already who can say to his wife 'We must have bloody noses and cracked crowns' (II. iii. 89). This mocker of the 'certain lord' and his refined manners will display the same irritation when he has to endure the courtierly refinements in Glendower's castle:

> I had rather be a kitten and cry mew
> Than one of these same metre ballet-mongers.
> I had rather hear a brazen canstick turned
> Or a dry wheel grate on the axletree,
> And that would set my teeth nothing on edge,
> Nothing so much as mincing poetry.
>
> (III. i. 127–32)

When he finds his wife using the genteel language of the court with 'sarcenet surety' for her oaths and the 'pepper gingerbread' of 'Sunday citizens' (III. i. 244–59), we recall his contempt for the 'many holiday and lady terms' of the perfumed exquisite at Holmedon. This certain lord, whom we see so vividly though he never comes onstage, has no weighty significance in the plot, but the report of him sets up our experience of Hotspur and feeds into all of his subsequent appearances onstage until he becomes himself a 'slovenly unhandsome corse' (I. iii. 44) who is only food 'for worms' (V. iv. 85–6).

Many critics have indicated that II. iv is not only one of the most complex and delightful scenes in the play but is also a turning-point in the action

Table 1.1 Act II, Scene iv – structure

Segment	Lines		Description	Lines devoted to report in real and fantasy versions	
(a)	1–34	(34)	Hal reports to Poins his popularity with the commoners.	4–24	(21)
(b)	35–106	(72)	Hal and Poins rag Francis. In preparing to roast Falstaff about the robbery Hal does a parodic imitation of Hotspur.	97–104	(8)
(c)	107–235	(129)	Falstaff's version of the deeds at Gadshill	108–235	(128)
(d)	236–68	(33)	Hal's account of the robbery and Falstaff's reaction.	236–51	(16)
(e)	269–82	(14)	Falstaff exits to receive news from court.		
(f)	283–309	(27)	Falstaff's companions reveal the deceptions used to sustain his account of the robbery.	283–97	(15)
(g)	310–54	(45)	Falstaff brings news of rebellion which provokes speculation about war.	317–43	(27)
(h)	355–411	(57)	First informal play: Falstaff plays king and insists the fat man must never be banished.	371–411	(41)
(i)	412–57	(46)	Second informal play: Hal's indictment of Falstaff ignores his plea for protection and unfolds the fate of banishment.	412–57	(46)
(j)	458–500	(43)	The Sheriff arrives seeking Falstaff for the robbery. The prince protects Jack from discovery.		
(k)	501–23	(23)	Falstaff is discovered asleep, his tavern bills are discussed, and Hal reveals his intention of serving the king.	508–13	(6)

Note: Part 1 (1–309, segments *a–f*), recall of past events in conflicting versions; Part 2 (310–523, segments *g–k*), anticipation of future events in conflicting versions.

signalling for the audience a key step in the transformation of Hal. Little can be added to the generally available accounts of the complex permutations of lies and trickery in the scene. It is worth outlining, however, the way that the moods and tones of the scene are firmly anchored and related in the structure of its various segments. Mark Rose in *Shakespearean Design* (pp. 50–9) has looked at the scene's structure in an analysis that is replete with insights into many of the connections between its various parts. I share many of his views about the overall aims of the scene, but my division of its segments is somewhat different, as is my focus on its use of reporting offstage events, and its interweaving of theatrical elements. As Table 1.1. indicates, the scene is developed in two distinct halves: (1) the recounting of events we have witnessed, which culminates in a contrast between fantasy and realist versions, (2) the imaginative projection of future events, which also juxtaposes fantasy and realist accounts. The specific passages of report which review the past or anticipate the future occupy 308 lines (60 per cent) of the 523-line scene. The reports, which are spread across this pivotal scene, are related to the complex issues in the play as a whole about role-playing, about what is true and what is false, about the nature of valour, about the nature of the heir apparent and the kind of king he will become.

There are interconnections between the various segments which can be summarized in a simplified diagram of the scenic structure:

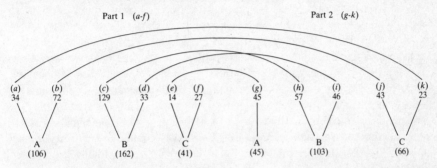

Each of the two parts has a tripartite structure with segments of preparation for the central confrontations within each part. Falstaff and Hal develop their contrasting versions of the past (the robbery) – the calling-to-account of Falstaff (c) (d), and their contrasting versions of the future (h) (i), which are supposed to be the calling-to-account of Hal by the king for his association with Falstaff, but which turn out again to be an indictment of Sir John himself. Since Falstaff is dedicated to theatrical fantasy we find distortions by Falstaff optimistically featuring himself as hero in the connected segments (c) and (h). Because Hal is much more concerned with reality we find parallel sequences in (d) and (i) in which Hal ruthlessly cuts Falstaff down to size. Both of Falstaff's versions are special pleading for a dream-world that can never be. Both of Hal's versions are informal trials of Falstaff, one for the specific crime of robbery and the other for his more general position as parasite from whom the prince must in the end separate himself. Segments (a) and (k) are the related opening and closing brackets of the scene. At the opening (a) Hal indicates how he has been winning friends and influencing the commoners, setting aside his socially distinctive role as heir apparent to pass as 'a Corinthian, a lad of mettle' – one of the boys – thus defining very clearly one aspect of his Janus-headed role. The scene closes (k) with his determination to return to the court, putting behind him his role as madcap truant, and to take on his other role as responsible heir apparent, the figure who, in line with his earlier declared strategy, will emerge 'like bright metal on a sullen ground ' (I. ii. 200). Segments (b) and (j) are related together as another pair of brackets to the scene, in that in (b) at the outset Hal is looking forward to exposing Falstaff's cowardice by acting as his severe judge (in the ruthless style of behaviour associated with Hotspur, 97–106), intending to call him to account in private. In segment (*j*) the Sheriff arrives as the representative of official law to call Falstaff to account for the robbery, but Hal again adopts a role, this time to protect Falstaff from immediate arrest, for he has already sentenced Falstaff to ultimate banishment. Segments (*e*) and (*g*) are related in that Falstaff goes offstage in (*e*) to hear news from court and returns in (*g*) to deliver it. Everything about this scene and its contrast of tavern and court is designed to emphasize the different ways that Hal and Falstaff look at the world and the different ways they act in it. In this scene we are dealing with a character, Falstaff, who regards what happened or could happen as having no connection with probability, as a dull and unattractive reality infinitely less preferable than the dazzling world one can embellish in the projection of one's wildest dreams. The connection, therefore, between offstage and onstage is not dependent simply on eyes which were 'there' bringing news 'here'; it is shaped by the mind's eye, the imagination which makes up a 'there' and brings it 'here' and makes us see it, even though we know it never was and never could be. Early in the play (I. ii. 183–205) Hal makes it clear that he is a man employing a mask, an actor gulling the world in a strategy which will allow him to emerge as a dazzling and effective king.

I would now like to look a little more closely at some segments of this scene to indicate other connections binding it together. The reported facts, the theatrical fantasies, and the projected reports of the future produce a richly layered contrast of the two worlds in which Hal performs.

(*a*) In his report to Poins of his success with the 'leash of drawers' Hal is flushed with success at a theatrical skill he has just exercised in gulling the groundlings offstage, building up a faithful following in his performance as a king of courtesy.

(*b*) Hal exhibits his craft further in the 'undeclared play' in which he gulls Francis. Hal, as ordinary customer, employing easy conversational familiarity appropriate to a man who has just received a pennyworth of sugar as a present from the drawer, initially compels no more faithful service than the importunate voice offstage demanding attention from Francis. That Hal is given little more deference than the customer (Poins) offstage underlines his success in passing himself off as one of the boys. The Janus-faced Hal knows that he will use his concealed role as heir apparent when it is most to his advantage. He brings his game with Francis to a climax when he unfolds the possibility of his princely generosity as bait to the bewildered drawer. Hal's proposition is clearly related to the circumstances of the Gadshill robbery to be discussed shortly when he asks Francis 'darest thou be so valiant as to play the coward with thy indenture and show it a fair pair of heels and run from it?' (44–6). The lad of mettle to whom it is possible to give a pennyworth of sugar is also the man who can offer you a thousand pounds (58–9) as recompense for the gift. Hal here is as much of a liar as Falstaff will be for he has as little intention of giving Francis a thousand pounds as Falstaff has of giving an honest account of the robbery. This is simply a preliminary demonstration of Hal's skill at stepping into and out of the role of heir apparent whenever it suits him. This curtain-raiser theatrical prologue in which Francis does not know what kind of man he is dealing with merely paves the way for a varied demonstration of Falstaff's discoveries of the same problem. The baiting of Francis has something gratuitously cruel about it which alienates our sympathies somewhat from the prince. Hal is so full of himself (89–91) that the audience is, perhaps, prepared to extend its sympathy to Falstaff if he can find some way of wriggling out of the humiliation that is being prepared for him.

Hal's slippery nature is defined for the audience not only by his 'now you see it now you don't' performance as heir apparent, but also by a satirical performance of what he is not. The blunt, guileless warrior Hotspur is the polar opposite of Hal. Hal is not ready to be a hot-headed tyrant hungry for action but he can deliver a comic vignette of Hotspur at breakfast (97–104). This parody catches a good deal of Hotspur's erratic behaviour and his wife's inability to get behind his nonchalant resistance to her inquires. It is not far from the exchanges we witnessed in the previous scene (II. iii) and will experience in the next scene (III. i). Hal does not want to be like the blustering Hotspur but declares himself willing to play such a role in tormenting Falstaff. Ironically, it is Falstaff who will take upon himself, in his account of Gadshill, the heroic posture, for just as Hotspur dispatches 'some fourteen' (103) enemies as a tuning-up exercise in Hal's fantasy, so Falstaff copes with the same number (eleven in buckram, three in Kendal green) in the arithmetical progressions of his own fantasy.

(c) The robbery itself was very much a staged affair, a play-within-a-play of which Falstaff was unaware. He enters determined to assert his own version of events, and Hal holds back his own report so that Jack will be the more effectively exposed as a liar and coward. Because the audience witnessed onstage the events on which the report is based it is able to concentrate on the audacity of Falstaff in his careless mathematical readjustments. These are the result of his belief that he is making a report to those who were offstage during the enactment of the robbery instead of to key participants in it. Falstaff counterfeits a hero in the hope of getting it accepted as true coin to gain personal glory for himself. We are aware, however, that his methods are not remarkably dissimilar to those of Hal who, with the leash of drawers and with Francis, has counterfeited being a common man in order to gain greater glory when he emerges as a warrior prince. Their role-playing has directly opposite effects, for Hal is able to manipulate and modify the real world, while Falstaff can modify the temporary play-world which has substance only in his imagination. Falstaff tries to embody the role of the *miles gloriosus*, the stage-braggart, to pass off theatrical illusion as reality. He makes a reference to his stage-progenitor, the Vice (128–31), in threatening to beat Hal out of his kingdom with a dagger of lath. His implication is that Hal's behaviour has been so shameful that, far from being a true prince, he is an ineffective player-prince worthy only of being beaten off the stage. The audience observes Falstaff, as fraudulent hero who believes himself to be undetectable in his role, accusing Hal of being an actor performing instead of being a real prince. This, like all the other strategies in the scene, reinforces our awareness of Hal's complex theatrical skills. Yet the more outrageous Falstaff grows the more we enjoy him and the way he is stealing Hal's fire, even though he is moving ever closer to exposure.

(d) In face of this fantastic tale Hal's closely held little secret of the truth seems to diminish in potency. Even so when Hal punctures this balloon of lies we might expect the enormous bulk which fabricated the lies to suffer some diminution and be shamed into silence. That, of course, does not happen. The way Jack, in response to Hal's report of the robbery, turns the tables is a master-stroke which Shakespeare had carefully prepared for earlier in the gulling of Francis. Hal juggles the roles of commoner and prince to suit himself. In the robbery he had undertaken the role of common thief undetectable to the victims and to the robber Falstaff whom he dispossessed of his booty. Falstaff's report fabricates an elaborate scenario which the prince reveals to be false. But with breathtaking impudence Falstaff takes advantage of the role of heir apparent which Hal alternately conceals and reveals. He spikes his accuser's guns by fastening on the duality the prince has fashioned for his own advantage. Falstaff now pretends to have detected him as heir apparent in order to extricate himself from the corner in which Hal believes he has him trapped: 'By the Lord, I knew ye as well as he that made ye. Why, hear you, my masters. Was it for me to kill the heir apparent? Should I turn upon the true prince?' (253–5). This is not a matter of Falstaff expecting anyone to believe that he did recognize Hal, but rather of outflanking him by his audacity in expanding his theatrical fantasy instead of abandoning it. If Hal wants to pretend to be a common thief Falstaff can go him one better by asserting that he went along with the game to humour Hal even though he saw through the disguise. This is complex enough in its juggling of roles, but it is only a step along the way to more elaborate juggling later in the scene. Falstaff, however, abandons the theatrical and fastens on what is real and important to him when he says 'But, by the Lords, lads, I am glad you have the money' (260–1), which is rather as if Falstaff is trumping Hal's ace. To Falstaff games, tricks, lies, shame all fade in the prospective glint of real money. This moment crystallizes the difference between Hal and Falstaff as performers. The money is of no consequence to Hal, any more than the leash of drawers or Francis are. His interest lies only in the exploitation of situations for his own amusement and power and the Machiavel's delight in the control which a mask gives him. Falstaff invests energy in furbishing up his image as the brave Sir John only so far as it brings immediate reinforcement and never brings him to the dangerous point of having to live up to it. Though a coward on instinct at Gadshill he believes the robbery to be a success for, whatever else was lost, the money was not and that, translated into sack, is all-in-all to Jack.

(*f*) The prince, baulked to some extent of an extended roasting of his Manningtree ox, turns to easier meat in questioning Peto and Bardolph during Falstaff's absence. They supply us with a report of offstage activities, very much in the nature of tiring-house preparations undertaken by Falstaff to support the performance he has just completed of 'The Epic of Gadshill'. The hacking of the swords with a dagger, the inducing of nose-bleeds with spear-grass, the beslubbering of garments with blood, all bolster our complex apprehension of Falstaff as a creature of stage-illusion.

(*g*) This is supplemented by Hal's greeting of Jack on his return as a 'sweet creature of bombast' (311). Bombast is the padding that could be used by actors to give the impression of fatness, so the reference reminds the audience of the theatrical illusion it is watching, since the actor of Falstaff is probably using such padding, and, within terms of the play's reality, suggests that Falstaff's substance is no more than theatrical, as fraudulent an illusion as an actor in padded costume. This is another of the ever-multiplying suggestions that the real world is, can be, ought to be an imitation of the theatrical world.

On his return Falstaff delivers his report of the news he has received from the messenger about events in the real world of the gathering rebellion. Such news might supply a sobering cold draught in this world of jesting were it not for the fact that Falstaff delivers it in terms of the imaginative fantasy of romance and the fustian stuff of the stage which echoes Hal's earlier performance of Hotspur. The characters he describes are not quite the generals we know or will come to know but are rather in the vein of the extravagant ranter and stage-braggart Falstaff has performed in his account of Gadshill. Percy is 'the mad fellow of the north' (319), Glendower has given the devil 'Amamon the bastinado, and made Lucifer cuckold, and swore the devil his true liegeman upon the cross of a Welsh hook' (320–2), and Douglas is one 'that runs a-horseback up a hill perpendicular' (326–7). Falstaff translates those who threaten the realm into the kinds of characters we find in old plays who bear the same relation to reality as the spectres who haunt Don Quixote's mind. Falstaff's inventions may seem to be excessive fantasy but, when we encounter these rebellious generals squabbling in the next scene (III. i), we find that in their bragging competition they are not altogether unrelated to Falstaff's performance as, and description of them as, the *miles gloriosus*.

(*h*) The scene reaches its climax in two further theatrical improvisations. So far we have been given stage-related accounts of offstage events and of events onstage that we have witnessed. We are now given juxtaposed accounts of events we will, in the unfolding of the story, witness on the stage. The king of the tavern and of all the sins of excess for a brief scene can present a parody of that sober and most responsible role – the King of England. With an ale-house chair as throne, a dagger as a sceptre, a cushion as a crown, and Mistress Quickly as a queen, Falstaff endeavours to turn the Eastcheap tavern into his own benign vision of the power-centre of the realm devoted to his welfare. The specific scene he anticipates is III. ii where Hal will receive a wigging from his father for his truancy but will extricate himself from his ignominy by role-playing as effectively as Falstaff brushed off the shame of his behaviour in the Gadshill robbery. Shakespeare in these contrasting versions of Henry IV's court now reaps all the rewards he had prepared for so carefully by distinguishing between Hal's and Falstaff's methods of play-acting.

Falstaff is true to his own concept of acting for he does not portray a king but a player-king. He acknowledges the illusion of his performance by asking for a cup of sack to make his eyes red so that he will have the appearance of weeping for his erring son. He declares that he will perform in King Cambyses' vein (369), an old play in the ranting style suitable to his own thespian leanings. Mistress Quickly reinforces our awareness of his acting when she says 'O Jesu, he doth it as like one of these harlotry players as ever I see' (377–8). His parody, in fact, turns out to be aimed at the highly elaborate figures of John Lyly's euphuistic style. Falstaff aims to amuse by playing a theatrical king who mocks the kind of theatrical kings with which the Elizabethan audience would be familiar. His performance has as much to do with the real role of king as his description of the battle of Gadshill had to do with the actual robbery. But in addition to angling for laughs there is a sense that Falstaff would prefer the world of theatre to reality because that illusory world puts no bounds on the imagination. In the theatre anything is possible. Henry IV can suggest Falstaff as a virtuous model to his erring son and Jack can never be banished because the world can be made into whatever you want of it from one moment to the next. Falstaff is much safer in such a fantasy world than in the real world of politics which is already knocking on the door. But we do not need to come out of the play-world to contact reality as Hal's restructuring of the scene goes on to demonstrate.

(*i*) Falstaff has tried to imagine himself a king at court, a place that is offstage and off-limits to him. The court world is not off-limits to Hal. We have not yet seen him there but we will shortly do so and we know that he will take the central role there in time. No audience of this play ever forgets the chilling significance of Hal's soliloquy at the close of I. ii. We always know that he is upholding the unyoked humour of idleness only for a while. The jesting he is indulging in at this tavern is essentially offstage (though the king knows of it and mourns for it) from the role he will soon embrace at court. Because we are aware of how self-consciously Hal shapes his roles our reception of his performance here is qualitatively different from Falstaff's. When, as king, he issues a long string of invectives against Falstaff he uses some theatrical terms drawn from old morality plays to classify his companion: 'that reverent vice, that grey iniquity, that father ruffian, that vanity in years' (431–2). He acknowledges Falstaff's theatrical nature but finds for him a role different from the one Jack had appropriated for himself. There is no chance that Jack will ever have the power to shape the world according to his own taste. He will play in the morality drama, which Hal intends to make of his life, that Vice figure who, though he may cause much mischief, will, before the close of the story, go down in defeat in the face of the reasserted forces of law and order. Falstaff, pretending to be the heir apparent, pleads for the indulgence of the fat man. He thinks he is acting the real Hal who, whatever tricks he gets up to, Falstaff believes loves him. But he is, in fact, playing only Hal, the actor, the indulgent, rascal prince who conceals his true nature, a nature of which Falstaff knows nothing but which is revealed to him in an electrifying, heart-stopping *coup de théâtre*. When Falstaff says 'Banish plump Jack, and banish all the world' and Hal replies 'I do, I will' (456–7) Shakespeare reaches the climax for which the whole scene has been a preparation. All the accumulating paradoxes of role-playing lead to this final, stunning irony. For most of the play Hal wears a deceptive mask. Only in this play-within-a-play, on the face of it a remoter level of illusion, does he fully reveal his true self to his companions as the pragmatic, ruthless king he is shaping himself to become. His theatrical game is invested with a potentiality beyond that of Falstaff's for he can turn it into reality. His use of two tenses ('I do, I will') brutally underlines that fact. The bragging fat man could, to save face, joke his way out of his fantastic description of the Gadshill robbery by claiming to have a tender consideration for the heir apparent. The heir apparent will eventually, to safeguard his image and his state, have no tender consideration for the man with whom he is here willing to share the stage. Hal's performance is a premonitory report on the last judgement on Falstaff (*Henry IV, Part 2*, V. v. 48–72) when he will be despised as a dream of as little substance as the fantasies he has projected in this scene.

(*j*) In the tavern games Falstaff still has enough confidence to ignore the ominous knocking on the door. The Sheriff is hot on his trail for the robbery at Gadshill, but Falstaff does not give a fig for reality and the law. He would prefer to pursue the illusory theatre in which Hal has just revealed his ultimate fate: 'Play out the play. I have much to say in the behalf of that Falstaff' (460–1). The complexity of Hal's various levels of role-playing are embroidered in the way he protects Falstaff by lying to the Sheriff: 'Now, my masters, for a true face and a good conscience' (476–7). His use of 'my masters' is the form of address used often by actors, especially of the Vice, to the audience of morality plays. The same address was used by Falstaff in trying to extricate himself from accusations of cowardice (254). Falstaff has acknowledged his progenitor to be the Vice; Hal has accused him of being the Vice and has signalled the punishment and defeat he will receive at the close of his theatrical career. All along, however, we have become aware of

Hal's Vice-like propensities which he openly acknowledges here as he is about to practise trickery on the Sheriff. It is easy to forget that technically Hal is as guilty of theft as Falstaff. It is typical of the way the two play their roles that Falstaff's theft should have been detected while Hal's has not. Hal's counterfeiting outflanks everyone until he is ready to emerge as the true gold of the dazzling sun. At the beginning of the scene he reports he had hidden his role as heir apparent among the leash of drawers in order to pass as a commoner. At the end of this scene he exploits his status as heir apparent to ensure that he is not now to be treated as a commoner. The Sheriff is obliged to be properly deferential and to desist in his search. Much of the scene has seemed to be a sort of relay-race in which Hal and Falstaff appear to co-operate in turning the events and characters in the world outside the tavern into theatrical illusion. Hal has tried on many parts in this scene – commoner, prankster, Hotspur, thief, judge, player-prince, player-king, Vice, but the audience is never allowed to forget that behind all the manipulations of his role as heir apparent he is, indeed, the heir apparent who is elusive to everyone around him.

(k) We know how completely Falstaff is deceived about Hal's real nature. How much he trusts Hal we can see in the ending of this scene. In spite of the threat of danger from the Sheriff he has fallen asleep behind the arras. It is a perfect conclusion to a scene which has so amply demonstrated that he lives for the present moment. He clearly believes that the anarchic play-world he inhabits is immune to threats from the real world because the sweet wag who shares his pranks can, as heir apparent, vouchsafe their continuance by the protection he extends to him. The bill found in Falstaff's pocket itemizing his varied intake of food and drink is one final oblique report of the excesses of Falstaff. The intolerable deal of sack that drowns but one halfpennyworth of bread is very much like the inflamed fantasies, which sack engenders, overwhelming the crumb of truth for which Falstaff has such little regard. The free and easy disorder and illusion which constitutes Falstaff's life is, however, we learn in the final lines of the scene, under threat of closure by Hal's long-range goals. Hal will go to court, the stolen money will be paid back with interest, Falstaff will be given a charge of foot, and everyone must anticipate work in the approaching war. Falstaff has survived by a combination of wit and fantasy and has not registered the long-term threat prophesied for him. He will continue to survive for some time and he sleeps blissfully ignorant of short-term threats to his comfort. The audience has been made very forcibly aware, however, that the heir is ready to become not only more apparent but more real, to play his role not merely in a tavern but on the stage of history. Falstaff's reports are of what he would like to have happened in the recent past and what he hopes will happen in the future. They are juxtaposed to Hal's account of what happened and what will happen.

All's Well That Ends Well

In *All's Well That Ends Well* there are three reports of action offstage which are all designed as part of a general strategy to elicit sympathy from the audience for Helena. For a variety of reasons Helena is an exceptional figure among Shakespeare's comic heroines and is more than usually vulnerable in her determined pursuit of Bertram. Helena is pursuing a marriage across class lines to a star out of her sphere. In Shakespeare's day when social ranking was of great importance in marriage an alliance between partners from widely disparate classes was possible but not generally practised. We get some commentary on this in several of Shakespeare's plays: in *The Merry Wives of Windsor* Page objects to Fenton as a socially inappropriate partner for his daughter Anne; the Duke has similar objections to Valentine as a match for his daughter Silvia in *The Two Gentlemen of Verona*; Bassanio's borrowing from Antonio to pursue the rich heiress, Portia, is shadowed by an awareness that he must make a show equal to the other titled suitors in his pursuit of this 'golden fleece'; the financial bidding involved to secure a rich prize is also seen in the competitive auction bids Lucentio and Gremio make to Baptista Minola for Bianca's hand in *The Taming of the Shrew*; in *The Winter's Tale* an unconventional marriage across class lines seems possible when Florizel and Perdita flee from Bohemia to Sicilia to escape the objections of Polixenes to his son's marriage to a 'sheep-hook', but it turns out, of course, that no social proprieties are violated when Perdita is discovered to be a princess after all. The considerable enhancement of one's social status by means of marriage was certainly not proscribed in Shakespeare's time but it was evidently still possible to suffer opprobrium as a social climber. If Helena is to be successful in her aim and win the sympathy of the audience it is very important that she should not be isolated nor generally stigmatized as a fortune-hunter. Throughout the play we find Shakespeare taking great pains to protect her from the kind of reflex condemnation he might have anticipated. In comedy there are often aged, blocking figures standing in the way of young love. In this play there are three aristocrats who might be expected to supply that function – the Countess, the King, and Lafew – especially in consideration of the fact that one of the young lovers is of a lower rank striving to marry into a noble family. But these figures, as critics usually note, are not at all like the irascible figures we meet elsewhere in Shakespeare such as Egeus in *A Midsummer Night's Dream* or Polixenes in *The Winter's Tale*. The three figures become allies of Helena and guarantors for the audience of her exceptional worth, defining her as a remarkable woman that any young nobleman ought to consider himself lucky to marry. The blocking figure in this play is Bertram himself. It will take a good deal of wit to outflank someone so priggishly full of self-regard. The three reports I wish to examine all help to generate a special sympathy for Helena. Instead of the old working against the young banning a socially unacceptable match, we have the alliance of the old *with* a young woman who wishes to break the conventional rules of marriage and *against* a young man who adheres to them.

It is in I. iii that this unusual alliance is first established. Shakespeare unfolds the news of Helena's love of Bertram to the Countess in a somewhat circuitous manner. The Steward enters at the opening of the scene and is asked for news of Helena. He would seem to be about to indicate what he has overheard from her when the scene diverges into the concerns in love of Lavatch, the clown, for 74 lines (I. iii. 8–91). In *As You Like It* Shakespeare had already set up a parallel structure between the loves of his main characters and the carnal inclinations of a clown (Touchstone). Much the same structure seems to be about to be invoked here, but it is never developed in any extended detail. The sequence here, however, does indicate the democratic nature of love and its operation at all social levels. Surrounding what becomes the high-flown self-regard and concern for honour which defines Bertram we have many more down-to-earth, workaday responses to the stings of carnality. We have already had the reduction of virginity by Parolles to a market commodity (I. i. 106–59) in a sequence which exhibited Helena's spirited nature and her witty capacity to handle the sexual innuendo of Parolles. This exchange has won Helena some brickbats from scholars who believe Shakespeare's heroines ought to be demure, respectable ladies unstained by any tinge of ribaldry. Lavatch, in his declared determination to marry Isbel, is shown to be remarkably liberal in his views on constancy in marriage. He seems to be quite willing to have other men cuckold him since he takes it to be the inevitable lot of men. His speech has a levelling effect that is relevant to concerns about disparity in social ranking later in the scene. For Lavatch it is of no significance that men are separated and differentiated on many matters since, in their carnal lust, they are part of a common herd (I. iii. 40–52). One of the broader ironies of the play, which relates to Lavatch's views, is that Bertram, driven by his carnal needs, will consider himself to be enjoying some extra-marital sport when he is, in fact, consummating his marriage and will thereby be forced to live up to more than the mere form of marriage. Instead of fleshing his will in the spoil of Diana's honour he commits a legal act which will spoil his own concept of his untouchable honour.

The by-play with Lavatch also has the important function of establishing the liberal tolerance of the Countess for her unusual clown. We will find Bertram to be a figure very unlike the girl who loves him for she values the impulses of the heart more than the social conventions that are impediments to her. To him matters of rank and birth are of primary importance in choosing a marriage-partner though they are of no significance in choosing a bed-partner. We might assume that Bertram's values have been formed in his family and that his disdainful hauteur has been bred into him. Shakespeare deliberately isolates Bertram by making it clear that this is not the case. The old, now deceased, Count of Rousillon was the model of chivalric magnanimity and genuine courtesy. The King cites him as an outstanding figure of a worthier age that is now passing (I. ii. 26–48), a man who 'Might be a copy to these younger times' (46), but who, it rapidly becomes clear, has not been copied by Bertram.

The Steward's report of Helena's love for Bertram (I. iii. 100–18) centres on her anguish about the social disparity between them: 'Fortune, she said, was no goddess, that had put such difference betwixt their two estates; Love no god, that would not extend his might only where qualities were level' (105–6). We have seen Bertram on stage in I. i taking leave of his mother and have been made aware by Helena of her attraction to the young man, which we may suspect is not fully reciprocated from the fact that he addresses only a few words to her on his departure (71–2). On the surface the report of the Steward is a simple anticipatory device, an advertisement for coming action. The Steward's motivation may be the protection of the family's honour. His words 'sithence, in the loss that may happen, it concerns you something to know of it' (113–14) are a little ambiguous. He could be implying that if Helena succeeded in marrying Bertram the family might be brought into lower esteem, or that, in pursuit of her goal, Bertram might take advantage of her (as he imagines he is doing with Diana later), and so the girl might lose her honour and the Countess might lose a servant. But we see, in any case, that the Countess has anticipated the news (115–18). The Steward simply resolves the issue since his evidence comes from overhearing Helena in an unguarded moment. The Countess has not been spying on Helena for the Steward renders his account from duty and not from prior instructions. The audience already has had some hint that the Countess regards Helena to be an unassuming figure who deserves exceptional rewards: 'Her father bequeathed her to me, and she herself, without other advantage, may lawfully make title to as much love as she finds. There is more owing her than is paid, and more shall be paid her than she'll demand.' (I. iii. 95–9) This gives us some indication that the Countess may not find the aspirations of one of her household servants for marriage to her son and heir to be socially inappropriate. The exchange with Lavatch makes it clear that she is not a conventional figure with rigid standards of propriety. Her reaction to the news, before she approaches Helena, is also related to the views expressed by Lavatch. Far from being outraged by the presumption of the girl she indicates how natural and universal the affliction of love is to the young. Implicitly she recognizes the democratic equality of all lovers when she admits that the pangs Helena is suffering bring back the remembrance of her own youthful passion (I. iii. 121–9). The report enables the Countess to set a trap for Helena and to bring the matter out into the open by teasing her into a confession. Helena has not had the temerity to make her aspirations publicly known and is in danger of letting concealment, like a worm in the bud, feed on her damask cheeks. We can deduce that, since the Countess does not wish to humiliate a presumptuous servant, she must be forcing the issue because she believes that Helena might make an excellent partner for her son.

We have already had signs that Bertram may be a cause of worry to the Countess. The first scene of the play has juxtaposed her opinions of the two young people. Her speech at I. i. 56–67 seems to indicate some apprehension about Bertram as 'an unseasoned courtier'. She solicits Lafew's aid in knocking him into shape and hopes that he will succeed his father 'In manners, as in shape' (I. i. 57), which seems to imply that, though he may look like his father and share his noble blood, he has yet to exhibit a virtue worthy of his heredity. She does not have such confidence in sending him forth that she can resist giving him advice on how to behave. The precepts are traditional enough, but if Bertram had the ability to follow any of them he would behave much less foolishly and churlishly than he does. His nature is all the more clearly outlined in that it is set against the prior description and unambiguous praise of Helena by the Countess (I. i. 35–41).

The Countess does not instantly become Helena's ally in her pursuit of Bertram, but there is no reflex condemnation of her aspiration as presumptuous. We know that Helena is a determined young woman and believes in self-help (I. i. 208–21). She might be thought a little too forward, however, had she voluntarily revealed her plan to the Countess and actively solicited her support. The Steward's report allows the Countess to assert ingeniously that she is a mother to Helena and thus draw from her a horrified rejection of a relationship that would make her a sister to Bertram rather than a woman unconnected to him and thus, at least theoretically, still eligible as a marriage-partner for him. The delicacy of presenting the matter in this fashion is Shakespeare's invention, for there is in the source no figure such as the Countess. It also provides an opportunity for Helena to make it clear that, despite her love for Bertram, she is fully aware of and takes seriously the impediment of social distance which stands between them (I. iii. 147–51). That Helena is so fearful of revealing her love, aware that others might regard her as presumptuous, and the fact that, with the Steward's advance warning, the Countess has to trick her into voicing her aspirations, makes her seem unnecessarily cautious, the more especially so because the Countess indicates no objection to the match. When Helena eventually confesses (I. iii. 184–210) she does so with attractive humility. She does not rule the match to be impossible but does indicate that she would seek to deserve him even though she is unclear as to how 'that desert' can be achieved. Her appeal to the Countess, on the common grounds of humanity and vulnerability to love, echoes the note struck by Lavatch earlier in the scene. The Countess is shrewd enough to recognize that Helena's proposed trip to Paris is not entirely altruistic, and the young woman is allowed to win our sympathy by honestly admitting that her plan to aid the King was prompted by thought of Bertram (I. iii. 225–8). The Countess does not state openly that she approves of the match, but, when she supports Helena's expedition to Paris in the knowledge that her chief motive is to be near Bertram, we can see that she is not opposed to it. Her last line, 'What I can help thee to, thou shalt not miss' (249), implies an offer of aid, since she is to be supplied with means and attendants to carry the Countess's greeting 'To those of mine in court' (246), of whom Bertram is clearly the principal figure.

Bertram will make a great deal of fuss about the gulf in rank which makes marriage to Helena humiliating to him. The Countess in this scene under-mines the argument based on nobility of blood and honour before it is made by acting very much like a mother to Helena and indicating that the girl's virtue and her own affection make her worthy of being her daughter no matter what distinction blood may make (I. iii. 135–46). It is the Countess, and not Helena, who broaches the idea that if being her daughter is impossi-ble she might still be her daughter-in-law (160). This scene establishes the first of the alliances between women in the play. There will be later ones between the widow and Diana and Helena as they try to cope with the capriciousness and vain self-regard of the men who bray about honour in public and act dishonourably in private. The Countess will become, besides Helena herself, the figure most obviously distressed by her son's behaviour (III. iv. 25–42). She will send letters to him in Florence berating him for his graceless behaviour, that are stern enough to disturb even someone as complacently self-righteous at Bertram has become (IV. iii. 1–6). She becomes so fond of Helena that the girl becomes as valuable to her as her own son (III. iv. 38–40).

The Steward's report provides the Countess with an advantage in ferreting out the truth, and thus provides an unusual alliance in comedy between young and old. In a more conventional structure, as I have suggested, the Countess might have discovered Helena's love in a direct exchange and determined to block it. Or, having been forewarned of the love by the Steward, she could have led Helena into a trap by eliciting a confession and then dismissing her. A similar structure is employed in *The Two Gentlemen of Verona* when the Duke, forewarned by Proteus of Valentine's intention of using a rope-ladder to gain access to his daughter and steal her away, craftily entraps Valentine, uncovers his plot, and banishes him. Shakespeare could have developed the scene with the Countess, having no forewarning, gradually uncovering Helena's desires. That would have been more cumbersome, may have required a longer scene, and would not have focused the audience on the Countess's strategy of deliberately provoking the confession and then providing aid which will expedite Helena's aims. This way of handling the matter allows Helena to voice all the conventional objections to the match in anticipating the censure of the Countess. The absence of any word of censure indicates that for the Countess, in the juxtaposition of values which riddles virtually every scene of the play, virtue and good deeds are as important in determining worth as noble blood, good breeding, and a lofty sense of honour.

Helena has some special skill in charming the wise and experienced characters of the play. Her trip to Paris is accomplished with the aid of the Countess. On her arrival in Paris Lafew becomes her ally. Lafew was invented by Shakespeare to act as a critic of the decayed nobility, of the young men at court, and specifically of Bertram who is green enough in judgement to be taken in by the fraudulent pretender to bravado, Parolles. Lafew is established as a shrewd judge of character, a man who can pick out virtue wherever it appears without allowing the claims of blood and social ranking to muddy his judgement. He appears not merely as a figure sympathetic to Helena but, in his report to the King of her arrival at court (II. i. 72–87), as her character-reference and promotional agent. Lafew's behaviour in II. i is calculated to seduce the King from his morbid commitment to death to the consideration of another proposed cure. Shakespeare makes a good deal more of the skills of Gerard de Narbon than we find in the source story and thus endows Helena, by association, with a slight touch of the aura of a mage who can do the impossible. It is Lafew's report which indicates her powers are almost unearthly and that her qualities make her outstanding and beyond compare even to an old man of his long experience. By providing her with an enthusiastic spokesman Shakespeare can thus maintain his image of her as a modest young woman which can be further unfolded in her subsequent interview with the King.

This is a very considerable change from the figure in William Painter's source story. Giletta exhibits an aggressive self-regard and is the sole originator and promoter of the plan to cure the King. Helena is more voluble than Giletta in ascribing her healing powers to the skill of her father (II. i. 101–14). She is neither as confident nor as insistent as Giletta. In the source it is the King who considers the young woman may be sent by God (Bullough, vol. II, p. 390). In Shakespeare it is Helena who modestly reminds the King of God: 'He that of greatest works is finisher/Oft does them by the weakest minister', reminding him that miracles can come from the unlikeliest of sources (II. i. 136–44). She continues her religious arguments in a way which places the emphasis not on her own skills (as Giletta unambiguously does), but on a faith in a skill that comes from God's grace (II. i. 148–58). Shakespeare develops the spiritual quality, suggested in Lafew's report, as a key element of her character. There is a worldly quality about many of the characters in the play, and especially about Bertram, Parolles, Lavatch, and the Lords in IV. iii. who talk about man's sinful nature (IV. iii. 60–9). Helena stands out against these figures, and Shakespeare puts such emphasis on her spiritual qualities because he is aware that ultimately, in the bed-trick, she will be involved in an action which is very earthy and pragmatic. We see in Helena a combination of the spiritual and the physical, a modesty and a lack of presumption that is nevertheless allied to a shrewd and determined temper to get what she wants and what is hers. These are qualities which the Countess, Lafew, and, ultimately, the King find attractive.

Shakespeare could have presented, had he so wished, the King's miraculous recovery onstage, but I believe its effect is more stunning by keeping it offstage. We have seen the King in a couple of scenes, and he is, in most productions, presented as physically very weak indeed, on a litter, in a wheel chair, or in need of much support. His mental condition is that of defeated submission to death rather than seeker after life. The report at the outset of II. iii. 1–37 indicates that the miracle has happened. But Lafew's report is presented in an oblique fashion because of the mannered, absurd interruptions of Parolles's importunate chatter. Lafew is addressing Bertram but Parolles completes Lafew's sentences so often that Bertram manages to get only three words into the entire exchange. We come upon the exchange as a conversation already in flow about a miracle that has occurred. We have a clue about what it is when Lafew says 'To be relinquished of the artists' (10) which we can deduce from the reply of Parolles is a reference to physicians. Only at the statement 'That gave him out incurable' (14) can we be certain that the King is the subject of the exchange. Thereafter Parolles is so bent on interrupting and so concerned to use impressive, though not illuminating, vocabulary and constructions that we are mystified. There is no clear statement of the King's recovery for 35 lines, and it could be argued that the exchange is a deliberate lack of preparation for the King's astonishing transformation, for the confusion is cleared up finally by the King's entrance. Most productions take the hint from the text, 'Why, he's able to lead her coranto' (41–2) to give the King a sprightly dancing entrance, so that, in his rejuvenation, he is almost unrecognizable, which helps further to underline Helena's exceptional powers.

Lafew's report is so confusingly extended that it cannot be seen as an abridgement of the action for reasons of dramatic economy. It is of course economical in other less direct ways. Apart from its ostensible function to report a miracle, its more important purpose is to initiate the relationship of Lafew and Parolles. The audience has already had a taste of Parolles and has reason to distrust him in his jesting with Helena (I. i. 95–207), and in his exchange with the Lords and his advice to Bertram (II. i. 24–60), but it is in this scene that we get a fuller picture of this counterfeit warrior. In his chatter with Lafew we find an affected self-regard that is reminiscent of Osric in *Hamlet* and of Lucio in *Measure for Measure*, three roles which might well have been played by the same actor in Shakespeare's company. It becomes even clearer that Bertram has not followed his mother's parting advice, 'Love all, trust few' (I. i. 59), and his association with Parolles underlines his lack of judgement. It is important that this is most clearly established in this scene where Bertram is so resistant to being tied to Helena, whom he considers so far beneath him, a figure regarded by everyone else as exceptional. Bertram shows no awareness of how, in Lafew's eye, and eventually in the eyes of everyone else, his reputation is galled by his association with Parolles, a hollow figure of no substance. The introductory exchange Parolles has with Lafew is the opening bracket of the scene which will be balanced in a closing bracket by another conversation between them wherein the wise old aristocrat comprehensively exposes Parolles as a fool (II. iii. 183–258), and Bertram continues his reliance on this shallow creature (II. iii. 259–94). In the face of Lafew's insults to this 'window of lattice', this 'general offense' that every man should beat, any true man of honour would call his tormentor to account and demand the issue be resolved in combat. Parolles is so cowardly that he absorbs every unambiguous aspersion on his character with only feeble verbal protestations and dares only to resort to insulting replies or threats of physical revenge when Lafew is offstage (II. iii. 230–6, 259–60). Shakespeare is here again protecting Helena and exposing Bertram. Lafew's introductory report is not entirely necessary for the transmission of information but does serve the purpose of showing Parolles at his most absurd. Should anyone in the audience be inclined to think Helena overly aggressive or Bertram's rejection of her as partially justified either because she is socially inferior, or because he is given no choice in the marriage, then they are reminded before and after how absurd Bertram's insistent claims about his honour are given the fact that his closest friend is a dishonourable, ungentlemanly fraud.

I have suggested some of the ways in which Shakespeare consistently presents Helena as a modest young woman by providing her with allies who promote her exceptional qualities. We can see this more broadly in the way he modifies the source story, the thirty-eighth novel in William Painter's *Palace of Pleasure*. Helena's prototype, Giletta, is an independent and resourceful woman who would rejoice the heart of any modern feminist. It could be argued that in modifying and softening the character Shakespeare is cleaving to the conservative instincts of a patriarchally ordered society. It can also be argued that the level of realism aimed at in the fantasy world of romance and folk-tale is not particularly demanding. Shakespeare may have wished to present a modified figure, acceptable in the relatively more realistic stage world, to support the refreshingly subversive contention that honour has nothing to do with rank and that marriage across class barriers can be a healthy way of rejuvenating a decaying society. Shakespeare seems to have felt that Painter's heroine was not realistically credible. He quite consistently reworks the story so that the figure isolated in it is not the woman but the flawed man, Bertram.

Giletta, in pursuing her secret love of Bertram, keeps her kinsfolk in ignorance of her intentions and has no allies. There is no sign in Giletta of Helena's awareness that her aspirations for a nobleman may be thought presumptuous, for Painter deals scarcely at all with the problems social disparity among marriage partners could cause in the real world. Helena is given allies in the aristocratic rank she will join by marriage so that, even though she is independent and determined, her worth is recognized by others and promoted by them. She wins the unambiguous gratitude of the King whereas in the source story 'The king was very loth to graunt him [Beltramo] to her' (Bullough, vol. II, p. 391). The young lords in court in Shakespeare's II. iii may not seem very eager to be chosen by Helena, but the only figure in the play fully sympathetic to Bertram's disdain for her is Parolles. Shakespeare adds a touch, that is not found in Giletta, when Bertram informs the King that he will not have her. Helena is willing to drop her request and withdraw from the bargain: 'That you are well restored, my lord, I'm glad./Let the rest go' (II. iii. 146–7). The marriage is insisted on not by Helena (she says nothing further before she departs) but by the King who considers *his* honour to be at stake. Nor is there, in the source, any disparagement of Beltramo comparable to Shakespeare's exposure of the flaws in Bertram. The French lords in IV. iii show little sympathy for his callous behaviour, and the sympathy of Parolles taints him rather than exempts him from blame. In IV. iii we can see that however supportive Parolles may be to Bertram's face he acknowledges the young man's faults behind his back. With this constant adjustment of detail Shakespeare makes the audience allies of Helena as she pursues her task of catching out her arrogant young colt of a husband. This is especially emphasized at the conclusion.

In Painter the Countess, Giletta, arrives home from Florence with the two children she has conceived in the bed-trick to provide her husband with incontrovertible evidence. In Shakespeare the King, the old Countess, and Lafew, assembled at Rousillon, intend to revert to type by allowing Bertram to marry Lafew's daughter now that (unlike the source) his first wife is reported to be dead. To the one ring of the source Shakespeare adds another, and unlike Beltramo convinced by his twin infants, Bertram is involved in extended complications. He double-damns himself by compounding his earlier lies, and by his dishonourable attempt to conceal his sexual exploits. He is censured by his mother, the King, and Lafew, and even the despised Parolles is allowed opportunity for some small revenge in testifying that Bertram did pursue Diana. Diana and the Widow are brought along as further allies to expose Bertram's feckless behaviour. Bertram paints himself into a corner and is in a much more perilous position than Beltramo in making himself almost a shameful pariah. He can only be rescued by the patient, ingenious woman who resurrected as it seems from the dead, has the grace to take him back as her husband. Bertram has made himself ineligible as a marriage-partner by his dishonourable behaviour, for, as Lafew says, before anyone knows Helena is alive, and even before the full extent of Bertram's duplicity in the past and his disgraceful evasions in the present are revealed, 'I will buy me a son-in-law in a fair, and toll for this. I'll none of him' (V. iii. 148–9).

The strategy in developing Helena is consistent, and the reports I have commented on are a small but significant aspect of all of the elements modified from the source. It is true that Helena is not as assertive a figure as Giletta, but Painter does not give a picture of a society that is, in its particular details, as complex as the one Shakespeare presents. Shakespeare devotes a good deal of space to displaying the masculine arrogance and snobbery of several of the men in the play, making Bertram a vivid portrait of a predatory, immature young aristocrat. Helena does not merely win back her husband, as Giletta did, she is the only one charitable enough to rescue him from the complete social ignominy his feckless behaviour has incurred. Helena, like many of Shakespeare's other comic heroines, is overwhelmingly talented, especially compared to the men around her, and she is able to prevail in spite of the handicap put in her way. Of course prevailing in this society does not mean competing equally – these women cannot win independence, they can only win the husbands they have been reared to pursue. These husbands are often quite unworthy of them, and we are often left with a sense that it is the woman's task, in a society crippled by reflex male-chauvinist values and patriarchal dominance, to improve matters by using their ingenuity in trying to make silk purses out of sows' ears.

Much Ado About Nothing

The most significant report of offstage action in *Much Ado About Nothing* occurs at III. iii. 133–51 when Borachio recounts to Conrade the deception he has practised on Don Pedro and Claudio in making them believe Hero to be a wanton by wooing at her window Margaret in the guise of Hero. Geoffrey Bullough in *Narrative and Dramatic Sources in Shakespeare*, vol. II, p. 76, has speculated about Shakespeare's handling of this sequence:

> It is truly remarkable that Shakespeare does not present the scene . . . for [it] is found in all the analogues. These scenes have a weakness in that the hero must not be allowed to rush from his hiding place and make his accusation then and there; but Shakespeare could have got over this as Bandello did . . . The Cambridge editors suggest that there may have been such a scene in an earlier version (by Shakespeare) of the play. I cannot believe that if there ever were a scene so dramatic, so central, it would have been omitted even to make room for Beatrice and Benedick to manoeuvre. Shakespeare refused to use it, I suspect, in order to draw attention to his major theme of hearsay and false report.

This sequence given in report is of a scene that, it is apparent, Shakespeare could have placed onstage, for, as Bullough points out, there is a somewhat similar and even more complex scene of overhearing in *Troilus and Cressida* (V. ii) when Troilus and Ulysses, overseen by Thersites, observe from hiding the seduction of Cressida by Diomedes. There is no disguise involved, but there is something of the same stunning reversal of perspective in a young man's attitude to a woman he has trusted. Eavesdropping scenes are, in any case, common enough in Shakespeare (from the sequence of overheard lovers in *Love's Labour Lost*, to the gulling of Malvolio, to Othello as a peeping Tom) for Shakespeare to have had little difficulty with it. Indeed, two of the most effective overhearing scenes have already occurred in this very play when Benedick (II. iii) and Beatrice (III. i) are both taken in and fail to penetrate the trick being played on them. Thus to stage the wooing of Margaret as Hero by Borachio would clearly fit the style of action. But Shakespeare was always aware that too much of a good thing might diminish an effect, and that is a plausible explanation of why the sequence is kept offstage. To put Borachio's ruse onstage would have meant presenting three overhearing sequences in a mere four scenes. It is not as if Borachio's ruse would have completed the sequence of scenes based on false appearances. Shakespeare has other scenes to come in which surprising reversals and revelations will occur. Claudio will appear in church where everything seems set fair for a happy marriage until he stuns everyone by proclaiming Hero to be 'a rotten orange' and 'an approved wanton'. After discovering his error Claudio will attend a second marriage ceremony where again things are not what they seem, and instead of marrying, as he expects, a total stranger will be united with the woman he had humiliated and thought dead. There are, I believe, a variety of reasons for keeping Borachio's ruse offstage, and an explanation of them involves an examination of many aspects of the design of the whole play.

There are a number of problems about the plausibility of the wooing at the window, which suggest than an audience's willingness to suspend disbelief might be less challenged by a report than by a direct witnessing of the sequence onstage. It could be argued that Shakespeare so habitually exploits conventional elements of folk-tale without worrying about whether they are realistic or acceptable to an audience that objecting to this sequence is akin to straining at a gnat after swallowing a camel. If the bed-tricks in *Measure for Measure* and *All's Well That Ends Well* have to be swallowed would Borachio's ruse strain an audience's belief even if, unlike those other tricks, it were put onstage? What is credible in drama varies with dramatic conventions, and it is pointless to judge the drama of other ages by the standards of the realist dramas of more recent times. It is my belief, however, that Shakespeare often goes to considerable lengths to make some incidents, as they appear in his sources, more acceptable. Certainly, one of the most questionable sequences in *Much Ado About Nothing* from a realist viewpoint is the wooing-sequence with Margaret, the hinge on which much of the action turns. Critics often note the anomalies in this sequence and the problems it does not fully answer. Few of them, however, have examined how many functions it serves and how many more problems would have been raised by presenting it onstage.

One of the reasons for keeping the ruse of Borachio's wooing offstage has to do with the effect on the audience's attitude to Margaret, and ultimately, as I shall suggest, to our view of the men as opposed to the women in the play. Margaret is eventually to be declared innocent of any complicity in Borachio's devious plotting against her mistress, Hero. Yet Borachio's initial explanation of his scheme to Don John in II. ii makes it seem, on the face of it, that she could not be totally innocent. Borachio asserts that he will perform a deception at Hero's window for the bystanders Don John will bring along, and they will 'hear me call Margaret Hero, hear Margaret term me Claudio' (II. ii. 37–8). We may wonder what arguments Borachio used to Margaret for this little show in which they would play the roles of Hero and Claudio without raising the girl's suspicions that something underhand was going on. The fact that she is attracted to Borachio, whom we hear she has favoured for a year (II. ii. 11–13), tells us something about her nature. Her comments on the wedding morning, in broad sexual innuendoes, about the pleasures of the wedding night (III. iv. 24–33), and her ability to tease double meaning out of Beatrice's remarks (III. iv. 39–84) which shows that she can match wits with her betters, fill out our knowledge of her lively character. Margaret is protected, to some degree, from any sense we may have that she is deeply practised in deception by Shakespeare's ensuring that, in the gulling of Beatrice in II. iii, it is Hero and Ursula who are the principal role-players. Margaret is only asked to draw Beatrice into the trap and after her exit (at line 14) has no further part in the trick.

The only explanation one could imagine that Borachio could give to Margaret as to why she should hang out of a window pretending to play Hero to his Claudio is to persuade her to join him in some horseplay, a below-stairs satirical mockery of the courtly-love pretensions of their social superiors, indulging his playful and, perhaps, drunken humour. That still sounds rather thin, though many things in comedy are thin. Shakespeare usually avoids focusing our attention on transparent elements in his plot by maintaining a judicious silence. We may also note that Shakespeare's silence and his keeping the scene offstage conceals another problem. If Claudio hears Borachio call Margaret Hero and she calls him Claudio then he must conclude that Hero is a very confused young woman or that she is in some playful collusion with her lover in mockingly referring to him as the suitor she is betraying. Borachio never explains how he will persuade Margaret to play the role nor does he explain how she could have remained innocent. It is possible to believe that she had no knowledge that Don John, Don Pedro, and Claudio would overhear her performance with Borachio. But after the humiliation Hero is subjected to at her wedding ceremony, even though Margaret is not onstage to witness it, it seems likely that afterwards she must have heard the nature of the accusation and must tumble to the fact that her involvement in Borachio's apparent jest must have led to the catastrophe. She holds key information that could clear Hero. If we suppose that she may deliberately conceal her role in Hero's shame then we can guess why. To confess her own tomfoolery might, given the irascible, erratic nature of Leonato, lead to her dismissal from her position and would certainly get

Borachio into trouble. Whatever speculations the audience may involve itself in, Shakespeare ensures that he does not provoke them, for he offers no immediate comment on the nature of Margaret's involvement. We may, in a similar way, speculate about why Emilia remains silent about her passing of Desdemona's handkerchief to Iago. We can only speculate that she gives him the handkerchief to please him. We know that she is unaware of his villainous nature, and she does eventually recognize her own instrumental part in causing Desdemona's death and compensates by risking and losing her life in order to clear the name of her mistress. It is hard to imagine that Margaret could have remained as innocently ignorant as Emilia, but Shakespeare does not give us much time to think about the matter. Don John flies the town, Borachio is put under arrest, and we are absorbed in the way the watch overhears the story and follows a devious path in uncovering the truth, so that our attention is distracted entirely away from Margaret.

In V. i Borachio redeems himself somewhat by revealing his crime to Claudio and Don Pedro. He does so partly, we may suspect, because Don John has abandoned him, because he has been driven to distraction by the circuitous bumbling of Dogberry, and possibly because of remorse or a shrewd determination to gain credit for repentance by confessing what Dogberry might, after several hours, be capable of revealing (V. i. 219–31). In III. iii. we hear Borachio assert of Margaret 'she leans me out at her mistress' chamber window, bids me a thousand times good night' (135–6) – which implies some mocking and satirical exaggeration. In V. i Borachio adds a detail, which must obviously have been involved if the victims were to be successfully gulled, that he was seen to 'court Margaret in Hero's garments' (226). In this full-scale dress performance we can envisage Margaret's innocence only as part of some tipsy prank with Borachio encouraging her to join him in 'sending up' the lovers on their wedding eve. On several occasions we hear that Borachio did the trick for money, but he is man enough once found out to admit his treachery. He is excused to some degree by Leonato, who indicates that he cannot bear the blame for the deception alone, because a 'pair of honourable men' (V. i. 253), who were taken in by the trick, are guilty too. Leonato forbears to mention that he, who did not witness the trick in person, was even more foolish, for he was convinced it was true and his daughter faithless only from a report. Borachio wins a little more respect by chivalrously exempting Margaret from any blame when Leonato accuses her of being 'packed in all this wrong' – 'No, by my soul, she was not;/Nor knew not what she did when she spoke to me;/But always hath been just and virtuous/In anything that I do know by her' (V. i. 287–90). It is worth remembering that in a number of the sources and analogues the maid is embroiled in scheming from devious motives of her own. In no version is the innocence of the maid attested to and insisted upon as it is in Shakespeare's handling of Margaret. At this point, of course, we may wonder how much a man such as Borachio can be trusted to tell the truth. At the moment when we might speculate how innocent Margaret could really be Shakespeare sheers right away from the issue by having Dogberry immediately proceed to a comic embroidery of this resolution by insisting on revealing his deeply held grievance that he was called an ass. The constable insists that this matter should not be forgotten in assessing Borachio's punishment, any more than that fantastic creation of mishearing, Deformed, should be overlooked.

I am not suggesting that the issue of Margaret's guilt is a major one for the audience. It is handled discreetly by Shakespeare to eliminate matters that could cause unnecessary distraction, as Bullough has suggested (vol. II, pp. 72–3):

> The dramatist does not explore her behaviour, for in a romantic tale women do strange things for their lovers, and she obviously thinks nothing of it as her behaviour next morning shows (III. 4). Shakespeare makes her 'just and virtuous' because he does not want to overwhelm Hero by treachery from within as well as from outside the house. The evil is to be concentrated in one small group, not a tragic perversion of the whole atmosphere.

In comedy loose ends are rarely left untied. We do not want the harmony of the ending to be clouded by the punishment of a servant who has played only a dubious marginal role. In the last lines of the play we hear that the major villain, Don John, is captured and returned for punishment, and Borachio, his agent, will receive punishment, though we never hear what it is to be. Margaret is not forgotten, for at the end of V. i Leonato indicates 'We'll talk with Margaret/How her acquaintance grew with this lewd fellow' (316–17). In the very next scene (V. ii) we can see that Margaret has either survived inquiry or that no serious question of her honesty remains, for she is onstage with Benedick who is begging for her help in his pursuit of Beatrice. Margaret is neither chastened nor subdued but as capable of bandying words with Benedick as she was with Beatrice in III. iv, and this exchange of bawdy innuendo signals her acceptance as part of the continuing community of comedy. The last we hear of her part in Borachio's ruse occurs in the final scene: 'But Margaret was in some fault for this,/Although against her will, as it appears/In the true course of all the questions' (V. iv. 4–6). That she did not act with malicious intention and is therefore forgiven is underlined by the fact that she is onstage in this last scene. It is part of the pattern of Shakespeare's comedies that she should be exculpated, for the women in them are very rarely malicious, and that allows the audience to see more clearly by contrast the folly of the men.

I have focused first on the problems Shakespeare avoided or carefully manœuvred around, especially Margaret's involvement, by choosing to present Borachio's supposed wooing of Hero at her window as an offstage event. I turn now to that sequence framing the matter in a different way by indicating the problems which would have arisen had it been presented as an onstage action. In Bullough (vol. II, pp. 134–9) there are passages from *Fidele and Fortunio*, an analogue by M. A. [Anthony Munday], in which some of the structures required to carry off this deception are indicated. But the story and intention in this play are different in many ways, and the scenes do not cover the functions Shakespeare would have required had he decided to conduct the gulling onstage. Shakespeare does, elsewhere, write a scene in which a figure in hiding is led to false conclusions about a woman's faith when he observes other figures engaged in misleading conversation. Iago's plot, in the peeping Tom scene in *Othello* (IV. i), is in danger of coming unstuck if at any point it becomes clear that his exchange with Cassio is not, as Othello believes, about Desdemona at all. Bianca's arrival with the handkerchief turns out to be a bonus which further convinces the hidden Othello of Iago's story. Bianca is not in Margaret's situation, for she is playing herself and not Desdemona in disguise. The scene is one of extraordinary suspense carefully set up by an earlier sequence with Bianca and several passages about the handkerchief which provides it with a loaded dramatic potential. In wishing to preserve the innocence of Margaret Shakespeare would have been presented with a problem had he decided to present onstage the seduction at Hero's window. If Don John brought on Claudio and Don Pedro to observe from a distance then the colloquy between Borachio and Margaret could not have hinted that she believed she was involved only in an innocent, joking game because that would have disabused the two victims the sequence was intended to convince. I can suggest how the scene could have been written to solve some of Shakespeare's problems while registering the fact that an onstage presentation might have caused as many problems as it solved.

(a) In order to reassure the audience that Margaret is innocent of any evil intent the scene would have to open with a sequence between Margaret and Borachio in which it becomes clear that she has been persuaded to dress up in Hero's clothes and to imitate her mistress only as a sort of satirical lark to humour Borachio and that she has no awareness that she will be overheard.

(b) Don John brings on Claudio and Don Pedro to observe the mock-wooing as Margaret ardently says farewell to her lover. Yet if she is completely innocent and playing a game it is hard to see how the scene could be conducted in entire sobriety without her cracking up or commenting on the joke of sending up the aristocrats. She cannot continue to be a giddy Margaret for the audience and a convincing Hero for the onlookers onstage at the same time.

(c) When the wooing and farewell appears to be completed Don John can justify his concern for the honour of Claudio and Don Pedro. We can hardly suppose that Claudio and Don Pedro could depart without their sense of outrage being expressed and some declaration of their intention to shame Hero in the chapel. (Iago and Othello review the sequence Cassio and Bianca have innocently performed, and Othello confirms his determination to take revenge, (IV. i. 168–207). But this would cause problems because it would diminish the impact of the chapel scene. The outrage Claudio and Don Pedro must necessarily express there, in explaining their behaviour to a shocked assembly, would have been already partly exhibited to the audience.

(*d*) The scene could conclude with the return of Borachio and the re-appearance of Margaret on the balcony to laugh at the play-acting they have been involved in. This would reaffirm our sense of Borachio's craft in bringing off the scene without Margaret ever having realized how she has been used.

Structured in this way it could be argued that Shakespeare, with great care in timing and phrasing, might have put the action onstage instead of handling it in report. It would, however, have required a major scene and greater time and prominence than Shakespeare was willing to give it. It could have unequivocally established Margaret's innocence, but Margaret is not such a significant character as to justify so much attention.

The most significant aspect of presenting the matter thus onstage in a few hundred lines instead of in report as offstage action in 19 lines would be the effect it would have on our view of Claudio and Don Pedro. Othello hunts for ocular proof, and though the audience knows it to be false, we can see how, in his eyes, it becomes convincing. It is very important that the audience has a direct experience of how plausibly he is convinced that he has caught Cassio in an admission of his treachery. To see Claudio and Don Pedro being gulled onstage by a plausible performance would give the audience the kind of ocular proof Shakespeare does not want us to have. We would be focused as much on how they are taken in, on their victimization, as on their reactions to the trick played on them. There would be more visible evidence of the villainy of Don John and the subtlety of Borachio which would change the play considerably. I have indicated already the lengths to which Shakespeare goes to protect Margaret. Further consideration of the reasons for keeping Borachio's ruse offstage indicates that the choice is related to the shaping of the attitudes of the audience to the men in the play who all share various degrees of foolish gullibility and a distrust of women.

It was easy in the Elizabethan age – for many even automatic – to blame everything on women by regarding them as daughters of Eve and a continuing source of all trouble. Claudio and Don Pedro are only too willing to believe Hero guilty; Leonato as a reflex assumes his daughter to be in the wrong and her accusers in the right; Benedick seeks to avoid any problems in his life by disdaining women and professing contempt for the married state; Don John has a rooted hatred of marriage; and Borachio's trick is based on a common assumption of woman's fickleness. Many of these men have to have their attitudes changed and to learn that trouble stems from their own reflex assumptions and their excessive prickliness in regard to their honour. It would have damaged Shakespeare's exposure of men's folly and punched a hole right through the case he so consistently builds, if the trouble were shown, as it is in the sources, to stem from the fickleness of a maid as a guilty co-conspirator in gulling her superiors. Shakespeare takes considerable pains to shut off that loophole by exempting Margaret from all blame. It was much easier to do that by keeping the sequence at Hero's bedchamber window offstage. Shakespeare can assert, what it might have been difficult to maintain onstage, that Margaret was herself a victim of Borachio's duplicity.

Our view of Claudio and Don Pedro and their gullible submission is affected to some degree by the way Don John is drawn. In the first place Shakespeare could have made Don John a much subtler and less detectable villain. Had he been given more of Iago's deceptive skills the audience might more easily understand the ease with which Claudio and Don Pedro are taken in. But Don John is one of the most broadly drawn villains in Shakespeare and a man so openly brooding and bitter that we are a little surprised that he could take in anyone. Beatrice and Hero comment about how little care he takes to conceal his bitterness (II. i. 3–5) in the scene immediately following our first view of Don John where, with his two followers, his corrosive nastiness is fully revealed. We hear from Conrade that Don John, who has languished in disfavour because of his opposition to Don Pedro, is only recently taken into his brother's grace (I. iii. 17–23). Don John rages against the politic behaviour Conrade counsels him to adopt and expresses his splenetic envy of Claudio – 'That young start-up hath all the glory of my overthrow. If I can cross him any way, I bless myself every way' (I. iii. 58–60). We can gather from other passages in the play that Don John is no expert at undetectable villainy in trying to pass himself off as an honest man. Benedick's response to the insult Hero receives in church indicates that, despite the general confusion, he has a shrewd idea of how the mischief has been set up to gull Don Pedro and Claudio: 'if their wisdoms be misled in this,/The practice of it lives in John the bastard,/Whose spirits toil in frame of villainies' (IV. i. 185–7). On the same day that the marriage is wrecked Don John flees town, and he thus confirms the story of villainy the watch has uncovered. Don Pedro, on hearing a true account of the ruse Borachio practised, asserts, with no evident surprise, the malign nature of his brother: 'He is composed and framed of treachery,/And fled he is upon this villainy' (V. i. 236–7), which may cause us to wonder how, when he stood outside Hero's window, he could so easily be taken in by Don John. Everything seems to point to the fact that Don John is a splenetic figure of very little skill, especially in view of the fact that all the schemes proposed in the play come from the brains of his servants and are largely performed by them. We have to come to the conclusion that the presentation of Don John as a saturnine, nasty, and not very bright villain is part of a larger design organized principally to affect our view of Claudio and Don Pedro.

Claudio and Don Pedro are not very winning characters. Bullough notes that Quiller-Couch considered that the decision not to present directly onstage the ruse whereby Borachio woos Margaret tends to weaken audience sympathy for Claudio in the chapel scene, and he observes that this may not be a flaw in the design but intentional:

> Shakespeare does not want us to enter deeply into Claudio's mind. He is not meant to dominate the action; he is a figure in a group dance-pattern, important, but not a soloist. Our sympathies are to be with him only in so far as he is temporarily a victim of deceit and delusion.
>
> (Bullough, vol. II, p. 77)

In my view that is to cast Claudio in far too favourable a light. Shakespeare, with the wooing scene, is negotiating a very delicate problem. If he had put it onstage then it could have been presented in two ways. Either the performance of Margaret and Borachio has to be so bad that we think Claudio and Don Pedro fools to submit to the deception, in which case their later behaviour so compounds their initial folly that they are unlikely ever to recover the good will of the audience. Or the performance is so good that we can believe they could be taken in, which wins for them rather more sympathy than they deserve. It is important that the audience believe they have been taken in, and that, from what we already know of them, it does not surprise us. But it is also important that we do not share their viewpoint or sympathize with them. The only way Shakespeare can have the best of both worlds is to keep the wooing offstage, and this preserves to a considerable degree the shock effect of Claudio's rejection of Hero in IV. i. The advantage of having Borachio report the wooing is that he can also reveal Claudio's intention of shaming Hero in church. This means that Shakespeare does not have to exhibit any of the outrage of Claudio and Don Pedro before the chapel scene. The self-righteousness and brutality of the two in that scene can therefore not only shock those onstage but seem excessive to the audience. I would not, therefore, merely speculate as Bullough does, that Shakespeare might have intended to diminish our sympathy for Claudio by keeping the wooing scene offstage, I would assert that that is one of its principal functions and fits in with other elements of design throughout the play.

Shakespeare intentionally structures the play to underline the fact that Claudio does not know Hero very well. His first inquiry about her has to do with the wealth that is attached to her (I. i. 262–3). That can hardly have been unusual in Shakespeare's age, and young men such as Petruchio and Bassanio are presented initially to some degree as fortune-hunters, but they are given other attractive qualities to supply some sense of balance, a practice that is not undertaken for Claudio. When Don Pedro indicates that he will depart for Arragon immediately following the wedding Claudio proposes, as a courtesy, to accompany him, which argues no very great passion in Claudio for Hero. Don Pedro has to insist that would be 'as great a soil in the new gloss of your marriage as to show a child his new coat and forbid him to wear it' (III. ii. 4–6). The comparison of Claudio to a child may be accidental but it does not seem inappropriate. The ruse which Don John tries early in the play at the masked ball in arguing and convincing Claudio that Don Pedro is wooing Hero for himself can only serve the purpose of revealing to the audience how gullible Claudio is. The matter is quickly resolved but only after Claudio's sulking and a display of his insecurity. This misfired plot is crucial to the second scheme that Borachio proposes to Don John. We are not surprised that Claudio is again taken in because we have been given no evidence that there is much substance to his relationship with Hero. We scarcely see them together for any length of time, and they have very little to say to each other. Every detail suggests that this is very much closer to the arranged matches of Shakespeare's day than some of the more openly romantic relationships in other plays. Many of Shakespeare's young male lovers are foolish, and some of them, such as Proteus and Bertram, not very attractive. Claudio may be deceived by a villain but he has been established as a priggish young man who cannot woo for himself and is mocked as something of an inexperienced pup by Benedick. In the chapel scene he behaves as a cad and is very fortunate in the end to be rescued from his dishonour and folly by the Friar's plan. The audience will be hard pressed to find him acceptable and does not need additional direct evidence of his folly in watching him being duped by Borachio. If a happy ending is to be achieved it is important not to put the central figures beyond the pale of forgiveness.

There are a number of elements which contribute to the protection of Claudio so that he never quite becomes irredeemable. He is not much, but then neither is Hero, who is muted and not possessed of the fiery spirit of many of Shakespeare's heroines, and is, for most of the play, dominated by her elders. There are other fools in the play besides Claudio, and that prevents the audience from singling him out for censure. Shakespeare only makes some minor uses of attitudes presented in the versions of the story by Bandello and Belleforest that the man is condescending to marry a woman of a lower social station. In Belleforest Timbrée (Claudio) tries to seduce the young woman for some time because he feels that she is not of sufficient rank to match him. Shakespeare's Leonato is a governor, and though there is no evidence that he is of a lower rank than Claudio, there is a feeling that he seems to view the marriage of his daughter to the protégé of the Prince of Arragon as something of a social coup. This tends to confirm the impression that this arranged match has as much to do with status as with love. In the chapel scene (IV. i) Leonato's lamentations are not at all initially for his daughter. He is willing to believe all accusations brought against her and trusts these visiting aristocrats and their sense of honour above his own flesh and blood. The play throughout underlines the vulnerable position of women, and it is most apparent in this scene when Leonato succumbs to the stereotyping of women, and the general male-chauvinist compact, in his belief that a noble offer of marriage to dignify his daughter has been paid back with the fickle duplicity of a woman. He is so concerned about the shame to his family honour that he scarcely registers Hero's anguish. In making Leonato have so little faith in his daughter Shakespeare goes beyond several of his sources. In some of them the father is prone to trust the men's sense of honour rather than the woman's. In Bandello, however, the parents and the citizens of Messina do not believe tales about the unchaste deception it is claimed Fenicia (Hero) has practised. Only when the Friar and others speak up for Hero's innocence is Leonato willing to reconsider, but even then his concern is less for his daughter than for clearing his family's besmirched name (IV. i. 188–98). When he and Antonio, in V. i, confront Claudio and Don Pedro they all behave like proud, self-righteous buffoons priggishl·concerned with honour. The audience has a hard choice to make about which pair is the more absurd – the two old men eager to fight things out or the insultingly cocky and disdainful aristocrats who refuse to be drawn into a brawl. Even if Claudio is not of a superior rank he certainly behaves as though he has the right to treat Leonato and his family with rough condescension. Perhaps the favour Don Pedro shows him makes him behave with impetuous haughtiness. He is affable enough when he is pursuing a woman who, he is assured, is Leonato's sole heir, but when his honour is at stake his veneer of courtesy begins to disappear. Yet despite Claudio's priggish behaviour the audience can accept Leonato's eventual forgiveness of him and his willingness to proceed with the marriage. This is not only because Hero is proved to be innocent but because Leonato has been a choleric, erratic figure of folly whose loss of faith in his daughter was expressed in an even more amazing display of masculine, arrogant, self-righteousness than Claudio and Don Pedro had exhibited. We can never be completely alienated from Claudio because we recognize that his behaviour is only one example of a more general, characteristic, masculine habit of worrying about the figure they will cut in this world. The egregious error the young man makes is one shared by the older and wiser Don Pedro who knows a good deal about his brother's villainous and mischievous nature.

We have also observed the elaborate means required to draw Benedick from his bachelor posture disdainful of women. Benedick and Beatrice are more fully drawn and more attractive figures than Claudio and Hero, but in overshadowing the young lovers they also protect them to a degree from our censure. The deception to which Claudio submits is less reprehensible in that we have observed the brightest and wittiest characters in the play taken in by deceptive appearances as they are converted into lovers and take on the roles they have mocked for so long. Shakespeare's choice of showing us in extended detail onstage the way in which Benedick and Beatrice are deceived, and of keeping the deception of Claudio off the stage, serves the purpose of ensuring that the audience cannot isolate the young man as being any more gullible and foolish than those around him. Here, as in his other comedies, Shakespeare is intent on illustrating how easily people can be deceived and how, from instant to instant, they can be subject to a radical instability as they change their opinions, behaviour, nature, and identity. Nor are Benedick and Beatrice presented merely as credulous fools. In contrast to the gullible submissions of Claudio and Don Pedro to a belief in Hero's wantonness, we have to admire, by contrast, the absolute trust that Beatrice has in her cousin. There is also something reassuring in the way that Benedick is drawn by his love for Beatrice into an act of faith in Hero's innocence and can separate himself from Claudio and Don Pedro so that he seems wiser and less self-regarding than they.

I have suggested that Shakespeare avoided several problems by presenting the pretended seduction of Hero offstage. But that is merely to look on the negative side. He also makes this way of handling matters pay off in many positive ways. Shakespeare does save time in one way the better to exploit it in another. The report of the incident at Hero's window becomes part of a rich and complex development. The report carries a lot of freight, as we can see if we list the sequences connected to it:

(a) II. ii. 7–49 (43) Borachio proposes his scheme of wooing Margaret as Hero to Don John.

(b) III. iii. 88–167 (80) Borachio gives his report of the wooing to Conrade and is overheard by the watch. This indicates that Borachio is scarcely a very accomplished villain, since his trick, undetected by Claudio and Don Pedro, is uncovered by one of the least imposing group of law enforcers ever invented.

(c) III. v (59) Dogberry brings news to Leonato that he has 'comprehended two aspicious persons' (43), but his report is constantly sidetracked by malapropisms, by irrelevant observations, by patronizing attempts to put Verges in his place. This impedes the delivery of a straightforward report which would prevent a great deal of subsequent error, so that in 48 lines of interaction with Leonato he manages to convey to him no information whatsoever.

(d) IV. i. 1–152 (152) Leonato, Claudio, and Don Pedro and others therefore proceed in a manner in which they are written down by Shakespeare as asses, their behaviour in the chapel scene stemming from the supposed wooing.

(e) IV. ii (79) Dogberry undertakes the trial of Borachio but pursues tangential and irrelevant issues. He is more concerned to be written down as an ass than to focus on the nature of Borachio's actions. His faulty sense of priorities in putting his own self-importance before any serious attempt to find out what has happened is, of course, very much like the behaviour of Claudio, Don Pedro, and Leonato in the previous scene.

(*f*) V. i. 198–245 (48) Dogberry persists in confusion when he tries to report matters to his superiors, and the true story is only brought out when Borachio gives an account of the nocturnal duping of Claudio and Don Pedro. Borachio is able to emphasize our sense, to which all these scenes contribute, that the difference between Dogberry and the two aristocrats is not as great as they might like to think: 'What your wisdoms could not discover, these shallow fools have brought to light' (221–2).

(*g*) V. i. 284–90 (7) Leonato indicates his intention of examining Margaret, but Borachio asserts that she was entirely innocent.

(*h*) V. i. 316–17 (2) Leonato says he will inquire of Margaret how she became involved with Borachio.

(*i*) V. iv. 1–6 (6) The figures involved in the wooing scene, save Borachio, are exempted from blame. Margaret was 'in some fault' but since it was unintentional it does not appear that she will be punished.

These passages (which total 476 lines) anticipate, relate back to, arise out of, or are attempts to deal with the wooing that is presented as offstage action. The overhearing of the report is an economy in stage time which introduces the watch as the figures who uncover villainy while their social superiors posture and rage like prize turkey cocks. The deliberately rambling sequence of scenes which ensues is a comic harvest for the audience and serves to show us how the aristocrats, with their grand speeches, and the clown, with his stumbling words, have an equal capacity to get hold of the wrong end of the stick. The watch may be slow, but were it not for their tenacity the lives of the aristocrats would never recover from the humiliation, alienation, acerbic charge and counter-charge, challenge and baseless self-justification, into which they fall.

It must be pointed out that this deeper perspective is found only in Shakespeare's version. Only the slightest hints for this group of bumbling watchmen exist in one of the dramatic analogues. The light they cast on the aristocrats by their action is entirely Shakespeare's invention. In several of the versions of the story the deception practised by maids or rivals in love, which is the basis for the false wooing plot, is detailed and vivid, but Shakespeare chose not to use stage time to present it directly, but instead embroidered the idea of deceptive appearances by broadening the social range of his characters. Shakespeare placed the head of an ass on Bottom and yet demonstrated that asinine behaviour can spread quite generally beyond humble mechanicals, and he does something similar with Dogberry. Bottom, of course, had enough wisdom to keep his mouth shut about his dream, and Theseus had enough wisdom to deal charitably with the dramatic efforts of the mechanicals. Dogberry is as full of himself as Bottom but not ultimately as shrewd. That is understandable in a play in which the ranking figure, Don Pedro, lacks the charity of a Theseus and is accompanied by a young prig, Claudio, who is as touchy and self-righteous as Lysander and Demetrius, but has less excuse because he is misled by a coarse malcontent, Don John and his ruffian, Borachio, and not by the impish, quicksilver magic of a figure such as Puck. We find a wide range of characters taken in by false reports, mishearing, and misinterpreting, their errors of judgement invariably resulting from self-interest and excessive self-regard. We have to acknowledge that not all dissimulated role-playing is bad. The one enacted sequence placed offstage by Shakespeare for a variety of reasons almost has tragic consequences for Claudio, Hero, Don Pedro, and Leonato, which are averted when the truth comes out. But there are two sequences of simulated activity, placed onstage by Shakespeare which lead to a fruitful sense of renewal and harmony. Beatrice and Benedick eventually learn that the reports they overheard were also deliberately deceptive, and yet this deception brings them out of disdainful isolation to discover that the lies pressed on them contained a truth which they had refused to recognize.

2

'There is a world elsewhere': The functions of stage absence in the structure of Shakespeare's plays

In this chapter I wish to focus on the way dramatic roles can be shaped by long absences from the stage and how Shakespeare uses such absences or delays in the initial appearance of a character for specific effects in the structure of his plays. In some plays long absences find a ready-enough explanation in the plot. *The Winter's Tale* deploys two plots in two different countries which explains the long period Leontes and Paulina are offstage. Even a character such as Hermione whose role appears to be concluded in Act III can yet emerge in miraculous resurrection to take part in the conclusion of the play. In other plays without such plotting exigencies the large number of characters requiring doubling from a limited number of actors might seem to be a practical and adequate explanation for such absences and delays. If we accept that as an answer, it is still useful to note the ways in which Shakespeare made a virtue of necessity to augment the broader aims of his play. A character, whose appearances onstage are widely separated or whose initial entrance is long delayed, may serve to provide a new perspective, may give the audience a jolt by presenting the reactions of a character who has not been part of the ongoing process of development in the play. Sebastian in *Twelfth Night* and Lodovico in *Othello* are used for this effect. Characters who appear at the beginning of a play, disappear, and then reappear only towards the conclusion, as in *The Comedy of Errors* and *A Midsummer Night's Dream*, serve a specific structural function, in addition to the advantages of doubling that they probably involved. When we examine central roles such as Angelo's in *Measure for Measure* or Antonio's in *The Merchant of Venice* it is clear that doubling requirements are not the most obvious, likely, or persuasive explanations of their absences from the stage, and that we must search for more complex reasons in the nature of the characters and in the deeper structural patterns of the plays. I will eventually examine the strategically used stage absences in the roles of major characters in the tragedies where doubling is certainly not a consideration and where it is unwise to conclude that exigencies of plot determine the shape of the play.

I turn first, however, to the simplest and most straightforward uses of stage absence.

Twelfth Night

Sebastian first appears in II. i establishing that he is alive, that he has won the admiring friendship of Antonio, and that he is on his way to Count Orsino's court. His appearance onstage occurs immediately following the scene (I. v) in which Shakespeare has broached initial complexities connected to the disguise of Viola as a man. The audience is thus forewarned that there are liable to be ensuing confusions involving the twins but that things are likely to be resolved happily when they each discover that the other survived the shipwreck. After his 38-line appearance, which is something like an advertisement of a coming attraction, Sebastian disappears from the play for 771 lines until he re-emerges in III. iii. By that time Viola is involved in deeper complications, and the play is ready for the fillip of the second twin to compound the confusions. Shakespeare had already demonstrated in *The Comedy of Errors* that it is possible to string out mistakes of identity around two sets of twins for most of a play. The reappearance of Sebastian promises further fun but it also opens up the possibility of a resolution to Viola/ Cesario's problems which have tangled her up between Orsino and Olivia and, in III. ii, have just promised to draw her into a duel with Sir Andrew. Sebastian's re-emergence does not, as in some of the other examples I shall examine, supply the audience with the sense of imminent closure, but it does make us aware that after more agreeable plot-twists a solution is at hand because the mathematics of the situation is evened out. In comedy every Jack must have his Jill, and to this point we have been stuck with the unsatisfactory number of three, Orsino loving Olivia, Olivia loving Cesario, Viola loving Orsino. At Sebastian's entrance in III. ii we have the confirmation promised in II. i, and the audience can murmur, in the vein of Puck, 'Two of both kinds makes up four'. Sebastian adds a further complication to the play in which we have already seen disguise and deception operating at a variety of levels. In both plots key figures are being misled by deliberate deceptions. Sebastian confuses matters by entering as an innocent who intends to deceive no one. There has been a good deal of resistance to overtures of love – Olivia to Orsino, Cesario to Olivia, Olivia to Malvolio, and Sir Andrew of course believes he is undertaking a campaign to win Olivia whose resistance he can eventually overcome, though Olivia knows nothing of his campaign. Sebastian, taken by everyone to be Cesario, turns out surprisingly to be very pliant in love and very resistant in battle. Everyone else is deviously trying to shape the world according to his own will and to satisfy his own expectations. Sebastian reverses everyone's expectations by acting straightforwardly, by calculating nothing, by being himself. His naïve enthusiasm is refreshing in this world of mannered posturing and devious disguises.

Shakespeare has already exploited confusions of identity nigh unto fears of madness in the experience of the Syracusan twins in Ephesus in *The Comedy of Errors*. Ideas of madness and excess intermingle throughout *Twelfth Night*, and Sebastian is given one of the most significant speeches in this vein in the soliloquy which opens IV. iii (1–21), which fixes effectively the irrational nature of the various loves we have been pursuing. In the hierarchy of awareness Sebastian has as little information about what is going on as Malvolio or Sir Andrew. He proceeds quickly to a marriage ceremony to a woman he has just met, a woman who, despite her strange behaviour, he assumes, cannot be mad because she is in charge of her household. Sebastian lacks pretension, responds to his instincts, and is set in effective contrast to Orsino, Sir Andrew, and Malvolio. His scarcely premeditated marriage to Olivia clears the way for his sister's happiness in achieving Orsino. In the play we watch a variety of characters involved in a confusion of roles taking considerable time to achieve any degree of self-knowledge, and any certainty about what they want, or what it is appropriate for them to have. Sebastian has no disguise but finds himself in a situation in which everyone else supplies him with one. He is a breath of fresh air in the play: when attracted he loves, when challenged he fights. He can feature in this straightforward fashion because Shakespeare has kept him offstage for all but 38 of the first 1380 lines of the play. By the time he appears in the Ilyrian city, where Orsino's court is situated, 58 per cent of the play is already completed. Viola, as Cesario, has been dogged by difficulties in both plots because she is a woman pretending to be a man. Sebastian inherits her problems but is able to resolve them in ways that are unavailable to her.

It is quite possible that the actor of Sebastian could have doubled the role of Valentine or of another follower at Orsino's court (although not Curio who comes onstage at V. i. 7 only 7 lines after Sebastian departs at the end of IV. iii). But if there were practical reasons for this stage absence they were dovetailed with the needs of the play's structure. Shakespeare had already presented the dual nature of Prince Hal whose whole political strategy was to appear in one role as mad-cap wastrel and then to eclipse it by his emergence as responsible heir apparent when it could be used for maximum advantage in his career. It is hardly surprising that Shakespeare would do the same thing with twins, who are a double nature that can be confused as one person but must eventually emerge as two, bringing forward the second figure when it will be of maximum advantage to his play.

The ending of comedy and the 'bracket' role

The resolution of comedy frequently involves unfolding to the characters secrets which may long have been in the possession of the audience. Though surprises are possible for the audience the endings usually focus on the reorientation of the characters as the veils of illusion which have bemused them are drawn aside. Characters emerge from their disguises, and those who thought them to be elsewhere, offstage, and far away, discover that they have instead been interacting with them and even, in the revelation of bed-tricks, been sexually engaged with them. Characters may discover that instead of being absent and offstage as undetected eavesdroppers they have, in fact, been stage centre as dupes of others. Figures whom the other characters, and even the audience, considered to be permanently offstage (that is dead) re-appear to the surprise of all. Those who have been taken to be men turn out to be women, those a character thinks he has been taking advantage of in their absence have been the principal witnesses of his selfish, foolish, or criminal activity. Life is conceived to be a stage, and the surprise of comic endings results from the correcting of false assumptions about what actions have been on and offstage and about the nature of the characters with whom the stage has been shared. We have to recognize that stage absence and the variation of actions on and off the stage work at two levels. The absence of characters from the stage on which the play is performed affects the audience watching it. But we are also given a supplement to that experience, for within the play-world itself, where the stage is such an obvious metaphor for life, we see how the characters are affected by their assumptions and errors about the nature of the story they are in.

Shakespeare uses the long absence of characters from the action in a familiar, straightforward, and conventional manner in some of his plays. There are two figures in *The Comedy of Errors*, the Duke of Ephesus and Egeon, who appear together in the first scene for its 158 lines and then disappear from the action until their re-emergence together in the final scene (V. i. 130–409). They are thus onstage for a total of 438 lines of the 1756 lines of the play – about 25 per cent of the action. Egeon at the outset tells his long narrative of the separation of himself and his wife, of the two sets of twins, and of himself from the set of twins he raised. In revenge for Syracusan statutes against Ephesian merchants the Duke pronounces sentence of death on Egeon for his trespass but allows him a day to produce the ransom that will save him. The play then proceeds to the various misadventures of the two sets of twins who stumble into ever wilder confusions to the point where the Syracusan twins have to seek sanctuary in an abbey and the Ephesian twins are bound and taken away by Dr Pinch to be exorcized of the devils it is believed are oppressing them. Egeon re-emerges at the end of the play, apparently having wandered the city all day without ever encountering any of the twins who could rescue him from the impending threat of death. I have seen productions which underline this point by bringing Egeon onstage, though there is no warrant for it in the text, in several scenes in the middle of the play where he just misses possible confrontations with various twins. Such appearances may be inserted by large modern companies which are not constrained by doubling requirements, but they thereby alter the intention of

Shakespeare in structuring this stage absence. The Duke and Egeon are, in effect, the brackets of the play. They establish an initial problem that hangs suspended over the play and which we expect will be resolved with all the other confusions at the end. When they reappear the audience is aware that the unravelling is about to occur. They are very clear signals of closure. But Shakespeare exploits Egeon for a little more than that. By the time we get into the final scene the audience is convinced that the confusions of identity have been stretched as far as ingenuity will allow and that no more comedy can be squeezed from the sequence of errors. Egeon, however, has been held in reserve since the opening scene and is able to add yet a further level of confusion, for when he reappears he comes upon not the Syracusan twins he has raised but the Ephesian twins who cannot recognize him because of the quarter-century that has elapsed since they were separated from him.

If the absence in *The Comedy of Errors* of the Duke and Egeon was occasioned by doubling then there are some incidental characters along the way which the actors of these 'bracket' roles could have played, but the most prominent ones would be Balthazar, the Merchant in III. i, and Dr Pinch in IV. iv. It is possible that the actor of either Egeon or the Duke could double Dr Pinch since he exits at IV. iv. 128 which is 156 lines before either of the 'bracket' roles are resumed. It might have seemed a neat joke that the actor of Egeon, a figure driven almost to madness by his troubles, could have taken the role of the eccentric Pinch, the exorcizer of apparent madness in Egeon's long-lost son. A subdued connection is made in the text when the Ephesian Dromio failing to recognize Egeon asks him 'You are not Pinch's patient, are you sir?' (V. i. 295) which, if Egeon and Pinch were doubled as I suggest, the audience would certainly recognize and could register as a theatrical joke, since the actor could hardly be performing a role as Pinch's patient if he has just completed a performance of Pinch himself. Egeon is, of course, unaware that he is speaking to twins he has not seen since their childhood rather than to the twins from whom he has been separated for seven years, and so he speaks a number of lines of irrelevant explanation about how his careworn life has changed him to make him unrecognizable (V. i. 298–301, 308–19). 'It is a wise father that knows his own child' is a saying ironically commented on here, for Egeon has made the same mistake everyone else has been making throughout the play. That a man can look the same and yet be two different people from one minute to the next is the basic joke of the play. Such jokes on identity are compounded with great ingenuity throughout Shakespeare's plays, and it is worth remembering that the jest at the level of the play's reality is enriched at the practical theatrical level. In this play two men turn out to be four. In the exigencies of doubling audiences in Shakespeare's theatre constantly see characters who look different with dress, make-up, and voice and are established as having entirely separate identities but who are, nevertheless, played by one actor.

Shakespeare caps his sequence of surprises with one that he has deliberately hidden from the audience by keeping a character off the stage to emerge for the first time in the final scene, and whose real identity is revealed only at V. i. 342–6, about 100 lines from the end of the play. That figure is, of course, the Abbess who has given sanctuary to the Syracusan twins and emerges as Emilia, Egeon's wife. The discovery of Emilia adds a further surge of joy because neither the characters nor we have been prepared in any way for this surprise. The play is like a scrambled jigsaw puzzle in which many pieces seem to be displaced, but most of them are recovered as we expected they would be. Finally the one missing piece whose absence would spoil the whole picture and give us a nagging undertone of a completeness not entirely fulfilled is suddenly discovered and deftly inserted into place. A writer of comedies, like a good magician, must show us dazzling and effective tricks, but he often builds up to his final trick, topping himself with a flourish of something we can scarcely have suspected.

The device of the 'bracket' role is one that Shakespeare used again in *A Midsummer Night's Dream*. Theseus, Hippolyta, and Egeus appear in the first scene for 127 lines and establish a threat of punishment to be visited on Hermia unless she can bring herself to yield to her father's demands within the specified period of four days. They then disappear from the play for 1397 lines (66.3 per cent of the 2106 lines of the play) to re-emerge at IV. i. 102, waking up the lovers from their dreams and bringing them from the woods of Athens back to the court for the entertainment that will accompany the nuptials. The confused couples have tried various permutations in their relationships in the woods, due to Puck's mischief, until matters are worked out satisfactorily. The reappearance of the court figures signals the approaching closure which will involve a return to the social world as an appropriate setting for the marriages. The only obstacle remaining to be removed is the objection of Egeus, broached in the opening scene to Duke Theseus, and that is disposed of in fewer than 90 lines after their re-entry. This resolution clears the stage for the concluding entertainment by the mechanicals. The actors of these 'bracket' roles could certainly have doubled any of the numerous roles involved in the world of faerie in the woods outside Athens, but they also provide the useful framing device of the court world in which the action opens and concludes.

In *The Merchant of Venice* much of the major business of the play appears to be concluded by the end of the trial scene (IV. i), but that is not a note on which a comedy can end. The news of their good fortune has to be brought to Lorenzo and Jessica in Belmont, and the revelation of the disguises undertaken by Portia and Nerissa must be made. The business with the rings is developed to supply a sunny resolution. The husbands are tested, thus supplying a third trial to add to those of the caskets and of Shylock, so that they may know what ingenious wives they have married and that they were indeed onstage in Venice when they thought them offstage in Belmont. There remains, however, the melancholy and lonely figure of Antonio for whom the onstage events have produced no available marriage-partner nor any other decisive resolution beyond the saving of his life. He cannot be fully included in the harmony but he cannot be entirely left out. He has received half of Shylock's wealth, and Shakespeare resorts to the offstage world which has caused him so much trouble, the uncertain fortunes of the high seas, for details that will bring a satisfactory resolution to the merchant's fate. Letters arrive to inform him (V. i. 273–9) that three of the argosies he had thought lost are safely in harbour. Though there are no bracketed roles to signal closure here that offstage world of mercantile adventure does supply a symmetry to the play, for it was speculation about the fate of Antonio's rich argosies which opened the play (I. i. 1–45).

In *The Winter's Tale* most of the separations and broken relations have been knitted back together by the final scene, but rather surprisingly they have taken place offstage, seeming to deny the audience experience of the joyous resolutions. Shakespeare has kept in reserve the crowning trick of his magical conclusion. He has denied us any knowledge that Hermione is alive but has allowed Paulina to hint at it. He has prompted us to anticipate the seemingly impossible by excluding us from the direct experience onstage of the recon-ciliations of Leontes, Perdita, Florizel, and Polixenes and supplying only reports of the happy occasions from various gentlemen lucky enough to witness them. An audience familiar with the comic structure (and Shakespeare) knows that we cannot be left with such an anticlimax and that there must be some surprise in store. Shakespeare produces his most audacious bracketed role when Hermione, who disappeared from the play in the middle of III. ii returns after an absence of 1665 lines (56.4 per cent of the play), and completes the reconciliations in her acceptance of Leontes and her greeting of Perdita.

In *The Tempest*, after all the major problems are resolved, there are still figures who have been held in reserve so that in their emergence they may swell the harmony and underline the comprehensive justice of the conclusion. Stephano, Trinculo, and Caliban return to the stage so that we may see that despite the tricks played on them they have come to no harm. The return of the boatswain as a bracketed role signalling closure is an obvious example of the way Shakespeare picks up all the strands to supply a completed weave of events. The actor playing the role may well have had other roles, possibly in Prospero's magic shows, but Shakespeare does not overlook the satisfying sense of completion that is provided by ending his long stage absence. The boatswain is characterized forcibly in the first brief, spectacular scene. He disappears after only 58 lines of the play have elapsed and reappears only 103 lines from the end of V. i, and his forthright manner, which provides an instant sense of *déjà vu* of the tempest, reminds us of the journey we have travelled since the opening of the play.

Measure for Measure

In *Measure for Measure* several roles, developed in sequence around varying kinds of stage absence, signal the approaching resolution of the problems raised in the play. Angelo sinks to the depths in II. iv. when he confronts Isabella with the alternative of sacrificing either her chastity or her brother's life. In the ensuing action we are aware that Angelo is attempting to maintain his reputation for gravity through false seeming. Shakespeare keeps him offstage for a considerable absence as the Duke unfolds his elaborate counterplots to cope with the 'swelling evil' of his deputy. Angelo leaves the stage at II. iv. 170 and does not reappear until IV. iv – an absence of 992 lines (37.1 per cent of the play). He becomes, appropriately for a man involved in the dark bed-trick, a creature of the shadows. This is an absence which may have had little to do with doubling requirements. The actor playing Angelo could double the role of Abhorson who leaves the stage in his last appearance over a hundred lines before the deputy re-emerges. At the theatrical level it would add a touch of irony to have an actor, who plays the fastidious and proud deputy so deeply concerned for his reputation that he shrouds his actions in mystery, also playing the role of the executioner who is to carry out the deputy's strict decrees. Abhorson is also a proud man and worries that if Pompey is appointed as *his* deputy the mystery of his profession will be discredited. But whether or not such doubling was used there are sufficient reasons for keeping Angelo out of sight. He is given power at the outset of the play and wields it for most of the action. Even after the Duke's return he is allowed to think he has sufficient power to protect himself. The audience has known from before he ever reveals his desire to Isabella that he is in the Duke's power. Vincentio has to be resourceful to keep up with Angelo's duplicity, but we have no doubt that his hypocrisy will be exposed. Angelo's power is, therefore, more apparent than real, and in some sense for the audience he is a spent force before half the play is over and can be plausibly kept offstage while the Duke sets his trap. In fact, much of his role in terms of lines is over by his exit in II. iv. Angelo speaks 294 lines in the play, and 228 of them (77.5 per cent) are spoken by the time of his departure in II. iv. He is onstage for a total of 1091 lines. He has been onstage for 544 of them (49.9 per cent) by the end of II. iv, and almost all the rest of his time onstage occurs in the long final scene. Another way of stating this is to note that at his exit at II. iv. 170 the play has run 1084 lines (40.6 per cent of its length of 2670), but Angelo has already spoken 77.5 per cent of his lines.

During this almost 1000-line absence of Angelo much of the action is related to him as the characters onstage deal with and respond to his various manœuvres. There is no shifting of place in the play (this is not Lear wandering on the heath), or a shift in the action to England as in *Macbeth*, or Coriolanus exiled from Rome, Romeo banished to Mantua, or Hamlet sent to England. All of the action here takes place in Vienna with Angelo sending his orders to prison from close by, shrouding himself from sight as he pursues his criminal path in the hope of remaining undetected. In the 992-line absence there are 145 references to him which would average out at about 1 every 7 lines. The references are, in fact, contained in 121 lines (12.2 per cent of the lines in his absence) and come from the mouths of the Duke (most frequently), Isabella, Claudio, Elbow, Lucio, Escalus, and the Provost on a fairly regular basis, as we hear of his secret bargains, his instructions, and responses to them. [The references: Angelo (36), he (35), him (26), his (23), deputy (9), himself (3), me (2), and 1 each for the judge, substitute, combinate husband, this man, ungenitured agent, my brother, brother-justice, Lord, pardoner, you, my].

Angelo can be absent from the stage not because his role is so taxing that the actor needs a pause but because he is not the only focus of Shakespeare's attention. Shakespeare is interested in the development of Isabella, in drawing Mariana into the plot – a figure who becomes of central significance in the final scene, and in the devious skills of the Duke which are developed as he learns of the corruption at all levels of his society fostered by his negligence. In Angelo's absence various sub-plot characters are developed – Mistress Overdone, Lucio, Pompey, Abhorson, Barnadine. Angelo is a fallen figure but he has a good deal of company in this society. The Duke is involved not only in catching out Angelo but in becoming aware of the need for his responsibility in leadership over figures at all levels of this society. Angelo is not, after all, a very complex figure. He has a narrow view of the world and has known himself and the potentialities of his carnal nature very little. His absence does not simply serve Shakespeare's purposes in developing other characters; it also helps Shakespeare to shape the response of the audience to Angelo. We hear of all his shadowy, criminal manœuvres, but that is very different from directly witnessing him undertaking all these dishonourable actions. He is part of a comic structure in which he will be forgiven, married, and reconciled to a life within a renewed community. The audience knows throughout that because he is outflanked his actions are not as criminal as he believes. His absence from the stage, therefore, is one of Shakespeare's shrewd silences. If he were pursuing his corrupt actions, even guilt-stricken, on the stage, he would be much more visibly a criminal, which might make his forgiveness at the end of the play more difficult for the audience to swallow. We may not feel entirely sorry for him, but because the focus is so constantly on the Duke's strategies we do come to see Angelo as something of a puppet manipulated by the ingenious Vincentio, and this prevents us from becoming irretrievably alienated from the deputy.

It is necessary that we see Angelo again before his re-emergence into the public spotlight and his attempt to brazen out his criminal behaviour. We need some sense of how he is reacting to his protracted secret dealings. They are so secret, or so Angelo believes, that they can only be revealed in soliloquy, which Shakespeare provides in IV. iv. By decreeing that those who crave redress of injustice should assemble with the deputy at the city gates the Duke has already brought Angelo to a state of the jitters, and his soliloquy (18–32) uncovers a complex sequence of anxieties. Angelo is fully aware of his own shameful perversion of the law, but he is relying on Isabella's sense of shame to keep his sexual conquest a secret or, failing that, on his own reputation for probity which will confute any accusation she dares to make. His revelation of his motive for 'killing' Claudio despite the bargain he has made indicates the circumspection of a Machiavel alert to any loophole that will expose his scheming. His concluding wish that he had spared Claudio, and his self-disgust at being so deeply ensnared in corruption, indicate to the audience that he is not lost beyond recovery. In the final scene he will be put in a position where he must receive from others what he has been incapable of practising – forgiveness.

Shakespeare is aware that he has not created a very appealing character whose forgiveness an audience can easily accept, as we can see from the way he handles Angelo in the final scene. Shakespeare has protected him to a degree by keeping him offstage. He persists in this strategy in a different way be keeping him, when he does return to the stage, very nearly mute. The less Angelo says in defending himself in the long final scene, in hypocritically pursuing a cover-up to sustain his reputation, the more acceptable he becomes to an audience. He makes some efforts to brush aside accusations but for the most part he is so sickened with the terrifying prospect of a public humiliation that he seems almost paralysed. Most of the volatile accusations, slanderous lies, and mistaken judgments come from the mouths of Lucio and Escalus. Angelo remains harrowed by fear, then by self-disgust, and finally makes a penitent plea for death. The last scene is devoted almost entirely to interpretations of his character, and yet in its 534 lines, in which he is present for 514 of them, he speaks only 39 of them (7.3 per cent).

Shakespeare works out an intriguing variation of the 'bracket' character in this play. Here for the characters onstage there is a figure apparently long-absent from Vienna. Duke Vincentio, as far as most of his subjects are concerned, disappears from view after only 75 lines of the first scene. He is still *in propria persona* with Friar Thomas in I. iii, but thereafter he is unrecognizable to everyone, save the members of the audience, until the opening of the final scene (V. i). His absence as far as his subjects are concerned thus stretches for 1811 lines (67.8 per cent of the play). We observe throughout the Duke interacting, in the guise of a Friar, with a variety of the subjects he has hitherto neglected. His re-emergence as Duke seems to signal the approaching closure for both his citizens, who have many grievances they want redressing, and for the audience aware that he has all the information to prevent the miscarriage of justice which Angelo hopes both to sustain and keep concealed. The resolution of the play is at hand, but it is an extremely complex unravelling full of surprises, which allows Vincentio to return to his disguise as Friar and re-emerge a second time as Duke. It is worth noting that this 'bracket' role builds on and extends the functions of such roles used earlier by Shakespeare. Such roles, as I have indicated, can signal closure, add further complications, add surprise, and supplement the surge of harmony building towards a resolution. Duke Vincentio's return to the play does all of these things and operates on two levels of awareness – that of the characters and that of the audience. In his first return he seems to continue in the role of neglectful ruler who passes difficult administrative problems to others as he had done at the outset. In his second re-emergence, after Lucio has had the misfortune to be 'the first knave that e'er mad'st a duke' (V. i. 352) Vincentio seems, in his peremptory judgements, to become the kind of severe and punitive administrator we have come to know in Angelo. But neither of these roles can supply appropriate behaviour for the new Duke, who has learned to combine compassion and a sense of responsibility for his subjects and to encourage them to apply it to each other. The ending of the play is only finally approached when most of the injustices have been resolved and when another figure long absent from the stage reappears. Claudio disappears at III. i. 172, is absent for 1336 lines (50 per cent) and reappears at V. i. 474, which is only 61 lines from the play's conclusion. At this point it becomes clear to the characters that the worst intentions of Angelo's severity in the service of protecting his own reputation have not been fulfilled.

Stage absence may serve the purposes of the play in forewarning us of closure, but the characters for so long out of our sight may have undergone no change. When they return, however, circumstances may have changed so radically that the problems they originally broached tend to dissolve in the reshaping of society. Before turning to stage absence in the tragedies it is worth remembering that Shakespeare can produce change in character in a variety of ways, by keeping characters onstage under extreme pressure, by taking them off for brief intervals, or by allowing them a lengthy offstage absence.

On many occasions Shakespeare chooses to show a radical change in a character in the unbroken flow of action within one scene. Although such scenes are carefully prepared in the structure of a play it often seems that Shakespeare is undertaking a *tour de force* with a magician's flair, as if priming the audience with a confident 'and now, ladies and gentlemen, before your very eyes', when he produces such transformations. Some of the most memorable transformations within one continuously flowing scene and without the aid of stage absence are: Gloucester's seduction of Lady Anne (*Richard III,* I. ii) and of Queen Elizabeth (IV. iv); the change in Shylock from a figure confident of revenge to the broken man subdued to his ruin (IV. i); the conversion of the plebeians from their faith in the explanations of Brutus about the assassination of Caesar to the howling mob determined on revenge under the impact of Antony's skilled rhetoric in the Forum (III. i); the movement of Laertes from a position in which he seeks honourable redress for his injuries to the secretive plotter tamed by the cunning of Claudius into his agent for the murder of Hamlet (IV. vii); the conversion of Othello by Iago from a contented, loving husband into a man so obsessed with the madness of jealousy that he is determined to kill his wife and her lover (III. iii). Such scenes show the dramatist working at the height of his powers revealing characters under pressure in the detailed process of change. In only one of these sequences is a character under continuous scrutiny for fewer than 200 lines (i.e. Laertes). Most of them present an uninterrupted experience of a character from well over 200 to almost 400 lines.

Shakespeare also frequently produces radical changes in character by frequent segmentation into short scenes and by moving characters offstage to break up the audience's continuous experience of them so that change may be produced in a series of steps. Macbeth is moved in a sequence of short scenes (I. v to II. iii) from initial resistance to the murder of Duncan, to complicity with his wife in a plot, to its accomplishment, to his horrified reactions, and to his attempts to conceal his involvement in face of the thanes who uncover the murder. It is a technique that Shakespeare employs in many of his battles by structuring short scenes with frequent entrances and exits to reflect the varying fortunes and clashes of the combatants – a method which is the focus of the next chapter in this study. Change can be produced more easily by arranging for the extended absence of a character from the stage, another method that I will analyse in detail later. Here I will only deal with a couple of the simplest and most practical exploitations of stage absence to produce a change in character.

The Two Gentlemen of Verona

Shakespeare is aware, even in his early, highly conventional and stylized comedies, that the audience might find a radical transformation of character difficult to accept if it is presented as a sudden volte-face. In *The Two Gentlemen of Verona* Proteus, whose name might seem to provide warrant for constant and rapid change, enters, in II. iv, as a firm and loyal friend to Valentine. The two friends, when last they met in Verona, were in different situations, Proteus being in love with Julia and subject to the amused raillery of the as-yet-unattached Valentine. Proteus discovers in Milan that his friend has fallen in love with Silvia. He meets her briefly (97–118) and is encouraged by Valentine to be a fellow-servant in adoring, after the manner of the courtly-love code, his mistress. In the ensuing exchange

Valentine makes vain boasts about his mistress as a nonpareil, is censured by Proteus for his braggardism, and reveals his plot to steal her away and marry her. Proteus may be able to signal to an audience that he is dazzled by Silvia, but his defence of the qualities of his own Julia and his attempt to calm the excessive zeal of Valentine do not give him extensive opportunity to unfold the transformation that is going on within him. Only when he is left in soliloquy at the end of the scene do we discover that his loyalty to Julia and to Valentine is wavering under the new compelling attraction to Silvia he now experiences. That young men are subject to a sudden veering of affections and to love at first sight is not in life, and certainly not in Shakespeare's comedies, going to seem unacceptable to most people. But the burgeoning love of Proteus is complicated by his attachment to Julia sealed by an exchange of rings in a scene (II. ii) which concluded only 151 lines (II. iii, II. iv. 1–93) before he claps eyes on Silvia. To pursue the new love, as he is immediately aware, threatens to violate the terms of the code of friendship which he and Valentine have shared hitherto.

Shakespeare considered, perhaps, that to have Proteus change from lover and loyal friend to a sinister, underhanded betrayer in one fell swoop might make him even more feckless, shallow, and reprehensible than he will eventually become. His solution was to break the transition into two steps. The soliloquy in II. iv gives us an initial view of Proteus discovering and revealing his new feelings. He is given 24 lines (187–210) to express alarm at the conflict within his breast. In amazement he questions his reasoning, endeavours to resist the temptation, but ends by asserting that if he cannot do so he is prepared to pursue the means to 'compass' Silvia. At that point Shakespeare takes him offstage, and the time interjected here provides the gap in which the audience may suppose Proteus is brooding further, becoming more agitated and less capable of resisting the temptation of behaving treacherously.

It has to be noted that this is a relatively crude and artless exploitation of the device since the only material Shakespeare has to hand is to parallel the meeting of the two gentlemen with the encounter of their servants, Launce and Speed. This does not have to be placed at this point and it cannot be said that II. v provides any material that is imperative to the plot. The 50 lines of the scene simply provide an opportunity for clowning and some sexual innuendoes as one of several examples of variations in tone between loyalty, love, service, duty, and betrayal at the level of the gentlemen and at the level of Speed, Launce, Launce's woman, and his dog, Crab. The servants exchange news of the love of Julia and Proteus, which the audience does not need, and the only ironical reflection one can glean from the scene is that Speed's account of his master as 'a hot lover', though correct, is not yet abreast of the new object of that heat. The scene transparently, in showing the servants on a journey of no particular significance to an ale-house, is placed only to give Proteus some offstage time.

Proteus returns in soliloquy at the opening of II. vi much more deeply in the toils, still debating his conflict, now at greater length, but setting aside loyalty and clearly yielding to treachery as he determines to uncover Valentine's plot of elopement to the Duke. The soliloquy which occupies this scene is 43 lines long and, though some of it is a repetition of the conflicts outlined in the earlier soliloquy, a presentation of them uninterrupted would have covered 67 lines. The interruption allows an actor to present his submission to his appetite in distinct phases rather than in one continuous transition. The anxiety of Proteus in II. iv can still be presented under relative control as he resists betrayal. In his return in II. vi, after the corrosive fire of desire has been at work, though he can still censure himself for his submission to the lure of treachery, he feverishly improvises more and more reasons for pursuing benefits that will make his losses seem of no account. We are not given any clear sense that a number of hours have passed while Proteus has wrestled in torment with his conscience. Shakespeare, by interjecting Speed and Launce, simply provides a gap of stage time that allows the audience to absorb the change in two phases.

As I hope to show in another study elsewhere Shakespeare was able eventually to use brief stage absences in sequences to develop the role of a major character such as Macbeth. His story, with its breathtaking speed in producing radical character change, relies to a considerable degree on the serial presentation of Macbeth in short scenes. He returns after each brief stage absence more firmly committed to the task he initially resisted. This phasing of the action allows for his accelerated submission to corruption as he plots to murder Duncan, reacts with horror to the deed, and then remorselessly seeks to shore up his power. Each time we see him he appears to have moved measurably into more desperate isolation in his cold-blooded desire to sustain his grasp on the crown for which he has sacrificed his soul. In the following section I am concerned mainly with extensive absences, but it is always useful to remember that they often work in combination with a sequence of shorter absences.

Stage absence in the tragedies

In most of Shakespeare's tragedies, and almost invariably in his major tragedies, the central figure is given a lengthy absence from the stage that is strategically placed, often in Act IV. These absences are unlikely to have been shaped in response to requirements of doubling. It is possible to see, however, the advantages Shakespeare gained in the dramaturgical practice. Many of these roles make exhausting demands on an actor's resources, and the insertion of a stage absence allows him to conserve his strength at a point where he may need it just before scaling the emotional heights demanded in the final movement of the play. The absence can also minimize the problem of over-exposing the concerns of the central figure to the audience. In the hero's absence the dramatist can take the opportunity to introduce variety by developing other characters and other plots that may be necessary in the resolution of the play following the hero's return to the stage. During the absence we are usually kept in touch with the hero's actions and with responses of other key characters to them, which serves to give us a sense of the potency of the central figure around whom actions are orchestrated. Shakespeare's practice in handling this break, however, varies considerably depending on the shape and structure of the individual play. In the statistics in Table 2.1 I give evidence from several plays for comparative purposes. I supply some data from three early plays where Shakespeare had not yet completely crystallized his strategy. I supply evidence also from most of the major tragedies. I will examine the effect of the hero's absence in several of them, both here and in Part 2 to demonstrate the variety within Shakespeare's development of this strategy. I have also examined the use of stage absence in *Macbeth*, *King Lear*, and *Antony and Cleopatra*, but I will present these findings in another study which is devoted to a comprehensive analysis of the structural strategies of these and other plays. I include data from two of these plays, however, for purposes of comparison.

Table 2.1 Positioning of the hero's absence

Play	Total lines	Before absence		Length of absence		After return	
Macbeth	2079	1401	(67.4%)	429	(20.6%)	249	(12.0%)
King Lear	3195	1989	(62.2%)	501	(15.7%)	705	(22.1%)
Hamlet	3776	2656	(70.4%)	499	(13.2%)	621	(16.4%)
Coriolanus	3293	2376	(72.1%)	438	(13.3%)	479	(14.6%)
Othello	3228	2477	(76.7%)	380	(11.8%)[a]	371	(11.5%)
Titus Andronicus	2521	1835	(72.8%)	285	(11.3%)	401	(15.9%)
Romeo and Juliet	2993	1983	(66.3%)	585	(19.5%)	425	(14.2%)
Richard II	2755	2311	(83.9%)	274	(9.9%)	170	(6.2%)

[a] Not a continuous absence.

There is obviously a significant variation in the placing of the hero's absence and the length of it. The longest absence as a proportion of the whole play is that of Macbeth. Othello's absence is only a little more than half as long and is not, if fact, a sustained continuous break, as all the others are, for reasons that are particular to its plot. The proportion of the play which comes before the initiation of the hero's absence does not vary radically, and what remains of the play after the hero's re-emergence is for the most part within a reasonably similar range. Such variations as occur are related to the number of plots or strands of action in the play which have to be resolved. The plays which leave the least amount of time after the hero's re-emergence are usually those, such as *Macbeth*, *Coriolanus*, and *Othello* which have one central focus of interest, instead of multiple plots, to wind up. As I will indicate in subsequent analyses in greater detail the uses to which the hero's absence is put varies considerably. Coriolanus is offstage for 438 lines, and yet almost all those lines are reactions to his absence and his joining-up with Aufidius so that his indispensable nature is impressed on us. In *Romeo and Juliet* we have long gaps in news of the banished Romeo as the action turns to Juliet's brave determination to be reunited with him. In *Macbeth* the action moves to England and to the delineating of the two figures who are defined in reaction to the hero's tyranny and who combine together to end it. In *King Lear* the stage is so crowded with action that we lose track of the central figure during his absence. We are told (III. vii. 14–19) that he is on his way to Dover, and Gloucester's aid in sending him thither is confirmed soon afterwards (III. vii. 50–8). We have no further information about Lear's whereabouts until we hear from Kent (IV. iii. 38) that Lear has arrived in Dover. Thus some 267 lines pass (III. vii. 59 – IV. iii. 37), over half of Lear's absence from the stage, during which we are denied information about his welfare. We observe the eagerness with which others exercise the power they have taken from Lear, and his diminished potency is underlined by the fact that his whereabouts, let alone his welfare, have become a marginal issue of little concern to most of the characters.

It could be argued that my suggestion that this break in these major roles can, in part, be explained by Shakespeare's consideration for his actors in allowing them to husband their resources, is not sustainable since this absence does not occur in all of the major tragic roles. There is no very extensive break in the role of Timon, but this it seems to me is one of the explanations of the flawed structure of *Timon of Athens*. The play lacks a variety of focuses of interest, and, in exposing the audience to Timon first as philanthropist and then as misanthropist, it fails to develop enough complexity to sustain our interest in the development and the fate of its central characters. In *Antony and Cleopatra* the same strategy was not required since the two figures alternate absences and share the load of the play, and, of course, Antony dies in Act IV at which point the focus turns to Cleopatra for the final movement of the action. There are similar reasons for an alternation of shorter absences in *Julius Caesar* where the play's focus is divided between three major characters. Even though none of the roles is as weighty as that of the major tragic heroes there is an absence in each role which allows a renewal of resources for Brutus and Cassius before their great quarrel scene and for Antony to recover from his weighty role in the forum scene and subsequent events before the final battle scenes. Brutus is offstage for 299 lines from III. ii. 61 to the opening of IV. ii. Cassius is absent for 381 lines from III. ii. 10 to IV. ii. 32. Antony is absent for the 360 lines of IV. ii and IV. iii. Richard III is given only one lengthy absence early in the play, but thereafter he is given short breaks until the end. It may be that a plot so focused on this central manipulator demanded his presence throughout most of the action. As an evil controller of all of the play's action Iago has the same type of omnipresent role. Neither Richard nor Iago have to scale the same kind of emotional peaks as Othello, Lear, Hamlet, or Macbeth. *Richard III* occurs early in Shakespeare's career, possibly before he had fully developed the means of distributing the load among his actors and of finding plausible stage absences for actors carrying the major roles. It is possible, of course, that the taxing demands of the central roles were not such a problem for Burbadge as a young man. Reviving the part later in his career may have been more demanding, though, as I have indicated, there are several significant offstage breaks in it. The roles written for Burbadge after the turn of the century were paced at a less continuously sustained clip, and this may be a result, in part, of consideration for the actor, but also stems from Shakespeare's increased skills in threading plots together which serve a variety of other purposes that are useful for an audience.

Critics have endlessly analysed Shakespeare's plays to indicate his extraordinary strengths as a writer, citing his skills in the image-making of his poetry, his insight, his creation of character,etc. I am drawing attention here to something a little more basic – the professional skills which make his work so playable. Plays can be easy or hard on an actor, and an actor of a major role has to find ways of adapting to the draining demands of a script. This is very much a matter of pacing and energy, knowing how much to give to one section of the script and how much to save for another. A skilled actor endeavours to achieve something like a perfect arc or graph of emotional effects in calculating his impact on an audience, for, like a politician, he must ensure that he does not peak too early. If he invests too much energy too early he may exhaust us and himself. If he holds back too much he may forfeit our interest and leave himself too much to do in too short a space. I have seen an actor playing Othello submit to wild jealousy almost as soon as Iago begins to poison his mind and having started too high too early exhaust himself and the audience in trying to go higher; I have seen an Othello who raved so much in the first part of the play as to lose his voice and be reduced to whispering his lines in the last two acts; I have seen a Lear who thundered so mightily in the heath scenes as to have no strength left for the rest of the role. These are huge roles as can be seen in Table 2.2 outlining the proportions of the plays devoted to the major parts with other significant roles provided as points of comparison. From the figures it can be seen how much weight these central characters often carry, especially in comparison with the supporting roles. The major roles may contain from 20–38 per cent of the lines of a play and the actors of them may be onstage from 45 up to as much as 70 per cent of a play. It is possible to see also that when they are onstage they are carrying much of the weight of the play, speaking usually close to 50 per cent and as much as 60 per cent of the lines, whereas other supporting roles usually have less than 40 per cent of the lines during their stage lives. An actor's role, like the production itself, must have a strong architectonic structure built scene by scene, moving from peak to

Table 2.2 Major roles in several of Shakespeare's tragedies

Play	Total Lines	Role	Lines Spoken	As % of play	Lines Onstage	As % of play	% of lines spoken when on stage
Hamlet	3776	Hamlet	1428	37.8	2411	63.8	59.2
		Claudius	520.5	13.8	1398	37.0	37.2
Othello	3228	Othello	794.5	24.6	1716.5	53.2	46.3
		Iago	1022.5	31.7	2278.5	70.6	44.9
		Desdemona	343.5	10.6	1205	37.3	28.5
King Lear	3195	Lear	707	22.1	1450	45.4	48.7
		Gloucester	308.5	9.6	1160	36.3	26.6
Macbeth	2079	Macbeth	647	31.1	1043.5	50.2	62.0
		Lady Macbeth	226	10.9	539	25.9	41.9
		Malcolm	187.5	9.0	524	25.2	35.8
		Macduff	148	7.1	487	23.4	30.4
Coriolanus	3293	Coriolanus	791	24.0	1606	48.8	49.2
		Menenius	509	15.4	1574	47.8	32.3
		Aufidius	250	7.6	637	19.3	39.2
Titus Andronicus	2521	Titus	711.5	28.2	1473	58.4	48.3
Romeo and Juliet	2993	Romeo	591.5	19.8	1562	52.2	37.9
		Juliet	527	17.6	1537	51.3	34.3
Richard II	2755	Richard	747	27.1	1399	50.8	53.4
		Bolingbroke	404.5	14.7	1412	51.2	28.6

peak with the actor taking any opportunity to recharge his batteries in order to meet the challenging demands of the role. I have seen many actors fail to meet the basic physical demands of these roles, and this may be a result of a lack of training or sufficient preparatory fitness. I wish to emphasize here the very considerable help Shakespeare gives to the actors handling his roles. These scripts have constantly attracted the world's best actors, and one of the simple explanations for this is that the roles, though demanding, are well proportioned. Shakespeare's skill in balancing out parts for his actors also inevitably pays dividends in the balancing of demands made on the audience's attention. Human beings seem to revel in variety, and one of the central appeals of Shakespeare's plays is the variety of character and plot which so effectively engages our attention. Shakespeare manages to make his artistic choices serve the needs of his plots, his actors, and his audience. Shakespeare used the absence of his hero from the stage in different ways tailored to the requirements of each play in his characteristic manner of hitting several birds with one stone.

Titus Andronicus

A brief glance at *Titus Andronicus* indicates that very early in his career Shakespeare had found ways of introducing variety into his action so that a major character was not required to undertake continuous exposure onstage but was given intermittent respites. Although the play is not a long one compared to some of the later major tragedies the role of Titus is considerable and makes large emotional demands on an actor. Titus speaks 711½ lines which at 28.2 per cent of the play is a greater proportion than Coriolanus, Lear, or Othello speak in their respective plays. Titus is onstage for 58.4 per cent of the play, which, though less in terms of lines, is larger as a proportion of the play than any tragic figure save Hamlet and Richard III. Shakespeare provides some significant offstage breaks in the role. In II. iii Titus is absent for 258 lines and he is off again for 181 lines from IV. i. 122 to the end of IV. ii. The final absence towards the close of the fourth act, from the end of IV. iii until V. ii. 9, lasts 285 lines and is something like the pause in the later major roles before the drive to the conclusion occurs. Of these 285 lines 117 are concerned with Titus – Tamora's plans against him and Aaron's revelation of his stratagems against Titus and his family. [In his absence we are kept in touch with Titus in 52 specific references to him – great/old Andronicus (7), Titus (2), his (21), him (7), he (6), father (4) and 1 each for thyself, thee, thy, villain, frantic wretch.] Shakespeare uses this interlude to bring in Lucius as the leader of the Goths and a threat to Saturninus, and to show the capture of Aaron as he reveals and revels in all the villainous tricks he has played.

Richard II

In *Richard II* instead of the absence in Act IV found in many of the major tragic heroes we find a sequence of absences distributed across the play. The play entwines the fates of Richard II and Bolingbroke and it alternates, and to some degree overlaps, offstage absences for them as they engage the audience's attention in their related decline and ascent. The structure of the plot requires the absence of Bolingbroke from England as a result of his banishment, and also the absence of Richard to fight his Irish wars which provides Bolingbroke with his opportunity to return. Shakespeare situates all of his action in England showing us nothing onstage of Bolingbroke in exile or of Richard in Ireland. After Bolingbroke's banishment the action focuses on Gaunt's death-bed and Richard's seizure of Bolingbroke's inheritance to finance his Irish wars. During Richard's absence we become aware of the disaffection of the nobles at the king's actions, the support Bolingbroke receives on his return, and the dismay of Richard's allies at the vulnerability of his kingdom. The stage action is, therefore, entirely focused on responses to the two absent figures and to the shaping of the confrontation which will lead to the deposition and beyond. Much of the play centres on the conflict of these two figures but most of its effect is achieved indirectly instead of presenting them in direct confrontation onstage. When the king leaves at I. iii. 248, after banishing Bolingbroke, they do not meet again onstage until

III. iii. 62 – a separation of 1094 lines (39.7 per cent of the play). In the entire
play they share the stage alive for 711 lines (25.8 per cent of the 2755 lines).
Their four scenes together are divided into two mirrored pairs, two with Bolingbroke in Richard's power and two reversing the situation. Richard sets up a
situation (I. i) in which he can dismiss Bolingbroke from his realm (I. iii), and
Bolingbroke returns the favour in setting up a situation (III. iii) which obliges
Richard to yield his kingdom to the man he originally banished from it (IV. i).

In the stage absences early in the play Bolingbroke leaves at the close of
I. iii and returns at the beginning of II. iii after an absence of 514 lines (18.6
per cent). During his absence there is a good deal of discussion of him.
Aumerle reports on his parting from Hereford and Richard comments on
Hereford's courtship of the common people (I. iv). Following Gaunt's death
in II. i, York complains of Richard's confiscation of Hereford's inheritance,
and we hear of the intentions of Ross, Willoughby, and Northumberland to
support Bolingbroke on his return. In II. ii the queen and Richard's
supporters discuss with York the growing strength of Hereford following his
return, and he seems to be moving into an unassailable position before
Richard's return from Ireland. In the 514-line absence there are 107 lines
(20.8 per cent) specifically devoted to Bolingbroke and his situation and there
are 68 actual references to him in 58 of these lines. [The references are:
Hereford (12), Bolingbroke (5), him (9), his (16), he (8), kinsman (3), heir
(2), our cousin (2), and 1 each for our, his son, children's, theirs, Harry,
himself, royal prince, banished duke, enemy's, both, t'other].

Richard leaves the stage at II. i. 223 to go to Ireland and returns to the
stage on the coast of Wales at the outset of III. ii and is thus absent for 465
lines (16.9 per cent). Of these lines 126 (27.1 per cent) are directly related
to Richard's situation, and there are 72 specific references to him in 60 of
these lines [The references are: king (27), Richard (3), his (10), he (9), him
(5), himself (2), thy (4), sovereign (2), lord (2), and 1 each for my lord,
husband, both, kinsman, whom, majesty, prince, happy gentleman.] There is
no sub-plot to occupy the attention of the audience, and so we are, during
these absences, tied very closely to the varying fortunes of the two key
figures by the responses, hopes, and apprehensions of their different
supporters. The play could not be sustained for very long in the absence of
both its key characters, and Shakespeare contrives to overlap their periods
offstage in such a way that the time when neither of them appears in this
sequence occupies only 226 lines (8.2 per cent) – II. i. 224 to the end of
II. ii, which is fewer than half the lines that either of them is off separately.

This considerable absence early in the play helps to explain to some extent
why, despite the fact that the role of Richard is large, no continuous extended
absence, such as those given for most of the later major tragic heroes, is
situated late in the play. Richard is given an offstage break in III. iv and
IV. i of 268 lines just before his prominent role in the deposition, and he has
another break in V. ii, V. iii, and V. iv of 274 lines before the events

which lead up to his death. This final absence is not as strategically placed, in providing an actor opportunity to husband his resources, as in the major tragedies, for the play has only 170 lines to run when Richard returns, although this re-emergence in V. v does start with a 66-line soliloquy, one of the longest in the drama of the period. This final pause in Richard's role gives the audience the sense that after all his struggles he is being pushed aside, as the focus switches to the troubles which assail the new monarch in the plot of which Aumerle is a part. During this sequence the only lines directly concerned with Richard are the opening 42 lines of V. ii, and then all reference to him is dropped until Exton's lines in V. iv, immediately before Richard's re-emergence in prison at Pomfret. Aumerle is involved in a conspiracy because of his allegiance to Richard but it is not presented in specific reference to him. In effect, therefore, there are 230 lines with not a single reference to Richard (V. ii. 43 – V. iv. 9). The 14 specific references to Richard in the 174-line absence occur in the 42 lines after his departure and in 2 lines before his re-emergence. [The references are: Richard (4), him (3), his (3), he (2), king (1), foe (1)].

The sequence devoted to Aumerle's involvement in conspiracy may seem to be tangential to the major concerns of the play, and in performance it is often edited or cut entirely. It has, however, a specific purpose in the play's structure of providing the audience with a distinct sense of *déjà vu*. As soon as Bolingbroke has moved triumphantly into power he finds himself in something like a parodic version of a scene in which he was a condemned man, accused before Richard at the outset of the play. As he says himself: 'Our scene is alt'red from a serious thing,/And now changed to "The Beggar and the King"' (V. iii. 79–80). We can vividly remember how recently it was that competing figures accusing each other of treachery, (Mowbray and Bolingbroke) stood before Richard trying to win his favour. Richard dealt arrogantly with the figures mutually accusing each other of treachery, and that was his first step along the path which led to Bolingbroke's ascendancy. Treachery rears its head again in the almost comic competition between York and his wife as they assert and deny the treachery of their son, Aumerle. We can see York as the consummate trimmer who censured Bolingbroke for daring to challenge the authority of an anointed king (II. iii. 87–112) and who, to prove his loyalty to that same Bolingbroke, is willing to reveal his son's treachery against the newly appointed king who has usurped Richard. There is another subdued parallel in the circumstances of the two kings. At the outset we gathered from Mowbray that he disposed of Gloucester, a figure troublesome to Richard, but received no reward for it. Exton pursues the same inexorable process of reaching for advancement by undertaking a king's dirty work and will at the end of the play find himself as forcibly rejected as Mowbray was at the outset.

There is another suggestion of a parallel recurrence, though at one step removed, in the pattern of the play. At the outset we were given a clear sense of Richard's irresponsibility as a playboy in thrall to figures such as Bushy, Bagot, and Green. In the strict Bolingbroke there is no such weakness, but he perceives a threat to the realm in the playboy propensities of his son which he laments (V. iii. 1–22). Shakespeare will eventually develop the dangerous parallels in Hal's re-enactment of Richard's disastrous career in *Henry IV, Part 1*, (III. ii. 60–96). Richard's absence from the stage in Act V is thus exploited by Shakespeare to indicate how, in a variety of ways, despite the fact that they are temperamentally very different, Henry as king is, from the very outset, beset by some of the troubles that have brought Richard to ruin.

The two figures dominate our attention throughout the play, but the disposition of their roles is quite different. Richard speaks 747 lines (27.1 per cent) of the play, almost twice as many as Bolingbroke with 404½ lines (14.7 per cent). Bolingbroke, however, is onstage for slightly more lines – 1412 (51.2 per cent) – than Richard – 1399 (50.8 per cent). The way their appearances are organized is significant. Until the end of III. i Bolingbroke has been onstage for 685 lines and has spoken 228 lines (56.4 per cent of his part). Richard has been onstage for slightly fewer lines (665) and has spoken 209½ lines, or only 28 per cent of his part. From that point onwards in the confrontations with Bolingbroke at Flint Castle (III. iii) and in the deposition scene (IV. i) Richard carries much of the burden of the play. From the opening of III. ii to the end of V. i (at the point where Richard begins his final stage absence) there are 970 lines (35.2 per cent) in which the climactic events occur. Richard speaks 442 of those lines (45.6 per cent) – and it is worth remembering that he is absent continuously in III. iv and IV. i for 268 of them, so that of the 616 lines he is onstage in this section Richard speaks a massive 71.7 per cent of them. During this same confrontation sequence Bolingbroke speaks only 90 lines (9.2 per cent), or, if we count only the 529 lines he is onstage during this transfer of power, he still speaks only 17 per cent of them. Shakespeare prepares for this sequence in which Richard is not only prominent onstage but is given the lion's share of the lines by supplying a long offstage absence early in the play in Act II, another break before the climax, and one immediately following his loss of power, before returning to the resolution of Richard's fate in V. v.

Hamlet

The absence of Hamlet from the stage in Act IV is important in the structural design and part of a strategy used throughout the play. The mingling of onstage and offstage appearances is a significant element in developing mystery around the figure of the Ghost. The numerous reports and the various behind-the-scenes manœuvres indicate a complex awareness in the characters themselves about where they are, or consider themselves to be, in their cat-and-mouse stratagems. The adoption by the prince of an antic disposition is a staging-device to deceive Claudius, and the play constantly develops scenes in which things are never quite what they seem and in which participants are at a variety of levels of understanding about what is going on. There are formal and informal plays-within-plays which make the matter of where onstage and offstage are for the characters one of great complexity.

A sequence which indicates complex choices related to moving characters on and off the stage occurs at the opening of *Hamlet* in the way that the prince and the Ghost are only gradually brought into confrontation. From the point of view of speeding up the action in what is a very long play it could be argued that the first scene could be cut entirely. The play could start with the presentation of Claudius (I. ii) or could open with Hamlet, brought to the battlements, as Horatio is in I. i, by reports of earlier visitations, ready to meet the Ghost at the outset. The report of the action of I. i which Horatio and the soldiers present in I. ii, could be entirely dispensed with. A moment's speculation, however, makes it clear that this complex riddling towards bringing Hamlet and the Ghost together, though it does not serve purposes of direct dramatic economy, does establish the dominant structural method of indirection wherein scarcely anything happens in the play as an immediate confrontation.

In the opening exchanges of I. i the central problem of uncertainty is touched on in the momentary confusion of establishing identity as the guards change the watch. They move on immediately to the broaching of a mystery when Horatio asks 'What, has this thing appeared again tonight?' (21). It is not initially clear what is being referred to. Marcellus and Horatio have already discussed it, and the latter has asserted it is the creation of the soldier's 'fantasy' (23). It is called a 'dreaded sight' (25) and then 'this apparition' (28). Horatio is clearly established as a sceptic, and any doubts members of an audience may entertain about the existence of ghosts can be set aside when this educated scholar submits to belief in it by the direct experience of its presence. Horatio confidently asserts ''twill not appear' (30), and the soldiers assert that his ears are fortified against their story though they have seen it twice. They begin to settle down to provide, in report to Horatio, the experience at second hand of an offstage happening when they are interrupted by the entrance of the Ghost (39). It is one of the most arresting entrances in Shakespeare, occurring as it does only a few minutes into the play and as if the fearful report of the soldiers had conjured up its very reappearance. The conventional expository account is aborted and replaced by a direct and terrifying experience that harrows the hitherto sceptical Horatio with fear and wonder. In this first encounter one salient fact in the mystery is established – the Ghost to all eyes bears the likeness of 'the buried majesty of Denmark'. But the Ghost departs before they can elicit any further information. The stunned figures on the battlements are left to speculate about the causes of the Ghost's wandering, seeing it as an omen of troubled times which is connected, in expository report, to the current political troubles in Scandinavia (67–125). This conversation does provide a political framework for the story we are to witness, but, when we look back on it later, we have to recognize it as a red herring, an explanation that is entirely irrelevant to the real reason for the Ghost's stalking mysteriously around Elsinore.

This attempt to dispel mystery, this providing of explanations that are wildly off the mark is the establishment of the method of the play. Hamlet will provide a series of red herrings and send Claudius unprofitably up blind alleys when the king tries to uncover the causes of his nephew's antic disposition. This is a world where men can only 'by indirections find directions out' and the explanations which Horatio and Marcellus offer for the Ghost's wanderings are far too direct for the devious puzzling secrets that will lock Hamlet and Claudius in mortal combat.

The Ghost makes a second appearance in this first scene as if it would challenge the straightforward explanations on offer, posing itself as a puzzle which invites further investigation. The audience might expect some movement toward the resolution of the mystery, but the enigma is maintained by the crowing of the cock which summons away the Ghost at a moment when Bernardo believes it was about to speak. The decision to impart their knowledge to Hamlet closes the scene. The resolution of the mystery is delayed by a variety of other matter. The Ghost will only reveal its secret to Hamlet, and much of the pressure of the play is created by the fact that Hamlet is isolated in his possession of that secret. The Ghost's story is of an extraordinary secret – undetectable murder. Hamlet will spend much of the play speculating on whether he can believe the Ghost, whether it is a spirit of health or goblin damned, and devising a test of its revelation. The divided world in which Hamlet must operate is unfolded as he approaches the Ghost's story which is interspersed with affairs of state, threats from Norway, diplomatic missions, the everyday events of Polonius' family, the farewell of Laertes to Polonius and Ophelia.

Hamlet is certainly melancholy and guarded when we first meet him. He is isolated to a degree from those around him. We hear of his love for Ophelia, his love of his dead father, his disturbance about his mother's remarriage, and sense tension in his attitude to Claudius *before* he is drawn into the dark tormenting world of uncertainty by the Ghost's revelation of its secret and its demand for revenge. We can sense his loss of the normal possibilities of life when we see him at the outset as a figure already set apart who is moved into a total and extreme isolation by the Ghost's story.

We can see why Shakespeare does not move quickly to resolve the mystery he broaches in the first few dozen lines of the play but chooses instead to allow this questionable shape to embroil and surround Hamlet and the audience. After the Ghost disappears for the second time in the first scene, therefore, the puzzle it poses hangs fire for a lengthy period. There are 192 lines in the second scene which pass before news of the Ghost is brought to

Hamlet. The 136 lines of I. iii turn to the sub-plot, and only after 38 lines of I. iv does the Ghost reappear. The gap between the onstage appearances of the Ghost from I. i. 143 – I. iv. 38 is 465 lines. At the point where the Ghost is ready to unfold the mystery with which the play began, at the opening of I. v, 660 lines (17.5 per cent) of the play have elapsed. The Ghost is making its fourth entrance onstage in the three scenes in which it has appeared. It has been onstage for 78 lines without speaking a word. Before it unfolds its tale it has been summoned away by cockcrow, assaulted with swords, been the topic of much speculation, the subject of 70 lines of detailed report (I. ii. 189–258), has beckoned to Hamlet to accompany it for a private revelation which led the prince's companions to restrain him and warn him against the danger and madness that might ensue. By moving the Ghost on and offstage, by accumulating reports and speculations around it, Shakespeare has made a very potent dramatic mystery. When the Ghost insists that Hamlet lend 'serious hearing/To what I shall unfold' (I. v. 5–6), the prince's reply 'Speak. I am bound to hear' voices, after the sequence of delays, the similarly rapt attention of the audience. The Ghost in its horrible tale certainly lives up to its advance billing. We can see at once that all the guesswork speculations of its significance to this point have been off the mark. Such potency and mystery have been related to the Ghost that it haunts the play and the audience's mind and recovers a vivid theatrical life when the Player King in 'The Murder of Gonzago' re-enacts for Claudius the story revealed to Hamlet in I. v.

The Ghost leaves the stage at I. v. 91, speaks from beneath the stage until finally the 'perturbed spirit' rests at line 181 – after 841 of the 3776 lines (22.3 per cent) of the play has elapsed. The Ghost does not reappear until III. iv. 102, an absence from the stage of 1492 lines (39.5 per cent of the play). This absence lasts from the point where Hamlet takes on the task of revenger, persists through his attempt to satisfy himself that it is an 'honest ghost', and ends just as Hamlet has made revenge more difficult by killing Polonius, an act which leads to his being shipped off to England. Given the extended battle of wits between Hamlet and Claudius it is difficult to see how the Ghost could have been brought on again before the play scene. One cannot easily imagine Hamlet explaining his delay to the Ghost by indicating that he was trying to establish whether it was 'a spirit of health or goblin damned'. The reappearance could not have occurred much later because it is only about 200 lines after the end of III. iv that Hamlet leaves for England and is himself absent from the stage for a considerable time. When Hamlet returns from his adventure at sea he is much more clearly committed to the fateful task and the doom of being a revenger imposed on him by the Ghost.

The reappearance of the Ghost seems to be prompted in a subliminal way by Hamlet's failure to kill the unprotected Claudius at prayer in the previous scene (III. iii). The reappearance is even more telling in that it occurs almost immediately after Hamlet has confronted his mother with 'The counterfeit presentment of two brothers' (III. iv. 55), the pictures, the descriptions, and the contrasts between the former king and his usurper. Hamlet scourges his mother: 'Have you eyes?/Could you on this fair mountain leave to feed,/And batten on this moor?' (III. iv. 66–8). In doing so he provides evidence against himself because the contrast between the brothers is so stark that it would seem to argue that Hamlet should have been able, as he asserted to the Ghost, to 'sweep to my revenge' (I. v. 31). Hamlet has only just established the veracity of the Ghost's story and has missed an opportunity to accomplish his revenge because the thought of sending the soul of Claudius to heaven as recompense for killing his father has impeded him. When a second opportunity seems to present itself he stabs through the arras to accomplish his revenge on the spying Claudius, only to find that his killing of Polonius postpones his task.

Hamlet has failed not only to undertake the task which the Ghost demanded but is in the process of violating another of its difficult injunctions. The Ghost had insisted that Denmark should be cleansed of the incestuous union into which Claudius and Gertrude have entered:

> Let not the royal bed of Denmark be
> A couch for luxury and damned incest.
> But howsomever thou pursues this act,
> Taint not thy mind, nor let thy soul contrive
> Against thy mother aught. Leave her to heaven
> And to those thorns that in her bosom lodge
> To prick and sting her.
>
> (I. v. 82–8)

In III. iv Hamlet has much to say to Gertrude about avoiding that incest, has indeed just provoked the pricks and stings (89–92, 95–7), but he has not, by his actions, made it impossible for her to continue that damned union. The whole bedroom scene, without the inserted complications of an Oedipus complex, indicates the continuing problems Hamlet has in coping with his mother's hasty and, to him, inexplicable marriage. The Ghost seems to appear not only to remind Hamlet of his 'almost blunted purpose' but to interrupt Hamlet's mounting harangue of his mother. Hamlet's problems are expressed vividly in the structure of the scene in the way he is caught in the cross-fire of his parent's eyes. Hamlet looks on the Ghost, the Ghost begs him to comfort his amazed mother, and Gertrude cannot see the Ghost of her husband, the cause of her son's agitation. The fragmentation, the mystery of the breakdown of the family, which was such a central cause of Hamlet's melancholy before he ever met the Ghost and which has not ceased to trouble him since, is fixed for the audience in this extraordinary spectral reappearance. We are reminded that Hamlet has considerable and unresolved problems about his mother's behaviour before the Ghost complicated matters much more deeply by indicating the manner of its death, which left the issue of Gertrude's complicity with Claudius entirely ambiguous. It is this issue which Hamlet has just been trying to resolve: 'A bloody deed – almost as bad, good mother,/As kill a king, and marry with his brother' (III. iv. 29–30), wherein he tried to confront Gertrude with the opportunity to reveal her guilt inadvertently. As soon as Hamlet turns to the issue which has long troubled him the Ghost reappears to interrupt his pursuit of it. Although Hamlet has, with only a few moments of relief, scarcely thought or talked about anything else but his task since the Ghost's last appearance, he indicates guilt at his delay as soon as it re-emerges (III. iv. 107–10).

The Ghost may consider Hamlet's blunted purpose needs whetting, but the audience can scarcely concur, and its reappearance serves functions that are outside its own concerns. We do remember the long passage of time since Hamlet first met the Ghost but we remember also the sustained effort the prince undertook to test the Ghost's story while Claudius surrounded him with spies to inquire into the true causes of his antic disposition. We can see that the Ghost, in its self-concern, wandering in pain, believes that very little has happened in its absence and that it still urgently awaits the accomplishment of the task it commanded. We are aware that less than 80 lines before its reappearance Hamlet has lunged with his sword at the arras to accomplish that revenge. The dead figure, in reasserting its demand, prompts us to recognize that the living have claims on our sympathy too. We are obliged to acknowledge how much more fully, in the Ghost's absence, we have come to apprehend the irresolvable problems of the revenge code. This scene itself broaches a revenge which will complicate the issue further. Laertes has, by Hamlet's action, just been given a motive to seek revenge for his father, an issue that will be pursued in the prince's enforced absence and surprise return. The issue here depends not on the dubious testimony of a ghost, nor any deep ambiguity or uncertainty of evidence, yet even Laertes, with all the drive of a reflex revenger, will not proceed to an open confrontation, but will become embroiled in a dishonourable plot that is even more sinister than the original murder undertaken by Claudius. The Ghost confirms, from its point of view, the drive to revenge in the plot, at a point at which it has to be postponed as the dangerous forces around Hamlet regroup themselves. Everything in the play supports the view of revenge as a subterranean and bewilderingly complex issue for any intelligent man who cannot respond with reflex bloodlust, and even for those, like Laertes, who assert a straightforward intention. The Ghost, in its reappearance, indicates no awareness of such difficulties and thus confirms the sense that our involvement in the unfolding of the complex issues gives us a *human* understanding of events that is beyond the simple view the Ghost has been able to maintain because of its long absence. The play seems to demonstrate that involvement in its action leads to destruction, even for figures like Ophelia, Polonius, Rosencrantz, and

Guildenstern who have a marginal involvement or no very clear idea of the complexities in which they are caught up.

In consideration of the disposition of a long absence in the appearances of the Ghost from a practical viewpoint it is necessary to speculate about other roles that the actor of the Ghost might have doubled. There are roles of gentlemen and court members which the actor could have fulfilled in several scenes. The actor could not easily have doubled the roles of Cornelius, Voltemand, or Reynaldo. The possibility exists for doubling the role of the Ghost with Fortinbras, the Captain of the Norwegian army in IV. iv, or with that of either of the gravediggers in V. i, or with Osric. The most captivating possibility however, if doubling was required, would seem to involve one of the players and especially the Player King. It would supply one of the subdued pleasurable jokes of doubling if we observe Hamlet hearing from the Ghost of the horrible murder that took place in his orchard and the same actor performing the role of the victim in the 'Mousetrap' played before Claudius. It would certainly provoke a vivid response from Claudius if the Player King (possibly with the connivance of Hamlet, we might speculate, to ensure the success of his trap) were made-up to look very much like old Hamlet. This would, in terms of face, beard, and stature be very much easier if the roles were doubled, a practice which has often been tried in productions. Claudius thereby watches not simply an imitation of his secret crime but must experience something very much like a return to the scene of the horrible crime itself performed in public. This might receive some slight support from the fact that Hamlet observes of his 'old friend', probably the leader of the troupe, who would perform the role of Player King, that 'thy face is valanced since I saw thee last' (II. ii. 413) indicating the addition of a beard which might already, therefore, remind him of his father whose beard we know 'was grizzled', 'a sable silvered' (I. ii. 240–2). It is not beyond the bounds of possibility that one of the ways Hamlet is prompted to thoughts of a play as a trap is a recognition that the leading player looks very much like his father. The player is greeted by Hamlet some 530 lines after the end of the scene in which Hamlet said farewell to his father's spirit. The Ghost's adjuration 'Remember me' may thus seem to receive fortuitous reinforcement when a figure, very similar in appearance, emerges to provide occasion for a test in which Hamlet can find out how much Claudius remembers.

Hamlet is not able immediately to sharpen what the Ghost has called his 'almost blunted purpose'. After his killing of Polonius he is obliged to submit to the king's plan to send him to England. We see him commenting on his own cause of revenge when he observes the forces of Fortinbras on their way to Poland. He departs from the stage at the conclusion of IV. iv and is absent for 499 lines until his re-emergence in the graveyard scene (V. i. 58). From quite early in the play we have observed Claudius using a variety of spies in trying to tease out the mystery of Hamlet's antic disposition. As soon as he understands in the play scene that Hamlet has knowledge of his fratricide he undertakes measures to get him out of the kingdom and to his death. Claudius does not, of course, reveal to anyone the deadly nature of the journey to England, though the audience gathers his intent from his soliloquy at IV. iii. 57–67. After Hamlet's departure, therefore, he is convinced that the issue has been resolved, but the audience intuitively knows that the play cannot be completed without Hamlet's return to confront Claudius.

During Hamlet's absence the action turns towards the sub-plot characters as Ophelia's madness is revealed and Laertes returns to pursue the revenge of his murdered father. We are not very far into this sequence when we discover, as we suspected, that the plans of Claudius have misfired and the prince has returned to Denmark. We have witnessed Claudius acting as a statesman, deploying spies, and wrestling with his troubled conscience, but we have not yet seen him fully at work in the deadly process of winding others into a murderous plot. He has already lost some of his instruments of spying and treachery – Polonius, Rosencrantz, Guildenstern, and Ophelia. The only major figures remaining are Horatio and Gertrude, neither of whom can be drawn into a plot against Hamlet. It is at this point that Laertes returns to Denmark demanding revenge. In Hamlet's absence, therefore, Shakespeare can develop Claudius more fully as an opportunistic schemer and he can unfold a character, Laertes, who was only briefly outlined early in the play. Laertes, who has lost his father and has to confront his mad sister and then hear of her death, can be set up as a bloodthirsty revenger in vivid contrast to the introspective Hamlet. The action soon has to turn to a consideration of how to deal with Hamlet when he returns to Elsinore. One member of Polonius' family is despatched before Hamlet's departure, another dies during his absence, and the circumstances that will ensure the death of the third member of the family on the prince's return are plotted during his absence. The period of Hamlet's absence also helps to widen the implications of the tragedy by embroiling others in a conflict that originally concerned only Claudius and the prince. All of the deaths (eight) in the play result, as Horatio puts it, from 'purposes mistook/Fall'n on th' inventors heads' (V. ii. 373–4). The plotting which leads to these deaths stems directly or indirectly from the stratagems of Claudius. There is, in this 499-line sequence, no danger of a loss of dramatic tension since we hear of the devious three-pronged attack being prepared for Hamlet's reception, and attend to the complete unfolding of two of the three characters who are the principal figures in the final bout of sword-play.

References to Hamlet are initially sparse during his absence, but the focus switches more to him as his return becomes imminent. In IV. v only a couple of lines (80–1) are concerned with him before the return of Laertes and the madness of Ophelia becomes the focus of attention. News of Hamlet is a central topic in IV. vi and 17 lines of the scene (13–29) are Hamlet's own words in the letter from him which Horatio reads aloud. In IV. vii Claudius explains to Laertes, in the opening 21 lines, his method of dealing with Hamlet. The scene is refocused on the present when another letter from Hamlet is delivered. References to the prince multiply (36–75), and Hamlet's own words are read by Claudius from the letter (43–7). Claudius turns the talk to the recent visit of a Norman, Lamord, his account of Laertes' skills with the sword, and Hamlet's envy thereat, as an introduction to his development of a plot against the prince (123–61). In the graveyard scene (V. i) there are no references to Hamlet before his reappearance (58). In the 499 lines Hamlet is absent, 125 lines, containing 39 specific references, are devoted to him, and 22 of these lines are Hamlet's own words in the reading-aloud of his letters. [The references are: Hamlet (8), his (11), him (10), he (9), your son (1)]. Shakespeare feeds our need to know of Hamlet's offstage movements even as he intermingles it with new matter.

There is always a danger in drama, but especially in such a long play, of overextending the central tension on which it is built. In organizing his play around the struggle between Hamlet and Claudius, as each tries to test and outflank the other, Shakespeare shrewdly builds tension not by presenting them in lengthy confrontations but by keeping them apart save for brief and telling clashes. No final struggle to the death rises out of the revelations of the play scene, and so Shakespeare varies the tempo and turns to other matters before tuning up the tension for the conclusion. When Laertes re-enters the play he looks very much as if, in leading a *coup d'état*, he might be an even bigger threat than Hamlet to unseat Claudius from his throne. We recognize, however, the masterful fashion in which the king redirects the energy of the avenger to serve his own purposes. We are obliged to note how easily Laertes can, in contrast to Hamlet, be caught and trapped. Claudius has been struggling for most of the play to deal with Hamlet and the mystery of his antic disposition. Some 2656 lines (70.3 per cent) of the play have run by the time Claudius despatches Hamlet to England, thinking he has resolved his problems. Hamlet escapes from that trap and returns to Denmark, and, though he will be trapped again, he is aware that he will probably lose his life in ensuring that he takes his revenge on Claudius. In contrast, it takes Claudius 161 lines (IV. vii. 1–161) to bend Laertes to his purposes. Laertes forfeits all sympathy, of course, when he becomes not only a tool in another's scheme – the unbaited foil and the poisoned chalice arranged by Claudius – but also himself an author of an underhanded trap in anointing the unbaited foil with deadly venom. The juxtaposition between Hamlet and Laertes, first presented in I. ii, is completed here. Hamlet in that scene could scarcely bring himself to speak to Claudius, and he makes it clear how irksome any association with him is. Laertes proved to be much more pliable and susceptible to flattery as Claudius, relishing the exercise of power, encouraged him to beg a favour (I. ii. 42–63). This impetuous young man is kept by Claudius, and indeed by Shakespeare in the terms of the deployment of his plot, in the manner Hamlet contemptuously asserts to Rosencrantz 'like an ape, in the corner of his jaw, first mouthed, to be last swallowed' (IV. ii. 17–19). Laertes is not a large role, for he has only about 180 lines to speak. He has fewer than sixty of them in the two scenes in which he appears at the outset (I. ii, I. iii), and nearly all of them are spoken in farewell to Ophelia and Polonius. It is necessary to draw him into the dangerous struggle of the main plot between the 'fell incensed points/Of mighty opposites', and Shakespeare achieves this with lightning economy in IV. v and IV. vii. During those scenes he is onstage for 300 lines, and, though he speaks only about 80 of them, he is very much at stage centre in his threat of a *coup d'état*, in his response to the madness of Ophelia, and as the object of the flattery of Claudius and his ally in the development of a sinister plot to accomplish his revenge. Nearly half of the role of Laertes is developed during the absence of Hamlet.

It is also during Hamlet's absence that the role of Claudius is more fully unfolded. We are aware throughout of Claudius as one of the 'mighty opposites' of the play, yet the 520½ lines that he speaks are only a little more than one-third of the lines spoken by Hamlet. He is the dominant figure in only 4 of the 11 scenes in which he appears (I. ii, IV. iii, IV. v, IV. vii), 2 of which are his dealings with Laertes during Hamlet's absence. Almost 40 per cent of the lines he speaks are in these 2 scenes (191½ of his 520½). The 193 lines of IV. vii constitute the longest time we see him onstage. We already know of the lengths to which Claudius will go to rid himself of Hamlet, but only in his spider-like weaving of a web around Laertes do we get a fully developed demonstration of all his devious political skills.

In terms of the rhythm of the play this offstage sequence provides for the actor of Hamlet a pause in what is one of the longest roles in the classical repertoire. Hamlet is onstage for 2411 of the play's 3776 lines (63.8 per cent). Of the 1365 lines Hamlet is not onstage this one continuous break of 499 lines provides 36.6 per cent of them. Hamlet speaks 1428 lines which is 37.8 per cent of the play. All of the action during Hamlet's absence is connected to him in one way or another, but it develops other centres of interest and brings to prominence another young man lamenting the loss of his father. On his departure Hamlet, as a man of action, is implicitly compared with the adventurer, Fortinbras, who leads his army across Northern Europe to fight for a piece of ground not big enough to provide burial for those who will die in dispute of it. In the final movement of the play, after Hamlet's return, we have the revenger Laertes as a point of comparison. He allows himself to be used, and himself behaves, in a treacherous and dishonourable fashion and will die without ever understanding most of the details of the plot in which he is involved in his attempt to revenge the deaths of his father and sister.

By using Hamlet's absence to complete all the details of the plot prepared for his return Shakespeare allows himself space to build up a more extended unfolding of Hamlet's character in the graveyard scene. The Hamlet who returns to Denmark is very different from the one who left it, and it is his absence which provides the opportunity to affect this essential transition and the graveyard scene which fully reveals it to the audience. The action on Hamlet's return does not press urgently towards the final duel. The graveyard scene with its battle of wits, its dark philosophical speculations, its nostalgic recall of earlier innocence, and Horatio's concern to deflect Hamlet from his macabre jests, allows us to recognize the prince's state of mind, his awareness of the impending shadow of death, and prepares us for his resigned acceptance of his fate. When Hamlet reveals the plot Claudius fashioned for his reception in England we know that he has already been brushed by the wings of death. When he absorbs the shock of Ophelia's death in the graveyard scene we sense that, in her loss he recognizes the end of any possibility of a normal life for himself. When he jumps into the grave and struggles over Ophelia's dead body with Laertes he anticipates the occasion, not far removed, when he will lie in his own grave. We are aware of a great sense of loss in the sacrifice of his life that Hamlet must make, but we are freed from some of the tension because of his meditations on death and the way he consciously submits to his fate. Hamlet's experiences during his absence offstage produce this necessary change of focus. Our experiences of the events onstage during his absence empower us with a full knowledge of the danger he is in. In both cases the hard terms of the revenge code, the accomplishment of the task at the cost of death, are gradually recognized to be unavoidable. But the audience's sense of apprehension is mitigated by a countervailing feeling of relief. The prince speaks to Horatio about his submission to his fate as he defies augury, finds 'special providence in the fall of a sparrow', and declares that 'the readiness is all' (V. ii. 205–12). The superior knowledge we possess here does not make us feel victims helplessly witnessing actions we would prevent if only we could. In some sense we know that Hamlet has at last come to the end of the long journey he has been pursuing since the Ghost first revealed its terrible secret.

The audience has to accept from the outset, in the nature of the Elizabethan interpretation of the revenge code, that the completion of his task will cost the prince his life. The tension in the final scene then is not concerned with whether Hamlet will survive, but whether he can against the odds, and in losing his life, nevertheless complete the revenge he has long been pursuing, whether his action can be one of triumph in defeat. Benetted round with villainies he still manages to have 'the engineer hoist with his own petar'. The king has, on only one occasion, been vulnerable and unprotected before Hamlet, but in a posture of prayer that led Hamlet to turn away from his opportunity. Claudius is never likely to give Hamlet any open opportunity again to catch him alone and undefended. Yet, by a stunning irony, in setting up a seeming innocent bout of swordsmanship as a deadly trap he provides Hamlet with the weapon and the chance to kill him in full view of the court. The prince has been pursuing this long journey because of the cunning, secretive skill of the murder of old Hamlet and is able to complete his task only because a cunning, secretive murder against himself provides him with his chance. That the resolution should come in public in a bout of sport which is yet another play-within-a-play is entirely appropriate to figures who have been fencing with each other throughout in feints and parries presenting 'onstage' versions of themselves while they worked 'offstage' to riddle out each other's secrets.

The final irony in the play concerned with stage absence has to do with the figure of Fortinbras. The Ghost's initial appearance is thought to be connected to the activity of the young Norwegian (I. i. 95–111). The Ghost is a portent of quite different matters and imposes a task which leads to the deaths of eight people. Fortinbras is offstage for 98.7 per cent of the play, all but 50 lines of it. He makes one appearance of 8 lines in IV. iv as he leads his army across stage to fight in a battle which has nothing to do with the action of the play, save that the exploit becomes one of the occasions that informs against Hamlet in his pursuit of revenge. The Ghost's connection with Fortinbras is tenuous, but they both, as a result of their absences, have little knowledge of or sympathy for the complexity of the events which unfold in the Danish court. In a very indirect manner, which is the way all events develop in this play, it is the Ghost's agency which leads to the tragic loading of the stage and to the circumstances wherein Fortinbras can take recompense for old Hamlet's slaying of his father and the lands which were thereby forfeited (I. i. 81–95). Fortinbras is little more than a stranger to the audience when he re-emerges 42 lines before the conclusion of the play. He has had no onstage interactions nor any reported offstage exchanges with any of the figures of the Danish court. It is very difficult to be onstage in this play and survive its action. Horatio does so because Hamlet ensures that he is no more than marginally involved. Fortinbras is offstage for almost the entire play and yet can inherit the kingdom by returning to it at an opportune moment.

Othello

Shakespeare writes *Othello* in such a way that it has a cumulative wearing effect on the nerves of the audience. It supplies us, as it does not supply any of the victims of Iago, with information that could undo his plot and it makes us watch helplessly as all opportunities to avert tragedy pass by. Major contributions to the fine-tuning of the tension of the play come from the way Shakespeare handles the relationship between onstage and offstage events and the offstage absences of his characters. I will consider Othello's offstage absence in detail but I want first to examine the way a significant turning-point is created by keeping offstage, until quite late in the play, a figure who is significant in its conclusion.

Lodovico makes his first appearance (IV. i. 209) after the play has already run 2317 lines (71.8 per cent) of its total of 3328. He appears in 4 of the last 5 scenes, is onstage for a total of 256 lines (7.9 per cent), speaks 69 lines (2.1 per cent), and performs quite specific and important functions that Shakespeare required at the climax of the action. A director could, of course, choose to have Lodovico onstage as a mute super among Brabantio's kinsmen in I. ii. and I. iii, but no mention is made of him nor is he referred to in any stage directions before his first appearance in IV. i. Though the cast of *Othello* is not large some doubling may have been involved. The Duke of Venice and some of his Senators appear only in I. iii, Brabantio appears only in the first 3 scenes, Montano appears only in II. i., II. iii., and V. ii, and Gratiano only in the last 2 scenes. There are various figures such as sailors, gentlemen, a clown, and messengers who were probably involved in doubling. One actor could have taken on the roles of the Duke of Venice and Gratiano, another actor could have played a Senator in I. iii, Montano, and perhaps other minor roles along the way. It is possible that one actor doubled the roles of Brabantio and Lodovico.

It does not matter very much that the audience does not know Lodovico before he appears in IV. i. because he comes to the play in ways that have a symbolic significance at least as important as any definition of his individual character. He is the voice of Venice, an administrative functionary of the white world which had such need of Othello's warrior skills that it even tolerated his marriage to a white woman in spite of the protestations of one of the Duke's council, her father. Lodovico comes also as a kinsman of Desdemona who, in her marriage, is moving into ever greater peril. I have suggested before that an audience can operate on two levels in its acceptance of a character and in its separate recognition of one actor doubling various roles. If the doubling here were as I have suggested there may even be an advantage in recognizing that Brabantio and Lodovico are performed by the same actor. Lodovico is, in some sense, Brabantio returning to the play, and a recognition of the connection is important to the function that this handsome kinsman performs. We are told later (V. ii. 205–10) that Brabantio is dead, and we can recognize that Lodovico is not quite the rabid racist we found in Desdemona's father. His shocked reaction to the treatment Desdemona receives is, however, very much the shock of official, aristocratic Venice and of a kinsman who, like Gratiano, another member of the family, may believe that Desdemona's unorthodox match was a mortal blow to her father.

As observers of Othello's subjugation to Iago's plot we have been taking it in as such a steady, unremitting experience that we may be in danger of getting inured to it. We are so familiar with Iago's manipulation of everyone around him that we may begin to find the sickening monotony of his success so predictable that we can no longer measure the full extent of the transformation he has wrought. Lodovico's entrance into the play is deliberately designed to be something like a dash of cold water in the face of a mesmerized victim for it provides us with an instant sense of *déjà vu*, a flashback to the Senate in Venice where we had our first experience of Desdemona and Othello together. We can remember the romantic commitment of Desdemona and Othello, the eloquence of Othello's speeches and his calm nobility, and Desdemona's urgent plea to be allowed to hazard the danger of sea and war in order to be with her husband. We can recall the Othello who, when attacked in the streets, could say 'Keep up your bright swords for the dew will rust them' and who, confronting charges that he practised witchcraft, with impressive confidence unfolded his 'whole course of love'. Lodovico remembers only the Othello he knew in Venice and, with no experience of him in Cyprus since Iago set to work, he is stunned by the Moor's transformation into a complete stranger.

There is another major effect resulting from Lodovico's late arrival in Cyprus and in the play, and that is the way it modifies our attitude to Desdemona. We have known about Iago's sinister intentions since the opening of the play. We have seen him undermining Othello almost unchecked since he began his campaign at line 35 of III. ii. for 856 lines (III. iii. 35 – IV. i. 209, where Lodovico enters), and much of the effect of this sequence is to isolate Desdemona and to give us an increasing awareness of her vulnerability. Cyprus is very much alien territory to her, and her isolation there, bereft of her kin, is a considerable aid to Iago's plotting. It is not that she is without friends. Cassio likes and needs her, and Emilia has great affection for her, but they have both been instrumental in placing her in situations which make her vulnerable to Iago's intentions. In addition this long sequence has proved to be remarkably claustrophobic because of the secretive interviews with Cassio, Emilia's muddled attempt to please Iago, and Iago's manipulation in private of Othello and Cassio. As characters quite unconsciously volunteer to play roles which further the success of Iago's plot, and as every accident connected with the handkerchief contributes to his destructive agency, there must seem to the audience, in the ensign's skilled handling of his victims in the separate compartments of his scheme, little chance for his monstrous strategy to be brought out into the open. Any hopes we have that Emilia might speak up about her knowledge of the loss of the handkerchief, which has become loaded with such sinister significance, are squashed in III. iv. Any hope we have that a confrontation between Desdemona and Othello might dispel the nightmare are dashed in III. iv and will be again in the 'brothel' scene (IV. ii) and in the murder scene (V. ii) when at last Othello reveals the full nature of his suspicions. It is only in IV. i, with the arrival of Lodovico, that the tight circle of those involved and misled by Iago is breached. Those within the tight circle have no clear idea of what is going on because Roderigo, Cassio, Emilia, and Desdemona have all been supplied with a variety of misleading explanations, so that Othello's behaviour remains a mystery they cannot penetrate. Emilia has guessed something of the problem, but her jaundiced view of men leads her to believe that whatever suspicions Othello entertains are probably groundless (III. iv. 159–62). We may hope for some confrontation between Othello and Desdemona which will bring his dark suspicions into the light where they may be challenged or, failing that, some public demonstration of Othello's tormented fury which will alert outsiders to the dangerous state of mind he is in. Lodovico's appearance and the gross public insult Othello gives to Desdemona in his presence would seem to supply such an opportunity. We can hope that someone who registers a sense of her injury, someone whose sense of decorum is appalled by Othello's erratic behaviour, someone to whom Othello has become unrecognizable, might be alerted by the serious-ness of the situation and come to Desdemona's defence by raising questions about her treatment. Who could be better for this purpose than a kinsman of Desdemona who has no knowledge of what has been going on in Cyprus?

The sequence with Lodovico, instead of providing the audience with a sense of release at the possibility of the discovery of the plot, slams the door shut again cutting off another escape path from the ever-narrowing road leading to the tragic resolution. Everything that happens serves to confirm Othello's suspicions. The poisoning of his mind has been a co-operative effort as Cassio, Desdemona, Emilia, and even unexpected bit-part players like Bianca, contribute to the improvised play Iago has fashioned for them to elaborate and support the story he has imposed on Othello. Lodovico, far from putting an end to this endeavour, becomes a part of it. His first inquiry about Cassio leads Desdemona to the hope that her kinsman can patch up the 'unkind breach' that has fallen between her lord and his lieutenant (IV. i. 217–19). Othello's fury begins to mount, and Lodovico fatally persists, leading Desdemona to what must, to her husband, sound like an unambiguous confirmation of his suspicions: 'I would do much/T'atone them, for the love I bear to Cassio' (IV. i. 225-6). Othello has been assured by Iago that he does not know very much about Venetians, but this must sound like an exotic custom indeed for it seems to be a scarcely veiled acknowledgment from a wife/mistress that she likes her lover to be friends with the husband she is cuckolding. Under what he must regard as cruel provocation Othello barely holds back from an unchecked explosion of temper. Lodovico adds, however, the final touch when he indicates that Cassio has been deputed in Othello's place (228–30) and Desdemona warmly declares her pleasure. Othello's belief that Cassio has already taken his place in bed makes what looks like her indiscreet celebration of it unendurable, and so he strikes her.

Lodovico's reaction to the striking of Desdemona sounds a note of outrage barely restrained by gentlemanly decorum: 'My lord, this would not be believed in Venice,/Though I should swear I saw't. 'Tis very much./Make her amends; she weeps' (IV. i. 235–7). The whole sequence serves to isolate Othello, for the bewildered Desdemona gives only the mildest of replies to

Othello's increasingly uncontrolled agitation, and thus his anger seems to have no justifiable basis or any ready explanation (IV. i. 227–34). Othello, who had appeared to be magisterially calm in the Senate where the white man, Brabantio, had featured as a mad irrational figure of excess, now seems to be a strange, barbaric man possessed by passions that are incomprehensible to all but one of the restrained Europeans surrounding him. In a matter of fewer than 50 lines (IV. i. 209–56) Lodovico has to cope with Othello's extraordinarily erratic temper, his wild, distracted speech, his public, physical abuse in slapping Desdemona, and his scarcely veiled and humiliating treatment of her as a puppet who, like a whorish actress, will turn a trick in anyone's bed while brazenly sustaining a pretence of innocence.

Lodovico, in his bemusement at the stranger he has just encountered, seeks an explanation, after Othello's departure, from Iago, that 'honest' figure to whom everyone turns at some point in the play. He again very specifically refers us back to the figure he and we knew in Venice but whose transformation he has not, as we so helplessly have, witnessed. He forces us to register the dimensions of the change:

> Is this the noble Moor whom our full Senate
> Call all in all sufficient? Is this the nature
> Whom passion could not shake? Whose solid virtue
> The shot of accident nor the dart of chance
> Could neither graze nor pierce?
>
> (IV. i. 257–61)

The exchange with Iago serves to underline how undetectable the ensign's agency has been, and the secret triumph he can take in it, in the dry, appalling understatement he gives in reply: 'He is much changed'. We are simultaneously forced to register Lodovico's shock, understandable since he has seen nothing of Othello since Venice, even as we also acknowledge that no one else save Iago has any explanation of the radical change in Othello despite their continuing contact with him in Cyprus. Iago is so secretly exuberant about the change he has wrought and to which Lodovico's response bears tribute that he is not so discreetly evasive as usual. He is so charmed by his success that he takes no elaborate pains to soothe Lodovico's suspicions, which range from speculations about lunacy in Othello to guesses at disturbing news in the letters he has brought from Venice. Iago's laconic replies (IV. i. 262–74) do not give very much away. One may suspect that his refusal to allay Lodovico's alarm comes from his deeply malicious envy which makes him enjoy the power of exposing Desdemona to danger and capable of maintaining a common man's enigmatic disinterest before her aristocratic kinsman. Iago, in his hatred, needs not only to bring down the alien Moor he despises but also, perhaps, the Venetians ranking above him. His joy in mocking Brabantio, whose refined daughter submitted to being 'covered by a Barbary horse', and to 'making the beast with two backs', threatening to spawn into this noble family 'gennets for germans', was clear evidence of the common man's contempt for his supposed betters who could stoop to relationships with which he would not sully himself. We know also of his contempt for the gentlemanly class and his contempt for their privileged education in his attitude to the 'great arithmetician', Michael Cassio, and in the pleasure he takes in exercising his scarcely veiled contempt in bilking and exploiting Roderigo. He enjoys having Lodovico bewildered and confused as much as he relished prodding Brabantio, and bringing them down a peg is a bonus in his strategy of destroying three figures, Othello, Desdemona, and Cassio, who, in his view, are unworthy of the various blessings and privileges they have received.

Shakespeare does provide us with further evidence that Lodovico, despite what he has seen in the mistreatment of Desdemona, will not enquire further and will leave the problems of the marriage to those directly involved. At the outset of the 'willow' scene (IV. iii) Lodovico comes briefly onstage with Othello as Desdemona prepares for bed on the evening that we know has been designated for her murder. There is no very compelling reason why Lodovico appears and no obvious function that he serves. He is onstage for 9 lines which serve to indicate that whatever anxiety the Venetian visitor felt (in IV. i) has been partially allayed. Othello, now determined in his course, is not so visibly agitated for, as Emilia says, 'He looks gentler than he did' (IV. iii. 10). Othello's courtesy to Lodovico seems to be reassuring enough, and the Venetian departs with no mention of any apprehension about Desdemona's safety. Any hopes we may have harboured that Lodovico would probe the issue further are dismissed here, which clearly signals that Desdemona is bereft of any protection against the fate approaching her. This is the more clearly underlined in her willingness to follow her husband's instructions to dismiss Emilia: 'We must not now displease him' (IV. iii. 16). Everything dovetails to the advantage of Iago's plot.

We hear, in the willow scene, the women's gossip about Lodovico as 'a proper man', 'a handsome man', a man for whom 'a lady in Venice would have walked barefoot to Palestine for a touch of his nether lip' (IV. iii. 34–8). The refreshing innocence of this reminds us of the world from which Desdemona came, a world evoked in several speeches, where she could, as her father asserted, have chosen any of 'the wealthy curled darlings of our nation' (I. ii. 68), men of the same social class as Lodovico, but selected instead the exotic, romantic figure of Othello. A method actor, deeply immersed in sub-text, might bring himself to believe that Lodovico does not show excessive concern for his kinswoman because, if he were of the same stripe as Brabantio, he might feel, even in face of Othello's bizarre behaviour, that since she has made her bed she must lie on it. His stereotypical reaction to her might, after all, not be far from that of another Venetian, Iago:

Not to affect many proposèd matches
Of her own clime, complexion, and degree,
Whereto we see in all things nature tends –
Foh! one may smell in such a will most rank,
Foul disproportions, thoughts unnatural –

(III. iii. 229–33)

The text does not give direct warrant for such a view but it does not pass over entirely Lodovico's failure to pursue the issue very far. His speculations about Othello's treatment of his wife imply that husbands who physically abuse their wives were not uncommon. He asks Iago about the striking of her 'Is it his use?' (IV. i. 267) and wonders whether the contents of the letters from Venice might have provoked him to unusual violence. This suggests that habitual violence might be just as ready an explanation as a particular motive. In the willow scene itself we also have Emilia's views that erratic, violent husbands are not especially unusual, and it seems quite possible, given Iago's suspicions and his contemptuous treatment of her, that she speaks from personal experience:

Say that they slack their duties
And pour our treasures into foreign laps;
Or else break out into peevish jealousies,
Throwing restraint upon us; or say they strike us,
Or scant our former having in despite –

(IV. iii. 86–90)

Lodovico's shock at Othello's behaviour may be not so much at the physical blow but at the fact that such lack of control is shown so publicly.

The explanation for Lodovico's acceptance of Othello's behaviour without extensive enquiry comes not merely from the apparent mildness of Othello at the opening of IV. iii, but, of course, from Desdemona's own willingness to put up with it. She, inside the relationship, is as surprised and confused about Othello's behaviour as Lodovico is outside of it. Her guesses as to its cause are as wildly off-the-mark and indeed the same as those of her kinsman. In the brothel scene she has been called a whore but has been provided with no evidence that she can challenge. She seems determined to be obedient and to placate Othello. Lodovico, observing this compliant behaviour, must inevitably believe that if no one makes a fuss about it and she seems not to be outraged then it is none of his business. Desdemona does, of course, seek out an explanation of Othello's behaviour after Lodovico's arrival, but naturally it is not from her kinsman who is so new to the situation. That she turns to Iago for comfort only underlines how little she knows about what is going on. We cannot, however, simply see Desdemona as beauty at the mercy of the beast, a vulnerable female in need of help, for it is possible that even if she had any inkling of the danger she

118

was in, she might not look to Lodovico for help. In choosing Othello she stood out against the prejudices of her society. Even in the willow scene, after her bewildering experience of being treated as a whore, when Emilia suggests a more jaundiced view of men she refuses to accept her ideas. It is her individuality and independence that make her attractive and her trust which makes her unaware of danger. Even with her dying words she tries to protect her husband. Lodovico's function in the play is to underline for the audience that all the 'insiders', those who have witnessed something of the rapid transformations in Cyprus, are really outsiders and helpless to understand or interfere. This makes it more forcibly clear that the only insiders are Iago, who turns all potential enemies to his plot into allies which ensure its success, and the members of the audience who understand everything but are also helpless to interfere.

The relentless pace of this play required that Shakespeare modify his habitual practice of supplying, in the later stages of his tragedies, relief for the actor of the hero's role by handling Othello's stage absence in an unusual manner. In almost covert fashion Shakespeare allows Othello an offstage interlude that is not continuous but which, nevertheless, provides the actor with some relief. Shakespeare developed the structures of many of his other tragedies so that the action reaches a natural pause in which there can be a change of focus and a regrouping of characters when the hero is removed from the central locale of the play. I have already examined such natural pauses in the role of Hamlet and will do so in later chapters with the roles of Romeo and Coriolanus. In *Macbeth* the tyrant's murderous acts culminate in the slaughter at Fife, and, though the hero does not move out of the country, the action can plausibly focus on the gathering of those forces outside Scotland which will lead to Macbeth's fall. In *King Lear* the mad king moves increasingly out of contact with his few companions of the heath, allowing the focus to shift to those wrestling for the power he has given away, before the king is reunited with Cordelia, and before his hopes of a peaceful retirement with her are finally shattered.

Shakespeare handles the plot of *Othello* in a way that produces an unbroken drive to the action which flows without any perceptible pause through Act IV and into the last scene of the play. Shakespeare radically alters the time-frame of Cinthio's novella from events spread over months and then years until the discovery of villainy long after the murder. The fragile nature of Iago's plot and the speed with which it must be accomplished before any evidence arises that could undermine it presupposes that there can be no break in the time-frame nor, given Othello's passionate urgency, any extended period in which the key characters can be absent offstage. Iago cannot be offstage for long because much of the almost unbearable pressure of the play arises from the oppressed sense those watching the action have that they, no more than his victims, can escape his incessant attention.

Othello cannot be allowed to escape from Iago's supervision for long nor can he be kept for any length of time out of view of the audience because the determination to resolve matters in murder and in haste stem from him. There is no banishment, no change of locale, no completion of one phase of action, no natural pause in the journey to the tragic conclusion. In Act IV the murderous plots which will occupy Act V are still hanging fire but the audience is aware of the relentless approach to catastrophe. Yet even though Shakespeare does not want to break the drive of the play or relax its tension he does, in a variety of ways, contrive to produce a change of focus and develops scenes which produce something like the equivalent of the pause I have looked at in other tragic structures.

Iago's, of course, is a larger role even than Othello's, and he is given no extended respite from the action. Because he is at the centre of his spider-web he must be constantly active in fitting his victims into the roles for which he needs them. The role of Iago, however, is not as taxing as that of Othello in terms of the emotional range it demands. Iago is successful because of his apparent normality and a cool-headed lack of emotion against which the volatile Othello must play. Iago has 1022½ lines to speak (31.7 per cent of the play) and Othello speaks 794½ lines (24.6 per cent). Iago is onstage for 2278½ of the play's 3228 lines (70.6 per cent), and Othello is on for 1716½ lines (53.2 per cent). Both of these characters speak almost half of the lines when they are onstage. In comparison to these giant roles Desdemona is onstage for 1205 lines (37.3 per cent) and has only 343½ lines to speak (10.6 per cent). Iago is onstage at some point in 13 of the play's 15 scenes (he is absent only in the herald's scene (II. ii) and the willow scene (IV. iii)). Othello is on in 12 scenes, missing only I. i, II. ii, and III. i. There are not many occasions when the audience can escape Iago's corrosive presence; and perhaps, in Shakespeare, only Richard III is as ubiquitous (though he is absent for 324 lines – I. iv, Clarence's murder (278), and the beginning of II. i (46), and also for the first 135 lines of IV. iv). Until the end of III. iii, by which time the play has run 1907 lines (59.1 per cent) Iago is never offstage for as much as 100 lines at one time (II. i. 1–82 is his longest absence). Only four times in the entire play is he absent for more than 100 lines – III. iv. 1–106 (106), IV. ii. 1–109, IV. iii (104), and his longest absence, V. i. 1–168 (168), when Othello is completing the murder he has designed. Othello is absent for several intervals before he gets to the modified pause Shakespeare shapes for him in Act IV – I. i (182), I. iii. 301 – II. i. 179 (277), II. i. 211 – II. ii. 11 (107), II. iii. 12–152 (140), II. iii. 249 – III. i. 55 (177). At the very heart of the play, however, there are demands made on the actor of Othello for a sustained, concentrated, and emotionally draining performance that have only a few parallels even in Shakespeare. In III. iii, III. iv, and IV. i the audience witnesses Othello onstage under Iago's pressure with only scattered and brief lapses of relief, and, from the opening of III. ii to IV. ii. 94, a sequence of 1056 lines (32.7

per cent), Othello is never offstage for as much as 40 lines continuously.

In this central sequence the audience may begin to feel that the only chance Othello has to escape from the snares in which he is caught is if he could talk to Desdemona alone for an extended period. In such circumstances he could fully reveal, instead of obliquely hinting at, the suspicions Iago has imposed on him, providing Desdemona with an opportunity to expose the flimsiness of Iago's story. Yet we recognize the skill of Iago's 'evidence' and that its strength lies in the fact that it cannot easily be checked. The key element, the handkerchief, is a detail we know she cannot disprove. She is unaware that when she dropped it it passed from Emilia to Iago to Cassio to Bianca. She could only assert again that she has mislaid it which seemed so feeble an excuse to Othello that it served to confirm his suspicions.

We can still recognize, however, that Othello, under the spell of his memories and even in his greatest anguish, retains the capacity to love the innocence in Desdemona which first charmed him, as several passages testify (III. iii. 278-9, IV. i. 175-6, 180-2, 184-7, 192-3, 200-2). We can still hope that without Iago's interference Othello might recover some experience of her innocence. In IV. ii. Shakespeare allows Othello and Desdemona to meet for 71 lines without Iago's poisonous presence. We very quickly perceive that Iago is, nevertheless, implicitly present in the scene, having taken up residence, to a degree, in Othello's mind. Othello endeavours to play the role of the customer of a brothel, one familiar with the tricks of Venetian women, and he talks very much in Iago's vein.

If we look back over the play we recognize how rarely Othello and Desdemona are alone onstage together. This strategy is designed by Shakespeare to underline our sense of how little time, after their whirlwind courtship, marriage, and removal to Cyprus, they have had to settle down and gain a knowledge of each other, which reinforces our understanding of why Othello is so vulnerable to Iago's scheming. The newly married reunited couple have an intimate exchange of ecstatic declarations of love in their arrival in Cyprus (II. i. 180-210), but this 31-line exchange is on a crowded stage and with Iago's 'aside' (197-9) to remind us of the havoc he intends to wreak. Even when they are together offstage and presumably consummating their marriage (II. iii), while Iago is encompassing the downfall of Cassio, they are left uninterrupted for only 141 lines (12-152). In III. iii they share an exchange (41-89) of 49 lines, but they are in the presence of Iago and Emilia. Later in III. iii when Othello brushes aside her proffered handkerchief they have an exchange of 12 lines (278-89), but Emilia is present. In III. iv Othello questions Desdemona in Emilia's presence for 68 lines (31-98), and in IV. i, in the greeting of Lodovico they are onstage for 45 lines (209-53) for only spasmodic and distracted communication. In IV. ii, therefore, they occupy the stage alone for *the first time*. Emilia is, of course, only just beyond the door to 'Cough or cry hem if anybody come' (29). By this point (IV. ii. 31) the play has run 2413 (74.7 per cent) of its

121

lines, and this is only the first of the two occasions in the play when husband and wife are alone. The longest interaction between them hitherto has been the 68-line cross-examination about the handkerchief (III. iv), and in fact the total of their direct interactions before the brothel scene is under 200 lines or around 8 per cent of the play to that point.

This sequence in IV. ii, when they are alone at last, would seem to be their only chance to clear up the problems which have brought Desdemona to within a few hours of the death planned for her. The exchange lasts 60 lines (31–90) until Othello summons Emilia to pay her for the privilege of spending time alone with his wife, a privilege which convinces him that she is a cunning whore with an imperturbable mask of pretended innocence he cannot penetrate. This initial time alone with her onstage confirms his need to be alone with her once more. In V. ii they are alone for the longest period they ever spend onstage together after their testimony before the Venetian Senate (I. iii), a sequence in which they are not involved in direct interaction. In V. ii they are onstage together for 106 lines but alone for only 62 lines of conscious interaction, from the point where Desdemona awakes to the point where Othello begins to respond to Emilia's urgent knocking on the door (23–84). Shakespeare manages to structure the play in a manner which presents the husband and wife alone onstage in direct interactions for a total of 122 lines, which constitutes 3.8 per cent of the play. The point I want to make is that though there is an unbroken flow in the time frame of the story and the drive of its murder plot, there is by the end of IV. ii an almost irreversible fatalism attached to the play. Whatever hopes we may have had that Othello and Desdemona could clear things up if left alone are dashed by the brothel scene.

When left to confront Desdemona and Emilia alone Othello cannot break out of the net Iago has woven around him. He has already witnessed, so he believes, Cassio crowing about his conquest of Desdemona (IV. i). Othello by IV. ii. 94 has undertaken all the observations, cross-examinations, and tests he needs to ensure himself that the retribution he intends to visit on his wife is justified. I have indicated that there are some impediments to sustaining a long, unbroken offstage absence for the hero of this play, but after the confrontation alone with Desdemona in IV. ii Shakespeare can develop the action to give Othello as much of a pause as can be managed. We no longer have any hopes that the catastrophe can be averted by any inquiries Othello might make. Any flickering hopes we sustain can only attach themselves to Emilia as she begins to work her way towards the truth that some villain has caused the transformation in Othello. Shakespeare does supply something of a pause in the role of Othello in which an actor can gather his strength for an assault on the emotional peaks in the conclusion of the play. He is onstage throughout the 371 lines of V. ii and he speaks 182 lines (49 per cent) of that scene (a few lines more than he speaks in the play's longest scene III. iii (480)). In the scene he contemplates murder, struggles with his terrified wife, murders her, discovers the details of the plot of which he has been a victim, laments the errors and the loss it has caused him, manages only to wound Iago before he is disarmed, and finally commits suicide.

In *Othello* Shakespeare follows a path he had taken earlier in his other play about Venetians when Antonio in *The Merchant of Venice* breaches a long absence briefly on one occasion, a strategy I will examine in a later chapter. Othello breaches his lengthy absence briefly on two occasions.

(a) IV. ii. 95–241 following Othello's departure in the brothel scene there is a discussion between Desdemona, Emilia and Iago about the Moor's strange behaviour and then Roderigo's confrontation with Iago about his disappointed hopes. *Othello is offstage for 147 lines.*

(b) IV. iii. 1–9 Othello and Lodovico say goodnight to Desdemona. *Othello is onstage for 9 lines.*

(c) IV. iii. 10–104 Desdemona and Emilia converse in the willow scene.

(d) V. i. 1–27 Iago and Roderigo assault Cassio in the streets. *Othello is offstage in these two scenes for 122 lines.*

(e) V. i. 28–36 Othello comes on and registers that Iago is undertaking his part of the plot before he departs to kill Desdemona. *Othello is onstage for 9 lines.*

(f) V. i. 37–129 Iago continues his botched murders, is discovered, and tries to cover his tracks before the news is sent to Othello. *Othello is offstage for 93 lines*, until he returns in V. i for the final 371 lines of the play.

The sequence then is off (147), on (9), off (122), on (9), off (93) – so that in the 380 lines Othello only has to appear for 18 of them.

What we find in this absence, breached by brief appearances, is a variety of matter which is developed to enlarge our sense of the approaching tragedy from several angles. When the women are left nonplussed after Othello's departure in IV. ii they, like everyone else, turn to Iago for enlightenment. Iago has separate interactions with all of the main contributors to his plot – Cassio, Roderigo, Emilia, as well as Othello. But apart from his bantering exchanges with Desdemona on their arrival in Cyprus (II. i. 102–59), and despite having spoken incessantly about her to Cassio, Roderigo, and Othello, he has spoken directly to her hardly at all. After her departure in III. iii. 89, when Iago begins to work on Othello, until Desdemona's encounter with Iago in IV. ii, 977 lines pass in which he constructs a completely false picture of Desdemona for her husband. In this core of the play Iago is onstage with her in III. iv. 107–40 (34) and IV. i. 209–53 (45) for a total of 79 lines, and in this period he speaks only half a dozen lines (III. iv. 134–9) which may be directed to her as well as Emilia. One of the bleakest moments for the audience, which seems to extinguish all hopes for her safety, is when Desdemona begs for Iago's help in winning back her husband (IV. ii. 148–50), kneels 'by this light of heaven', and swears her faith. This reminds us with savage irony of how Othello had knelt with Iago and sworn a vow 'by yond marble heaven' (III. iii. 460) and of how Iago swore by 'you ever-burning lights above' (III. iii. 463) to destroy Desdemona because of her betrayal of her faith. The tragedy seems to have a momentum that is beyond recall, and Iago's flimsy plot seems to survive all tests because he is called on by his victims for explanations which allow him to disassociate himself from any agency in the events that trouble them. Iago has spent considerable periods with Othello, Cassio, and Roderigo, providing them with hopes, plausible roles and motives, and reasons to rely on his advice and insight, so that we have little hope that any of the men will penetrate behind Iago's mask. This scene gives us evidence that, at this point, there is no hope that the women will see through Iago either.

As soon as he has been able to reassure the women Iago has to deal with Roderigo. We begin to get the impression, however, that Iago has to keep his eye on too many things at once. The pressure that is building on Iago comes at first from the figure who, from the very outset, he has been able to handle most easily. As a poor dupe Roderigo never has any lengthy exchanges with the other characters and in this scene he is clearly beginning to chafe against the bondage in which Iago has kept him. Outraged by the lack of return he has received for all the jewels he has yielded up in the siege of Desdemona, he threatens to reveal his plight to her (IV. ii. 196–9). The worm is at last beginning to turn, and Iago has to spend 70 lines (IV. ii. 172–241) calming Roderigo down. Iago manages to turn the occasion to his advantage by suggesting that his petulant dupe murder his 'rival' Cassio.

Othello comes onstage briefly for 9 lines at the opening of IV. iii as Lodovico bids Desdemona goodnight and she is counselled to dismiss her attendant. It could be argued that Othello's appearance here is not completely necessary, but the sequence performs a couple of important functions. As I have argued earlier, Lodovico's appearance here and apparent amity with Othello indicates to the audience that nothing is going to come of the alarm he showed earlier, for he is reassured by the fact that the Moor's erratic behaviour has given way to calmness. It is useful for the audience to see this calmness, however briefly, because it reminds us how settled Othello now is about the task he is going to undertake and how imminent the murder is. It also serves to set up the ensuing willow scene in all its innocent charm because it reminds us yet again how privileged and private our knowledge is and how little the women know that behind Othello's new-found calmness in proposing an evening stroll with Lodovico lies a settled and murderous intent.

The clearest evidence that Shakespeare is, to some degree, following a familiar pattern in the Act IV-pause in the tragic hero's role, wherein he gives the audience a new focus by presenting it with some hitherto relatively undeveloped character or interaction, is the conversation between Desdemona and Emilia in IV. iii. *Othello* is the most dramatic of Shakespeare's major tragedies, and yet because of the relentless pressure of Iago's plotting we have little time devoted to the innocuous routines of daily domestic life. We are heavily embroiled in the masculine world in Othello's generalship, the drinking-session which destroys Cassio's lieutenancy, the cynicism of Iago about women, Cassio's attempts to fight off the tenacious Bianca, and above all in Othello's suspicions, fostered by Iago, that he has been cuckolded. The play is, to a degree, stifling for an audience because we are oppressed for so long and in so many issues with masculine insecurities and given only intermittent fragments of Desdemona's generous, open nature. Even in those moments we get little unalloyed relief because her innocent behaviour is so often being misinterpreted by Othello to confirm his belief in her guilt. I have noted above how little time in the play is devoted to a straightforward celebration of the love of Othello and Desdemona. In IV. iii, on the eve of her murder, we remember that our last experience of their relationship, undistorted by Iago's version, was the 49 lines (III. iii. 41–89) when Desdemona importuned her husband to reconsider his dismissal of Cassio, and we recognize the comfortable beginnings of the routine give-and-take of married life. It was only 3 lines after Desdemona's departure that Iago began in earnest, and none of the exchanges of husband and wife thereafter (III. iii. 278–88, III. iv. 31–98, IV. i. 209–53, IV. ii. 24–94) are noted for domestic tranquillity.

As Desdemona grows more bewildered by her husband's behaviour she is left ever more isolated. In leaving Venice she has lost contact with her father and kin, and because Cassio has disgraced himself she can have only fleeting meetings with him to reassure him that she is urging his return to favour. The only figure left for her to associate with, save for Iago whom she appealed to in IV. ii and Lodovico who has been taken off for a walk by Othello, is Emilia. The close relationship between the two women is an addition Shakespeare makes to his source. It is crucial to the outcome of the play because Emilia, at the climax of her role, has a choice of loyalty to her mistress or her husband and chooses Desdemona though it costs her her life. The audience has to be prepared for Emilia's brave defiance in the final scene. Iago exploits his dupes with skill throughout, but the one he takes most for granted, the one who turns out to be the loophole in his scheme and can name him as villain, is his own wife. She is a woman who knows the base suspicions to which men can stoop, and, though her realistic view of the way men act towards women is not as cynical or contemptuous as Iago's view on women, it comes from a direct experience of neglect, jealousy, insult, and abuse.

When we review the consummate economy with which Shakespeare develops her role we can see how important IV. iii is for our understanding of her. Desdemona is committed through Iago to Emilia's care by Othello's order (I. iii. 296–7), but Emilia does not appear onstage until the arrival in Cyprus. She is onstage in that scene (II. i) for 129 lines (82–210) and has to endure Iago's bantering abuse of her in particular among his general slander of women. She speaks only 1½ lines, but we get some sense of an alliance between herself and Desdemona as Iago mocks women of all temperaments and appearances. She is offstage for 541 lines until III. i. 41 when she greets the dispirited Cassio, who wishes to win Desdemona as his advocate to Othello. She is present at the beginning of III. iii, though she only speaks 3 of the 89 lines, when Desdemona promises aid to Cassio and then appeals to Othello on his behalf. Later in the scene (III. iii. 278–320) – and fatally for her mistress as well as indirectly for herself – she picks up the handkerchief dropped in negligence and initiates its eventful journey. Because she has no knowledge of the deadly use to which it can be put she stands silently by in III. iv when Othello confronts Desdemona about the handkerchief, concealing her 'borrowing' of it to appease the whim of her wayward husband. Iago's plot could collapse at this point, but Emilia will only expose her husband as a villain when she understands her own instrumentality in the death of her mistress. In III. iv she is onstage for the first 168 lines and speaks only 16½ of them, but it is only in this scene that we witness for the first time a private exchange between the two women. They discuss the possibility of Othello's jealousy (23–31) and continue in the same vein after Othello's demands for his handkerchief drive him to fury (99–106). They conclude the interaction on the speculations about the cause of Othello's distress after Iago's entrance and departure (140–68) in which Cassio remains a mute witness of the conversation for all but 3 of these 29 lines. In the brothel scene (IV. ii) she speaks 41½ lines in the 103 she is onstage (1–19 (19), 24–30 (7), 91–106 (15), 110–71 (62)). For only 12 of these lines is she alone with Desdemona (95–106), but throughout it we get a very clear sense of her loyalty to and concern for her mistress, as she asserts Desdemona's honesty in the face of all Othello's suspicions. She comforts the dazed Desdemona when Othello has left and condemns his outrageous behaviour much more severely than her mistress when they inform Iago of what has occurred and seek an explanation from him. Emilia comes measurably closer herself to uncovering the mystery of the Moor's behaviour (IV. ii. 15–16, 130–3, 139–44, 145–7). It is her assertions of faith here which seal the compact we have seen growing between the two women and prepare us for the willow scene. There is a considerable amount of what might be called deep preparation for IV. iii, a scene which has to do a lot of work in the play's structure.

The willow scene is one of the most effective in all of Shakespeare's work in changing pace, mood, and focus. It is the only extended sequence, after Iago has begun to poison Othello's mind, in which we are not concerned with the suspicions, puzzlement, and lies that arise from Iago's plot. It is an intensely domestic scene and, after the claustrophobic atmosphere created by scenes of almost unbroken deception, anger, and abuse, it strikes us as remarkably normal. Even though it is not free of the anxiety which the shadows of suspicion have induced, it is almost an island of relief for an audience. The open generosity and sympathy between the women is a breathtaking contrast to the corrupt, sinister, and violent attitudes and aims of the men. It is as if – briefly – we are allowed to wake from a nightmare to remember how straightforward life can be. The preparations for sleep, the unpinning and brushing of Desdemona's hair, the laying-out of her nightgown, her memory of her mother's maid Barbary and the sad fate of her love, the singing of the song, the frank exchange of views about Lodovico's attractiveness, the discussion about the nature of men with Emilia's somewhat jaded views of their faithfulness, the clear assertions of Desdemona about the value of loyalty – all of these contribute to our sense of the survival of attractive, healthy, uncomplicated views and domestic pleasantries in a play which has progressively lost touch with tranquillity, trust, and faith. Emilia here speaks 44 of the 95 lines they are alone together in their amiable chat.

If we add up all the lines in the play where Othello is in direct communication with Desdemona (albeit that he is at times distracted and their exchanges are not continuous), they add up to 329. Othello is onstage alone with Desdemona for 168 lines, and I have noted that in the two scenes (IV. ii. 31–92, V. ii. 1–106) he is involved in direct exchanges with her for a total of only 122 lines. Emilia is onstage alone with her mistress for 124 lines (III. iv. 23–31 (9), III. iv. 99–106 (8), IV. ii. 95–106 (12), IV. iii. 10–104 (95)), and for 26 more lines (III. iv. 140–65) when Cassio is onstage but takes no part in their conversation. With a few other scattered remarks (III. iii 3–5, 29, V. ii. 121–6) her direct interaction with Desdemona amounts to 160 lines – 77.5 per cent of which are when they are alone. Not only does she spend as long alone onstage with Desdemona as Othello does, but in the willow scene has a longer unbroken period of conversation with her (95 lines) than Othello ever enjoys. This scene between the two women is the most sustained, uninterrupted exchange either of them experiences in the play, and this indicates the weight the scene carries and its importance in showing us sides of these women that we have only glimpsed hitherto. The play is very much concerned with the conflict between the sexes and the differing views they have of each other. We have had fragments of the women's contrasted views of the men (III. iv. 99–106, 140–64), but the willow scene gives us an open, extended exchange uninterrupted by men. It is the only scene in which a preponderant share of the speech is by women. It is the only scene which concludes with the exit of women; Emilia exits with Cassio at the close of III. i, but otherwise here only with Desdemona is the one occasion on which she closes a scene and is not simply an incidental presence within the ongoing flow of masculine concerns. The willow scene serves slightly to redress the balance in a play which is filled with the slander and abuse of women by men. It is the culmination of our awareness that, in the second half of the play, Emilia is closer to Desdemona than Othello is. The growing relationship between the women is an essential perspective on the growing alienation between the sexes which develops because of masculine suspicions of and contempt for women, from which Cassio in his treatment of Bianca is not exempt nor Roderigo in his hope of buying Desdemona. The lengths to which men are willing to go in their treachery to each other – Iago with Othello, Cassio, and Roderigo; Roderigo implicitly with Othello and actively with Cassio; and Othello with Cassio, are only highlighted in relief by contrast when Emilia sacrifices her life for Desdemona in asserting the unsullied faith of her mistress and in revealing Iago's villainy.

When we look at the proportions of Emilia's role we see how significant her relationship with Desdemona is. Emilia is onstage for 924 lines (28.6 per cent of the play). Her interactions with Iago amount to fewer than 100 lines, which is less than the space devoted to her exchanges with Desdemona. It is worth remembering that we only ever see Emilia alone with her husband once for the 21 lines (III. iii. 300–20) when he snatches the handkerchief from her, and this is less than one-quarter of the time she spends alone with Desdemona in the willow scene and a sixth of the time she spends alone with her in the play. Emilia speaks 219 lines in the play (6.8 per cent) and nearly one-third of them (70) are directed to her mistress – a few more than she speaks to her husband.

Table 2.3 Othello's role

Scenes		Lines	Othello onstage		Othello speaks	
(a)	II. ii.–IV. ii. 94	1056	836	(79.2%)	377½	(35.7%)
(b)	IV. ii. 95–end of V. i	380	18	(4.7%)	12½	(3.3%)
(c)	V. ii	371	371	(100%)	182	(49.0%)

When we look, in Table 2.3, at the proportions of the latter half of the play in which the destruction of Othello and his wife are accomplished we can see that it develops in three phases, which provides a significant pause in Othello's role even though he continues to live in the house where most of the action takes place. In the 380 lines when Othello is not quite continuously absent there are 102 lines devoted to talk of him, which contain 46 specific references [Othello (4), the Moor (3), he (14), him (10), his (7), my Lord/thy Lord (7), this gentleman (1)]. The importance of the willow scene (IV. iii) as a pause in which we can momentarily relax from our concern with Othello is underlined by the fact that for 85 lines of that scene (20–104) there is no direct mention of him, which is the longest gap in such references in the 380 lines. But though the absence of concern about Othello in the amiable gossip of the women may provide relaxation in one sense, in another way it makes us, as in all the other sequences I have examined, more vulnerable to the tension we can never fully escape. That the women can chat with such ease reminds us how innocent they are of any real understanding of the disaster which is about to strike. Their normality is refreshing, but it is also appalling testimony to Iago's skill in bringing Desdemona within the shadow of death without arousing deep enough apprehensions to make her rattled, suspicious, fearful, or defensive. Othello's absence from the stage provides temporary relief even as it sustains the underlying tension, because we know that his return to the stage will bring death to the gentle, faithful, and attractive woman now being shown to us in most sympathetic detail.

The willow scene, then, is the core of this relative pause in Othello's role. The Moor makes his second brief appearance (V. i. 28–36) in the midst of Iago's ambush of Cassio in the streets. After the pause of the willow scene we know that the murderous plotting is in motion again, and it is necessary to have Othello briefly onstage to indicate that he is proceeding to his murder, for the tension is finely tuned to wear on the nerves of the audience members. Through the remainder of V. i and the dark confusion we are aware that Othello is on his way to his task and through the opening of V. ii we know that Emilia is on her way to the bedchamber to inform Othello of what has transpired in the streets. The 9 lines of Othello's appearance are not absolutely necessary but they confirm the essential structure of murders committed in tandem in an overlapping time-frame which brings Emilia into the room in time to witness Desdemona's expiring words but not to save her.

We have seen Iago throughout in command manipulating others with ease, but when he is called upon to execute a key part of his plot he becomes a victim of the confusion he has unleashed. It only dawns on Iago when it is too late that he has got himself into a situation where Desdemona must die, and Roderigo must die or he will demand a restitution of his jewels, and Cassio must die before he finds out that the Moor suspects him with his wife. A double murder has been planned, but it turns out in the event that four deaths are required. One murder is botched and two murders are not accomplished effectively enough to ensure that Iago can survive his plot undetected. Iago desperately attempts to implicate Bianca as a cause of violence and makes the fundamental error of sending Emilia to inform Othello of events, which allows her to discover enough of the truth to expose the villainy. But in any case Cassio survives, Roderigo testifies against Iago before he dies, and letters in Roderigo's pockets confirm Iago's plotting against Cassio. Othello's relative inactivity allows us to focus on Iago's bungling. His brief appearance in V. i is set up quite deliberately as a contrast to Iago's behaviour and anticipates his re-emergence onstage in the citadel in V. ii when he attempts, with magisterial calm, to accomplish what he believes is the necessary sacrifice of his wife.

A good playwright can make us feel that our acceptance of helpless, inactive observation in return for privileged insight is very costly indeed. *Othello* works so powerfully on an audience because we are forced into complicity with Iago's plot. We are aware how flimsy his plot is, how far from the truth of it some characters are, how close others (like Emilia) are, and how little information it would take to destroy the plot. We are simultaneously aware that we are the only people in full possession of all the relevant information. It is not surprising that there are many recorded instances of audience members shouting out to warn characters of the predicament they are in and of the lies being pressed on them. Most audiences endure the ordeal silently as they wait for release from the privileged information with which Iago burdens them. When the characters do finally share the knowledge the audience has been burdened with they are not helpless like us but are quite capable of asserting values which extinguish the views Iago has hitherto been promoting. He has been skilled at exploiting others through their strengths as well as their weaknesses. His own weakness is never to have understood the strength within his wife that can be used to expose his villainy. Lodovico's late insertion in the play helps us to see more clearly the transformation Iago has wrought. Othello's absence from the stage provides opportunity for Desdemona and Emilia to show us friendship that is a crucial factor in bringing the villainy to light, as is Iago's bungling of his part of the plot. The secret offstage world of lust Iago has induced Othello to believe in dissolves and, like an insubstantial pageant faded, leaves not a rack behind. We are released from the pained privilege of our offstage immunity when we observe the faith and courage of those onstage in coming to terms with the delusions which have ensnared them.

3

'Are those my tents where I perceive the fire?': The structure of Shakespeare's battles and their onstage/offstage action

When we examine Shakespeare's practice in orchestrating battles we find that martial encounters, with their potential for frequent display of physical combat, draw from him the greatest versatility and flexibility in selecting what is to been seen onstage and what is to be reported as offstage action. In such sequences we usually have a large number of actors shuttling on and offstage in a mosaic of short segments which signify battle in a judicious apportioning of physical and verbal components. It could be argued that in the shaping of his battles Shakespeare is most clearly pursuing his practice of making a virtue of necessity. We do not know the duration of onstage physical combat prescribed in the battles. The Elizabethans enjoyed the skills of the swordsman and the onstage fights in which it was displayed, and the dramatists did not shy away from this activity. But even if we suppose that more extensive physical action was presented than is indicated in the brief stage directions of the text it is clear that actual fighting does not take up a preponderant amount of stage time in the battles. This representation of battle principally by verbal means we could ascribe to the limitations of the stage and especially to its small number of places for entrances and exits, or to the limited size of the company of actors, but the emphasis on speech-making is a central aspect of Shakespeare's unfolding of this masculine activity as being deeply imbued with self-dramatization and public display, with proud challenges and the rhetoric of defiance. The plays do not suggest that such masculine assertions in war are a great deal of sound and fury signifying nothing (though they are quite vividly that on occasion), but the warrior certainly endeavours to establish his identity and prowess as much with his mouth as with his sword.

What is notable, in the evidence of the texts, is that Shakespeare did not routinely include onstage fights in his representation of battles. In some plays there are three or four episodes of physical combat onstage, in others there are none. In some plays all the battle action is presented as offstage events, and this may seem to be justified by the evidence in the sources, as in the case of the sea-battles in *Antony and Cleopatra* where onstage presentation is precluded. Occasionally Shakespeare presents unnamed soldiers in combat onstage, but his fights are more usually between named characters and often between generals on each side. In *Julius Caesar* much of the battle action is presented as reports from those onstage gazing at events which only they can see offstage. The quotation in the title of this chapter is taken from one such moment, and such reports are not merely supplements to the onstage action. A misinterpretation of those events offstage leads Cassius to believe his cause is lost and to commit suicide. In fact, in this play we see none of the principal figures in physical combat, and Shakespeare concentrates not so much on the clash of forces at the battle of Philippi as on the sense of fatality which overwhelms Brutus and Cassius and drives them to their Roman deaths. In *Troilus and Cressida* there is an extensive sequence of onstage fighting, but it does not so much enhance the image of battle-prowess as question it. The play focuses on the disparity between what men say they believe and what they actually do, and this is underlined by the despicable butchery of Hector by Achilles, or by Thersites scuttling away from Margarelon. We have to register a similar significance at the battle of Shrewsbury where, out of all the action Shakespeare could have chosen to show us, two of the key elements he selects for onstage presentation are Falstaff playing dead while Hotspur is made food for worms. In some plays the battle-rhetoric seems to be conventionally acceptable, unshadowed by irony. In *Troilus and Cressida*, however, the storied heroes, who have spoken so extensively about honour, range across the battlefield bellowing for each other like enraged beasts. The satirical tendency brutally obvious in this play is potentially there in many battles and may be created by the handling of its proportions. In circumstances where there is so much talk backed up by little action the warriors can appear to be strutting peacocks with feral instincts and absurd pretensions. The St Crispian's Day speech or rallying-calls such as 'Once more unto the breach' are not presented satirically in *Henry V* as the boasting jingoism of a fanatic, but they are set in a context which makes it clear that the magic of such speeches does not work on everyone. If we accept the fact that audiences can enjoy physical combat between skilled actors and that it would seem wise to present some episodes of onstage fighting when a battle is, as often in Shakespeare, long anticipated as the climax of the play, then denying an audience such action would seem to require strong reasons.

We could speculate that there might be a practical, reasonable, though not very thrilling, explanation of this choice of staging if some of Shakespeare's leading actors begged to be let off any strenuous physical activity. With such a stable company over so many years it is clear that Shakespeare was able to tailor his plays to the skills and attributes of the members of his company. Did a young, athletic Burbadge revel in roles involving physical combat but resist such demands as he aged? A brief glance at the plays indicates that there is no progressive diminution in the fighting designated onstage in the protagonists Burbadge probably played. The battle in *Richard III*, one of Burbadge's famous roles, certainly contains a fight in which Richard is killed onstage and it may have been a lengthy, athletic combat, but the battle, which contains only one fight, is one of the shortest in the canon. In *Henry IV, Part 1*, as Hal, Burbadge had to fight Douglas and to fight and kill Hotspur. In *Henry V*, however, there is no onstage fighting for the king, nor is there for Brutus in *Julius Caesar*. Hamlet, 'fat and scant of breath', has a sword-fight which, in its several bouts of passes, is one of the most detailed and in terms of stage time, possibly the longest physical combat in Shakespeare. In *Macbeth* the hero has four bouts of fighting – one with Young Siward and three with Macduff. In *King Lear* and *Antony and Cleopatra* the protagonist engages in no fighting onstage. In *Coriolanus*, on the other hand, there is an elaborate battle in Act I which seems to demand a good deal of fighting from the central figure. The demands in terms of physical combat wax and wane across the whole of Shakespeare's canon in no fixed pattern. Burbadge played many roles as a warrior-leader, but Shakespeare did not consider it necessary to define them always in physical displays of skill. This is a bonus a writer for a repertory company can count on. An actor may in one role display his skills with a sword, and an audience which knows the actors of a repertory company well can take such skills of the actor for granted when he is employed in another role as warrior. If for various reasons it did not serve Shakespeare's needs to show Antony as a great warrior in action, even though he is involved in battles which cover considerable parts of the play, the audience will not doubt his martial courage and physical skill even when his battle strategy proves faulty. We hear accounts of Antony's campaign-hardened life in the speech of Caesar (I. iv. 55–71) and the awareness of others of his potency as a warrior. The play does not need to show us Antony's skills as a warrior in physical combat for the focus in these events is on the corruption of his military judgment as he subjects himself to Cleopatra's demands, and the shame he experiences from his resulting failures in battle. Shakespeare accomplishes the remarkable feat of presenting a sequence of battle scenes without any physical combat by registering the reactions to the ebb and flow of battle in the eyes of those onstage to events that are entirely offstage. Antony's followers are appalled by the decline in his judgement and they prepare us for his self-laceration in shame and for his fury at Cleopatra. When he recovers his spirit and moves towards a momentary triumph his resurgence is shown as he arms for battle and not in his actual deeds on the battlefield. Shakespeare's handling of battle is usually a complex weave of actions and reactions, of actual fights and reports of fights. An enormous proportion of this play is devoted to reactions to events occurring elsewhere – how Romans react to events in Egypt, how Cleopatra in Egypt reacts to Antony's absence when he is in Rome. The characters are very conscious that they are public figures, and it is of central importance to these world-beaters how they appear in their own eyes and in the eyes of their friends. In the necessary economy of dramatizing a story spread over considerable time and space Shakespeare decides that we do not need to see the actions in which they fail to live up to their own self-images but concentrates rather on the anguish they experience at having let themselves down. Nor do we need to see Octavius in action for he is not so much a great warrior as a calculating politician. We do not experience directly any of the encounters of the various battles but we develop the very direct sense, from the accumulating reactions and reports, that it is not so much that Octavius wins them as that Antony loses them. We hear of the battles and recognize them as the catalyst of what we must concentrate on – the sense of disintegration induced in Antony by his losses.

Shakespeare's practice in handling battles, then, is considerably varied. There is only one play, *Troilus and Cressida*, in which all of the action is situated within a continuing and unresolved war. In some plays, such as *Henry V*, a battle may be anticipated very early and preparations for it occupy virtually all of the ensuing action until a climactic clash of arms. In *Henry IV, Part 1*, a battle is anticipated early, but the approach to it is intermingled with other matters. The fate of major characters may be resolved in a climactic battle, though in *Coriolanus* events develop out of battle rather than towards battle. Not quite half of Shakespeare's plays contain battles or sequences related to battle, and from them I will examine a few in detail to indicate the range of his practice and the way battle can be a mere incident occupying a few minutes of stage time or can be the organizing principle for a large segment of a play. I will reserve until Part 2 of this study an examination of three plays in which the structure of the battle is more effectively examined as a central part of the broader strategies of onstage/offstage action in the play as a whole.

The actual events of a battle are often only a small part, frequently the smallest part, of all the elements related to battle in the plays and for purposes of analysis it is useful to recognize that there is a regularly repeated structure of four parts which, though they may vary radically in their proportions from play to play, are almost invariably present. The four parts are:

(a) *The political build-up before the action moves to the battlefield*. In this phase the opposed factions which are to join battle forge alliances, air their grievances, justify their intentions, may quarrel among themselves, or be involved in aborted attempts to avoid war.

(b) *Preparation on the battlefield itself*. The opposed factions may count their strength, receive news of allies coming or failing to come to battle, discuss the strategy to be used in the battle, or be involved in embassies and diplomatic manœuvres back and forth between the generals of the opposing armies.

(c) *The battle itself*. It opens with an alarum and ends when a retreat is sounded. Not only does Shakespeare build up to and down from battle, but the actual battle-sequence is composed of a mosaic of elements in which physical activity is only one of the modes of expressing it. In my analysis of each battle, broken down into its constituent segments and presented in summarizing tables, I provide one column headed 'Category' which designates the type of battle-activity by number corresponding to the following elements:

1) challenges and speeches of defiance from the various combatants;
2) fighting in hand-to-hand combat;
3) orders sent to other forces and reports of fighting from other parts of the battlefield as offstage events. In these pauses, often between bouts of physical activity, warriors recount their deeds, reflect on battle and its losses, or urge each other on;
4) processions of armies, excursions, and stage directions which register the sounds of battle;
5) speeches by dying warriors and by victors in elegy of beaten foes.

In practice some of these categories can, on occasion, overlap and be mingled in one segment.

(d) *Resolution of issues after battle*. This involves celebration, reports on the dead, the punishment of surviving foes, the reward of the service and heroism of loyal allies.

In most of my analyses of battle I indicate the proportions of the play which may be occupied by these distinct and successive phases. It has to be acknowledged that this use of lines as a rough guide to a proportion of the play's running-time may not always be adequate or illuminating because some of the activity of battle is registered in the stage directions and not in the counted lines of the play. It is possible that the excursions of armies or the individual combats may have taken up a good deal of time, but even if we grant that, it is obvious that in many of Shakespeare's battles physical activity in extended combat plays very little part and in some plays none at all. Even if the few bouts of duelling were quite elaborate, in none of the battles would they, in terms of stage time, be the predominant element of what we see. In modern productions battles are often very elaborate and may be specially arranged by a fight choreographer as assistant to the director, supplementing the combat of the principals with physical clashes, not indicated in Shakespeare's text, among the various supernumeraries, which a director chooses to include. In some of the battles staged by the Royal Shakespeare Company or the Stratford Festival Company in Ontario it is possible to see skirmishes among two dozen or more common soldiers in addition to the combats Shakespeare indicates for the named characters. Shakespeare did not have the resources of such modern companies and, in his ingenuity, gives the impression that he does not need them. It is here that the weaving-together of onstage and offstage events produces, by an elaborate sleight-of-hand, the impression of complex action. The essence of the magician's skill is to divert the audience's attention so that it fails to register, at the critical moments, how the trick is being performed. I am trying to indicate here the versatility of Shakespeare's approach to battle, wherein he can give a great deal of space to political anticipations and manœuvres related to battle, to extended preparations of the battlefield, and to the consequences of battle, impressing the audience with the weightiness of the issue without having to rely very heavily on any extended display of physical combat. It may be that only half a dozen of the actors, or even fewer engage in actual fighting on the stage, but the combats are surrounded by such a wealth of other details that we do not focus on the schematic and conventional nature of the sequence. Even in modern productions, with all their choreographic inventiveness and their marshalling of teams of supernumeraries, the battle sequence, from alarum to retreat, is usually not a very large part of the running-time of the play. In the scores of productions I have seen in a variety of theatres I would assert that in a three-hour production the actual battle-sequence – (c) in the outline above – even in those plays where there are extensive details and a number of physical combats, rarely lasts for twenty minutes. In the time devoted to the rich variety of battle-events the sequence of physical combats rarely lasts as long as ten minutes and in most of the battles it is much less than that. In Shakespeare's day, when the fighting onstage was probably limited to that indicated in the stage directions, it is unlikely that any more time or even as much was devoted to the actual clash of swords.

We are, of course, submitting to a whole variety of conventions when we are willing to accept that the confusion of thousands of men in a battle such as Agincourt can be translated into twenty minutes or so of stage time. The events of the battle itself are only a small part of the action situated at Agincourt. By the time he wrote *Henry V* Shakespeare had developed a recognizable strategy for presenting battles and he devotes two acts of this play to the events at Agincourt which convinces audiences that Henry V is Shakespeare's pre-eminent warrior-king, even though, if we look a little more closely, we have to recognize that we never actually see him strike a blow in anger. The figure in the play he comes closest to fighting onstage is one of his own soldiers, Williams, but even that promised combat is turned into a joke. The play devotes all of its action, save for the 44 lines of the Chorus at the opening of Act V, to events at Agincourt from III. vii. 1 – V. i. 81 which, with the exclusion of the above-mentioned Chorus involves 1208 lines (38 per cent of the play). Of these lines the events of the fighting itself stretch from IV. iv. 1 – IV. vii. 81 – a total of 218 lines, only 18 per cent of the total sequence of events in the battle camps at Agincourt and 6.8 per cent of the entire play. It is by coming to terms with these kinds of proportions, which are quite characteristic of Shakespeare's practice, that we can understand how careful the weaving is of the mingled yarn of the battle-sequences. I reserve a detailed analysis of *Henry V* to Part 2 of this study and start here with a play which has a good deal of physical combat in its battle scenes.

Henry IV, Part I

The action in *Henry IV, Part 1* is predominantly concerned with the political build-up on both sides which will eventually be resolved 'in the intestine shock/And furious close of civil butchery' of the battle of Shrewsbury. The only contemplation of peace in England in this play, when the nation is not under threat of rebellion, occurs in the opening scene where there is 'a time for frighted peace to pant' (I. i. 2), though there is immediate anticipation of 'new broils/To be commenced in strands afar remote'. This plan (I. i. 1–30) has to be postponed because of threats of war within the realm, so the build-up to Shrewsbury begins, in effect, at I. i. 34 with news of Glendower's success against Mortimer. The news from the north is of Hotspur's triumph over Douglas, but there is warning of trouble to come in Percy's refusal to yield up his prisoners. I will outline, therefore, the various segments of the play which compose what I have called section (*a*) of Shakespeare's dramatization of events related to battle. These events are initially developed intermittently along with other matter related to the antics of the prince and Falstaff, though at the end of II. iv they are already looking ahead to battle.

(*a*) *The political build-up in events which occur before the action moves to the battlefield*

(i) I. i. 34–108 (75) Reports on the various battle actions in the realm.

(ii) I. iii. 1–299 (299) The kings warns Worcester and the Percies that they must yield to him or expect the consequences, implying a battle (118–24). Hotspur speaks of revenge for their wrongs (180–7), and Worcester fleshes out a strategy which will build an alliance to confront the king (257–99). He speaks specifically of raising an army (281), of taking up arms (295), and Hotspur eagerly anticipates battle 'O, let the hours be short/Till fields and blows and groans applaud our sport' (298–9).

(iii) II. iii. 1–61, 89–90 (63) Hotspur reads a letter from one queasily unwilling to join the rebellious plot. His wife, Kate, gives us an account of his troubled rest whereby Hotspur, in his dreams, is already in the midst of battle.

(iv) II. iv. 517–23 (7) Only after the lengthy exposure of Falstaff's lies about the robbery at Gadshill does the sub-plot acknowledge any concern for the battle when the prince determines to go to court and announces that he will obtain Falstaff 'a charge of foot' (519) for 'We must all to the wars' (517).

(v) III. i. 1–188 (188) is directly concerned with the issue of battle as the rebels anticipate the time after their triumph when they will divide England between them.

(vi) III. ii. 1–180 (180) Much of the scene involves the king's censuring of his son and his recall of history in comparing Hal, in his truancy, to Richard II, but it is, especially in its juxtaposition of Hal and Hotspur, a build-up to Shrewsbury, for it is here that Hal moves from his idle pranks into the political arena. The king outlines Hotspur's accomplishments in battle and the threat he now poses (101–20), and Hal presents himself as the counterweight promising to meet Percy in battle and redeem his reputation (132–61). The conclusion of the scene brings us much closer to the battlefield when Blunt and the king outline the forces on each side preparing for a martial clash (162–80).

(vii) III. iii. 178–97 (20) After some jesting in the Eastcheap tavern the sub-plot characters are again turned towards battle as the prince informs Falstaff of the charge of foot he has obtained for him and makes arrangements to set off to the battlefield.

Shakespeare effectively stretches across three acts of his play preparations for the battle which will not occur until the final act. The private endeavours of Falstaff and the prince intermingle with the political concerns until they are drawn into the orbit of battle so that by the close of Act III all of the characters have left London and are on their way to the clash at Shrewsbury.

This phase then occupies three acts, 2084 of the play's 2954 lines (70.5 per cent). This slow build-up is carefully handled reaching the point where the rebels plan to confront the king at the close of I. iii which is 612 lines into the play, and the moment when Hal is ready to abandon his wayward pranks in order to join his father, at the close of II. iv, which is 1444 lines into the play and a little less than half of it. The action then moves through the rebels' anticipated division of the spoils and Hal's reconciliation with his father so that by the end of III. iii. we are nearly three-quarters of the way through the play when we come to the battlefield. We will in fact be only 265 lines from the end of the play before the commencement of the battle itself. In this first phase there is the mingling of the two strands of action which will be woven together on the battlefield. There are lengthy sequences in this opening phase which are not directly involved in preparation for, or discussion of the strategy of, the coming battle: (i) discussion of peace and a crusade to the Holy Land (I. i. 1–33); (ii) Falstaff and the prince prepare for the robbery at Gadshill (I. ii. 1–205); (iii) the build-up to the robbery and its enactment in II. i. and II. ii; (iv) Hotspur's bantering with his wife in II. iii, when he is trying to deflect her curiosity, is not directly focused

Table 3.1 (a) I. i. 1–III. iii. 197 – 2084 lines (70.5%)

Sequences building up to the battle as a result of the rebellion					Sequences concerned with private issues or not directly related to preparation for Shrewsbury			
					(i)	I. i	1–33	33
(i)	I. i	34–108	75		(ii)	I. ii	1–205	205
(ii)	I. iii	1–299	299		(iii)	II. i	1–94	
						II. ii	1–102	196
(iii)	II. iii	1–61	61		(iv)	II. iii	62–88	27
		89–90	2				91–113	23
					(v)	II. iv	1–516	516
(iv)	II. iv	517–23	7					
(v)	III. i	1–188	188					
(vi)	II. ii	1–180	180		(vi)	III. i	189–263	75
					(vii)	III. iii	1–177	177
(vii)	III. iii	178–97	20					
Total			832 (39.9%)					1252 (60.1%)

on battle plans; (v) the aftermath of the robbery (II. iv) which exposes Falstaff's lies and leads to the staging of informal playlets; (vi) the rebels turn to lighter social entertainment when their ladies appear in III. i; (vii) in the tavern (III. iii) Falstaff laments the picking of his pocket and jests with the prince. In Table 3.1 there is a summary of the passages involved in the alternating focus of the play in the events which occur before the action moves to the battlefield. Shakespeare entertains us with the antics of Hal and Falstaff for a good deal of this opening phase, for all but 158 of the lines not related directly to the preparation for Shrewsbury are devoted to their sub-plot. Many of the alternating sequences are of roughly comparable length save for II. iv, the climactic unfolding of the sub-plot. We have the sense that the energy, vitality, and private jests of the sub-plot give place to the broader national issue as the characters are caught up in it. Falstaff is too anarchic a figure to be brought under complete control and offers a comic commentary on events to the very end. In fact, the weighting on the pranks and private issues in this phase forces us to note Hal's turning towards the serious issues of the rebellion as, with precise political timing to gain the greatest impact, he steps over increasingly into the main plot 'redeeming time when men think least I will', as he prophesies at the close of I. ii. As we move closer to the battle itself the relationship of Hal and Falstaff is given very little stage time.

(b) Preparation on the battlefield itself. Discussion of battle strategy and negotiations to avoid battle – IV i – V. ii. 100 – 605 lines
(20.5 per cent of the play)

Consistent with the slow and intermittent build-up in the first three acts of rebellion and responses to it, there are, on the battlefield, extended reports of forces assembling for battle and negotiations to resolve the issue, in the

Table 3.2 (*b*) V. i–V. ii – 605 lines

Preparations for battle – the gathering of forces and consideration of strategy		Negotiations to avoid battles and reactions to diplomatic manœuvres	
(i) IV. i. 1–136. The rebel camp Northumberland and Glendower reported as unavailable and the gathering of the king's forces joined by Hal.	136		
(ii) IV. ii. 1–76. Falstaff and his abuses in recruitment	76		
(iii) IV. iii. 1–29. A dispute over battle strategy in the rebel camp.	29		
		(i) IV. iii. 30–113. Blunt tells the rebels of the king's offer to consider their grievances.	84
(iv) IV. iv. 1–41. Archbishop of York fearful for the rebels' cause, noting also Mortimer's absence.	41		
The day of battle			
(v) V. i. 1–8. The king prepares for battle.	8		
		(ii) V. i. 9–82. The king receives from Vernon and Worcester the rebels' reply to his offer.	74
		(iii) V. i. 83–103. Hal offers to fight Hotspur in single combat.	21
		(iv) V. i. 104–14. The king renews his offer of pardon.	11
(vi) V. i. 115–39. The king prepares for battle and so does Falstaff in his catechism on honour.	25		
		(v) V. ii. 1–71. Worcester and Vernon report on their meeting with the king but suppress the news of the offer of pardon.	71
(vii) V. ii. 72–100. Hotspur addresses his fellow generals in preparation for battle as the king is reported to be advancing.	29		
Totals	344 (56.9%)		261 (43.1%)

hope that the prophecy the king made at the opening of the play in his promise of peace (I. i. 5–18) might be sustained. The action moves back and forth from one camp to the other and weaves two strands of action together – sequences devoted to the sides readying for battle and sequences of negotiation to avoid battle which I summarize in Table 3.2. This section varies its material in a not-quite-even division of lines devoted to war and peace.

Before proceeding to an analysis of the battle itself I want to look back over the action in the two phases I have so far considered to indicate some characteristics of the staging which establishes a rhythm to which the audience becomes accustomed. In the battle scenes Shakespeare can take advantage of certain aspects of his stage and he can radically change the rhythm of the action so that it will stand out in contrast to what has gone on before battle. The open, bare thrust stage which, in the flow of action, can easily and swiftly represent a variety of locations is of especial advantage in dramatizing the here, there, and everywhere of action on a battlefield. Before battle in this play the stage has represented, according to the suggestions of most modern editors, without any elaborate modifications in decor, a varied range of locales: the court of Henry IV (I. i, I. iii, III. ii), possibly an apartment of the prince (I. ii), an inn-yard at Rochester (II. i), the highway at Gadshill (II. ii), Hotspur's castle (II. iii), a tavern in Eastcheap (II. iv, III. iii), Glendower's castle (III. i), the rebel camp at Shrewsbury (IV. i, IV. iii, V. ii), the road to Coventry (IV. ii), the palace of the Archbishop of York (IV. iv), and the royal camp at Shrewsbury (V. i). In 16 scenes it can, with little problem, represent 11 different locales. Battlefields have throughout history been confusing and chaotic places and, with various commanders in charge of different forces, we can, in a Shakespeare play, move from one wing of battle to the other, and from one side to the other in a series of short segments. We can be at various locales of fighting, and from minute to minute, be in the midst of fierce combat or in some momentary backwater away from the tide of action where warriors can rest and exchange news. In all the conventional stylizing of the fighting the most obvious limitation Shakespeare has to contend with is a lack of numbers. In these battles thousands of soldiers met in 'intestine shock' – we hear that at Shrewsbury the king has 30,000 troops and Hotspur considerably fewer. Shakespeare has at most a score of actors to present action that may have involved nearly 50,000 men. Most of his battles occur near the end of his plays when he has all of his actors available, and there is no impediment to any actor being used because of a need to re-emerge in one of the roles he is doubling.

Before the battle-sequences the plays have usually established a fairly regular rhythm of entrances and exits. Characters may be onstage for hundreds of lines without any impression of the bustling urgency which can be produced by a sequence of rapid movements on and off the stage. Such urgency may begin to build-up as a prologue to the accelerated pace of the battle scenes as messengers arrive with news, or as diplomatic embassies move back and forth between the battle-camps. A spectacular example of this increase in pace occurs at the end of IV. iv in *Richard III* and in the ensuing sequence of the ghosts (V. iii), producing a crescendo of pressure in their indictment of Richard in his dream on the eve of Bosworth. The increasing frequency of entrance and exit picks up the pace and gives a recurrent shift in the focus of our attention.

A brief glance at the action in *Henry IV, Part 1*, before battle indicates how frequently conversations last for dozens or even hundreds of lines. Hotspur, Worcester, and Northumberland share a conversation of 170 lines in I. iii; in II. iv the prince and Falstaff are onstage together and with others more or less continuously, save for a short break, for over 400 lines; the rebels in Glendower's castle are on together, with only Glendower absent for a brief spell, for over 250 lines in III. i; in III. ii Hal and his father are onstage without interruption for over 150 lines. In battle, the action is fragmented into a series of vignettes as changing groups of characters burst on to the stage for a mere handful of lines. This process of editing the battles into a sequence of short events is akin in some ways to the technique of montage developed in films. Before the battle we move from scene to scene from one camp to another. In the battle the accelerated flow gives us the impression that on the fixed stage we are jumping to different parts of the battlefield, now with the generals in combat, now with the generals resting briefly and talking of deeds elsewhere on the field, now with Falstaff avoiding combat, now with Douglas bellowing for an opponent. So the regular rhythm of lengthy scenes with uninterrupted conversations between a few characters may give place in battle to sequences of short segments of action with a constantly changing focus.

There is usually not only an acceleration in the frequency of entrance and exit but also rapid variations in the numbers occupying the stage at any given moment. As I have pointed out one of the limitations Shakespeare had to deal with in staging battles is a lack of numbers. It can, however, seem less of a lack if, for brief periods, there are a dozen or more characters onstage in, say, the procession of armies, or as many characters on and off in the quick sequences of action in battle. The visual impact of numbers registers the more readily in that we may, for long periods of the play, have seen no more than four or five characters onstage at once. With only a score of actors available Shakespeare was able to present plays that can have twice as many parts (*Henry IV, Part 1*, has 35 speaking parts). The Globe stage was of a considerable size, and it would take a large number of actors to give any sense that it was crowded. Because it was a thrust stage with the audience wrapped around it there would be problems in having large numbers of actors onstage together for long periods risking the masking of important action from segments of the audience. This would not be as serious an impediment in the staging of battles which often involve confusion, rapid movement in scenes which are broken into short segments of constantly varying focus.

It was not only the size of Shakespeare's company and the way the audience was wrapped around the stage that made it hazardous or difficult to have large numbers of characters on stage for extended periods; it was also the nature of access to this stage. In addition to the two major entrances, one on each side of the stage in the back wall of the public theatres, there were probably supplementary points of access from the discovery-space and the upper stage, but all of these places for exit and entrance were relatively close together and in the same plane of the tiring-house wall. One of the great virtues of this thrust stage was its flexibility which allowed for a constant flow of action unimpeded by curtains or changes of scenery. This flow could be imperilled if the plays were structured in a way which presented many characters onstage at once and required such large numbers to make mass exits together. We only have to look at Shakespeare's practice to discover how often he adjusted material so that mass exits were required as infrequently as possible. It is of course, probable that if we envisage alternation in the use of the two major accesses to the stage the characters opening one scene can cover to a degree the exits of characters from the previous scene. If we look through all the scenes of *Henry IV, Part 1*, before battle, using the indications of exits established in modern editorial practice, it is apparent that there are few scenes when large numbers have to get offstage at the same time. Mass entrances are not always such a problem because they are often ceremonial and the stage is set (as perhaps in I. i) with figures waiting expectantly for a central figure, such as a king, who can keep the characters and the audience waiting. This outline indicates how rarely, before battle, the stage is crowded with characters and how rarely when there are more than half a dozen characters onstage they are all required to exit together at a scene's conclusion. I indicate here how the entrances and exits would work with the use of two major accesses to the stage, though it is likely that more were available in the tiring-house wall.

I. i.   has 2 speakers of the 4 named characters and some mute supers as attendants, and they all exit together, Westmoreland despatched on his mission through one exit and the rest probably through another. In the ceremonial nature of this court scene a sedate procession at entrance and exit is probable.

I. ii.   has 3 speakers, but Poins joins Falstaff and the prince and stays after Falstaff has left. After Poins departs the prince is left alone onstage to conclude the scene.

I. iii.   has 5 speakers and other mute supers. The king and his followers depart (124), and this leaves sufficient time for any of the supers who are his attendants, and are required in subsequent minor roles, to prepare for reappearances in II. i and II. ii as Chamberlain, Gadshill, Peto, Bardolph, and the travellers set upon in the robbery. After the king's departure the three Percies are left to conspire and depart together, Worcester through one exit, Northumberland and Hotspur through another.

II. i.   has 5 speakers (only 4 appear onstage, the Ostler is off). Of these, 2 depart together in the middle of the scene, the remaining 2 depart through different exits at its conclusion.

II. ii.   uses 9 actors if we allow for 3 Travellers. Of these, 7 would have to exit together at 1. 84 if we assume that Falstaff's gang hustle the bound travellers off with them. This is not an insuperable problem in mid scene because Hal and Poins, who are stealthily observing the thieves in their exit, can attract our attention as they appear at another entrance and prepare to rob the returning thieves. It is, in any case, established that it is dark, and the prince and Poins are able to stand aside early in the scene without being noticed and so any overlap in the exit and entrance at 1. 84 would be acceptable. When Falstaff and his three fellow thieves return there are six characters onstage, but the four original thieves can be chased off and exit serially through the different exits, leaving Hal and Poins to exit at the conclusion.

II. iii.   Hotspur, on alone at the outset, is joined by his wife, and a servant enters and exits, to leave the husband and wife to exit together.

II. iv.   involves 11 actors, and there are numerous exits and entrances throughout. The only crowded exit would be after 1. 479 when Bardolph, Gadshill, Poins, and the Hostess leave together. At the scene's conclusion only Hal and Peto are left (Falstaff is asleep, but concealed) to exit together.

III. i.   has 6 characters and 5 are left at the end of the scene, with possibly Glendower and Mortimer leaving by one exit and the remaining 3, Worcester and 2 ladies, by another.

III. ii.   has 3 characters. Mute supers as courtiers come on at the opening but exit after only 3 lines. Blunt eventually joins the king and Hal, and they leave together at the close.

III. iii.   involves 5 characters, and by the scene's close Falstaff is left to exit alone.

IV. i.   has 5 characters, 3 at the outset, joined by 2 others, and they exit together, though the messenger is not required onstage after 1. 24 and could leave earlier.

IV. ii.   involves 4 characters, but by the end of the scene Falstaff is left to exit alone.

IV. iii.   involves 5 characters, and they leave together at the conclusion, Blunt probably by one exit and the 4 rebels by another.

IV. iv. has 2 characters who exit together.

V. i.   has 7 characters, but only 3 of them are required to make an exit together (the king, Prince John, and Blunt after line 120). After the prince departs Falstaff is alone onstage to make the final exit.

V. ii. requires 6 actors, and they leave together at the end, though the 2 messengers could plausibly leave earlier. The trumpet summons to battle covers the exit and the alarums, and the entrance of the king's power gives us other concerns for our attention.

In all of the above action 35 speakers are involved, and mute supers on several occasions, with as many as 11 speakers within one of the scenes. Shakespeare structures matters so that there are very few occasions when there are more than 5 actors onstage at the same time – 7 in II. ii, 8 in II. iv, and 7 in V. i. The scenes are also arranged so that there are very few cumbersome mass exits. In the 16 scenes before the battle the only occasions on which 5 or more characters are required to exit together are in I. i (5), II. ii (7 in the middle of the robbery), III. i (5), and IV. iii (5), and we could add IV. i (5) and V. ii (6) if the messengers do not exit after delivering their news. On the occasions when 5 or more actors are on the stage at the same time frequently such numbers are serially augmented and depleted avoiding mass entrances and exits. Even when 5 or more have to exit together matters are usually arranged so that more than one exit is employed. There are moments in battle, though not frequent ones, when Shakespeare may have used larger numbers of actors on the stage for brief periods, and such sequences would have a significant impact in the visual patterning of the play in serving as contrast to what we have seen before.

It is useful to remember, however, that if larger numbers were used in the battles they still could not be left onstage for extended periods without masking events from some section of the audience, and Shakespeare had to handle numbers carefully if he was to get actors on and offstage without impeding the necessary flow of battle. For the most part in battle he arranges a mosaic of brief episodes in which characters enter and exit serially. When he wishes to give the impression of numbers he usually arranges the procession of an army and could, in such instances, use a dozen or more actors moving across the back of the stage and using its two principal points of access. In such circumstances the mass exit would be less of a problem because the actors do not all have to exit together but, as a troop, could march across by twos and file out. They are not holding up the flow of action but embodying it. When the impression of numbers is thus established it can then be extended in the ensuing segments, not in crowding the stage at any one time but in having many characters on and off the stage in a short time – a rhythm markedly different from the action hitherto. The mosaic of episodes in *Henry IV, Part 1*, is, of course, especially rich because of the variation from seriousness to absurdity. The battle mingles among its elements not only many men in hot pursuit of physical combat but one figure involved in the deliberate avoidance of it. Falstaff seeks neither action nor honour but

Table 3.3 (c) The battle of Shrewsbury – V. iii (60), V. iv. 1–154 – 214 lines

(Segment) Description	Category	Entrance	Exit	Number onstage	Lines about action offstage
V. iii					
(1) S.D. *The king enters with his power.* Alarum to the battle.	4	12	12	12[a]	
(2) 1–13 (13) Blunt, dressed as counterfeit of king, exchanges defiance with Douglas.	1	2		2	3
(3) S.D. *The fight. Douglas kills Blunt* (1st Death).	2		2		
(4) 14–29 (16) Hotspur congratulates Douglas on his deeds. Douglas claims to have killed the king. Informed his victim is Blunt, one of the many counterfeits of the king on the field, Douglas swears he will kill them all and exits with Hotspur.	3	1	2	2 + (1)[b]	
(5) 30–8 (9) S.D. *Alarum.* Falstaff enters and, fearing for his life, looks on the dead Blunt and indicates most of his 150 recruits are dead.	4/3	1	1	1 + (1)	4
(6) 39–54 (16) Hal asks to borrow Falstaff's sword and reports many noblemen are dead. Boasting of his deeds Falstaff claims to have killed Percy. Hal asserts Percy still lives. Falstaff, unwilling to lend his pistol, offers his sword instead. Discovering a bottle of sack in Falstaff's ammunition case, Hal departs scorning his frivolity.	3	1	1	2 + (1)	7
(7) 55–60 (6) Falstaff, alone again, is not eager to confront Percy for he wants life and not Blunt's 'grinning honour'.	3		1	2 + (1)	
V. iv					
(8) S.D. *Alarum. Excursions.*	4	12	13	12 + (1)[a]	
(9) 1–15 (15) In a battle pause the king shows concern for Hal who has been wounded in action offstage. Rather than retire from battle Hal asserts the king must advance and he will himself continue fighting. He speaks of carnage on the battlefield. Westmoreland, with Prince John's encouragement, goes off to fight again.	3	4	2	4	2
(10) 16–23 (8) Hal asserts admiration for John. The king recounts John's lusty performance in fighting Percy. Hal returns to the action.	3		1	2	3

Table 3.3 *contd.*

(Segment) Description	Category	Entrance	Exit	Number onstage	Lines about action offstage
(11) 24–37 (14) Douglas finds the king alone and refers to the counterfeits he has already killed. The king refers to the bravery of his sons seeking out rebels.	1	1		2	4
(12) S.D. *They fight. The king being in danger, enter Prince of Wales.*	2			2	
(13) 38–42 (5) Hal defies Douglas and refers to deaths of nobles he intends to revenge.	1	1		3	1
(14) S.D. *They fight. Douglas flieth.*	2		1	3	
(15) 43–57 (15) Hall gives the king news of allies who need help elsewhere. The king acknowledges how much Hal has redeemed his reputation in battle. Hal declares how wrong those were who indicated he was only awaiting his father's death, for he could have let Douglas kill the king instead of fighting him off. The king leaves.	3		1	2	3
(16) 58–73 (16) Hotspur enters to exchange defiance.	1	1		2	
(17) S.D. *Hotspur and Hal fight.*	2			2	
(18) 74–5 (2) Falstaff enters and makes encouraging comments to Hal.	3	1		3	
(19) Douglas enters to fight Falstaff and he exits when Falstaff feigns death. The other fight continues until Hal kills Hotspur.	2	1	1	4	
(20) 76–85 (10) Hotspur utters a final speech and dies in mid sentence (2nd Death).	5			3	
(21) 86–100 (15) Hal speaks an elegy on Hotspur's bravery.	5			3	
(22) 101–9 (9) Finding, as he believes, Falstaff's dead body Hal speaks an elegy on him.	5		1	3	
(23) 110–27 (18) After Hal's departure Falstaff rises and justifies his pretence of death because it has secured his survival. He fears Percy may be counterfeiting, stabs his dead body, and intends to carry him off in search of credit for his 'bravery'.	1[c]			2	
(24) 128–54 (27) Hal and John enter. Hal expresses surprise that Falstaff is alive. Falstaff indicates he and Percy rose and fought until	3	2		4	8[d]

147

Table 3.3 *contd.*

(Segment) Description	Category	Entrance	Exit	Number onstage	Lines about action offstage
he triumphed over the rebel. Hal indicates to John he will go along with this story though he knows it is fantasy.					
(25) After 1. 154 a retreat is sounded indicating battle is over.	4		4		

[a] I choose a dozen actors for the opening of each scene to represent the army and the excursions because at least that number would be available for brief segments giving substance to the battle otherwise conducted in episodes with a few actors.

[b] I also assume that six of the speakers (king, Hal, John, Westmoreland, Hotspur, Douglas) enter and exit as forces involved in the excursions. Blunt's dead body remains onstage and could probably be carried off amid the excursions at the opening of V. iv.

[c] Falstaff's fearful commentary does not easily fit any of the categories I have defined, but is a kind of parody of the more usual speeches of defiance.

[d] Falstaff's story about his fight with Hotspur is not about any real action but it is offstage in that Hal and John did not witness it, and also for the audience which knows that it never occurred.

survival and the hope of profit through lies about his deeds. There are other battles in Shakespeare which have this counterpointed element: Thersites in *Troilus and Cressida*; Bardolph, Nym, Le Fer, and especially Pistol in *Henry V*; and Parolles in *All's Well that Ends Well*, whose ignoble actions are the only aspect of battlefield events the audience witnesses. Falstaff is the most vivid example of inaction, and he serves as a contrast to the constant entrance and exit of renowned warriors baying for blood. The various segments which constitute the battle – section (*c*) – are summarized in Table 3.3.

In this outline it is possible to see how the battle is composed as much of a rapid sequence of entrances and exits as it is of actual fighting. If the characters hurry on breathlessly we have the sense that a great deal of physical activity is occurring just out of sight offstage. The frequent insertion of pieces of news about fights and death elsewhere creates the impression that we are often in different parts of the battlefield at moments of temporary shelter from combat where the warriors, in brief respite, catch their breaths before returning to the fray. It is possible to open the battle with a relatively substantial show of numbers since 'the king's power' can embody those who have speaking parts in the preparation for battle and several of the actors who have been doubling a variety of roles throughout such as Poins, Gadshill, Peto, Francis, Chamberlain, the travellers (in II. iv), the Carriers, and the Sherriff. At no point in the battle sequence is the rebel army required to march across the stage as a massed force. In terms of speaking parts on the rebel side only two figures, Hotspur and Douglas, are required. In the excursions presented at the opening of V. iv soldiers from each side may chase each other back and forth across the stage and, it is possible, engage in brief sequences of the clashing of swords. The actors of Mortimer and Glendower

Table 3.4 Onstage and offstage in the battle

Character	V. iii (1–60) Entrances	Exits	V. iv (1–154) Entrances	Exits	Total Entrances	Total Exits	V. iii Lines on Stage	V. iv Lines on Stage	Total Lines on (out of 214)
King	1	1	2	2	3	3		1–57 (57)	57
Prince Hal	2	2	4	3	6	5	39–54 (16)	1–23, 39–109, 128–54 (122)	138
Prince John	1	1	3	2	4	3		1–15, 128–54 (42)	42
Blunt	2	1			2	2	1–60 (60)		60
Douglas	1	1	3	3	4	4	1–29 (29)	24–42 (19)	48
Hotspur	1	1	2	1	3	2	14–29 (16)	58–154 (97)	113
Falstaff	2	2	1		3	2	30–60 (31)	74–154 (81)	112
Westmoreland	1	1	2	2	3	3		1–15 (15)	15
Mute others	6	6	6	6	12	12		1–15 (15)	15
Totals	17	16	23	20	40	36			

were probably involved in doubling early in the play, and both of them could be used in the excursions. It is possible that one of them was doubling Vernon and the actor of Worcester was also available. Neither of them have speaking roles in the battle and are required to appear as prisoners at the opening of V. v. Since there are only 8 speakers involved in the battle there are plenty of available actors to serve as mute soldiers on the two indicated occasions of stage crowding. I assume that in each of these segments the speakers appear briefly to augment the numbers – i.e. in the procession at the opening of V. iii – the king, Hal, Prince John, Westmoreland, Blunt, and Falstaff. The first four of these characters, with the addition of Hotspur and Douglas, enter and exit in the excursions at the opening of V. iv before those required in the continuation of the action return to the stage.

If we look, therefore, at the 214 lines of the battle-sequence up to the retreat sounded at V. iv. 154, which leaves Hal, Prince John, and Falstaff still onstage with the body of Hotspur, we can see how much of the battle depends on the rapid sequence of episodes punctuated by the frequency of exit and entrance. In the two segments of stage crowding (1 and 8) I am counting the use of only 6 mute supers on each occasion to add to the speaking characters being used though it seems possible to me that the numbers could have been higher if all available actors were used. The way the characters are used in the onstage and offstage action is summarized in Table 3.4.

On neither of 2 occasions when the stage is (briefly) crowded would getting large numbers off the stage be a problem. In V. iii the procession of the army allows the numbers to file off, and the excursions in V. iv can be arranged to allow those involved to get off in rapid series through the exits. For the remainder of the 25 segments there are never more than 4 characters onstage at one time and, with the exception of segments 1 and 8, no more than 2 actors are ever required to enter or exit together. Only 1 of the segments (25) lasts for more than 20 lines, so we are provided with a constant change of focus.

In terms of stage time the battle is predominantly represented in speech with the bravery of Hal and the cowardly commentary of Falstaff comprising 64.2 per cent of the lines. The lines are divided between the 8 speakers as follows: Hal (82½), Falstaff (55), Hotspur (24), Douglas (22), King Henry (17½), Blunt (6½), Prince John (5½), Westmoreland (1). In terms of physical combat there are 5 fights indicated in the text. If we include all the possibilities of swordplay, assuming some in the excursions that open V. iv and Falstaff's stabbing of Hotspur, then in a simplified sequence we can see that these incidences of fighting activity are effectively spread across the battle:

(i)   V. iii. 1–13   (13)
(ii)   Douglas fights Blunt.
(iii)   V. iii. 14–60   (47)

(iv)	V. iv. Excursions may involve brief combats	
(v)	V. iv. 1–37	(37)
(vi)	Douglas fights the king.	
(vii)	V. iv. 38–42	(5)
(viii)	Hal fights Douglas.	
(ix)	V. iv. 43–73	(31)
(x)	Hal fights Hotspur.	
(xi)	V. iv. 74–5	(2)
(xii)	Douglas fights Falstaff simultaneously with the fight of Hal and Hotspur.	
(xiii)	V. vi. 76–126	(51)
(xiv)	Falstaff stabs the dead Hotspur.	
(xv)	V. iv. 127–154	(28)

There are, as I have noted, a large number of entrances and exits in both scenes, and yet in V. iii there is only 1 fight in 60 lines and 4 formally designated fights in the 154 lines of V. iv. Of the 8 speaking characters used by Shakespeare 7 of them are dedicated to fighting. Falstaff, dedicated to survival, provides variation as a counter-movement, and can provide a commentary on the only 2 characters who die onstage. Of the 8 characters, 5 are engaged in fighting onstage. The culminating fight in the sequence is that between Hal and Hotspur which resolves the battle at the political level though there is still room for Falstaff's private experience of battle to occupy our attention. It is worth noting the proportions here. Hal speaks 15 lines (V. iv. 86–100) in elegy on Hotspur, and 9 lines (101–9) on the 'dead' Falstaff. Falstaff is given 18 lines (110–27) to speak of counterfeits, to fear a revived Hotspur, and to 'kill' him. This conforms to the pattern of the whole battle, for considerable sections of it are devoted to Falstaff's outrageous boasts, his tempering of valour with discretion, and Hal's various reactions to him. In the 214 lines of the battle 86 of them (40.2 per cent) are devoted to Falstaff in the 4 episodes in which he is prominent [V. iii. 30–60 (31), V. iv. 74–5 (2), 101–27 (27), 129–54 (26)], and he is onstage for only a little less than Hal, the figure given most stage time on the battlefield, and for about the same number of lines as Hotspur.

There is, in the categories of battle I have defined, an interweaving of the various elements, and only after the death of Hotspur (V. iv. 76–109) is there a sustained sequence of one type (5), though even there the elegies over Hotspur and Falstaff are varied and set in contrast. The three categories involved in speech divide up as follows: (1) speeches of defiance in 5 different segments total 66 lines (30.8 per cent); (3) reports on battle, pauses for encouragement, and the recounting of deeds occur in 9 segments and total 114 lines (53.3 per cent); and (5) eulogies and elegies of the fallen in 3 segments total 34 lines (15.9 per cent). In the elements contained in the stage directions there are 5 fights, with Douglas involved in 4, Hal in 2, and the king, Hotspur and Falstaff in 1 each (constituting category 2). There are 4 segments which involve assorted physical activity and noises to represent battle – procession of soldiers, alarums, excursions, retreat. Of central significance in the arrangement of the sequence is the way the physical activity onstage is supported by speeches of defiance and by the insertion of news of events happening elsewhere offstage. This augments the impression that we are seeing many of the most significant events which are representative parts of the bustling chaos of a much broader battle.

There are 35 lines in total, inserted on 9 occasions, which supply news of the battle events just out of our sight. When Douglas fights Blunt onstage he asserts that he has already killed one figure, impersonating the king, Lord Stafford, offstage. From Falstaff we hear that he has led his regiment (offstage) into action, and he implies that this involved 147 deaths (since of his 150 only 3 are left alive). When Hal enters he has obviously been engaged in battle (offstage) for he has lost his sword, and he asserts 'Many a nobleman lies stark and stiff/Under the hooves of vaunting enemies' (V. iii. 40–1). Falstaff, who is almost certainly lying, asserts that he has accomplished (offstage) deeds worthy of Turk Gregory and has killed Percy (V. iii. 44–5), in parodic reflection of Douglas who asserted he had killed the king only a moment earlier. When Hal returns to the stage bleeding he has obviously again been involved in fighting (offstage), and he speaks of many deaths on that field 'Where stained nobility lies trodden on,/And rebels' arms triumph in massacres' (V. iv. 12–13). The king, in supporting Hal's admiration of his brother John, indicates how the young prince held Percy at bay in combat (offstage). When Douglas catches the king alone Henry speaks of his two sons roaming the battlefield in search of their enemies. The prince, in rescuing his father, challenges Douglas in the name of those killed onstage, Blunt, and offstage, Shirley and Stafford (V. iv. 40). He gives news of Gawsey and Clifton who require aid in other parts of the battlefield, and the king goes off to supply support. The battle comes to a conclusion when Falstaff describes his vigorous fight with the revived Hotspur, action which he claims to have undertaken when the two princes were offstage, but which we, as witnesses of the stage, know never occurred at all. Thus the events we observe are accompanied by accounts of events elsewhere, and to the two deaths we witness are added the deaths of several named noblemen and dozens of Falstaff's tattered recruits in action in other parts of the battlefield. It is not easy to get characters killed onstage off again. Blunt's corpse can be scrambled off amidst the mêlée of excursions, and Falstaff is designated to take up Hotspur's body and presumably to take it off to claim his reward. If we cannot see many deaths onstage there is certainly no impediment to the recording of casualties off it. There is more designated physical combat at Shrewsbury than in many of Shakespeare's battles, but it is evident that he depends on a variety of elements and that reference to events offstage is a recurrent device strategically alternating with the clashes of the major figures which are, for the most part, imaginative inventions added to the details available in the sources.

I have taken some care in trying to work out a detailed structure of Shakespeare's handling of this battle because it is important to recognize the limitations he was up against and how he exploited them The exciting choreography of battles in many modern productions by the RSC or by the Stratford Festival in Canada with their large companies and extensive resources can give us a false picture of the way the battles may have been staged in their original productions. It seems improbable to me that the original productions ever produced battles as busy as those on the modified thrust stage in Stratford, Ontario; and for obvious reasons. It is possible to find in productions at the Festival Theatre that as many as 30 to 40 actors rush about the stage in representations of battle. It is important to recognize why such extensive choreography can work effectively. There are 6 major points of access: stage left; stage right; at the centre beneath the balcony; at the centre above the balcony; and 2 more from the gutters at the front down beneath the wrapped around audience. There are often 2 more auxiliary accesses at left and right from the steps up to the balcony. There are also 5 aisles which can be used, leading out to the foyer, and they are used on occasion, sometimes in battles. There is, as in the Elizabethan theatre, a trap-door available for access to and from the underworld. The Festival Theatre thus has at least 14 accesses to its stage, and its 6 major accesses work on diagonals which allow for sallies back and forth across the stage. The public theatres of Shakespeare's day had considerably fewer accesses, and since there were not convenient diagonals to exploit it is unlikely that the stage could have been kept in such active turmoil. The battle of Shrewsbury, as written for the Elizabethan theatre and a company more limited in numbers than many of the leading and usually subsidized companies today, does indicate that varied physical activity could be used if it was judiciously spaced out, and if exits and entrances were worked out in serial additions and subtractions of one or two at a time so that large numbers were rarely required to clear the stage in a short period.

We can finally ask why Shakespeare shapes the battle of Shrewsbury in this manner with more fighting onstage than in many of his battles. We have to search within the structure of each play to understand the choices Shakespeare made in the presentation of his battles. It might seem that Shakespeare could have written the battle of Shrewsbury in the same manner that battle is handled in *King Lear* or in *Julius Caesar*, as totally or predominantly offstage action. In *Henry IV, Part 1*, however, physical combat is a necessary culmination of the way much of the play has been developed. Hal and Hotspur are juxtaposed almost from the outset as two forces kept apart who must eventually clash as a natural resolution of the issue between the rebels and the king and in a physical combat that is an inventive addition by Shakespeare to his sources. We need to *see* Hal in heroic action instead of merely hearing reports of his fights because it is the logical culmination of the image-making which Hal has carefully shaped to astonish his critics and had promised to the audience in his soliloquy in I. ii. To many in the play Hal has appeared to be an idle playboy, a figure detached from the serious business of protecting or sustaining the realm, and his behaviour has been criticized and lamented by his father. Hal can resolve all doubt about himself, as he makes quite clear in a pointed speech to his father (V. iv. 50–6), not only in words but by his action of driving off Douglas in the very moment he is about to triumph over the king. When we consider all the elements which build up Hotspur as an irascible, restless figure dedicated to the pursuit of honour in physical combat we can see that it is essential to show *him* in action. When Hal kills him onstage we have the climactic physical representation of Hal as a hero triumphant, the vivid culmination of an image he has manipulated and the moment for which he has prepared in his interview with his father in III. ii, in the negotiations before battle where he offered to decide the issue in a single combat, and in Vernon's glowing speeches about his transformation from madcap to warrior prince. That image can be thrown into sharper relief, 'like bright metal on a sullen ground', by having an unheroic Falstaff scuttling about the battlefield. Falstaff can avoid fighting, play dead, be terrified in his contemplation of the dead Hotspur, and thus throw the whole issue of honour, so extensively examined in the play, into broader perspective. When Falstaff claims reward for killing Percy we know that his presentation of himself as a hero is fraudulent, but we can also recognize that he has something in common with Hal, who did kill Percy, for they are both figures who quite consciously manipulate their roles to achieve maximum advantage.

*(d) Resolution of issues after battle. V. iv. 155–61 (7),
V. v (44) – 51 lines*

(i) V. iv. 155-7 (3) The princes, Hal and John, hear the retreat sounded and depart to hear of who is living and who is dead now the battle is over.

(ii) V. iv. 158–61 (4) Falstaff carries off the body of Hotspur in search of reward.

(iii) V. v. 1–15 (15) The king rebukes Worcester for causing the battle by refusing to convey the news of the regal pardon offered the rebels before the battle. The king orders the captives, (Worcester and Vernon) to be taken to execution.

(iv) V. v. 16–33 (18) Hal reports that Douglas, injured and abandoned by his troops, has been captured. Hal sends Prince John to free Douglas and, in a magnanimous gesture of chivalry, orders the waiving of any demand for ransom for this valiant warrior.

(v) V. v. 34–44 (11) The king divides up his forces to confront the remaining scattered rebel forces, some to the north to deal with Northumberland and Scroop, others to the west to deal with Mortimer and Glendower.

In this entire sequence we hear only brief references to the king's battle losses (V. v. 6–7). All the figures who have been involved on the battlefield, as well as those rebellious figures who failed to come to Shrewsbury, are swiftly accounted for in one way or another. The issue of whether Falstaff is successful in his claim for reward is not considered, and it is not allowed to complicate the rapid resolution of the play. One figure dangerous to the realm and to Prince Hal, whom he has used but as a factor to 'engross up glorious deeds' on his own behalf, has now been disposed of. The other parasitical figure, who will be exploited in the same way, is reserved for further attention in a sequel which may well have been already forming in Shakespeare's mind.

In the above analysis I have indicated how the presentation of the battle itself is here, as usually in Shakespeare, only one element in a complex four-part structure. It is the climactic sequence of the play which has been thoroughly prepared for and so vividly and completely resolved that it requires only a short sequence after battle to bring the play to its close. When we summarize the proportions of this structure it becomes clear how much time Shakespeare devotes to the preparation for battle so that the climax itself can be conveyed in the vivid, varied, and relatively short sequence of the battle itself. As I have noted earlier, the lines themselves cannot be directly equated to the running-time of the play since the physical action of battle is represented in stage directions which are not indicated in a line-count. The proportions, however, still indicate how much of the play is devoted to events which relate to battle but do not actually represent its physical action.

Henry IV, Part 1 – the play is 2954 lines long.
2084 lines are devoted to events before action moves to the battlefield – 70.5 per cent.
1252 of those lines are devoted to the private pranks of Hal and Falstaff (i.e. 60.1 per cent of the lines before action moves to the battlefield, or 42.4 per cent of the whole play).
In the sections related to the battle:

(a)	the build up to battle	832 lines	28.2 per cent of the play
(b)	preparation on the battlefield itself	605	20.5
(c)	the battle of Shrewsbury	214	7.2
(d)	resolution of issues after battle	51	1.7
	TOTAL	1702	57.6

Although about half of the play is related to the build up to and resolution of the civil war at Shrewsbury, the play devotes only 7.2 per cent of its lines to the depiction of those battle-events themselves. The proportions may vary from play to play, but there is never a radical modification from the practice we find here save in the direction of showing fewer incidences of physical combat onstage. There is, at Shrewsbury, as much sword-fighting as Shakespeare presented in any battle and considerably more than in most of them.

Macbeth

In *Macbeth* the outlines of the four-part structure related to battle are not as clearly articulated as in some plays. The point at which the forces make a decision to confront Macbeth in battle only gradually become apparent. It is clear that as his acts of tyranny spread the opposition gathers. We learn of the beginnings of a coalition that may confront Macbeth (III. vi. 24–49). As Malcolm and Macduff seek to raise an army in England Macbeth is reported to be preparing for war. Macbeth visits the witches and undertakes the murder of Macduff's family, but only in IV. iii. do we meet the two figures who will cope with the tyrant. For much of that scene, as Malcolm tests Macduff, it is not clear that the action is moving towards a resolution on the battlefield. Macduff encourages Malcolm to take the lead in calling Macbeth to account. It is only at IV. iii. 131 that Malcolm openly declares his willingness to fight. From that point the audience is aware that it is watching action that will lead to a resolution at Dunsinane.

> (a) *The political build-up in events as preparation before the action moves to the battlefield itself – IV. iii. 131 – V. i. 74 – 184 lines*

> (i) IV. iii. 131–240 (110). Ross's report on the slaughter of Macduff's family is implicitly a preparation for battle. As the bloodiest and final act of Macbeth's tyranny it gives Macduff an immediately personal pretext for revenge. Malcolm makes this point specifically when he says 'Be this the whetstone of your sword' (228).

> (ii) V. i. 1–74 (74). The sleepwalking scene is, indirectly, another sequence preparing for battle. Macduff has just been informed that he has lost his wife and family. As we observe the distracted and alienated queen in her sleep we recognize that Macbeth is now alone, and this prepares us for his facing of his enemies in almost total isolation, which it will turn out is the way that Shakespeare will dramatize the battle sequence. In summoning up the catalogue of crimes committed, Lady Macbeth, in a telegraphic manner, emphasizes her own guilt and the events which have led his countrymen to call Macbeth to account.

156

(b) Preparation on the battlefield – V. ii (31), V. iii (62), V. iv (21),
V. v (52), V. vi (10) – 176 lines

The sequence divides itself into preparations on both sides, the attacking forces approaching through Birnam Wood (V. ii, V. iv, V. vi – 62 lines), and Macbeth in his castle at Dunsinane (V. iii, V. v – 114 lines). We are given reports that Macbeth's forces are deserting (V. ii. 18–20, V. iv. 10–14) and we see Macbeth relying on the prophecies of the witches that he need have no fear of any man born of woman nor until Birnam Wood comes to Dunsinane (V. iii. 1–10, V. v. 1–7). We hear and see drums, colours, and soldiers marching and Macbeth's determination to compel allegiance among his dwindling forces (V. iii. 35–6), but the battle, which initially is shaped as a siege of Dunsinane, is not formally joined for some time. Macbeth insists on putting on his armour (V. iii. 33, 48) but Seyton asserts it is 'not needed yet' (V. iii. 33), and so he wearily asks to have it pulled off (54) and brought after him. In V. iv the advancing forces cut boughs in Birnam Wood. In V.v Macbeth is aware that 'The cry is still "They come"' (2) but remains in Dunsinane confident that he can repel a siege. Only at the end of V. vi is the commencement of the battle itself signalled when trumpets sound and the alarums indicate that the forces are now in position for action.

The approach to battle, with its short scenes and its frequent exits and entrances provides an acceleration of the action, an increasing sense of Macbeth being encircled, abandoned by his forces, and shows the erosion of his confidence in the prophecies on which he relies. Shakespeare develops the material of the preparation on the battlefield and the battle itself as a continuing sequence which highlights Macbeth's increasing weariness and disillusion as he oscillates from defiance to despair. The outcome of the battle appears more and more to be a foregone conclusion. Shakespeare's interest centres on the responses of Macbeth as his hopes dwindle and he approaches his unavoidable fate. The audience is not denied a battle or physical combat, but it is to be a battle of Macbeth against an army. The alienated position he has achieved in grasping the crown and the ensuing tyranny to secure it is graphically imaged in the structure of the battle itself. Shakespeare uses a mixture of the battle elements I have defined in *Henry IV, Part 1*, but the predominant element in language is in category 1, Macbeth's desperate speeches of defiance, as the encirclement established in section *(a)* is completed in the sequence of combats he undertakes.

It is clear that in the build-up to battle Shakespeare, as usual, employs available actors to give the impression of numbers. From V. ii onwards there are 14 actors required to play the speaking parts. Soldiers and attendants are designated in 2 scenes with Macbeth (V. iii, V. v) and in the 4 scenes with his enemies so that it would seem that perhaps 20 actors were required. If we divide the mute supers equally it becomes apparent that Shakespeare presents a disproportion between the two forces for there would be 12 figures representing the attacking forces and 8 figures on Macbeth's side. Accounts of the ending of *Macbeth* usually emphasize the increasing isolation of its hero. What I would like to point out are the details of the various techniques used by Shakespeare to produce our recognition of the way the hero drifts away from his peers to become a pariah. After III. iv he never again shares the stage with Lady Macbeth. He has no thanes as allies, and associates only with the witches and with minor characters. He talks increasingly to himself and to servants. This emphasis is deliberately exaggerated by the increase in numbers in the attacking forces, augmented by characters such as Angus, Menteith, Caithness, Siward, and Young Siward who have little or no part in the play prior to Act V, and whose few speeches could without difficulty have been given to figures such as Ross and Lennox. They dress the stage the better to set off Macbeth in Dunsinane whose forces are deserting, leaving him only with figures such as the 'cream-faced loon' who brings news of 'ten thousand' soldiers advancing, the doctor ministering to his dying wife, the messenger who brings news of the moving Birnam Wood, and Seyton. Whereas all of the figures attached to Malcolm are warriors, of the speakers attached to Macbeth only Seyton would appear to be a possible candidate to take part in physical combat onstage. It is evident that Shakespeare had plenty of actors available if he had wished to develop an extended sequence involved in combat as at Shrewsbury, or even had it meant using unnamed soldiers as he does at Philippi. But in developing an isolation around Macbeth he gives us a sequence in which the battle itself requires only 5 actors. Before battle Macbeth, Seyton, and some soldiers are ready to fight against what are clearly overwhelming odds. The only figure from Dunsinane that we see fighting on the battlefield is Macbeth himself. He is, in effect, his army.

In the preparation for battle Macbeth's role is shaped in a way which indicates that he must rely on himself without aid from any sources other than his faith in the witches, and this is most graphically presented in his conduct in battle. Not only are all of his exchanges increasingly plagued by distraction and by an oscillation in his moods, they are also seen increasingly to be involved in self-communion. He appears on the stage alone at the opening of V. iii. 1–10. In calling intermittently for Seyton he speaks wearily about the emptiness in his life (19–29). His defiant claim at the conclusion of the scene (59–60) seems to be an attempt to reassure himself as much as a statement to either Seyton or the doctor. In V. v he reappears defiant (1–7), and seems to be musing to himself rather than communicating with Seyton (9–15), as he does also in reflecting on the tedium of life in response to news of his wife's death (17–28), or in recording his loss of confidence (42–50). In the 112 lines he is onstage in these two scenes Macbeth speaks 94 of them, and for almost 60 of these he is either alone or musing in a manner which indicates he is lost in his own thoughts. He pulls himself back into contact with the minor figures hovering at the periphery of his attention only intermittently so that his opening lines in the battle itself (V. vii. 1–2) state

Table 3.5 (c) The battle of Dunsinane – V. vii (29), V. viii. 1–34 (34) – 63 lines

(Segment) Description	Category	Entrance	Exit	Number onstage	Lines about action offstage
V. vi Alarums continued at end of scene signifies battle.	4				
V. ii					
(1) 1–4 (4) Macbeth alone asserts he must fight but fears no man born of woman.	1	1		1	
(2) 5–11 (6½) Young Siward enters, brief exchange of vaunting speeches.	1	1		2	
(3) *Fight, and Young Siward slain*	2		1[a]		
(4) 11–13 (2½) Macbeth, with confidence in the witches' prophecy, exits.	1		1	1	
(5) 14–23 (10) *Alarums* and Macduff enters in search of Macbeth and determined to avenge his slaughtered family.	1/4	1	1	1	
(6) 24–29 (6) Siward assures Malcolm the castle is taken and victory near, for many of Macbeth's soldiers are deserting. *Alarum.*	3/4	2	2	2	5½
V. vii					
(7) 1–3 (2½) Macbeth enters alone and defiant.	1	1		1	
(8) 3–8 (5) Macduff enters and exchanges speeches of defiance with Macbeth.	1	1		2	
(9) *Fight. Alarum*	2/4			2	
(10) 8–34 (26½) Macbeth unfolds the witches' prophecy that he is invulnerable to any man of woman born. Macduff reveals he was ripped untimely from his mother's womb and taunts Macbeth into fighting again.	1			2	
(11) They fight again and exit. *Alarums.*	2/4		2	2	
(12) They enter, fighting still until Macbeth is slain.[b]	2	2	2	2	
(13) *Retreat and flourish.* The conclusion of battle.[c]	4				
TOTALS		9	9		5½

[a] It is unclear what happens to Young Siward's body after he is killed at V. vii. 11. There is no crowd of actors onstage to cover his exit until the entrance of the conquering army after V. viii. 34. If Young Siward falls through an exit in death the problem would be solved, and I assume that here otherwise the body would have stayed onstage. The implication of Ross's exchange with Siward about his son's death (V. viii. 39–53) and the comments of Malcolm indicate that the body is offstage otherwise the evidence about wounds on the body would be superfluous.

[b] Various editors have suggested that Macbeth might be killed by the discovery space or in the gallery to allow a curtain to be drawn for the concealment of the body. Macbeth's head is shortly to reappear in the hand of Macduff, and decapitation could not easily occur with the body in full view.

[c] In several editions, including the Arden, V. viii ends with the slaying of Macbeth and the remaining action is designated V. ix. In the Pelican V. viii continues to the conclusion.

clearly what his position has become and how he will behave in battle like a bear at bay tied to the stake to endure the assault of the hounds which have surrounded him. The segments which make up the battle action are summarized in Table 3.5.

This battle involves very few actors and does not use the variety of elements I have noted elsewhere. There are sound effects throughout, but in the battle itself no armies appear onstage, there are no excursions, and there are few reports of action offstage. We have been informed of the desertion of Macbeth's troops before battle commences, and one further report augments that impression. Macbeth is left alone to continue his defiance and then to register the unreliability of the 'juggling fiends' on whom he has counted so much. Because Macbeth evidently has no allies there is no action offstage to be reported as a supplement to what we see on it. Though the battle is not a complex mosaic it does afford Macbeth 3 bouts of physical combat (4 if we count the exit and re-entrance with Macduff as 2 separate fights). Only 3 figures are involved in sword-play, and 2 deaths are shown. Macbeth is shown more extensively in fighting onstage than any of Shakespeare's other battle veterans, save perhaps Hal and Coriolanus. This, too, confirms our sense of Macbeth's isolation. It indicates Shakespeare's flexibility in shaping a battle for his own purposes. In creating the impression of a mass of forces surrounding Macbeth it became possible for him to develop the battle itself with 4 figures on one side and his central figure as the lone representative of his army fighting a battle in which he is cornered, defiant and doomed.

(d) Resolution of issues after battle – V. viii. 35–75 – 41 lines

The death of Young Siward is recounted and his father reacts stoically to the news. Macduff enters with the tyrant's head and Malcolm, hailed as King, arranges for the state to return to order as he invites everyone to his coronation at Scone. As with everything else in the lightning-swift economy of this play matters can be resolved quickly for there are scarcely any outstanding issues. Lady Macbeth is dead – by 'self and violent' hands, we are told here as the only footnote to her demise. Macbeth has been defeated, and his isolation is further underlined in the fact that there are no surviving allies to whom forgiveness or punishment is to be applied. Seyton is not significant enough to warrant any special attention. The kingdom is purged of its evil as the head of Macbeth signifies.

Sections related to battle

(a)	Preparations before the battlefield	184 lines	8.8	percentage of
(b)	Preparations on the battlefield	176	8.5	the 2079
(c)	The battle at Dunsinane	63	3.0	lines of
(d)	Resolution of issues after battle	41	2.0	the play
		464	22.3	

Table 3.6 V. ii – V. viii. 75 – 280 lines

Character	Entrance	Exits	Lines on Stage	Total lines onstage	Lines Spoken
Macbeth's forces					
Macbeth	5	5	V. iii. 1–60 (60), V. v. 1–52 (52), V. vii. 1–13 (13), V. viii. 1–34 (34)[a]	159	126
Seyton	3	3	V. iii. 30–60 (31), V. v. 1–7 (7), 15–52 (38)	76	4
Doctor	1	1	V. iii. 1–62 (62)	62	6½
Attendants, Soldiers (3)	6	6	V. ii. 1–60 (60), V. v. 1–52 (52)	112	0
Servant	1	1	V. iii. 11–19 (9)	9	1½
Messenger	1	1	V. v. 29–52 (24)	24	7½
Malcolm's forces					
Malcolm	4	4	V. iv. 1–21 (21), V. vi. 1–10 (10), V. vii. 24–9 (6), V. viii. 35–75 (41)	78	34½
Macduff	6	6	V. iv. 1–21 (21), V. vi. 1–10 (10), V. vii. 14–23 (10), V. viii. 3–34 (32)[a], 54–75 (22)	95	30
Monteith	4	4		103	9
Angus	4	4		103	7½
Caithness	4	4	V. ii. 1–31 (31), V. iv. 1–10 (10), V. viii. 35–75 (41)	103	9½
Lennox	4	4		103	6
Soldiers (3)	12	12		103	1
Young Siward	3	3	V. iv. 1–21 (21), V. vi. 1–10 (10), V. vii. 5–11 (6)	37	5
Siward	4	4	V. iv. 1–21 (21), V. vi. 1–10 (10), V. vii. 24–9 (6), V. viii. 35–75 (41)	78	24½
Ross	3	3	V. iv. 1–21 (21), V. vi. 1–10 (10), V. viii. 35–75 (41)	72	7½
TOTALS	65	65			280

[a] includes exit, re-entrance, and exit in the fight of Macduff and Macbeth at V. viii. 34

Table 3.7 Disposition of forces

	Scene	The forces	Number on Stage
(b)	V. ii	Scottish forces allied to Malcolm	7
	V. iii	Macbeth in Dunsinane	6 (for 11–20) or less
	V. iv	Malcolm's army	12
	V. v	Macbeth in Dunsinane	6 (30–52) or less
(c)	V. vi	Malcolm's army	12
	V. vii	Battle	2 or less at any one time
	V. viii. 1–34	Battle	2 or less at any one time
(d)	V. viii. 34–75	Malcolm's army triumphant	10 (34–53), 11 (53–75)

When we look at the final three sections of this sequence, (b), (c), (d) – the action in and around Dunsinane which covers the last 280 lines of the play – it is possible to see how much Shakespeare emphasizes the role of Macbeth and his isolation. Though the battle itself is not complex, in the action surrounding it Shakespeare uses the numbers available to him to crowd the stage. There are 65 entrances and exits in this sequence, which are summarized in Table 3.6, if we assume that the soldiers and attendants are divided with three on each side and if Malcolm's forces in V. vi and V. viii, before and after the battle sequence itself, include all the actors who have had speaking parts in V. ii and V. iv. Only the actual speakers in these scenes need to come far enough forward from the back wall to distinguish themselves from the supers who can remain at the rear and move from one exit to the other in their advancing march. This use of numbers helps to emphasize Macbeth's beleaguered situation without requiring any extensive choreography in the battle itself. It may be that all of these entrances and exits were not required, but even if the numbers onstage were pared down it is clear that there is a great deal of activity onstage and the impression of the advancing numbers would remain. If the actors appear as I indicate then it is clear that 7 of them are onstage for 103 lines, though between them they speak only 33 lines. Macbeth dominates the scenes in which he appears, speaking 51½ of the 60 lines for which he is on in V. iii, and 42½ of the 52 lines of V. v; he is onstage in this sequence for 56.8 per cent of the lines and speaks 45 per cent of them. Shakespeare developed every aspect of this final sequence to give prominence to Macbeth. Macbeth does most of the talking and all of the fighting in his own cause. All of the other aspects of the staging are designed to emphasize the odds he is up against. The battle itself requires few actors but it allows Macbeth a number of combats. It is the whole sequence which gives this sense of disproportion in numbers between the two sides, as can be seen in Table 3.7 if we note the number onstage in these scenes and supply each side, as I have designated above, with 3 unnamed soldiers (though it would make more sense to diminish the numbers on Macbeth's side from V. iii. to V. v. since we are told of his dwindling numbers). It is the action surrounding the battle which provides the evidence of constant movement and impressive numbers in the wave of opposition by which Macbeth is engulfed.

King Lear

In handling the battle in *King Lear* Shakespeare departs from his usual practice, and it becomes not so much a climactic event after lengthy preparation as a deliberately anti-climactic event reversing the accumulating hopes which have been built up in the audience.

The analysis here is based on the conflation of Folio and Quarto in the Pelican edition. Those who believe that the Folio is Shakespeare's own revision of the Quarto will find their views reinforced by Gary Taylor's article 'The War in *King Lear*' (*Shakespeare Survey*, 33 (1980): 27–34). He makes some points similar to the ones I am arguing here, asserting that the battle is 'an aggressive disappointment: the author's defiant and conscious refusal to give us what we want', and he claims that the Folio omissions make this case even more effectively than a conflated text.

It is possible to distinguish four phases of action related to the battle, but the anticipation of a martial confrontation is only one strand among several in the weave of events. The resolution of the play does to some degree develop out of the battle, for Cordelia's death results from Edmund's control over her and Lear as prisoners. Albany uses Edmund's soldiership in battle and only turns on him and arrests him when it is over. The deaths of Goneril and Regan in their treacherous competition for Edmund are not directly related to battle. It would have been possible, perhaps, to have Edgar fighting in Lear's cause, triumph over Edmund on the battlefield. Shakespeare, however, separates it off as a formal tournament combat after Lear's cause has been lost. The battle is only an incident, and not a very prominent one, among many others in the resolution of the play. This is a consequence of the development of much of the middle section of the play in the diffused focus of a variety of locales as Lear and his followers disperse on the heath. Lear wanders from pillar to post in search of a healing rest that is denied him. At various times we follow Edmund's rise to power, Goneril's attempts to win him, attempts to establish contacts with Cordelia, the savage reprisal of Cornwall and Regan on Gloucester for his supposed treachery, the variety of communications between the competing sisters and Edmund, Edgar's care for his blinded father and his confrontation with Oswald, Cordelia's concern for her wandering father. As can be seen in the summary below the anticipation of battle is spread over several hundred lines. It is referred to intermittently in the midst of other action developed in several locales.

(a) *The political build-up in events which occur before the action moves to the battlefield – III. i. 19 – IV. iii. 55, IV. v. 1–40 – 846 lines*

(i)   III. i. 19–49 (31) The first news which points towards a possible resolution of issues in battle occurs when Kent talks of division between Albany and Cornwall, of spies from France gaining intelligence of this, of a power from France already secretly in the kingdom 'at point/To show their open banner' (33–4) and an assertion that Cordelia is with this power in Dover.

(ii) III. iii. 7–18 (11) Gloucester confirms this news when he speaks to Edmund about his intention to 'incline to the King' (12). He speaks also of division between the dukes and of a dangerous letter he has received in which he is connected with 'part of a power already footed' (11–12) which seeks to revenge the king's injuries. The news provides Edmund with the opportunity to betray his father to his own advantage.

(iii) III. v. 9–12 (4) Cornwall receives Edmund's revelation that his father is in contact with the forces from France.

(iv) III. vi. 86–95 (10) When Lear, sheltered by Gloucester, is threatened, the earl seeks to have him conveyed to safety with the French forces in Dover.

(v)   III. vii. 2–3 (2) Cornwall asserts that 'The army of France is landed'.
      III. vii. 14–19 (6) Oswald indicates that Gloucester has helped Lear to escape to Dover and that the king is accompanied there by some of his knights and Gloucester's dependants who intend to join up with the 'well-armed friends' of the invading forces.
      I am picking out here only those passages directly related to the coming battle. Much of the action relates to it in a general way, and the trial and torture of Gloucester arise from his aid to Lear and from the earl's connection with the French forces – III. vii. 41–57 (17). The blinding of Gloucester is also part of the process of change which separates Albany from his wife and her cohorts and brings Edgar to a position as challenger of Edmund.

(vi) IV. ii. 2–5 (3) News of the invading army and Albany's response to it is given by Oswald to Goneril.
      IV. ii. 15–18 (3) Goneril sends Edmund back to Cornwall to urge him to prepare for battle as she indicates she will have to take charge of her own forces.
      IV. ii. 55–9 (5) When she confronts Albany's contempt for her in her treatment of her father she reminds him of the need to confront the foreign forces.

(vii) IV. iii. 1–8 (8) The action moves to Dover but not yet to Cordelia. We hear from Kent that the King of France has returned home leaving his marshal, La Far, in charge of his forces. There is a report

of Cordelia's response to news of her father's suffering and of Lear's presence in the town and his unwillingness to see his daughter.
IV. iii. 48–9 (2) There is news that the forces of Albany and Cornwall are advancing.

(viii) IV. v. 1–18 (18) Regan, in Gloucester's castle, hears news of the preparation of various forces and of Goneril and Edmund.

In this long sequence, which develops action in scattered places as the characters on their various paths move towards Dover, we are constantly aware of personal motivations related only tangentially to the approaching battle. Lear seems to wander out of contact with the figures who have aided him, Edgar seeks to guide and help his father, Regan and Goneril are as much concerned about their private competition for Edmund as they are with the battle, Albany is so appalled by his wife's behaviour that he seems to detach himself from the plans for battle, Cordelia longs for the safety of her father and a reconciliation with him, Gloucester goes to Dover to pursue his personal intention of committing suicide unconnected with the issue of battle. Of the 846 lines in this section of the play only 120 of them (14.2 per cent) are specifically connected to the issue of battle. The audience is certainly kept in touch with the sporadic preparations for the confrontation, but we are concerned more immediately with the developing personal issues and relationships and above all with the long-anticipated reconciliation of Lear with his daughter. The audience has been induced to look forward to this event for so long that the battle seems subsidiary to it, and we may begin to believe that, in consonance with the sources, Cordelia's success in battle will follow swiftly on the restoration of a harmonious relationship with her father. There are, after all, signs favourable to such a resolution amid the preparations leading towards the battlefield – the death of Cornwall, the alienation of Albany from his wife, the threat of disunity between Goneril and Regan as they vie for Edmund.

(b) Preparation on the battlefield – IV. iv (29), IV. vi (281), IV. vii (97), V. i (69) – 476 lines

(i) IV. iv (29) We are at last with Cordelia in Dover. Drums and colours and attendant soldiers indicate that we are now in the camp where the foreign forces are readying for battle. Cordelia's concern is focused more on the recovery of Lear still at large in the fields than on plans for the coming battle.

(ii) The saving of Gloucester by Edgar near Dover and their subsequent meeting with Lear is not linked to the approaching battle.
IV. vi. 204–12 (9) Discussion of battle only becomes an issue after Lear's departure when Edgar talks to the Gentlemen and hears that the British forces are close by and Cordelia's forces have 'moved on'.

Edgar's fight with Oswald is separated from battle as a private issue. IV. iv. 279–81 (3) At the end of this long scene the drum of an advancing army is heard.

(iii) In Cordelia's camp the focus is on her moving reconciliation with Lear.
IV. vii. 85–97 (13) Reference to the battle is made only at the end of the scene in an exchange of confusing reports which indicate that the battle is now imminent.

(iv) V. i (69) For the first time the action presents us with the British camp where the soldiers under Edmund and Regan join forces with those under Albany and Goneril. Yet even as they move towards the battle the dominant issues remain the personal ones. Goneril indicates that she would rather lose the battle than Edmund (18–19). Edgar, in an exchange with Albany, prepares for his challenge to Edmund after battle is over. The letter he gives to Albany will lead to the duke's discovery of his wife's treachery. We hear also of the actions Edmund intends after the battle. The battle again features as a subsidiary issue, an interlude before more important matters are dealt with. In the 476 lines over which this section stretches, only 123 lines (25.8 per cent) refer specifically to the approaching battle.

(c) The battle V. ii. 1–4 – 4 lines

(i) The stage directions indicate the commencement of battle with alarums within followed by Drums, Colours, and the procession of Lear and Cordelia with the invading army across the stage.

(ii) 1–4 Edgar on the battlefield places his father in the shadow of a tree and goes off (we assume) to fight in the battle, or to hear news of it.

(iii) The sound of retreat follows an alarum, and the battle is over almost as soon as it began.

(d) Resolution of issues after battle – V. ii. 5 – V. iii. 327 – 334 lines

(i) V. ii. 5–11 Edgar brings news to Gloucester of the battle-loss and the capture of Lear and Cordelia.

(ii) V. iii In the complex unfolding of the final scene the characters meet their various fates.

The most obvious fact about the shaping of all the events connected with the battle is how radically they vary from the details in the sources Shakespeare may have used. In Geoffrey of Monmouth's account, in Holinshed's Chronicle, in *The Mirror for Magistrates*, and in *The Faerie Queen* King Lear returns to England with French forces and defeats his evil daughters and their husbands and is restored to power. When he dies after three years Cordeilla has to confront the children of her sisters, is captured by them, and kills herself in prison. Shakespeare not only telescopes these events by eliminating the three years of Lear's restored rule, he alters the outcome of battle and the causes of the deaths of both Lear and Cordelia. In terms of the old chronicle-play which brings matters to a happy resolution Shakespeare's alterations are even more stunningly fundamental. All of the events related to the battle in the old play are shaped in an entirely different manner, and Shakespeare either ignores or changes them in every detail. In scene 24 we have an elaborate reconciliation between Leir and Cordella and a determination to redress the wrongs done to the King by a resort to arms. In scene 26 we see the Gallian King and Leir preparing to embark from France with an army to invade England. In scene 27 the British forces on watch are more concerned with drinking ale than with invading enemies. The French advance on the English sleeping in a coastal town (scene 28). The British are surprised and their watchmen drunk so that they are scattered half-naked (scene 29). The prisoners under the control of the Gallian King indicate that Leir's return is welcome and the kingdom will yield to his rule. Gonorill and Ragan enter with their army and defiance is hurled back and forth (scene 30). The battle opens in scene 31 with alarums and excursions, but Cornwall soon enters to indicate that the battle is lost and the British forces are revolting to join the invaders. The scene indicates the scattering of the army and lasts 13 lines. After more alarums and excursions in scene 32 victory is sounded. This battle is a little more extended than in Shakespeare with its various excursions, but there is no formal fighting onstage. In combination with the invasion of the coastal town the action lasts about 40 lines with some emphasis on comic aspects of the rout. In the old play Leir's success in battle is the climax of a sequence of events which have long prepared the audience for his eventual return to power. It could be argued that the preparation for such an outcome is at least as strong in Shakespeare, but this movement towards a happy resolution is not only set at nought by the astonishing reversal of our expectations in battle but by the breathtaking swiftness of that reversal. In the old play Leir's victory is achieved with 32 lines of the play remaining, which are devoted to brief celebrations and thanks. In Shakespeare 334 lines are devoted to the consequences of the battle-loss. The audience is obliged to readjust its expectations and to penetrate deeper into tragedy as successive events which promise a happy resolution – Albany's ascendancy over Edmund, Edgar's defeat of Edmund, Edmund's repentance, the deaths of Goneril and Regan, the death of Edmund – fail to bring a restoration of order and leave us to confront the deaths of Cordelia and Lear.

It might be argued that a variety of practical considerations connected with doubling led Shakespeare to reduce this battle to virtual invisibility. Since most of the characters are still alive not many are available to double as anonymous soldiers to be engaged in battle. The Fool disappears from the play on the heath but there is a possibility that this actor also doubled the role of Cordelia. The actor of Cornwall is available, and Oswald has died in IV. vi. There are various minor roles which must have been doubled – the Gentlemen in IV. iii and IV. vi, the servant to Cornwall in III. vii, and the servants who help the blinded Gloucester, the old man in IV. i, the doctor in IV. vii, and various messengers. The miscellaneous roles could be performed by 3 or 4 actors which means that they would be available to fill out the ranks of an army in battle.

Another factor to consider is the fact that it would not have been easy to engage many of the named characters in direct physical combat. Three daughters are all in the battle but we do not expect to see them prominent in combat. Shakespeare does have Viola engage in a comic sword-fight and has Imogen on the battlefield at Milford Haven, but Joan de Pucelle is the only woman ever shown engaged in combat on a battlefield in Shakespeare. We do not expect the blind Gloucester to fight. Edgar has already fought Oswald before battle and he will fight Edmund after battle. Albany and Edmund are available to fight, but there are no named characters available whom they might fight. There is no point in having Edgar fight Edmund, since it must be inconclusive given the challenge to a tourney reserved for the last scene. We do not expect to see Albany fighting, for we know he has little stomach for a fight against Lear and is in the battle to stem the French invasion of England. But in the shadowy approach to battle Shakespeare has not distinguished any French soldiers as individual characters, and none are available to be engaged in combat. After all his troubles and his physical weakness in IV. vii we do not expect to see Lear wielding a sword. He may still have the strength to kill the slave hanging Cordelia at the end, but she is much dearer to him than his kingdom. In IV. vii when told by Kent he is in his own kingdom his reply is 'Do not abuse me' (77), which implies that he does not wish to submit again to the illusions of power. He wants some private haven with Cordelia, and his presence on the battlefield we can take as a signal that he is unwilling to be separated from her more than as any concern to regain his crown. The only named figure among the invading forces who is available to fight is Kent. It is possible that a fight between Kent and Albany or Edmund could have been staged. Kent had a brief exchange with Edmund at the outset but has not shared the stage with him since. Kent has never spoken to Albany and there is no tension or significance to be developed out of a confrontation between them. Albany is in any case to revert later to supporter of Lear and to attempt to restore him to his kingship, so there is little point in arranging a fight with figures who are going to end up on the same side.

In the way that Shakespeare has structured his plot it becomes apparent that none of the major characters could be involved in significant combat. There are six more deaths to come in the play, and only the death of Cordelia is to come from the consequence of battle, her imprisonment by Edmund. All but Lear's death will take place offstage, though the dead bodies of his three daughters will surround the King onstage, recalling their attendance on him in the bargaining for love in the opening scene. Yet even when we eliminate the named characters as likely combatants, it would still have been possible to engage some of the available extras in combat as anonymous soldiers. Even if no combat were to be presented onstage Shakespeare could have had characters onstage reporting on skirmishes between the armies offstage as he does in many battles. Shakespeare, however, employs none of these devices and does not even offer the formality of excursions. He goes to the other extreme presenting only the opening and closing sound effects and the procession of one army. The armies of Albany and Edmund are not seen *in* the battle but only before and after it is over.

This reduction of the battle to 4 lines is clearly the centre-piece in Shakespeare's very careful design of changing the end of the story as it was presented in the old play and as we have been seduced into thinking might be possible here. As I have noted there has been no consistent focus on the battle since we first heard of Cordelia's arrival in England (III. i. 30–4), but we have had no reason to doubt that the king would triumph and return to power as in all versions of the story hitherto. It is true that Lear's vicissitudes have been more punishing than anything in earlier accounts and his analysis of the illusions of power more penetrating, but his recovery in Cordelia's presence seems to promise his restoration to sanity and to a humility which he had lacked at the outset. The possibility of a happy outcome gathered strength consistently as it seemed likely that Albany might turn against the savage power-brokers, or that Goneril and Regan might as easily fall upon each other as unite against Cordelia. It turns out that all these details are false hopes of a new dawn deliberately softening up the audience for the moment when the reversal occurs with devastating swiftness. Between the moment when Lear and Cordelia are marching *to* battle and returning as prisoners *after* battle there are 11 lines of verse. There are no speeches of defiance, no reports on battle-deeds, no pausing for breath, no clash of swords, no exchange of news about the feats of combatants, no eulogy over the dead. Just as we are expecting to see Edmund, Goneril, and Regan repaid for their treachery and barbarous acts we find that the two figures who have only just been reunited are in the hands of Edmund who has already indicated an intention to kill them.

Shakespeare, no doubt, recognized that this reversal would be stunning but also ran the danger of being anti-climactic. The expected confrontation of good and evil forces is not denied to the audience but is worked into events surrounding battle. The absence of physical combat in battle is compensated for by fights outside it. Edgar's fight with Oswald before the battle is part of the false promise of a new dawn. Edgar begins to emerge as a possible saviour willing, after his efforts in helping Lear and his father, to confront the forces of injustice and its agents. Edgar not only kills Oswald but passes information to Albany which will expose the villainy of Edmund. His determination to confront Edmund in battle seems to indicate that he may emerge, in the manner of Prince Hal, redeeming time when men least expect it. Instead of having the two brothers meet on the battlefield Shakespeare presents them in single combat, leading the audience again on a false scent that all is not lost. Lear and Cordelia are in danger in prison. Albany has already ensured that Edmund's climb to power has come to an end, and Edgar seems to complete the process in achieving revenge. Along with the deaths of Goneril and Regan we are for a second time being prepared for the possibility of a happy ending which makes us even more vulnerable to the desolating resolution of the action. The battle is shaped, therefore, as only one part of the alternating current in the final sequence. The fight with Oswald before battle is part of the oscillation towards a rising hope that we expect to achieve finality with the victory of Lear and Cordelia. In the sharp jolt of the brief battle we oscillate towards despair, but recover hope in Edgar's triumph in combat, only to be finally crushed when it turns out that the one significant consequence of the battle-loss, Edmund's determination to kill Cordelia, has in fact been fulfilled.

Part 2

4

'Mangling by starts the full course of their glory': The legend and the reality of war in *Henry V*

In *Henry V* the campaign against the French is not one episode in a sequence of events; it is the substance of almost the entire play. An examination of this play will allow me to develop more fully the structural analysis of battles undertaken in the last chapter and to examine, in the deployment of one specific device, the Chorus, the relation of offstage events to those onstage which is the subject of this whole study. There are very few scenes in this play which are not directly related to battle. The coming war is not the topic of conversation in I. i where Canterbury and Ely discuss Henry's character, his sympathy for the Church, and the Church's determination to remain in his favour. Before this, however, the Chorus has already evoked 'a warlike Harry' (5), has spoken of 'the very casques/That did affright the air at Agincourt' (13–14), and the clerics are soon (I. ii) providing the legal basis for Henry's expedition to France. There are scenes which focus on other issues: the Eastcheap friends of Falstaff squabble among themselves (II. i) and react to news of Falstaff's death (II. iii). With these few exceptions all of the 3178 lines of the play are involved in preparations for war, reactions to it, events on the battlefield, and the consequences of Henry's victory. The play works towards the climactic confrontation of Agincourt but along the way it incorporates skirmishes, a siege, diplomatic negotiations back and forth, the episodic progress along the campaign road of the English across Picardy. If we look, in Table 4.1, at the geographical locale of the scenes of the play, as suggested by most modern editors, we find that a very significant proportion of the action is situated outdoors in the camps which are the bases for each side in the episodic campaign waged among the fields of northern France.

In no other play does Shakespeare go to quite these lengths in presenting an extended sequence of action related to a battle campaign. Between the opening and closing movements of the play virtually all of the action occurs in the camps preparing for battle or on the battlefield itself. All of the interactions and most of the language of the play is devoted to filling in the

Table 4.1 Locale of the scenes in *Henry V*

Choruses relating to peace	Scenes not on the campaign road and battlefield	Scenes on the campaign road	Choruses relating to war
			Chorus I (34)
	I. i } Within the (98)		
	I. ii } king's palace (311)		
	II. i. London (123)		
			Chorus II (42)
		II. ii. At Southampton, preparing to sail on the battle campaign (193)	
	II. iii. London (57)		
	II. iv. French king's palace (146)		
			Chorus III (35)
		III. i. Before the walls of Harfleur (34)	
		III. ii. Near Harfleur (130)	
		III. iii. Before the walls of Harfleur (58)	
	III. iv. French king's palace (57)		
		III. v. French camp at Rouen (68)	
		III. vi. English camp in Picardy (167)	
		At Agincourt	
		III. vii. French camp (152)	
			Chorus IV (53)
		IV. i. English camp (296)	
		IV. ii. French camp (63)	
		IV. iii. English camp (132)	
		IV. iv. Battlefield (75)	
		IV. v. Battlefield (24)	
		IV. vi. Battlefield (38)	
		IV. vii. Battlefield (173)	
		IV. viii. English camp (121)	
Chorus V (45)			
		V. i. English camp (81)	
	V. ii. French palace at Troyes (358)		
Epilogue 1–8 (8)			Epilogue 9–14 (6)
53 (1.7%)	1150 (36.2%)	1805 (56.8%)	170 (5.3%)

picture of this campaign to the exclusion of any other focus of interest. A survey of the component elements of the play would seem to indicate that Shakespeare is marshalling all of his talents to give us as detailed a picture as possible of a patriotic crusade against the French, a climactic moment of English history. Only when we examine these component elements can we see what a complex picture Shakespeare creates. Even though such a predominant section of the play is devoted to events in the battle camps and to the battle itself it is clear that Shakespeare is not structuring an un-ambiguous tribute to martial action or to the English success. Our perception of the war is regulated very clearly by what Shakespeare chooses to show us on the stage and by report of the events which occur offstage.

I have examined in many plays the way in which narrative matters related to offstage occurrences are woven into the texture of ongoing events. In this play we have a very specific device for the transmission of narrative detail prominently foregrounded. Because the Chorus has a very important function not only in what it reveals but in what it ignores, it is necessary to examine its deployment as one of Shakespeare's structural strategies in the play. When the Chorus claims to be serving a particular purpose, compensating the audience for the inadequacy of the stage, it is, in fact, doing something quite different. Shakespeare's devious use of the Chorus is one of the key devices in the play and it is part of a broader strategy of presenting us with a balanced picture of the battle in which war is neither glamorized nor satirized but is seen to be a mosaic of the heroic and the absurd, the famous and the obscure, the valiant and the cowardly, the selfless and the selfish, the warrior-king and the common soldier.

The use of the Chorus in *Henry V* is really central to the whole question of what Shakespeare is doing when he reminds us so deliberately of the illusory nature of the play-world. Does the Chorus speak directly for Shakespeare in lamenting that the glorious history of England can receive no fully worthy representation on a tawdry stage? It used to be a commonplace of criticism that any Shakespearian character who can be termed 'choric' may often be taken to be presenting the dramatist's own views on the action, inheriting the habit Seneca gave the chorus of passing on didactic messages to the audience. How natural, therefore, to assume that we have Shakespeare's own scarcely disguised voice when he came to present a formal Chorus. But surely if a writer is uncertain of success, and insecure about his technique, he does not strive to advertise his flaws and his fears throughout the play. Nor do any of the critics explain why Shakespeare felt no need of a narrator in, say, *King John*, which radically compresses historical time, sews several campaigns together, and bobs back and forth across the Channel like a tennis ball. Shakespeare's audience can never have expected the kind of panoply and 'realism' for the absence of which the Chorus in *Henry V* apologizes. If they had accepted the tents of Richard III and Richmond a few feet apart on the same stage with ghosts flitting between, they were hardly likely to feel the lack of prancing steeds and of flotillas for crossing a channel that they had been imaginatively o'erleaping these many years by means of the poet's evocative language. We must find some explanation for the function of the Chorus other than as a vent for Shakespeare's frustration at working with productions governed by severe financial limitations. The only inventions that would satisfy this literalist Chorus is the movie-camera. There is no evidence elsewhere of Shakespeare as an early D. W. Griffiths *manqué*. What there is evidence of everywhere is Shakespeare's overwhelming confidence that the simple, bare, thrust stage of his theatre could be used to present any kind of story in any kind of world whether real or imaginary.

As my analysis of battles in other plays indicates Shakespeare varies his practice very considerably showing extensive physical combat in some and scarcely any at all in others. It is true that his dramatization of battles involves some sleight-of-hand in the way battle-action is often embedded as only one element in the four-part sequence of political build-up and negotiation before battle and a resolution of issues after it. What we see onstage is often extensive preparation rather than extensive battle-action. We must assume confidence on Shakespeare's part in handling battle onstage when he chooses, in some plays, to use very much less than the resources evidently available to him in those plays where excursions, the procession of armies, and several physical combats posed no problems for him. At Shrewsbury Shakespeare certainly wants us to see the absurd side as well as the heroic side of battle, otherwise he would not have devoted so much stage time to Falstaff's ruses in scrambling for safety. In the campaign in France in *Henry V* we are shown war from a great variety of perspectives, and a good deal of the action does not contribute to a glowing image of heroism. The Chorus laments the limitations of budget and company size which reduces Agincourt to 'four or five most vile and ragged foils,/Right ill-disposed in brawl ridiculous' (Chorus IV, 50–1), but the Chorus is a character in the play, and it is not the theatre which undercuts him but Shakespeare. The dramatist could have shown us King Henry and his generals triumphing over the French. We hear about some noble endeavours by the high command but we do not see any of them. Nor does he put onstage much of the detail supplied in his source, Holinshed's Chronicle, about the king's battle-endeavours as he fought alongside his soldiers and his triumph in combat when he slew Alencon and two of the duke's men. Shakespeare does not give us even the four or five most vile and ragged foils for which the Chorus apologizes. He gives us no onstage combat at all. One of the major elements in this battle comes close to being a 'brawl ridiculous' in Le Fer's submission to Pistol; but that is not an accident due to Shakespeare's inadequate resources, it is a deliberate choice. It foregrounds an aspect of battle the Chorus would rather not acknowledge, but it is quite central to Shakespeare's treatment of war throughout the play. Shakespeare includes the Chorus not to advertise the limitations of his theatre but to expose the limitations of the view of history presented by the Chorus. I have argued that one of Shakespeare's great skills is to make a virtue of necessity. An examination of the function of the Chorus proves a supreme example of that skill.

The plays which Shakespeare presented on his bare stage were not naturalistic in the modern sense. Many critics, convinced that the acting style Shakespeare's company used was highly artificial and gestural, have ransacked books of rhetoric for evidence of a sort of formal sign language. Other scholars have argued that the actors eschewed the rhetorician's system and tended towards a more realistic portrayal. It is useful to remember that if characters were presented in an extremely formalistic manner many references within the plays become redundant and inexplicable. Shakespeare created a long string of characters who were frauds recognizable by their artificial and imperfect manners. Characters such as Osric, Sir Andrew Aguecheek, Lucio, or even Parolles can only be funny if there is some world of natural courtesy against which to measure their deviancy. Shakespeare was very much aware that the stage could present artificial fustian stuff and he puts parodies of such material into his own plays the better to set off a more natural world. The players' speeches in *Hamlet* parody the theatre in a way that tends to make us forget we are still in the theatre. Falstaff in his Cambyses vein, Pistol, or Don Armado, by their extravagant commitment to thespian displays, tend to emphasize by contrast the natural behaviour of those around them. The mechanicals in *A Midsummer Night's Dream* amuse us because of their fears of success in the naturalistic style. They are hopelessly unaware that their limited acting skills will make it impossible for the audience, however willing, to suspend its disbelief. We can laugh at the failure of one level of illusion only in so far as we submit to the success of illusion at another level. When Shakespeare points our attention to the theatrical he does not weaken its hold over us, he strengthens it. This could only be true, of course, in a society which feels that, far from there being an enormous canyon separating the real world from theatre, there is in fact considerable overlap, a blurring of the line of demarcation which gives the dramatist considerable latitude in manipulating the audience.

The Chorus in *Henry V* apologizes for the tawdriness of the stage and implies that we can recreate history only by a vigorous exercise of our imaginations. We are immediately into the rich paradox that reality is a product of imagination, and that turns out to be the chief irony associated with the Chorus. The Chorus has a very selective imagination; it will deal only with glamour and bravery. This narrative voice is borrowed from the chronicles, but it is familiar in the older drama. Chorus figures and presenters are quite common in the plays of the 1570s and 1580s, but, as the skill of the dramatists improved, this device (which belongs more to the

177

narrative forms of prose than to drama) began to disappear. The various tatters of older forms – allegorical figures, prologues, inductions, choruses, etc. were digested by the play proper and the material was presented more frequently in terms of character in a self-contained world. It is odd, therefore, that Shakespeare who had already written many plays without resort to these old-fashioned devices, should employ a formal chorus in the play which brings to a close his preoccupation with the history of England. Considering Shakespeare's complex skills by this stage of his career we have to assume some deliberate purpose in his employment of such an archaic device.

In *Henry V* Shakespeare broke the mould in which he had cast all his Histories hitherto. That repetitive cycle of rise and fall, of factious barons roaming England and France to seek out their advantage, is finally thrust aside. The last remnant of that struggle, in the treachery of Cambridge, Grey, and Scroop (II. ii) is an echo of the past. The king's decisive crushing of that conspiracy brings a whole era to an end. He advances on France with a united front, the factions having buried their enmity in a patriotic crusade. The concord among the nobles is remarkable and Shakespeare cleverly sets it off by relegating the conflict and factiousness to the commoners. He also contrasts the concord of the English high-command with the petty squabbles among the French barons.

The mixture of low-life comedy with the hallowed events of history was not Shakespeare's invention. In the source play, *The Famous Victories of Henry the Fifth*, from which he took many hints, we find a similar admixture. In the episodic nature of the source play there is little evidence of the unifying design, the total structure of ideas, that Shakespeare was to make of history. The source play does not relentlessly examine the traditionally received account of Henry's conquest; rather, it follows tradition and enlivens it with comic interludes. A central aspect of Shakespeare's drama is the placing of scenes, of setting up a contrast of attitudes which illuminates a structure of ideas regulating the play. For this purpose he elaborated much of Pistol's part, and invented the whole of Fluellen's part and the group of common soldiers present at one of the critical moments of the play. One of the ways of balancing the views presented by this sub-plot world was to introduce the Chorus.

The functions of this Chorus would at first sight seem to be straightforward. It provides narrative bridges and exhibits appropriately patriotic sentiments. But those critics who take the function of the Chorus for granted ought to realize that none of its speeches provide information absolutely necessary to our comprehension of the play, a fact noted by Johnson at the end of his 1765 edition of the play. In comparison, say, with the spare and obviously functional employment of the chorus in *Doctor Faustus*, or with its essential narrative importance in Dekker's *Old Fortunatus*, Shakespeare's Chorus is supererogatory. If we excised the part, however, we would radically alter the structure of ideas and the mood and atmosphere of the play. In the Chorus it seems as though England has at last found its true voice; it is an abstract extension of the function that Shakespeare had first essayed in Faulconbridge. The cause of battle seems, in the glowing rhetoric of the Chorus, to have passed from individual personality to the whole nation.

I am not suggesting that Shakespeare specifically allegorizes the Chorus, but he needed a voice that would represent one extreme of the spectrum of ideas on patriotism, as Pistol represents the other extreme. The king holds the balance. Henry cannot be the embodiment of patriotic zeal because he is faced with the human responses which separate men from their ideals.

But if the king is to be properly heroic then no other man must overshadow him by an unquestioning acceptance of the virtues of patriotism. Shakespeare chose, therefore, a figure lacking both in personality and involvement in the action of the play. Being immune to the world it observes, the Chorus is static; its lyric exuberance persists throughout because there is no dynamic principle involved in its depiction which can induce development. The Chorus presents a play-within-a-play, or rather a play within its own flow of grandiose rhetoric. The Chorus claims that the stage is not worthy to present reality but makes us aware that its own affinities are more with poetical transmutation, overblown hyperbole, than with reality. It begs admittance to perform as our guide and appears regularly before the opening of each act to speed us on our way. We can come to an understanding of the significance of these choric prologues by weighing them against the content of each act.

The Chorus in the Prologue to Act I paints a rose-tinted spectacle of historical events. In attempting to inspire us to reach out for a glorious reality the speech of the Chorus begs us to forget the stage in language that forcibly reminds us of it. Because the Chorus embodies an unquestioning belief in the glory of war it presents a vision which does not adequately cover any man's actual experience of war. Shakespeare has many scenes to exhibit which are far from the pomp and glory of which the Chorus speaks, scenes which are tawdry indeed, ragged men who on this unworthy scaffold hardly aid the swelling scene. A play which capitalized on the tawdriness of the stage, on the ordinariness of human response, might seem more like real life, more real, indeed, than the tantalizingly impossible vision the Chorus presents.

In Act I we turn from the florid invocation to the political details of how the expedition came to be undertaken. The king establishes himself at once as a shepherd of his people intent on securing authoritative support for a just war. Whether we find the genealogical ramblings of Canterbury comic or not, it is clear that Shakespeare devotes a whole act to establishing the unity of the Church and the barons in England's cause. Shakespeare clearly indicates that we are in an entirely new world and to that extent fulfils the picture of a puissant nation which the Chorus had celebrated at the outset. The scenes constantly invoke that golden age of Edward III and the Black

Prince so that our eyes are turned on this new king as a rising sun who will return England to its former glory (I. ii. 279–81).

The Prologue to Act II presents us with material designed for lyrical intensity, a patriotic hymn describing a nation girding its loins. The information concerning the conspiracy provides us with no material that we do not obtain by other means during the ensuing action. The information has a similar function to many of the Brechtian devices of anticipation. When we come upon the conspiracy, it does not disturb our faith in England's new-found unity, because the Chorus has already informed us that we will ship for France. Thus we can concentrate on the masterly fashion in which the king deals with it.

It must also be observed that the speech which serves as Prologue to this act makes no mention of the action which fills two-thirds of it. It can hardly be said that the scenes in Eastcheap contribute to the picture of an England transformed into an ideal state. Henry himself may be reformed, but Shakespeare saw no point in abandoning his unrepentant associates when they could be used to elaborate richly on the major concerns of the play. The Chorus throughout the play exhibits no knowledge of this world resistant to the poetic vision of a mighty nation eager to fall upon its enemies. We do not expect the hyperbole of the Chorus to acknowledge their pedestrian concerns. But though the Chorus can ignore these characters, the king cannot, and the comic scenes add up in the audience's mind to illuminate the king's contemplation of: 'the wretched slave/Who, with a body fill'd and vacant mind,/Gets him to rest, cramm'd with distressful bread;' (IV. i. 254–6).

In the Prologue to Act II we are prepared for the embarkation at Southampton: 'The king is set from London, and the scene/Is now transported, gentles, to Southampton;/There is the playhouse now, there must you sit,' (Prologue II. 34–6). The Chorus is interested only in the main line of the story, only in the king and his cause, not in any embellishments. There is even the implication that there is nothing further of interest in this narrative until the king appears: 'But, till the king come forth, and not till then,/Unto Southampton do we shift our scene,' (Prologue II. 41–2). The Chorus in elaborate manner rushes us forward to Southampton. It is with some surprise, then, that on entering Act II we find Shakespeare lagging behind in Eastcheap. Our sights have been set well above the Boar's Head tavern:

> Now all the youth of England are on fire,
> And silken dalliance in the wardrobe lies.
> Now thrive the armorers, and honor's thought
> Reigns solely in the breast of every man.
> (Chorus II. 1–4)

Shakespeare tempers this public eulogy with the private humours of Pistol and Nym, which aim at a little less than the reign of honour. This inconsistency might, perhaps, be more easily explained by assuming a late shuffling and addition of scenes or incomplete revision, were it not in line with the entire development of the Chorus, whose poetic vision is played off against the reality of the everyday world. Those critics who have assumed that the Chorus was designed to link an episodic narrative together and prepare the audience for rapid transitions might note not only that it is almost entirely superfluous in that role, but also that its function might often be more fruitfully examined as a deliberate lack of bridging and preparation for what actually goes on.

It cannot be accidental that the first scene in the Boar's Head parodies the rhetoric of politics in the court world that we have just left. There is division over the title and possession of a piece of property, Nell Quickly; there is an exchange of insults; there is a determination to fight it out, and concord is established by linking us back to the major theme in the resolve to bury the quarrel in France. The 'humorous' exchange between Pistol and Nym, with its absurdly overblown conceits and threats, is a comical reflection of the stern rebuttal of the dauphin's insulting joke. The contrast here, of course, is in the excesses of the bragging, flyting match, as opposed to the king's restrained and dignified retort to the French, and the lack of purposeful action that comes from the shouting match, as opposed to the king's resolute expedition to conquer France. The overblown battle-rhetoric of Pistol acts as admirable counterpoint to the genuinely ecstatic patriotism of the Chorus. The Chorus evokes images of an offstage world of fervent nationalists unquestioningly committed to a crusade. What we see onstage is rather more down to earth than the propaganda-posters the Chorus hangs up for our attention. Pistol's determination to profit by the war is a far cry from the honour which reigns in the breast of all the youths of England. It must be said, however, that the rogues, who give not a fig for honour, are gradually eliminated from the play. The Lord of Misrule, Falstaff, who had his being in more frivolous days, dies without being given the opportunity to make an impact on the crusade, soon Bardolph is hanged, later Nym is reported to have been hanged, and Nell Quickly is said to be dead. Only Pistol, soundly battered, crawls back to England. None of them interacts with the king, save Pistol in his encounter with Harry 'Leroy'. The new England offers no secure place for the former revellers. This, however, does not prevent us from recognizing that the version of events given by the Chorus is a considerable gloss on reality.

The Prologue to Act III contains 33 lines, and of these only 9½ at the most can be described as transmitting expository information; the rest is poetic embellishment. We have already learnt at the end of Act II that Henry is footed in France. The evocation of the channel-crossing in vivid pictorial imagery serves more as a transitional pause than for the contribution of information. The patriotic tone is reinforced with the description of a deserted England and the proud, invading army. Only at the close of the speech are we told rapidly about the siege of Harfleur as answer to the unsatisfactory

French terms. The two succeeding scenes are set in dialectical contrast, reflecting on this invocation. The king continues the martial rhetoric in his Harfleur speech, living up to the ideal set by the Chorus. The laggards from Eastcheap fall away from that ideal, tempering valour with very heavy doses of prudence. Bardolph's entrance, opening Act III, Scene ii, inevitably punctures the vein of resounding rhetoric that Shakespeare has sustained unbroken for almost 70 lines. Anything less 'Like greyhounds in the slips,/Straining upon the start' can scarcely be imagined. The rhetoric of the Chorus and Pistol is again juxtaposed; they both employ rhetoric of obviously literary origin. The Chorus aspires to the patriotic lyrical strains of a Spenser, magnifying honour to a point that ignores human weakness. Pistol borrows the fustian terms and epithets of the traditional stage braggart to hide his aversion to honour and to cover his human weakness. By providing this parody of heroism Shakespeare induces us to believe the more in the genuine heroism of Henry. That Pistol will twice get his pretence of bravery accepted – Fluellen's eulogy of his work at the bridge and Le Fer's submission – indicates how careful one has to be in recognizing true valour. All the world's a stage to Pistol, and he has his moments of glory even as he is also pelted with rotten vegetables when the audience, in this case Fluellen, sees through his performance. There are many scenes which carry on a ribald commentary on the glorious action, but Shakespeare carefully dissociates the king from all of them, despite his former proclivities, until late in the play. By that time, although we have not forgotten Prince Hal, we have had ample opportunity of recognizing the kind of king he has turned into.

This analysis of the function of the Chorus in the first movement of the play indicates the complexity of Shakespeare's strategy in balancing various forces against each other. The play has two battle-segments, and I treat the siege of Harfleur as the culmination of the first movement of the play which I have hitherto, in my analysis of battles in other plays, defined as section (*a*), the political build-up in events before the action moves to the battlefield. I continue to designate it in the same way here and summarize its various sequences in Table 4.2. It does contain battle-events – the siege of Harfleur (*a*2) – but in the broader pattern of the play they are part of the preparation leading towards Agincourt.

If I were not subsuming the siege of Harfleur under section (*a*) as part of the preparation for Agincourt it could be divided up itself into four segments associated with battle.

(i)   Political build-up. Chorus 1 – Chorus III. 24 (1028)
(ii) Preparation on battlefield. Chorus III. 35–43 (9)
(iii) Siege of Harfleur. Chorus III. 34 – III. ii. 125 (161)
(iv) Resolution of issues of battle. III. ii. 126 – III. iii. 58 (63)

It is evident that we do not have in this schema the pattern of the broad,

Table 4.2 Section (*a*) Preparation before the battlefield – 1553 lines

Subsections	Preparations in England and France for Agincourt		Scenes not directly related to the campaign in France	
*a*1. Chorus 1 – Chorus III. 33				
	Chorus I. 1–34	(34)		
			I. i.	(98)
	I. ii.	(311)		
	Chorus II	(42)		
			II. i.	(123)
	II. ii.	(193)		
			II. iii.	(57)
	II. iv.	(146)		
	Chorus III. 1–33	(33)		
*a*2. Chorus III. 34–III. iii. 58		(224)		
*a*3. III. iv–III. vi. 167*		(292)		
		1275		278

* Some skirmishes in Picardy are recorded as offstage action but they are developed mainly in connection with the intermittent unfolding of Fluellen's relationship to Pistol.

general political build-up followed by extensive diplomatic negotiation on the battlefield itself before the actual commencement of physical combat. This does not mean that there is no diplomatic negotiation before Harfleur, but it takes place at the French court where Exeter comes to seek terms (II. iv) and not at the site of the siege. We meet no characters on the battlefield before the fighting starts save the Chorus who announces the siege and is interrupted by its initial sounds before he departs. All of the diplomatic manœuverings on the battlefield are reserved for Agincourt.

I want to examine in a little more detail the handling of the siege of Harfleur to indicate the way it supports what I have been saying about the Chorus and establishes a method of dealing with battle which is more fully unfolded at Agincourt. At Harfleur there is physical evidence of battle in the sound of alarums and guns and the scaling-ladders brought on at the outset of III. i, but there is no evidence of physical combat designated onstage. Henry makes his rousing battle-speech in III. i, and it seems likely that this 43-line speech was delivered to citizens of Harfleur cowering in the gallery on the tiring-house wall. It opens with a question and addresses 'you men of Harfleur'. It is possible that the scaling-ladders were erected by the English soldiers against the tiring-house wall. The English would then have had access to the battlements of Harfleur, represented by the gallery, to attack the French. This staging is quite common in modern productions, but the script does not ask for it. What is presented after Henry's battle-speech does not enlarge on the description by the Chorus of a patriotic crusade, because the focus is on the rogues from Eastcheap away from the fighting, hanging back, as Falstaff did at Shrewsbury, to ensure that they avoid the danger of physical combat. It is possible that in practice Shakespeare's company added some physical combat, but in the script there are no named characters in conflict, and the focus is more on those who are not fighting than those who are. A clearer possibility of physical action, often suggested by modern editors in a stage direction, comes after III. ii. 18 when Fluellen catches up with the Eastcheap truants and forces them into the breach by driving them before him. This develops into the predominant method of the play's handling of battle whereby there is constant talk of blood and violence and heroism but what is seen onstage are parodies of fighting among minor characters on the English side which do occasionally break out in physical blows.

When we look at the 161 lines of the siege of Harfleur we find that it opens with 34 lines of Henry's battle-rhetoric and that action is represented principally by sound effects. There are 125 lines (77.6 per cent of the 161 lines over which the siege stretches) devoted to minor figures of captain's rank or lower who are not in the thick of the action. The sequence of Eastcheap lads tempering valour with discretion until driven to their duty by Fluellen (III. ii. 1–24), is followed by the boy's commentary on the rogues he serves, on their cowardice and criminal activity which hardly adds lustre to the glory of battle (25–49). Then follows (50–125) a discussion about the undermining of walls, a task which Fluellen believes is being carried out very badly. MacMorris exhibits confusion and irritation about the progress of the siege. He was called to the breach and to work on the mines, a retreat was sounded, which has left the battle in an uncertain stage of suspension, while the king discusses with his commanders his next move. MacMorris believes they should blow up the town and cut throats, but a parley ensues instead of a renewal of the siege. In the turmoil and uncertainty a disagreement between Fluellen and MacMorris comes close to physical combat.

In the siege we have the juxtaposition of the rhetoric of battle and the pursuit of glory with a rather seedy, very unheroic reality of the way many men respond to the challenge of battle. Shakespeare was aware that without any complex sub-plot in a play so totally focused on war it might be stretching the patience of the audience too far to have no indication of conflict until Agincourt. The presentation of the siege of Harfleur to fill out a long and difficult campaign has its own inherent danger. Presented as a complex issue in itself and with extensive physical representation it might impede the build-up to Agincourt and steal some of the thunder of that engagement. Agincourt must be the climax of the action, and so Harfleur concentrates on those not fighting, on marginal figures. This, we might expect, would leave plenty of space for reports of glorious battle-deeds and the presentation of physical combat of Agincourt. I make this as a sensible argument on Shakespeare's skill at presenting variety in his battle sequences such as he developed elsewhere. The fact of the matter is, however, that though Shakespeare does present variety he does not reserve Agincourt for the exhibition of glorious martial endeavour but pursues the complex weave of events established early in the play and at Harfleur.

(b) Preparations on the battlefield – III. vii. 1 – IV. iii. 132 – 696 lines

After the siege of Harfleur is resolved Shakespeare provides almost 700 more lines (21.9 per cent of the play) to filling out the picture of the mood and atmosphere of those gathered on the battlefield in the two camps. In III. vii we are given a picture of the overwhelming confidence among the French generals as they anticipate a day of sport in chastising the sick and depleted English army. The contempt and haughtiness of these competitive aristocrats is set in perspective by the foreknowledge of the audience of the stunning reversal of French expectations in the surprising outcome.

In the Prologue to Act IV we look again in vain if we seek vital narrative-information in the speech of the Chorus. We have seen the English offer a challenge to battle, we have heard of the sickness of their troops and we have observed already 'The confident and over-lusty French' despising their English opponents. The Chorus merely reviews this material, but it also creates that midnight calm, that pause on the brink of the storm, in which Henry's tour among his soldiers can take place. The Chorus utters that magic word in English history and raises the spirit of the times – 'The name of Agincourt'. The function of the Chorus here is almost that of a priest presiding over and ushering in this sacred ritual of patriotism, this re-enactment of a miracle. The magnificent imagery of this speech could have been divided up among the characters, but, isolated from the action, its cumulative impact swelling into a hymn of praise to the king helps to set up an atmosphere of reverence which causes the audience to pause and focus its attention. There is a sense here of ritual mimesis in which the priest-like Chorus announces the stages of the re-enactment, which are subsequently performed, thus bringing us to that sense of order and unity aimed at by religious rites. This hallowed atmosphere created by the Chorus is supported by echoes of Christian tradition in the action itself.

The king is something more than human in the speech of the Chorus. He is 'like the sun' with miraculous restorative powers; as he moves in the darkness – 'A little touch of Harry in the night' – he has affinities with Christ as the light of the world. The king is the saviour of the English. As Christ came down to earth and assumed the image of a humble carpenter's son, so the king walks among his men disguised, dividing his thoughts with them, attending to the humble almost as though they were his flock and he their shepherd. I am, of course, forcing to the surface those associations which must remain vaguely at the back of our minds as we watch these scenes. The imagery of communion, however, is obvious enough. Henry's famous battle-speech to his soldiers, as unlikely a band of crusaders as the fishermen-disciples themselves, emphasizes the significance of St Crispin's day and the ritual sharing of blood:

> We few, we happy few, we band of brothers;
> For he today that sheds his blood with me
> Shall be my brother. Be he ne'er so vile,
> This day shall gentle his condition;
>
> (IV. iii. 60–3)

The speech draws its strength, too, from the tradition of the *comitatus*, but in its emphasis on the few, on the chosen, it reminds us of the disciples in a hostile land. Henry is depicted as God's chosen instrument to subdue the pride of the French, who have little to say of God and are pictured almost as effete heathens hungering only for glory. The king's anguished soliloquy on the hard duties of being chosen leader is also perhaps, uttered in the loneliness of the night on the eve of a great trial, a very distant reflection of Christ's agony in Gethsemane. Finally, and more fancifully, there is a very faint echo of the journey to Emmaus in the exchange of Williams with Henry, for, having failed to recognize his master disguised in the night, the revelation comes as a shock later on with the king's bounty. These echoes work collectively to create a general atmosphere of religious dedication which is ultimately rewarded with a miracle, the battle-losses at Agincourt – 'O God, thy arm was here!'

A great deal of this atmosphere of ritual stems, as I have suggested, from the speech of the Chorus. But we must also note that there are other elements in the act which prevent it from becoming a totally formalized ritual and which place the battle firmly in the human sphere. We realize, if we think about it for a moment, that this version by the Chorus of Henry's tour among his soldiers is deliberate misdirection, a lack of preparation for the scene as Shakespeare writes it. The king does not appear like a sun to thaw his soldier's fear, but moves disguised, unknown to his soldiers, not to impress and inspire them but to be depressed and dispirited by them. His experience among them begins with comic familiarity and insults from Pistol and ends almost in a brawl with Williams. The Chorus invokes an offstage world that resides principally in its own imagination. What we see onstage is rather more complex than the simplistic vision of a unified host inspired by a heroic king into unquestioning allegiance.

I will look in closer detail at the structure and function of IV. i because it is a key scene and most clearly unfolds the general strategy Shakespeare is pursuing through the entire play. Large segments of the play, and especially the speeches of the Chorus, point us towards the glory of Agincourt, and much of the play is conducted at the levels of monarchs and noblemen negotiating as they move steadily closer to an armed confrontation. There is also a significant admixture of the views and actions of more ordinary men, and the play increases its focus on such matters the closer we come to battle at Agincourt. That concern leads to what is, in effect, almost as significant a climax as the battle itself when, in IV. i, the king confronts the views of his common soldiers. This scene is, with the exception of the extended genealogical ramblings in I. ii and the final wooing scene (V. ii), the longest in the play.

The king on the eve of battle spends only a very limited amount of time with his generals, 60 (20.3 per cent) of the scene's 296 lines. It is a complex scene with a careful symmetrical structure, and the core of it is Henry's various exchanges with and observations of the commoners and the debate with his soldiers in which he has to offer an elaborate theory of self-justification for his actions. He receives opinions rooted in the immediate fears of men far-removed from the theories with which the powerful seek to justify war. The 181-line sequence with the commoners (35–215) is longer than all the rest of the scenes in the play save the two mentioned above and II. ii. It is the longest sustained sequence of interactions the king ever has in the play, and it is augmented, of course, by 55 more lines of the king's brooding soliloquy (IV. i. 216–70) on the significance of the argument. It is the first time in the play that Henry has spoken to anyone beneath captain's rank. In the entire play to this point his exchanges with anyone other than the high command, prelates, and ambassadors have amounted to the 24 lines in his chat with Fluellen (III. vi. 86–109). This, of course, is in total contrast to our experience of Hal in *Henry IV, Part 1*, where he spends more time on stage with his Eastcheap comrades than with the aristocrats, and in *Henry IV, Part 2*, where, though he spends much less time with his tavern-mates, he still has significant interactions with them. This play has, despite the determination of the Chorus to ignore common men in anything other than general accounts of their patriotic fervour, been pressing the actions and views of an assortment of common men on the audience. As the play reaches its climactic moment it presents the king in a confrontation with his commoners. At the heart of all the rhetoric and negotiations and the urgent battle-speeches there is a recognition in the play that not all men have the unalloyed patriotic zeal possessed by the king. The king has to confront his lonely responsibility and to recognize the distance between 'thrice gorgeous ceremony' (252) and the wretched slave 'crammed with distressful bread' (256), and the structure of the scene fixes for the attention of the audience these juxtaposed poles of the play which, I have been indicating, are worked in so many of its details.

Structure of IV. 1:

Segment A: A1 The king and Gloucester and
  then Erpingham 1–34 (34)
A2 The king and Pistol 35–63 (29)
A3 Fluellen and Gower 64–82 (19) – 82

Segment B: B1 The king with Bates, Court, and
  Williams 83–179 (97)

	B2 The king and Williams make a challenge	180–215 (36)	– 133
Segment C:	C1 The king's soliloquy	216–70 (55)	
	C2 The king and Erpingham	271–4 (4)	
	C3 The king's prayer	275–92 (18)	
	C4 The king and Gloucester	293–6 (4)	– 81

The central section of the king's talk with the soldiers is introduced by a section of preparation and followed by one of reflection and continued preparation for battle of almost equal length. Segment A prepares in a variety of ways for the topics of discussion in Segment B, which, in its turn, provokes the brooding reflections of Segment C. The symmetry is underlined by the way conversation with Gloucester and then Erpingham open the scene, and comments and exchanges with these same two figures close the scene.

At the outset (A1) the king makes some general observations about how good can arise out of evil. Because they have to fight the enemy they have to get up early, which is healthy. We are also reminded that death is the end of all and in thinking on our end 'we gather honey from the weed/And make a moral of the devil himself' (11–12). Much of the argument of Segment B has to do with whether the king is responsible for the evil as well as the good that may befall the soldiers fighting in his cause. Williams suggests that the king must bear the burden of the unshriven sins of his soldiers (127–38), which is rather a reversal of what the king optimistically suggests at the outset since it is more like gathering weed from the honey. Henry argues against Williams that war is God's beadle paying out in battle those criminals who have thitherto escaped detection, and that assertion is a continuation of his comment at the outset that good can come out of evil. He also continues with the common soldiers his initial argument that battle makes men think of the necessary preparation they must make for death. We constantly need reminding that we should always be ready for eternity (8–10). The sinner whom death allows to escape his clutches can think on the greatness of God's mercy and can prepare, and remind others to prepare, for their ends (168–75). When the king exchanges greetings with Erpingham an idea is struck which is embroidered in the central segment of the scene. Aging Erpingham claims that he suffers no discomfort in sleeping in the fields for he can proudly assert that he is lying like a king (16–17). The king observes that this method of accepting pain by making a comparison to others is a useful device (18–23). But it is precisely that facility in easing the spirit which the king finds lacking in his common soldiers. Bates says that he believes the king would rather be up to his neck in the Thames than here in France and he would himself rather suffer such discomfort with the king than risk his life at Agincourt. When Henry asserts that the king must be happy where he is Bates wishes that he were in France alone so that he could be captured and ransomed thereby saving the lives of his wretched soldiers (109–15).

The entire scene concerns itself with the nature of the role of king, giving varied evidence on the issue of whether the king is a man like everyone else or whether there are qualities which separate him off from them. Erpingham asserts that he is glad to be as uncomfortable as a king. Bates is far from sure that such suffering is justified. Henry in his borrowed cloak puts on another identity. No longer awesome majesty, he descends into the everyday world and hears not the flattering public eulogy his presence can compel but the disquieting private opinions that men would hide from their king. With Pistol the king plays the part of Harry Leroy and is taken for a Cornishman. Pistol's behaviour here is perfectly calculated to the needs of the scene. He is the epitome of play-acting and, stuffed with fustian stage-rhetoric, is the very image of fake heroism. He is a kind of burlesque version of Henry and is intimately related to the discussion of honour which is featured in this scene. Pistol has no deeper sense of honour than Falstaff, and behind all of his blustering pretence he is, like fat Jack, and like Parolles, a survivor. The soldiers Henry meets later in the scene are not convinced of the justice of the king's cause but they will fight lustily for him, which is more than can be said for Pistol. In his description of the king as 'a bawcock', and a 'heart of gold,/A lad of life, an imp of fame' (44–5), Pistol reminds us of the madcap Hal. We recall how skilled a role-player Hal has been and how easily he passed in disguise among the common people. Here he is returning to that disguise so well that Pistol cannot recognize him. This segment with Pistol has two other details which help out the balance of elements in the entire scene. When Pistol finds out that Harry Leroy is kinsman to Fluellen he gestures contemptuously and leaves with an insult. Later in the scene Williams and the king almost come to blows and exchange gages to be worn in their caps so that they can seek each other out and settle the quarrel after battle. That detail here is anticipated in the king's advice in response to Pistol's boast that he will knock Fluellen's leek about his head on St Davy's day, for Henry warns him not to wear his dagger in his cap that day or he will come to harm. We are reminded that Pistol is a coward and Fluellen is not, and this is yet another way of developing the juxtaposition in the scene of those who are eager to fight and those who are not.

We might wonder why Fluellen makes an appearance here (A3), since he does not exchange any words with the king and does not aid in furthering the plot. Fluellen has an important function in the play of embodying, in contradistinction to several other characters, unquestioning loyalty to the king, a professional soldier's and a military historian's faith in the rules of war and in the ordered pursuit of honour. The battle will not be fought strictly according to the rule, but Fluellen, in his orthodox obedience and his faith in the king's cause, stands out clearly as an admirable foil to the other common soldiers. He is, in a sense, a comic parody within the plot of the homage to tradition that the Chorus presents outside it. But although there is something comic in his pride about his knowledge of the description of the disciplines of war there is something admirable about his simplicity, as indeed the king underlines when he comments that though he is 'a little out of fashion/There is much care and valor in this Welshman' (81–2). If all of Henry's soldiers were like Fluellen he would not have the disquieting conversations he experiences later on in the scene. Fluellen fussing about in the brief interlude, worried about the noise the soldiers are making, reminds us of the function he has performed throughout and, like the recurrence of a musical phrase, acts as a counterpoint to the section that immediately follows. On the warrant of Pompey the Great Fluellen knows that armies should be quiet on the eve of battle, for he is a stickler for 'the ceremonies of war'. But men in battle do not behave according to the book and tradition in which Fluellen believes any more than Shakespeare's play fills out the neat, highly edited version of events that the Chorus proposes. Fluellen, with his rigid code, reminds us how a man can become trapped by ceremony, by the need for things to be seen to be done properly. Fluellen is so concerned with how things ought to be done that in the ensuing battle he is stunned by the experience of the way things, in brutal reality, are actually done. It is in this scene that Henry at last realizes how much he is trapped by the ceremonial aspect of power which separates him from other men and makes him bow under the burden of responsibility for the nation. There is considerable irony in the juxtaposition of Fluellen and Henry, for the king gave himself an education as a seeming madcap which veered wildly from the dignity of the ceremonial role of heir apparent. Hal has become England's most successful king in this culminating play of Shakespeare's history cycle precisely because he threw the rule-book away, held ceremony at arm's length, and appeared either like the dazzling sun or like one of the boys as it suited him. Here is Fluellen talking about rules culled from books as his king walks in disguise among his soldiers. Yet Henry is pursuing, in his own way, a knowledge of what Fluellen calls 'the ceremonies of wars, and the cares of it, and the forms of it, and the sobriety of it, and the modesty of it' (72–4).

The king has learned, in his exchange with Pistol, that his borrowed cloak has made him seem merely an ordinary soldier who can be insulted as easily as the next man. Henry has known from the beginning what it took Richard II a lifetime to learn: that kingship is a role. The man who fills it has the immense task, in seeming to others more than a man, of reminding himself that as a mortal he must not delude himself into believing that he has special privileges which exempt him from mortal flaws and a mortal fate. As Henry asserts here:

I think the king is but a man, as I am. The violet smells to him as it doth to me; all his senses have but human conditions. His ceremonies laid by, in his nakedness he appears but a man; and though his affections are higher mounted than ours, yet when they stoop, they stoop with the like wing. Therefore, when he sees reason of fears, as we do, his fears, out of doubt, be of the same relish as ours are.

(98–106)

This is a step along the road in dealing with the illusions of power that will culminate in the assertion of Lear that a king is, like all men, no more than a poor, bare, forked animal. Henry, having laid his ceremonies by to walk as an ordinary man, finds resistance among the soldiers to his proposition. When he asserts that he could never die so contented as in the king's service because of the justice and honour of his cause he strikes no chiming echo of assent in the soldiers. The sour reply of Williams, 'That's more than we know' (122) measures the gulf between the king and his subjects. In serving without care or knowledge of ultimate consequences they refuse to act on their own independent convictions. The soldiers are soon arguing that if the king's cause is bad then punishment for his sin should be his alone and not shared with those who fight in his cause and he should also accept the blame for any sinners who die unshriven. He must make recompense for their sins because he led them to death in a cause for which they took no responsibility (123–38).

The scene indicates how far reality differs from the embellishment of tradition and memory that the Chorus is engaged in mythologizing. Here we have the situation, warts and all. Implicit in this is an answer also to the apology of the Chorus for the inadequacy of the stage in dealing with glorious events. We have found that the siege of Harfleur is not an unalloyed illumination to accompany the heroic text of 'Once more unto the breach'. We will find that Agincourt is not an unambiguous illumination of the text which rouses men to courage 'at the name of Crispian'. Shakespeare makes it clear that we must have all sides of the story and cannot afford to have less than the whole truth. It becomes evident in every aspect of the play that the tawdriness of the available theatre-furnishings and decor must serve as an appropriate supplement to the way Shakespeare develops his material as a necessary countercheck to the unbridled enthusiasm of the version of events pressed on us by the Chorus.

In setting aside his role Henry has come to a full recognition of the loneliness of his task. He can in disguise even be accused by his own soldiers of being a fool for naïvely trusting in the king's word. He almost comes to blows with them and involves himself in a challenge with Williams because he wants his soldiers to have faith in and share the king's cause. The soldiers are not really cynics; they are realists. If we think of all the deceptions and the breaking of faith among the mighty in the previous three plays of this tetralogy we realize that these soldiers have good cause to be wary. Prince John at Gaultree was typically presenting the two-faced application of power which runs through the plays, and so also was Henry IV with all his counterfeits infesting the battlefield at Shrewsbury. The idea that you should accept things at face value is something which Henry cannot convincingly argue since his whole success has been in his manipulation of masks. He learns the real opinions his soldiers have of their king precisely because he is right here not at all what he seems, because he is onstage and not as the soldiers assume elsewhere offstage.

In the king's soliloquy after the departure of his soldiers the dialectical arguments of the play are resolved. A man in a cloak can be taken for a fool and mocked when his privilege is set aside. When he throws aside the cloak and appears in the robes of majesty the same man can inspire fear and homage but he cannot know whether those around him are in disguise and merely showing him a deceptive surface of allegiance. The king is deceived if he believes that he always receives sweet and sincere homage rather than poisoned flattery. All of the ceremonial accoutrements of power can never give him security and peaceful sleep. His talk of pageantry and ceremony deals with surface appearances, that triumphant exterior view which the Chorus has so persistently promoted. In his talk with his soldiers the king has at last come in contact with its opposite, not the great patriotic crusade which all men joined with unquestioning enthusiasm, but the natural anxious care for the self unmindful of greater causes. The soldiers will do their duty, but not blithely with minds free of all doubts. It is the king's task to look at the larger issues and to do so without being blinded by the ceremonial trappings of his office. A king finally emerges from the cycle of Shakespeare's history plays who, by the nature of his strange education and his practical application of role-playing, comes to an understanding of himself and of man's limitations while he is still at the top of Fortune's wheel.

In this subdued parallel with the loneliness of Christ in Gethsemane when his disciples on watch fell asleep, we are not surprised that Henry soon turns in prayer to God for help in his heavy task. It may be that the uncertainty of Williams about the justice of the king's cause stirs up some flickering sense of guilt which his father, haunted by his usurpation of Richard II, passed on to him. Henry indicates the pains he has taken to expiate the crime. The play does not raise any questions about the legitimacy of Henry's claim to the throne, nor are we made to feel that England will suffer because the blood of an anointed king was spilt. We are reminded, however, that Henry has not forgotten and, we may assume, the common soldier has not forgotten, so that we can see why men found it so difficult to maintain faithful allegiance when those who held the crown came upon it in so many crooked byways. The gulf that exists between king and subject is always there, and in this scene Shakespeare gives ample evidence of how difficult it is to bridge that gulf. Given England's tortuous history we are made forcibly aware what a miraculous triumph Agincourt will be. There are rogues in the English army, though some have already been hanged, but there are loyal and precise men such as Fluellen, and blunt, workmanlike soldiers such as Williams and Bates. The king and his men have different perceptions of their responsibilities, but for once the English are not fighting each other in the seemingly endless, savage dynastic struggles. Despite disagreements and the threat of blows the English in the end have asserted their unity, for, as Bates puts it, 'Be friends, you English fools, be friends! We have French quarrels enow, if you could tell how to reckon' (210–11).

Table 4.3 Sections (*a*) and (*b*) – Focuses of Interest

The English court and High Command		The French court and High Command		The lower orders, captains, and common soldiers	
Chorus I	(34)				
I. i.	(98)				
I. ii.	(311)				
Chorus II	(42)				
				II. i.	(123)
II. ii.	(193)				
				II. iii.	(57)
		II. iv.	(146)		
Chorus III	(35)				
III. i.	(34)				
				III. ii.	(130)
III. iii.	(58)				
		III. iv.	(57)		
		III. v.	(68)		
				III. vi. 1–84	(84)
III. vi. 85–167	(83)				
		III. vii.	(152)		
Chorus IV	(53)				
IV. i. 1–34	(34)				
				IV. i. 35–215	(181)
IV. i. 216–96	(81)				
		IV. ii.	(63)		
IV. iii.	(132)				
1188 (52.8%)		486 (21.6%)		575 (25.6%)	

When we summarize the action in Sections (*a*) and (*b*) off and on the battlefield and before the opening of hostilities at Agincourt it is clear that the play has developed three separate focuses of interest indicated in Table 4.3. The greatest proportion of lines is given to the English high command with the king and his noblemen working out with the prelates and among themselves the strategy for, and justification of, the war. The Chorus devotes all of its attention to the king's cause and presents an image of a country united behind him with little space devoted to the French and none at all to any of the elements which do not fit into its harmonious vision of a united England. The play also gives attention to the strategy and preparation for war among the French high command. The third element of the rogues from Eastcheap and the common soldiers is something like an anti-masque, a view of war from the level of captain and below. There is some overlapping of these elements as when an English ambassador appears at the French court (II. iv) and the various scenes in the English camp where heralds and French ambassadors appear to negotiate terms. Sections (*a*) and (*b*), the preparation for Agincourt, involve 2249 lines (70.8 per cent) of the play. The siege of Harfleur sewn into that sequence is comprised of 161 lines, which is 5 per cent of the whole play or 7.1 per cent of the play until the battle-action

Table 4.4 (c) The Battle of Agincourt – Iv. iv. 1–IV. vii. 81 – 218 lines

(Segment) Description	Category	Entrance	Exit	Number onstage	Lines about action offstage
IV. iv					
(1) *Alarum. Excursions.*	4	6	6	6	
(2) 1–65 (65) Pistol threatens Le Fer who promises him money if he will show mercy.	1	3	2	3	
(3) 66–75 (10) The boy comments on Pistol's bogus bravado, indicates Bardolph and Nym are hanged, and refers to the vulnerability of the baggage train which is guarded only by boys whom he intends to join.	3		1	1	4
IV. v					
(4) 1–24 (24) The French generals in disarray anticipate defeat. *A short alarum.* Bourbon tries to arouse them from thoughts of despair and suicide.	3/4	5	5	5	6
IV. vi					
(5) 1–38 (38) *Alarum.* The king enters with prisoners, asserts that the fighting is not yet done, and receives Exeter's report of the deaths of Suffolk and York. As new alarums sound and the French return in force, Henry orders his soldiers to kill their prisoners.	5/4	8	8	8	34
IV. vii					
(6) 1–10 (10) Fluellen laments with Gower the massacre of the boys guarding the baggage train.	5	2		2	10
(7) 11–49 (39) Fluellen makes a comparison of his gallant king with Alexander the Great.	3			2	
(8) 50–60 (11) *Alarum.* The king with more prisoners vents his anger for the massacre of the boys, orders his herald to challenge the French to fight or 'void the field', and indicates no quarter will be given to the prisoners.	4/3	9		11	10
(9) 61–81 (21) Montjoy begs that the French be allowed to number and bury their dead. Henry indicates uncertainty about victory, but the battle is formally concluded when Montjoy asserts 'the day is yours'.	3	1		12	16
TOTALS		34	22		80

commences at Agincourt. There are 485 lines devoted to the English high command at the outset before the other elements mingle in. The other two elements become ever more significant as the action develops until, on the eve of battle (IV. i), the commoners are given more prominence than the generals. To a considerable degree the encroachment of this anti-masque material prepares us for the way that Shakespeare dramatizes the battle of Agincourt, which is summarized in Table 4.4.

This battle is not one of the more complex mosaics of action that Shakespeare wrote in his career. The only physical activity indicated, other than the flourishing of a sword implied in the text for Pistol, is the excursions at the outset of IV. iv. The battle involves 13 speaking parts, and I have indicated the use of 6 mute supers to play the French prisoners and the members of Henry's entourage, though these roles could be fulfilled by Warwick, Gloucester, and the herald for the English side. It is true of course that many modern productions present us with a lot of physical activity at Agincourt, and it is possible that the original production may have done so. The text does not present such action as central, and we have here Shakespeare's sleight-of-hand in giving us a mosaic of elements of the various ways that men respond to battle. The emphasis in the play is as much or more on the anticipation of battle as in the fighting of it. This is another clear example of one of the principles I have been pursuing in this study of how much Shakespeare relies on reactions as well as actions especially in his dramatization of battle. The mixture of elements here may seem similar to that presented at Shrewsbury. Falstaff's scuttling to safety and his pretended triumph over Percy was one element among several, but in *Henry IV, Part 1*, we did witness several physical combats between major characters. Hal was featured as a pre-eminent champion driving Douglas away, saving his father, and defeating Hotspur. This play dispenses with Falstaff, a figure who undercut the heroic action. Nym and Bardolph are soon disposed of. Agincourt is not, however, presented as a noble, patriotic crusade. We hear of noble deaths but we see none. We see, in fact, no fighting at all. We hear of a brutal massacre of boys and the threat of savage reprisal against the French prisoners. It is the proportions of the various strands of action in this battle that are, from all points of view, quite remarkable.

The play has devoted nearly three-quarters of its lines to the political build-up, the military actions, and diplomatic manœuvres anticipating the clash at Agincourt. There have been 696 lines devoted to an anticipation of battle in both camps on the battlefield before the fighting commences. The first scene devoted to the fighting presents, of all people, Pistol. The blowhard but cowardly Pistol triumphs over Le Fer, who is featured only in this scene (IV. iv) and is even more cowardly than his conqueror. Though the scene designates no clash of swords it is the only battle scene in which any physical activity could be required, as Pistol threatens to cut the throat of his captive, and it is the only scene in which the English and French face each other as warriors onstage. In IV. vii the king enters with Bourbon and other French-men, but they are already prisoners. The scene with Pistol is one of the most extensive burlesques of battle that Shakespeare ever wrote. Pistol demands 'egregious ransom' and makes absurd translations of his victim's trembling replies: 'pitié de moy', 'I will have forty moys'; 'le force de ton bras', 'Brass, cur?'; 'pardonnez-moi!', 'Is that a ton of moys?' Le Fer's comic grovelling and Pistol's swaggering add up to what the audience must accept as quite probably as much the common reality of war as the howling disorder of the French noblemen apprehending defeat in the following scene. The only evidence of glorious nobility and heroism is reported as offstage action when Exeter tells of the deaths of Suffolk and York (IV. vi. 4–32). This is the other pole of battle held in the same mosaic of events as Pistol's fraudulent heroism. It represents the ethos of the war-band which was evoked in the St Crispin day speech, the loving masculine embrace in death of this 'band of brothers'. It will be remembered 'with advantages' as a great feat of this day and will go down in the kind of history that the Chorus so exuberantly represents. But Shakespeare has mingled into his battle details that came from his invention rather than from the chronicles, the kind of details that glorify-ing legends often overlook. Pistol and Le Fer are given a scene onstage of 64 lines; the report of the noble deaths is of offstage action and is given 29 lines – less than half as much space. Indeed about one-third of all the lines in the battle are devoted to accounts of action offstage. We have to note that in addition to the 75 lines of IV. iv we also have another 49 lines (IV. vii. 1–49) devoted to another less-than-central issue, Fluellen's lament of the massacre of the boys and his eulogy of Henry's Welsh origins. These sequences which total 124 lines, constitute 57 per cent of all the action we see of the battle. Pistol is onstage for 65 lines, Fluellen for 49, and King Henry is onstage for 70 lines and speaks 28 lines, which is ten lines fewer than Fluellen speaks. The king is only one element among several in the mixed weave of the battle. This is not an anti-climax, for the whole approach to Agincourt has been a complex mosaic and we have been prepared for the varied endeavours of war in which Henry is given no more prominence than his loyal captain, Fluellen, and no more than Pistol who fights for his own advantage rather than for England's. The pattern will continue, as the private issue of the quarrel with Williams, which was invented by Shakespeare, is given as much prominence after battle as the political issues that are considered. The cumulative effect is to give the play a much broader range than was available in the chronicles, humanizing the king in a presentation of war from a variety of viewpoints.

(b) Resolution of issues after battle – IV. vii. 82 – end of play – 711 lines

The mingling of elements continues as the mood lightens towards comedy and the wooing which closes the play. The three centres of action narrow to two

Table 4.5 (*d*) Areas of interest

Henry's public concerns and the resolution at the French court	The commoners and the resolution of private issues
IV. vii. 82–7 The naming of the battlefield. (6)	
	IV. vii. 88–109 Henry's exchange with Fluellen about Welsh ancestry. (22)
IV. vii. 110–12 Henry sends for numbers of the dead. (3)	
	IV. vii. 113–73 Henry meets Williams, gives his favour to Fluellen, sends him after Williams, with Gloucester and Warwick in attendance, to ensure no harm arises. (61)
	IV. vii. 1–67 Fluellen argues with Williams. The king reveals that he was the figure Williams challenged on the eve of battle. He gives the soldier money and Fluellen tries to add a shilling to the reward. (67)
IV. viii. 68–121 Battle losses are announced, thanks given to God, and a return to England proposed. (54)	
Chorus V. The king's welcome in England and his return to France are reported. (45)	
	V. i. Fluellen resolves his quarrel with Pistol by making him eat his leek. Pistol determines to return home. (81)
V. ii. Henry woos Katharine at the French court. (358)	
Chorus: Epilogue (14)	
480 (67.5%)	231 (32.5%)

(summarized in Table 4.5), as the French court is no longer a separate sphere of interest but the place where Henry concludes his conquest. There is a continuation of the concerns of the commoners as relationships developed before the battle are brought to a resolution.

We can register the significance of this balance of material if we note that 57 lines are devoted to Henry's concern about his battle-losses while 128 lines are given to the prank he plays on Williams and Fluellen. Shakespeare capitalizes on the contact between the king and Fluellen before the battle (III. vi, IV. i), which is brought to fruition in IV. vii and IV. viii, when the challenge made with Williams in IV. i is turned to comic mischief. This bridge-passage prepares the ground for the lighter mood of the concluding scene and allows Fluellen and Williams to show their bravado, and the king to show his generosity to a common soldier. It also allows us to see that though Henry has been almost entirely serious in this play he still retains a taste for mischievous pranks. He was in disguise on the eve of Agincourt just as he was at Gadshill in *Henry IV, Part 1*, and in the Eastcheap tavern in *Henry IV, Part 2*. With Williams he is involved in the kind of ragging that he engaged in with Francis, the drawer, and with Falstaff and others before he became king. This provides an effective transition to the French court where he will jest wittily with Katharine and play the role of a king who is a plain, blunt, workaday figure – a man who can pretend to be not remarkably different from the common soldiers he has mingled with at Agincourt. It is his final performance in the three plays in which he has featured. He has never been the blunt, unsophisticated figure he pretends but he has been able to play it whenever it served his turn. Henry is never the simplified, distilled element of legendary heroism any more than war itself, in Shakespeare's handling, is a straightforward exhibition of noble deeds.

Summary of the sections of the play

(a) Political build-up before the action moves to the battlefield.
Chorus I – III. vi. 167 – 1553 lines — 48.9%

(b) Preparation on the battlefield.
III. vii. 1 – IV. iii. 132 – 696 lines — 21.9%

(c) The battle of Agincourt.
IV. iv. 1 – IV. vii. 81 – 218 lines — 6.8%

(d) Resolution of issues after battle.
IV. vii. 82 – conclusion of play – 711 lines — 22.4%

Before looking at the conclusion of the play and summarizing its structure I want to look at some specific techniques used by Shakespeare to vary his material which in some way compensates for the fact that a play which is primarily devoted to dramatizing a battle campaign does not devote much time to action on the battlefield itself – only 6.8 per cent of the play.

One of the major elements which relates the separate strands of action pursued in the English and French high commands is the sequence of embassies back and forth in the diplomatic manœuvres which seek to avoid the resolution of the issue in battle and the pleas which seek to halt the fighting once it has started. They are spaced regularly throughout the play and cumulatively add a sense of urgency to the action.

(i)   The French ambassador brings the insulting gift of tennis balls to Henry and thus confirms England's determination to undertake the campaign in France: I. iii. 235–98.   (64)

(ii) Exeter visit the French court as England's ambassador, asks for the French crown, and gains no clear submission: I. iv. 75–146.   (72)

(iii) Henry, with his threats of future bloodletting, forces the Governor of Harfleur to yield the town to him: III. iii 1–58.   (58)

(iv) Montjoy brings a demand from the French king that Henry must yield up ransom if he would avoid battle, but despite the sickness of his troops Henry refuses: III. vi. 110–62.   (53)

(v)   Montjoy returns to renew his request for ransom and is again refused: IV. iii. 79–127.   (49)

(vi) Montjoy returns for the last time to admit defeat and ask for permission to bury the dead: IV. vii. 61–86.   (26)

These formal appeals and demands give a rhythmic sequence to the action as the climax approaches. Shakespeare uses this device in many of his plays with battles but does not often organize the elements in a rhythmic sequence over such a long period. They contribute a total of 322 lines of negotiation or about one-tenth of the play.

Another of the most significant continuing sequences is the stream of speeches which provides the audience with images of war. They occur in many scenes building a cumulative sense of impending violence which serve in some sense as both a substitute for and a very elaborate extension of the experience of battle. I will list all of the relevant passages for, though they do not have an equal density or a continuously vivid level of imagery, there is a reiterated series of references to blood, violence, the eager preparation for battle, and the death and destruction which war brings. These speeches provide a recurring motif so that long before we get to Harfleur or Agincourt we are steeped in the language of war which supplements our experience of battle action itself. In this sequence I list all of the references to war but quote only some of the more vivid images and supply asterisks for those passages which are reports of actual events:

(i)   Chorus 1, 5–8 (4), 'the warlike Harry . . . at his heels,/Leashed in like hounds, should famine, sword, and fire/Crouch for employment'; 12–14 (3), 'the very casques/That did affright the air at Agincourt'; 26–7 (2) 'Printing their proud hoofs in the receiving earth'.

(ii) I. ii. 18–28 (11), 'how many now in health/Shall drop their blood in approbation . . . awake our sleeping sword of war . . . the swords/That makes such waste in brief mortality'; 100-16 (17), 'unwind your bloody flag . . . Stood smiling to behold his lion's whelp/Forage in the blood of French nobility . . . Awake remembrance of these valiant dead,/And with your puissant arm renew their feats'; 126–31 (6), 'Whose hearts have left their bodies here in England/And lie pavilioned in the fields of France'; 136–54 (19), describing the Scots 'Came pouring like the tide into a breach,/With ample and brim fullness of his force,/Galling the gleanèd land with hot assays,/Girding with grievous siege castles and towns'; 193–6 (3), even honey-bees are characterized in the terms of warriors 'Make boot upon the summer's velvet buds,/Which pillage they with merry march bring home/To the tent-royal of their emperor'; 262–7 (6), 282–9 (8), 'for many a thousand widows/Shall this his mock mock out their dear husbands,/Mock mothers from their sons, mock castles down'.

(iii)   Chorus II, 1–15 (15), 'honor's thought/Reigns solely in the breast of every man,/They sell the pasture now to buy the horse'.

(iv)   II. iv. 51–62 (12), 'When Crécy battle fatally was struck . . . and smiled to see him/Mangle the work of nature'; 97–109 (13), 'the poor souls for whom this hungry war/Opens his vasty jaws . . . the widow's tears, the orphans' cries,/The deadman's blood, the privèd maidens' groans'; 120–6 (7); 132 (1).

(v)   Chorus III, 25–7 (3), 'see a siege:/Behold the ordnance on their carriages,/With fatal mouths gaping on girded Harfleur'; 32–4 (3), 'the nimble gunner/With linstock now with devilish cannon touches,/And down goes all before them'.

(vi)   III. i. 1–34 (34), 'Once more unto the breach, dear friends, once more,/Or close the wall up with our English dead . . . when the blast of war blows in our ears . . . lend the eye a terrible aspect:/Let it pry through the portage of the head/Like the brass cannon . . . Be copy now to men of grosser blood/And teach them how to war . . . I see you stand like greyhounds in the slips,/Straining upon the start'.

(vii)   *III. ii. 1–9 (9), 'The knocks are too hot . . . sword and shield/In bloody field/Doth win immortal fame'; *50–123 (74), Fluellen and MacMorris discuss the mining of the walls of Harfleur and the confusion of battle.

(viii)   III. iii. 3–43 (441), Henry's speech, painting for the people of Harfleur the horrors of war that will plague them unless they yield, is the most concentrated passage of violent images and indicates how Shakespeare can call up for an audience pictures of war that cannot be presented on the stage. This is not a report of an actual event but an imaginative projection, from a plenitude of past experiences, of the violence and waste that accompanies battle:

> Therefore to our best mercy give yourselves,
> Or, like to men proud of destruction,
> Defy us to our worst; for, as I am a soldier,

A name that in my thoughts becomes me best,
If I begin the batt'ry once again,
I will not leave the half-achievèd Harfleur
Till in her ashes she lie burièd.
The gates of mercy shall be all shut up,
And the fleshèd soldier, rough and hard of heart,
In liberty of bloody hand shall range
With conscience wide as hell, mowing like grass
Your fresh fair virgins and your flow'ring infants.
What is it then to me if impious war,
Arrayed in flames to the prince of fiends,
Do with his smirched complexion all fell feats
Enlinked to waste and desolation?
What is't to me, when you yourselves are cause,
If your pure maidens fall into the hand
Of hot and forcing violation?
What rein can hold licentious wickedness
When down the hill he holds his fierce career?
We may as bootless spend our vain command
Upon th'enragèd soldiers in their spoil
As send precepts to the leviathan
To come ashore. Therefore, you men of Harfleur,
Take pity of your town and of your people
Whiles yet my soldiers are in my command,
Whiles yet the cool and temperate wind of grace
O'erblows the filthy and contagious clouds
Of heady murder, spoil and villainy.
If not – why, in a moment look to see
The blind and bloody soldier with foul hand
Defile the locks of your shrill-shrieking daughters;
Your fathers taken by the silver beards,
And their most reverend heads dashed to the walls;
Your naked infants spitted upon pikes,
Whiles the mad mothers with their howls confused
Do break the clouds, as did the wives of Jewry
At Herod's bloody-hunting slaughtermen.
What say you? Will you yield, and this avoid?
Or guilty in defense, be thus destroyed?

(ix) III. v. 48–55 (8), 'Bar Harry England, that sweeps through our land/With pennons painted in the blood of Harfleur . . . in a captive chariot into Rouen/Bring him our prisoner'.

(x) *III. vi. 1–15 (15), Fluellen's report of Pistol's bravery 'at the pridge'; 66–77 (12), Gower's description of how Pistol and cowards like him will show off at home about their pretended feats in battle; *87–96 (10), Fluellen's report to the king of the skirmish at 'the pridge'; 155–7 (3), 'We shall your tawny ground with your red blood/Discolor'.

(xi)   III. vii. 131–52 (22); the French generals discuss the folly of the English in pursuing battle like mastiffs and their capacity to 'fight like devils'.

(xii)   Chorus IV, 1–53 (53); this speech shows not the violence of war but the expectant activity on the eve of battle 'Steed threatens steed, in high and boastful neighs . . . busy hammers closing rivets up . . . lank-lean cheeks and war-woven coats,/Presenteth them unto the gazing moon/So many horrid ghosts . . . The royal captain of this ruined band . . . A little touch of Harry in the night'.

(xiii)   IV. i. 127–36 (10), 'all those legs and arms, chopped off in battle, shall join together at the latter day . . . some swearing, some crying for a surgeon, some upon their wives left poor behind . . . few die well that die in a battle'; 155–84 (30), 'gored the gentle bosom of peace with pillage and robbery . . . War is his beadle, war is his vengeance . . . every man that dies ill, the ill upon his own head – the king is not to answer it . . . when our throats are cut, he may be ransomed and we ne'er the wiser'.

(xiv)   IV. ii. 1–63 (63); the whole scene in the French camp is full of calls to arms and to the mounting of horses: 'Mount them and make incision in their hides,/That their hot blood may spin in English eyes . . . the shales and husks of men . . . Scarce blood enough in all their sickly veins/To give each naked curtle-axe a stain . . . our squares of battle, were enow/To purge this field of such a hilding foe . . . The horsemen sit like fixed candlesticks/With torch-staves in their hand . . . their executors, the knavish crows,/Fly o'er them all, impatient for their hour'.

(xv)   IV. iii. 44–8 (5), 'Then will he strip his sleeve and show his scars,/And say, "These wounds I had on Crispin's day"'; 61 (1), 'For he today that sheds his blood with me'; 87–8 (2), 'their poor bodies/must lie and fester'; 98–125 (28), 'Dying like men, though buried in dunghills . . . draw their honors reeking up to heaven,/Leaving their earthly parts to choke your clime . . . Our gayness and our gilt are all besmirched/With rainy marching in the painful field . . . they will pluck/The gay new coats o'er the French soldiers' heads'.

All of these evocative lines are before the reports we get of battle-action offstage at Agincourt and in addition to the actual battle-events we witness onstage.

(xvi)   *IV. vi. 4–27 (24), 'Thrice within this hour/I saw him down; thrice up again and fighting/From helmet to the spur all blood he was . . .

And York, all haggled over,/Comes to him, where in gore he lay insteeped,/And takes him by the beard, kisses the gashes/That bloodily did yawn upon his face . . . And so espoused to death, with blood he sealed/A testament of noble-ending love'.

(xvii) *IV. vii. 1–10 (10), 'Kill the poys and the luggage . . . Tis certain there's not a boy left alive . . . Besides, they have burned and carried away all that was in the king's tent; wherefore the king most worthily hath caused every soldier to cut his prisoner's throat'; *50–60 (11), 'we will come to them and make them skirr away as swift as stones . . . we'll cut the throats of those we have'.

(xviii) *IV. viii. 70–121 (52), 'Of princes . . . there lie dead/One hundred twenty-six . . . added to these . . . Eight thousand and four hundred . . . Here was a royal fellowship of death!/Where is the number of our English dead?/Edward the Duke of York, the Earl of Suffolk,/Sir Richard Ketley, Davy Gam, esquire;/None else of name; and of all other men/But five-and-twenty . . . Was ever known so great and little loss/On one part and on th' other?'

I have listed the passages so extensively to give some sense of the astonishingly complete and vivid picture of war which is presented in the play. Every few minutes the sounds and activities of war are being conjured up. Among all of Shakespeare's plays this is the one most steeped in the military world, the one which gives us the clearest sense of the range of its effects, from the stirring panoply of battle-preparation to its horrifyingly violent results. We hear of dismembered limbs, widows, and orphans not once but again and again in the mouths of aristocrats and commoners, and the tide of blood runs through the minds of characters everywhere in the play. The battle itself may last only 218 lines, but the images of battle are constantly mustered for us so that we become, like the characters themselves, almost hypnotized by the portentous ever-accumulating descriptions of war. The lines I have summarized above which present these specific pictures and situations of war amount to 650 lines or 20.4 per cent of the play's lines. The asterisked passages which refer to real events rather than imagined and projected images of battle, constitute 205 lines or only 31.5 per cent of the total. We can see, therefore, how much Shakespeare augments his presentation of Agincourt with poetic evocations which surround us with the experiences of war. It is interesting that the stirring, heroic bravery of battle has to compete with Pistol's absurd ranting, the dishonourable massacre of boys, the trembling terror of the French generals, and the savage disposal of the French prisoners. It is this kind of violence we have heard so much about in the play. I have not included among the passages referring to real situations any of the pictures drawn by the Chorus, and that is because I believe we are encouraged to weigh the evidence of the Chorus with some scepticism. It is true that the Chorus does talk of the lank-leen cheeks and war-worn coats of the English on the eve of Agincourt but it does so to establish its picture of Harry inspiring his pining, pale troops to exuberant patriotism – a picture that the subsequent action does not fulfil. The Chorus does, at the outset, speak of 'famine, sword and fire', but what is remarkable about the evidence it offers is that it is entirely devoted to the spirit-stirring aspects of martial endeavour and not at all to its horrors written so large in so many other passages in the play. The Chorus speaks of mighty princes, proud horses prancing, brave fleets with silken streamers, choice-drawn cavaliers. Its language of pith and puissance is constantly of the breast-beating kind, the promotional rhetoric of recruitment, of pluck triumphing against overwhelming odds. Not once in the 209 lines devoted to its prologues to each act does it mention the word 'blood', and it contributes nothing to the picture of the waste and desolation of war which is pieced together by several of the characters. The Chorus tries to work on our imaginations because the pitiful resources of theatre cannot be relied upon to stir up the enthusiasm appropriate to this ritual re-enactment of a miracle. We are advised to 'sit and see,/Minding true things by what their mock'ries be' (Chorus IV, 52–3). Shakespeare, however, gives us such a variety of evidence that the true and often unpleasant things we confront in the play indicate to us that it may be the speeches of the Chorus whitewashing the war which are to be taken as mockeries.

There is another connecting sequence of events in the play which is indirectly linked to the battle. There is, as I have noted, very little, if any, physical combat onstage in the battle and no designation of a fight between leading characters, a token of war that Shakespeare often exploits. I have indicated a variety of ways related to battle-rhetoric, negotiations, challenges, and the constant stream of evocative poetry which the dramatist uses to fill out the picture of physical action given to us. There is also, throughout the play, a general undercurrent of quarrelling among minor characters which occasionally breaks out into physical blows and often provides comic parodies of bravery before, during, and after the battle. This petty bickering provides a supplement of volatile temper and a threat of physical violence to the brief battle-sequence. This squabbling, boasting, and scuffling give us evidence of the proud stubborn nature of the male ego both at the level of commoners and among the aristocrats. The brush-fire of smouldering squabbles mingles honour and petty childishness to show why men are so prone to risk the chance of war and its desolation in pursuit of glory:

(i)   Pistol and Nym with their turkey-cock blustering bravado quarrel about Nell Quickly and unsheathe their swords in threats to settle the matter by violent means until Bardolph draws and calms them down: II. i. 27–77.   (51)

(ii)   Pistol and Nym fall into further argument and draw their swords once more but do not proceed beyond words of defiance: II. i. 94–109. (16)

(iii) When Bardolph, Nym, and Pistol retire from the fray at Harfleur, Fluellen, disgusted with their truancy, drives them back to the breach possibly with aid of a drawn sword: III. ii. 18. (1)

(iv) In discussing the strategy of the assault on Harfleur the proud, touchy nationals MacMorris and Fluellen fall into disagreement, threaten each other, and almost come to blows, when the trumpet-sound for a parley interrupts them: III. ii. 86–130. (45)

(v) When Pistol asks Fluellen to intercede for Bardolph, who is threatened with hanging for theft, he issues insults in response to the Welshman's punctilious regard for the disciplines of war. This quarrel only reaches a physical resolution after battle: III. vi. 24–58.(35)

(vi) In the competitive boasting in the French camp there is a good deal of friction though it does not break out into physical aggression. The dauphin is humoured, patronized, and mocked with a veiled contempt by his colleagues: III. vii. 1–86. (86)

(vii) On the eve of Agincourt Williams argues with the king so vociferously that they exchange gages with an agreement to fight matters out after battle: IV. i. 180–211. (32)

(viii) Fluellen is set up by the king with his gage, gets into an argument with Williams, and receives a blow from him: IV. viii. 1–67. (67)

(ix) Fluellen concludes his quarrels with Pistol and strikes him, possibly several times, and forces him to eat his leek: V. i. 1–71. (71)

Shakespeare, therefore, devotes 404 lines to these verbal altercations and challenges of a private nature separated from the issue of war. Swords are drawn on at least two occasions, and there are physical blows on two occasions. No sword-fighting is designated in the battle itself, but we have ample evidence elsewhere of the preening, blustering, aggressive male who is ever eager to show that he is on a short fuse and must not be trifled with. There is a comprehensive array of strutting eccentrics stretching from the lowest ranks up to the generals and not excluding the king himself. These vaunting figures are ever eager to display their mettle or to hope that a pretence of bravery will carry them through, and their quarrels give an urgency and edge to the action. We always have the sense that violence could break out among the tetchy combatants within the ranks of each army before they ever confront each other on the field of Agincourt.

The atmosphere of this play is overwhelmingly masculine. There are only four women in the play, and only in the last scene is a woman onstage for an extended period of time. If we add together what they contribute to the play we see what a minuscule proportion of the action is devoted to them:

		Onstage	Speaks
II. i.	Mistress Quickly	73	15
II. iii.	Mistress Quickly	57	27
III. iv.	Katharine	57	37
	Alice	57	20
V. ii.	Queen Isabel	98	14
	Katharine	358	27
	Alice	358	7

There are 545 lines (17.1 per cent) of the play when there are one or more women on the stage. Between them they speak 147 lines (4.6 per cent) in the play. If we consider the part of the play before the action turns to wooing we find the significance of the women almost negligible. In the 2806 lines before V. ii the three women appear for a total of 187 lines (6.7 per cent of those lines) and between them speak 99 lines (3.5 per cent of those lines). In the remainder of the 2619 lines before V. ii women are scarcely considered or even mentioned save as figures to be widowed or raped in the savagery of war. Only in that final scene is there a continuous female presence when Alice and Katharine are left alone with Henry (V. ii. 98–271). In those 174 lines we should note that the lines spoken are divided as follows: Katharine 27, Alice 7, Henry 140. The absence of women helps to emphasize those qualities shown from so many perspectives in the play, the quarrelsome, obsessively aggressive, and competitive masculine temperament.

Now that I have indicated some of the devices used by Shakespeare to tie his play together and enlarge on its martial spirit I turn in conclusion to the final contributions of the Chorus as they complete the structural pattern I have been trying to articulate throughout the play. We are given one more chance to weigh received tradition, and its method of editorializing history, against the way things might more realistically occur, in the speech the Chorus makes as a prologue to Act V. This speech is the most functional of all in terms of transmitting narrative material, and it is the only one which concentrates on abridging the story. Since we return to the English camp in France immediately, it could be argued that there was no necessity for recounting the king's return home and from thence back to France. Shakespeare is so free in his treatment of history that there seems to be no reason why Henry could not have proceeded straight to the French court. But such telescoping of events was not to Shakespeare's advantage here. Even if historically Henry had not in fact returned home, it would have been necessary for Shakespeare to find some matter to form a transitional pause here. The atmosphere of war which has coloured this play must be brought to an end for the change in mood to the gay courtship which concludes the play. The description by the Chorus of Henry's reception in London not only crowns the patriotic fervour which has built up throughout the play but also neatly rounds off the preoccupation with war by a celebration of the return to peace. Even so we must note that the Chorus in providing the narrative link suppresses, in fact, more than it reveals. We are told of the triumphant return to England and a second visit to France for the composition of a treaty. No mention is made of Henry's second invasion of France, a four-year battle campaign the treaty for which was not concluded until five years after Agincourt. Shakespeare had chosen to reduce the battles of five years to one swift and decisive campaign. This streamlining of events frees him to explore a subplot world and to elaborate a variety of moods and attitudes. The Chorus laments the inadequacy of the stage for transmitting history even as Shakespeare is using it to distort history in order to fit his own dramatic patterns.

Productions of this play in recent times have run to a variety of extreme interpretations. Olivier's film version, reflecting the miraculous heroism of the Battle of Britain, as the original play itself, many have claimed, celebrated the destruction of the Armada, appeared to operate on the assumption that Shakespeare's meaning was to be elicited from the attitude of the Chorus. A later London production was played in tin hats and gas-masks among trenches, and Michael Langham's production at Stratford, Ontario, in 1966 with its Brechtian emphasis, operated on the assumption that Shakespeare's sympathies lay with the informal 'chorus' of soldiers. By a rather brutally managed irony the formal Chorus thus appeared to be jingoistic, ludicrously out of touch, in the painting of pretty verbal pictures, with the agonizing realities of war. To interpret *Henry V* in either of the above manners is to be unjust to the balance of evidence in the play. If we assume the Chorus to be Shakespeare's spokesman, we are hard put to it to give sufficient weight to the evidence of the soldiers. If we emphasize the soldiers' views exclusively, then we have to interpret large sections of the play in terms of a crude and heavily obvious irony that is not characteristic of Shakespeare. Henry is placed in a central position to mediate the dialectical contrast. Shakespeare has shaped Hal through two plays with a kind of education unique among the English kings of whom he wrote, so that at last the glories and horrors of martial struggles can meet in the perception of one man. The plainest thing about the complicated structure of this play is that Shakespeare was not writing heavily weighted propaganda for one side of the problem or the other.

The Chorus, then, is throughout the play a strategically used device embodying the popular tradition which glowed, perhaps, in the memory of an Elizabethan audience. Tradition tends to rub away the encrustation of human detail, it glamorizes and has an infinite capacity to forget the human weaknesses among the human strengths. There is some truth still in tradition, but it is not the whole truth. Shakespeare did not wish to destroy the glory of Agincourt, but he realized that by injecting episodic detail he could make it more convincing.

The play is, then, like so many of Shakespeare's plays, a mixture of elements which fulfils the description offered by a Lord in *All's Well That Ends Well*, 'The web of our life is of a mingled yarn, good and ill together' (IV. iii. 66–7). Wars are not fought only by generals nor are all generals admirable. There are figures such as Pistol, Nym, Bardolph, and Le Fer in battle, and there are also figures such as Williams, Fluellen, and Gower. There are braggarts such as the dauphin, a figure not accidentally related to Pistol, and there are heroic soldiers such as Suffolk and York. There are traitors such as Grey, Scroop, and Cambridge and there are loyal warriors such as Erpingham and Exeter. We may not think much of the dauphin or the French king but we can admire the courtesy and decorum of Montjoy as Henry does.

In the final speech of the play the Chorus once again apologizes for the inadequacies of the stage, and yet we, who look back to such scenes as Pistol grovelling before Fluellen's leek, are unlikely to concur in the judgement of the Chorus: 'In little room confining mighty men,/Mangling by starts the full course of their glory' (Epilogue, V. 3–4). The great art of Shakespeare's version of the story lies in the ample room that he has allowed himself and his mangling by starts, in such a varied way, the full course of the action. The Chorus has very clear ideas about what is appropriate to the occasion and does his best to steer matters in the right direction even though he has very serious doubts about whether the theatre or Shakespeare are capable of providing the requisite material. Shakespeare, of course, does the Chorus proud in many circumstances but he embarrasses him in others. The shaping of the response of the audience results from the choices Shakespeare made about what to show onstage and what to keep offstage and transmit by report, and from the proportions of the various elements that are intermingled in the play.

'Is thy news good or bad? Answer to that': The use of reports and the structure of roles in *Romeo and Juliet*

The request Juliet directs to the Nurse (II. v. 35) which forms part of the title of this chapter is of a kind repeated again and again throughout the play. In most of the scenes of *Romeo and Juliet* someone is seeking for news about events that have happened onstage during their absence or events that have occurred elsewhere offstage on which their fate hinges. In this world of secrecy enforced by the poisonous feud much of the play develops around reports and reactions to them, and I will examine a selection of such sequences to indicate how varied Shakespeare's employment of this is and how much the relationship of offstage and onstage events shapes the tragedy. This process of narrative review is one of the most vivid ways of underlining relativity of viewpoint, of how reactions to events are shaped by the emotional attachments which are so strong in this feud-divided society.

We can start out with reporting in its most usual and straightforward function of providing expository detail. Shakespeare sometimes provides expository accounts of events that occurred before the opening of the action which do not seem directly relevant to an understanding of the plot. Though the accumulation of superfluous detail may not provide any dramatic economy in relation to the plot it may vividly serve for a swift unfolding of character. Our initial experience of the Nurse in *Romeo and Juliet* is keyed to her recounting of offstage events, to the transporting of the audience from 'here' to 'there' with vivid pictorial details that have only a marginal function in relation to the plot.

The Nurse has a speech of 33 lines (I. iii. 16–48), to which she adds in repetition 8 more lines (50–7) which are ostensibly devoted to establishing the fact that Juliet is almost fourteen. The youthfulness of Juliet is an important detail of the play, and yet in establishing that fact the Nurse's 41 lines of speech are superfluous because Lady Capulet (line 12) has already given her age. The Nurse's rambling, self-indulgent method of calculating Juliet's age by recalling Lammas Eve and her weaning at the age of three includes a sequence of memories that are situated eleven years in the past and that are not directly related to the business Lady Capulet is pursuing in the scene. We might feel that we do not really need the half of these details which the gossipy nurse fondly dwells on. We learn that the Nurse had a daughter, Susan, now dead, of the same age as Juliet, that Juliet was weaned in the sunlight under the dovehouse wall amidst the shaking of an earthquake at the time when the Capulet parents were in Mantua. We know that Juliet could already walk because of the jest the Nurse's now-dead husband shared when she fell down and bumped her forehead. The whole point of this vivid accumulation of information is that it seems to be superfluous, and an elaborate meander in arriving at the issue of the proposed match to Paris. The speech, however, serves a range of functions with quite remarkable economy. As the equivalent of what in film is called an establishing shot it conveys the full flavour of the Nurse's character in one fell swoop. It is one of the most vivid and compressed introductions of a character in world drama, and an actress given such a launching will require only grace notes thereafter.

The essence of the Nurse, which is fully exposed in two of her reports I will examine later (II. v, III. ii), is her gossipy attention to confusing or distracting irrelevances, her enjoyment of teasing Juliet, her earthy enjoyment of bawdy innuendo, her complacent assumption of a place of special trust in the family and of a closeness to Juliet in particular. All of this is established in this first extensive speech. The fact that she has lost her own child, Susan, who was of an age with Juliet, and that she is a widow suggests that she will have a special attachment to Juliet and to the family. The intimacy indicated in having breast-fed Juliet and in the weaning process establishes the easy familiarity they share and the indulgent way in which she aids in the plotting of the secret marriage to Romeo. The first thing we hear about the relationship of the Nurse and Juliet is in the tetchy falling-out in the weaning because of the wormwood on the nipple. As the experience of growing up and falling in love separates Juliet from her Nurse she will be left isolated to act courageously alone when she weans herself from the bitter wormwood of the Nurse's feckless advice to forget Romeo and marry Paris. In placing this speech about Juliet's infancy in the midst of a discussion about the selecting of her partner in marriage we are made aware of how she is still young enough to be reminded of her childish habits even though she is soon to be exuberantly in love, married, and facing a terrifying situation that would test the will and courage of any adult. The Nurse is asked by Lady Capulet to stop rambling on (49), a request which sparks a seven-line bawdy, leering repetition of her story, and she is only finally diverted from her chatter by Juliet. One can suspect that Juliet, who may be trying to maintain some poise as she approaches serious adult decisions such as the choosing of a marriage-partner, may find the Nurse's insistent recall of her infancy a little irritating and demeaning enough to draw her remark of impatient asperity (58) in heading off a story that the Nurse may often wearyingly repeat. So the interaction which arises from this over-extended story does prepare us for the frequent teasings which are at the heart of their relationship.

In a more general sense this speech and the space given to its garrulous repetitions helps to establish elements which are crucial to the atmosphere of the play. It is a vivid example of the domestic detail that is such an important element threaded through the play. It contributes to the sense we have of the enclosed and protected world of women that is situated almost entirely, before the last scene, within houses as opposed to the freer-ranging masculine society which can wander the streets. The fact that Shakespeare can give such space to details tangential to the immediate needs of the plot establishes the relaxed atmosphere which continues through much of the first half of the play in the teasing exchanges, the bawdy innuendo, and the bouts of wit. The speech, in its recall of the comfortable routine of life in the sunshine near the dovehouse wall, disturbed by the threatening rumble of an earthquake and the fall and injury of young Juliet is an emblem, in a sweet remembrance of innocence, of the whole process which this play will develop of an expansive world of comedy darkened by an encroaching tragedy. We may recall at the end of the play, when Juliet has fallen into a charnel-house and onto a dagger, that we first heard of her falling down as a child and getting 'A bump as big as a young cock'rel's stone'. The fate of falling backwards when she has more wit, predicted for her by the earthy, amiable husband of the Nurse, is not one she has been given much opportunity to enjoy. Because of this speech which creates for us a moment of her childhood the audience has an experience of Juliet that makes our sense of her loss all the more poignant because her transition from cradle to grave is so swift.

In *Romeo and Juliet* the central sequence and turning-point of the play occurs in III. i in the violent intercession of the feud which brings death to Mercutio and Tybalt and causes the banishment of Romeo. I wish to examine the way that Shakespeare develops a complex sequence of reactions in the transmission of reports to those who were offstage during the events the audience has witnessed onstage. In the scenes following III. i there is little forward movement of the plot, but in the intensive concentration on reactions Shakespeare first broaches what is to become a radical shift in the focus of the play as Juliet moves to the centre of our attention and Romeo is shifted to the margins. As I have indicated, reporting offstage and onstage events is not simply used as a practical device for keeping characters and audience abreast of the necessary details which amplify and drive the plot along. It may be at the very heart of the problem, on which Shakespeare's plays enlarge, about the difficulty of establishing what has happened, which we can gather from the varying reactions and versions of events of those observing and taking part in them. We can tell something of the problems of reporting, and the ambiguity, relativity of viewpoint, and assumed bias that can be associated with it, by noting the way Shakespeare uses reports, and reactions to them, of this central intercession of the feud.

Benvolio's account of the fighting and bloodshed in the outbreak of the feud is a report of 28 lines (III. i. 140–3, 150–73) to Prince Escalus of events which the audience has witnessed and which occupied 80 lines (III. i. 55–134). Benvolio was established as a reliable reporter of events in a previous intercession of the feud at the opening of the play (I. i. 104–13), and in his account of the lovelorn Romeo to the Montagues (I. i. 116–28). He has been featured as a sensible, peaceful youth in his attempt to head off dangerous street-fights and in his friendly, temperate advice to Romeo. Benvolio is not given to the kind of excesses we have observed in Tybalt and Romeo nor to the mocking raillery and energetic wit we find in Mercutio. He is a figure from whom, in the wild confusion and passionate juxtapositions of the brawling outbreaks of the feud, we might expect a fair and reasonably accurate report. He is, of course, now that Mercutio and Tybalt are dead, and Romeo fled, the only available witness of the sequence of events. It is just possible that all of the events in III. i could have been reported to the Prince before his entrance thus saving the audience from an account of events already witnessed. It can be argued that in the duelling bouts we have had a continuous crescendo of tumultuous events involving a rapid sequence of entrances and exits so that the audience is now ready for a breathing space in which there is some gradual reassertion of order and control. Benvolio's succinct summary of events provides this transition, like a bridge in music, from the violence of the fighting to the heavy judgement and sentence of the Prince.

Benvolio supplies a tight and almost completely accurate précis of a complex sequence of events. He makes sure that Romeo's resistance to Tybalt's encouragement to fight is given prominence. He records how Romeo reminded everyone of the Prince's penalties to be incurred if the feud were renewed – a reference to Romeo's lines at III. i. 84–8. Benvolio does not get the order of events quite right. Romeo warned of the Prince's displeasure after the fighting had begun, and it was during that intrusion that Tybalt took 'his envious thrust' at Mercutio under Romeo's arm. He does, nevertheless, include all of the pertinent facts. The audience can recognize that Benvolio's account is remarkably free of rancour and bias. It is true that he edits out much of the build-up to the fighting before Romeo entered. He says little of Mercutio's touchiness and the fact that, spoiling for a fight to defend his injured honour, it was the Prince's kinsman who drew first. His version of the events puts a good deal of the blame on Tybalt, but the audience can hardly believe that to be bias. Tybalt has, on all three occasions he has appeared, been the spark eager to set the feud alight. He came into this scene searching the streets for Romeo and eager to fight, pursued persistently a course of insults, and dishonourably killed Mercutio by taking advantage of the confusion. Benvolio could have painted an even more unsympathetic picture of Tybalt without straining the truth. He omits to mention also his own attempt to head off the danger of street-brawling (1–4, 49–52). He may do so, perhaps, to focus attention on Romeo's attempts at peace-making (162–7) in the hope of mitigating the severe punishment that his cousin can expect for disturbing the quiet of Verona's streets. The audience must feel, I believe, that Benvolio's report, given the danger Romeo is in, is remarkably straightforward and informed by balance and a sense of proportion. There is no one else in the play who could have presented it so objectively save, of course, Friar Laurence, the figure who will be called on at the end of the play to present a report to the Prince of the events surrounding the third outbreak of sword-play and the tragic complexity of events shaped by the deadly enmity of the feud.

This sequence does not, in fact, provide the audience with an account of events at variance with its own first-hand experience of them. What it does is to underline the reflex assumption that reporting can hardly be expected, in such passionate and involved events, to be objective. Lady Capulet inevitably and understandably assumes that Benvolio's report is 'false', biased as it must be in recounting the death of a Capulet by the hand of a Montague kinsman (174–9). She seems to believe that Tybalt may have been the victim of an ambush which Benvolio has deliberately failed to report when she asserts 'those twenty could but kill one life'. This encounter was not like the general mêlée in I. i, but, by suggesting that it was, Capulet's wife can shift the focus away from the central import of Benvolio's account that Tybalt was the provoker of the violence and slew Mercutio, the Prince's kinsman, by a treacherous, underhand manœuvre. The audience observed only four people involved in sword-play, but we can see how, in such deep enmity, Lady Capulet might come to believe more plausibly in her imaginative recreation of an event she did not witness than in any version a Montague might offer. Truth cannot be gauged only from the standpoint of the speaker; it is also evaluated by the auditor. The reception of a transmission is dependent on plausibility and probability. Lady Capulet projects her own sense of bias and by reflex dismisses the report of Benvolio. The fact that she is wrong serves a number of functions simultaneously; it underlines our privileged immunity as an audience, differentiating our perception from that of the characters, and making us aware that, in the normal flow of life outside the theatre, we are as prone as they are to mistake truth for lies and lies for truth; it further defines the unusual nature of Benvolio in this play which throws up the passionate excesses of those around him by contrast; it reminds us how little impact truth can make in a society riven by passionate excess, and it prepares us to accept the fact that the feud cannot be dispelled by the truth but only by the waste of lives resulting from the suppression of the truth. The reflex assumption Lady Capulet asserts of Benvolio ('Affection makes him false') becomes hauntingly true for Romeo and Juliet whose affection makes them false to their families as, at the cost of their lives, they remain true to each other. A skilful dramatist, far from being limited by the mechanical requirements of transmitting information, can exploit them to his own advantage. Benvolio's report, however, is only a brief preface to the remarkable scene developed entirely out of the confusions of reporting when the Nurse brings the news to Juliet in III. ii.

It is important to remember that the Nurse's account is not only set in elaborate contrast to Benvolio's report; it is very deliberately linked to an earlier scene of the Nurse reporting news to Juliet. The sequence in II. v is worked out of the arrangements the Nurse has made with Romeo about the marriage at II. iv. 169–82. Our witnessing of that exchange does not mean that its dramatic potential has been exhausted. The urgency of Juliet as she waits for the news and the torment she is put through in trying to extract it from the Nurse, who deliberately teases her by refusing to satisfy her anguished curiosity immediately, give us a vivid sense of youthful passion. The essential news which Juliet needs is delivered in 8 lines (II. v. 67–74), but the deliberate meanders leading up to the transmission of the report occupy 49 lines (II. v. 18–66). This method of stringing out the report is not a sacrifice of dramatic economy but an exploitation of it to provide a contrast, that is written large enough through the play, between the earthy, weary, somewhat callous and calculating Nurse and the excited, urgent, spontaneous, and courageous Juliet, a contrast which is part of a more general division between old and young in the play.

In III. ii we again have Juliet in a state of eager anticipation as she waits for news of Romeo's plans to consummate their marriage, completely unaware of events that have blighted their love at its inception. We have had Benvolio's brief and business-like report which gets an essential turn in the plot into place. A less inventive dramatist might have thought that an event onstage followed by one report of it, followed by yet another report, would be a cumbersome interruption to the flow of events. It would, after all, be quite possible to resolve the difficulty by bringing Juliet on in III. ii already fully in possession of the news, in tears and subject to the Nurse's solicitude. It is typical of Shakespeare's method of focusing on reaction as much as on action that he met the problem head-on and made a virtue out of necessity, giving us not a brief report of an action we have witnessed and transmitted already to those not present but a scene of 143 lines completely focused on Juliet at a turning-point in her life. In II. v we had an amusing and relaxed scene where Juliet was in confusion because of the wilful teasing and delay of the Nurse. In III. ii, after the passage of so little time, we have a scene fraught with tension where confusion results not from deliberate teasing and delay but from an overwhelming grief. In II. v the Nurse gasped out fragments of news as comic red herrings amid bouts of pretended irritation and irrelevant inquiries – her aching head, her aching back, 'Have you dined at home?', 'Where is your mother?', etc. In III. ii the Nurse, genuinely upset and wrapped up in her own grief, cannot recount events in any coherent fashion.

Shakespeare structures the scene in segments which alternate between hope and despair, an oscillation which is initiated by the Nurse's confusing transmission of the news:

(i) In soliloquy Juliet eagerly anticipates Romeo's arrival and assumes, on the Nurse's arrival, that she will receive news about his plans to visit her (1–35).

(ii) The Nurse starts out with news of Tybalt's death, but, in failing to name him, leads Juliet, who has asked for news of her husband, to believe that Romeo is dead (35–40).

(iii) Still failing to name Tybalt and blaming Romeo for his death the Nurse confirms Juliet's fears. In reply to Juliet's demands for clarity and certain knowledge the Nurse dwells, without distinguishing between the combatants, Romeo and Tybalt, on the latter's deadly wound (40–60).

(iv) The Nurse finally attaches the name of Tybalt to the corpse she has been lamenting, which is almost 30 lines after she entered in distress. Juliet, already convinced that Romeo is dead, absorbs this news of a second death as a further blow (60–8).

(v) The Nurse emerges from her emotional trance and finally clarifies the issue by stating that Romeo is banished for killing Tybalt (69–70).

Reports usually take characters and audience from 'here' to 'there', from 'now' to 'then', but the Nurse is ineffective in performing that function because her mind is so completely 'there' and 'then', caught in the tide of her own grief and anger, unable to disentangle itself from the horrible sight of Tybalt's dead body, that she cannot hold the event at a distance to provide a clear account to Juliet, who must wander in error toward the truth which remains concealed for almost 40 lines. Benvolio gave a clear and coherent account in 24 lines, but even after 40 lines Juliet knows only of Romeo's banishment for slaying Tybalt. She knows nothing of the detail Benvolio has supplied – the order of the violent events, the fiery behaviour of Tybalt, the initial unwillingness of Romeo to fight, the interposition of Mercutio, the treacherous killing of Mercutio under Romeo's arm, and Romeo's embroilment in the feud to avenge his friend's death. Since there is no evidence that she was present in III. i to hear Benvolio's account the Nurse says nothing and probably knows nothing of the motivations involved in the duelling. Her views have been formed from third-hand accounts amid the bias of the Capulet household. She says she swooned when she saw Tybalt's body. We can assume, in any case, that, like Lady Capulet, she would not be inclined to believe an accurate account of the violent feud. It is enough for her that if Tybalt is dead then the Montague is to blame. She dwells only on the two results that are significant to the different members of the Capulet household, but what she leaves out, or does not know about, is as significant for the audience as the confusing manner in which she delivers the news.

Juliet never finds out in this scene about the death of Mercutio and the issues of honour and responsibility for his death which embroiled Romeo in the feud. This serves Shakespeare's purpose in another way, for it allows him to exhibit the strength of Juliet's faith in and trust of Romeo. Her reactions indicate that she is torn in her emotional attachment and loyalties between Tybalt and Romeo. The Nurse, who has probably watched Tybalt grow up from childhood and is conditioned in her hatred of the Montagues, cannot be expected to have an objective view of Romeo's involvement in the feud even if she knew the details of it. Her attack on Romeo prompts Juliet to declare her faith in his honourable intentions (89–94). The events themselves would have justified Juliet's faith, but the fact that she can assert it without knowledge of them strengthens our awareness of her commitment to love, to the force which transcends the feud rather than to the rooted hatred which fuels it.

The play constantly juxtaposes the sterile values of the feud with the fruit-ful possibilities in the relationship of Romeo and Juliet. In the masked ball where the two first meet we have their delight in love set against the corrosive fury of the tetchy Tybalt. When challenged to a duel in III. i Romeo endured Tybalt's insults for the sake of his new-found love. In this scene, which reports on that confrontation, we again have the two forces set in contrast, and this is the true purpose of the scene in the extensive elabora-tion of news and the reaction it provokes. The Nurse represents the forces that assert a primary loyalty to blood-kin, to the maintenance of division, to the conviction that those on your side are unquestionably right. Juliet is a battleground for warring impulses. Her allegiance to her family and her cousin conflicts with loyalty to her new family in her marriage to Romeo. The contrast is effective because the opposed viewpoints are not, as they so often are in other plays, a result of differing levels of awareness. Once the story is straightened out the Nurse and Juliet are reacting to the same facts. The Nurse knows quite well that Juliet is married and yet gives less weight to that than she does to allegiance to the Capulet family. Juliet's ability to stand out against the imperatives of the feud is based on an ordering of priorities that is quite different from those of the Nurse. She is also being set in contrast to Romeo, for his reflex response to the deadly demands of the feud has led to the banishment which will separate him from his wife. Juliet struggles with warring impulses within her as Romeo did but she resolves them in favour of love rather than loyalty to family as he did not. Her initial reaction, which is a natural grief at her cousin's death, stems from her upbringing among the Capulets (III. ii. 71, 73–85). Yet even in elaborating her sense of outrage at a kinsman's death her description of his killer, Romeo, uncovers, in its sequence of oxymora, her ambiguous reaction ('Beautiful tyrant! fiend angelical!', 75); and it only needs the condemnation of Romeo by the Nurse to turn her into his stout defender. The Nurse's state-ment (85–9) is a blanket condemnation of all men as faithless. Juliet's response demonstrates that in some senses she is a characteristic product of her aristocratic ranking in society, in the high valuation she sets on honour. Without any evidence of what happened in the streets she is confident that Romeo must have been compelled to action in defence of his honour. In countering the Nurse's commitment to the bonds of kinship with her own response to the bond of marriage she works her way to a logical resolution of her sense of priorities (96–107).

The anguish of Juliet, as she recalls the second of the two details of the Nurse's report, Romeo's banishment, moves the Nurse to try to bring Romeo to her before he leaves Verona. Juliet indicates the depth of her grief and of her love when she asserts that it would have been easier for her to mourn the death of her father or mother along with Tybalt than to accept Romeo's banishment (116–20). She hears that her parents are wailing over Tybalt's corpse and she says that her own tears will be devoted to her loss of Romeo (128–31), and thus very clearly signifies her sense of isolation within her family to which much of the second half of this play is devoted. In Lady Capulet's reaction to Benvolio's temperate and fair account of the fighting we are aware that the feud poisons the possibility of seeing anything objectively. The Nurse's instinct in putting family first, though she knows of the marriage to Romeo, prepares the audience for her eventual suggestion that Juliet ignore her first marriage, forget Romeo, and accept the union with Paris that her father proposes, which will leave Juliet isolated from all counsel save that of Friar Laurence (III. v. 214–44).

By the end of III. ii we are still not done with the reports that stem from the action in III. i. Romeo in Friar Laurence's cell in III. iii does not yet know of his banishment, and most of the scene is devoted to his anguished reaction to that news and the friar's attempt to interpret his fate as an unexpected blessing of clemency. Like Juliet in the previous scene, who uses the words 'banished' and 'banishment' 6 times in 20 lines (III. ii. 112–31), we find Romeo obsessed with the word. He speaks these words 14 times in 56 lines (III. iii. 12–67), and the friar uses them 4 times. The despair of the two lovers is linked when the Nurse appears in the friar's cell to report on how Juliet has taken the news. Some of her report (III. iii. 84–7, 99–102) refers to the behaviour we have witnessed, but in the extremity of emotions described seems to refer to a developing despair and anguish after the conclusion of that scene.

If we look back over the whole sequence we can see how much time Shakespeare has devoted to reports and reactions to the climactic sequence of actions in III. i. It is one of the longest such sequences in his plays. The only arrangements of forward-looking action are those which will help Romeo to visit Juliet before he leaves Verona. Tybalt dies at III. i. 129, and reports on, reactions to, and the consequences of that event cover 384 lines [III. i. 130–95 (66), III. ii (143), III. iii (175)]. Only in III. iv do we turn to the new matter of Capulet's arrangements for the marriage of Paris to his

Table 5.1 The two main roles in the first half of the play

Act/Scene	Lines	Romeo onstage	Romeo's lines	Juliet onstage	Juliet's lines	Romeo and Juliet onstage together
Chorus I	14					
I. i.	236	83	61½			
I. ii.	103	59	28½			
I. iii.	105			101	6½	
I. iv.	114	114	31			
I. v.	144	112	25½	129	17½	112
Chorus II	14					
II. i.	42	42	2			
II. ii.	190	190	80	179	108½	179
II. iii.	94	72	23½			
II. iv.	204	167	48			
II. v.	78			78	42½	
II. vi.	37	37	12	22	7	22
III. i. 1–129	129	75	34			
T O T A L S	1504	951	346	509	182	313

daughter, though it, too, stems from the death of Tybalt, in that Capulet speeds on the marriage to distract Juliet from what he believes to be the dangerous grief she suffers from in lamenting her cousin's death.

The most significant factor structurally about this sequence is that it initiates a process which develops into a fundamental switch in the focus of the play. If we look at the play as being composed of two almost balanced halves arranged around a turning-point at the instant when Romeo slays Tybalt, where the audience knows that an ineluctable movement towards a tragic conclusion is set in motion, then we can see that there is a very distinct contrast in the two halves in the way in which Romeo and Juliet are featured onstage and in the number of lines they speak. In the first half, summarized in Table 5.1, we see a great deal of Romeo and much less of Juliet, proportions which are reversed in the second part. The focus in this first half of the play is weighted towards Romeo who appears in 10 of the 12 scenes. He is onstage for 63.2 per cent of the lines and he speaks 23 per cent of them. Juliet appears in only 5 of the 12 scenes, is onstage for 33.8 per cent of the lines, only a little over half as much as Romeo, and speaks only 12.1 per cent of them, slightly more than half as many as Romeo. They have been together onstage for 20.8 per cent of the play in its first half.

When we turn to the second half of the play we find that we are much more prominently concerned with the actions and reactions of Juliet in her desperate isolation amid her family. The change in emphasis in the two roles is summarized in Table 5.2. In the second half of the play Juliet appears in 7 of the 13 scenes, is onstage for 69 per cent of the lines, and speaks 23.2 per cent of them. Romeo is onstage in 5 of the 13 scenes, is onstage for 41 per cent of them, about 60 per cent of the time Juliet is onstage, and he speaks only 16.5 per cent of the lines. Perhaps of equal significance is the

Table 5.2 The two main roles in the second half of the play

Act/Scene	Lines	Romeo onstage	Romeo's lines	Juliet onstage	Juliet's lines	Romeo and Juliet onstage together
III. i. 130–95	66	5	½			
III. ii.	143			143	114	
III. iii.	175	172	69½			
III. iv.	36					
III. v.	244	59	24	244	103	59
IV. i.	126			109	47½	
IV. ii.	47			23	12	
IV. iii.	58			58	55½	
IV. iv.	28					
IV. v.	141			141[a]		
V. i.	86	86	69½			
V. ii.	29					
V. iii.	310	289	82	310[b]	13	310
TOTALS	1489	611	245½	1028	345	369

[a] I count Juliet as onstage for all of this scene though the Pelican edition indicates that curtains reveal her in her bed for only part of it.

[b] I assume here that Juliet is not concealed on her tomb in a curtained inner stage (as scholars once believed, although this now commands less support), since it seems to me unlikely that such important sequences (V. iii. 84–120, 144–70) could be played so far from the audience within the confines of the inner stage or a discovery space.

fact that Juliet has two lengthy periods in the opening half of the play when she is offstage. She does not appear until I. iii. 5 when the play has run 357 lines. She is absent again from II. ii. 186 until the opening of II. v, a gap of 302 lines. In the first half of the play Romeo is offstage only once for more than a hundred lines (I. iii). In the second half he is offstage for the 143 lines of III. ii and for 585 lines from III. v. 59 to his re-emergence onstage at the opening of V. i, a sequence I will examine next. They are onstage together in the second half of the play for 369 lines, or 24.8 per cent of it, but they are, of course, together in full consciousness and in mutual interaction only for the opening 59 lines of III. v, the scene of their parting.

This shift in focus begins to become evident in the sequence of reports and reactions to the central intercession of the feud. Romeo has committed the action which exiles him from Verona and from the action to which Shakespeare now chooses to give prominence. Our concern is to be with Juliet's desperate situation, her reactions to the banishment of Romeo, to the pressure put on her to marry Paris, to the friar's risky plot to reunite her with Romeo, to the potion that is the agency of the plot, and to the tragic failure of that plot. Romeo becomes a marginal figure out of touch with these events, who disappears from the play for almost one-fifth of its length. In this second half of the play we find 66.9 per cent of Juliet's onstage life in the whole play and 65.5 per cent of the lines she speaks in the play. So this sequence of reports is a very significant transition-point for both of the main characters. The scene she shares with the Nurse who brings her confusing and ultimately dreadful news (III. ii) contributes 9.3 per cent of her onstage life, and in it she speaks 21.6 per cent of all her lines. Before this scene she has spoken only 182 lines in the play, and in this pivotal scene she speaks 114 lines. Shakespeare supplies an opportunity for an extensive display of Romeo's reaction to news of his banishment which he receives in Friar Laurence's cell only a little before his farewell to Juliet and his subsequent extensive absence. In III. iii he is onstage for 172 lines (or 28 per cent of the time he is onstage in this second half), and in his despair he speaks over a quarter of all the lines he utters in it. I have indicated that there are ways, had Shakespeare chosen, to avoid this sequence of reactions and reports. Instead, he elaborates it as a structural pause and a redirection of the drive and focus of the play. Until III. i events have been ripening towards the possibility of a comic resolution. The violence of the feud shears through those threads of hope, and Shakespeare provides a lengthy interlude in which the characters learn of the disaster and count the cost of the damage. The consequences of one thrust of the sword generate almost 400 lines of reaction.

Romeo's absence towards the end of Act III and for all of Act IV in *Romeo and Juliet* is made plausible by his banishment from Verona, but since Shakespeare shows us some of the scenes in Mantua and was quite capable of showing us Romeo there at any time it is obvious that the absence serves other purposes. Romeo has not had any extended offstage absences in the first half of the play. He is absent for the 105 lines of I. iii, for the 78 lines of II. v, and for 207 lines from III. i. 135 to III. iii. 3. But since the weight of the play is divided between two characters Shakespeare is able to introduce an extensive absence for Romeo in Act IV as he turns to the developments revolving around Juliet in Verona, action which makes intermittent reference to Romeo as outlined in Table 5.3. In some tragedies, such as *Macbeth* and *Coriolanus*, we are given a sense of the hero's potency during his exile or absence from the play, but that is far from the case here where Romeo's actions have brought him banishment, separation, and despair. When Romeo has departed in III. v Lady Capulet enters to comfort Juliet, talking of the villain, Romeo, who has slaughtered Tybalt and the revenge they should seek against him (80–104). Juliet appears to go along with her ideas though her attitude to Romeo is phrased in double meanings perceived only by the audience. When Paris is proposed as a husband she asserts she would sooner marry Romeo, the Capulet enemy (123). Thereafter Romeo is not referred to again until the scene's conclusion when Juliet seeks the Nurse's advice (207–47). So a little more than one-third of this segment (67 of 185 lines) is devoted to talk of Romeo with a heavy concentration of specific references [Romeo (6), him (10), he (6), husband (2), your first (husband) (2), and 1 each of – the villain, traitor murderer, banished runagate, his, my lord – for a total of 31]. In IV. i we have Paris making arrangements for marriage

Table 5.3 References to Romeo during his absence

Scene	Lines	Lines referring to Romeo	Words referring to Romeo
III. v. 60–244	185	67	31
IV. i.	126	18	8
IV. ii.	47	0	0
IV. iii.	58	16	6
IV. iv.	28	0	0
IV. v.	141	0	0
T O T A L S	585	101	45

with the aid of Friar Laurence until Juliet enters seeking some remedy for her dilemma. All of this is designed to protect her marriage to Romeo, but he is only briefly referred to at 55–9, 88, 113–24 – 18 lines evoking Romeo with 8 specific references [Romeo (4), her (2), my sweet love, and thy lord, 1 each]. As Juliet agrees to the marriage to Paris in IV. ii there is no reference to Romeo. Left alone, in IV. iii, to take the drug Juliet invokes Romeo in 16 lines (24–35, 55–8) and 6 specific references [Romeo (5), thee (1)]. During the discovery of the 'dead' Juliet and the lamentation for her in the 169 lines of IV. iv and IV. v there is no reference to Romeo.

The sense we have that Romeo and Juliet are victims of forces beyond their control and of the well-meaning but disastrous plans others have for them is reinforced by the intermittent references to the absent Romeo as Juliet is swept along by events and allowed only brief periods to devote to thoughts of him and plans to reunite with him. All but 14 of the 45 references to Romeo are made in the continuation of the action immediately following his departure, and most of them are made when Juliet has to pretend to go along with her mother's views of him as a villain and murderer. In the 400 lines after that scene (III. v) until Romeo re-emerges only 34 of those lines, containing the remaining 14 references, are devoted to keeping him at the margin of the audience's attention. We do not, of course, forget Romeo, but the play is written in a way which impresses on us how tenuous are the hopes that things will turn out well. Romeo recedes out of contact as other concerns fill the stage, and in the period of more than half an hour that he is absent there are extensive passages in which he is not mentioned at all. Juliet's hope, Romeo, seems to flicker like a candle in the darkness, in danger of being extinguished by the press of events and the possibility of confusion, as indeed it turns out in the miscarried message. Romeo's absence, therefore, serves to underline what becomes now the chief focus of attention – the increasing isolation of Juliet. Bereft of her husband she is harangued by her parents, offered the Nurse's completely unacceptable advice to forget all about Romeo and supported only by Friar Laurence with his desperate plan. Because of the secrecy of the marriage only the Nurse and the friar know what a proposed marriage to Paris involves. To Lady Capulet Romeo is a banished murderer, and neither Capulet nor Paris refers to Romeo at all.

Shakespeare has plenty of material to develop during the absence of Romeo. Until the marriage the play potentially has the structure of comedy – the renewal of the wintry, sterile world of the feud with the blossoming fertility of young love. This promise is blighted when Romeo enters the feud, so that in the second half of the play we see how things progressively get out of control as well-meaning busybodies interfere and accidents occur in a combination which ensures tragedy. Once Romeo is banished there is no opportunity for revealing more of Juliet's character with her husband. The role of Juliet only comes into full focus in Act IV as she flies in the face of all the reflexes of her society, hazards all she has for love, strives to keep the light of hope alive in the darkening world of a society dominated by masculine values.

When we examine the whole play we find that, with the exception of III. iv, IV. iv, and V. ii, either Romeo or Juliet appears in all the rest (21 of 24) of the scenes of the play. They only appear together in 5 of the play's scenes and are only alive, or at least aware of being alive, in 4 of them. Romeo appears in 14 scenes and Juliet in 12. There is not a great deal of difference between the size of their roles – Romeo speaks 591½ lines and Juliet 527. In terms of the time they are onstage Romeo is before us for 1562 lines and Juliet for 1537. Thus in the 2993 lines of the play Romeo is before us for 52.2 per cent and Juliet for 51.3 per cent of the play. Their parts, however, are distributed quite differently. By the time Romeo leaves in banishment in III. v he has already spoken 440 (74.4 per cent) of his lines and he has been on for 1187 (76 per cent) of the lines he is onstage. By the time Romeo leaves Juliet has spoken 328 (62.2 per cent) of her 527 lines. It is during his absence that she is given greater prominence for then she speaks 185½ lines (35.2 per cent) of her part, and over one-third of the time she is onstage during the play is in his absence. She is onstage for 516 lines (88.2 per cent) of his 585-line absence. This serves to reinforce our sense of the cruelty of time and the pressures on the lovers in that we see them together for such a small proportion of the time they are onstage. In only one scene are they allowed to interact consciously and alone for more than a hundred lines (II. ii). When Romeo does at last return to the stage in V. i he is full of hope and describes a dream of how Juliet recovered him from death by kissing him (1–11), which ironically and cruelly relates to what will in reality be reversed as Juliet tries to achieve death for herself by kissing Romeo in hope that some poison still hangs on his lips (V. iii. 163–6). The news Romeo receives on his re-emergence onto the stage is of Juliet's death which leads him immediately to think of the means for securing his own death (V. i. 12–54).

Shakespeare uses the period of Romeo's absence to concentrate on Juliet's plight and in doing so is able to develop other roles that have only been sketched in in the first half of the play. Paris and Lady Capulet are given a significant amount of stage time, but the figure who, besides Juliet, is developed most is Capulet. Capulet speaks 262 lines and is onstage in the play for 609 lines. We are aware early in the play that Capulet is a wilful, capricious, and choleric figure. After he exits in the masked ball (I. v. 127) there is a considerable hiatus in his role. He does not appear again until the central feud scene (III. i. 138) some 814 lines later (27.2 per cent of the play), and he does not speak again until III. iv, some 1189 lines later (39.7 per cent of the play.) Capulet appears in 10 of the play's scenes, and 4 of these are in the 5¾ scenes of Romeo's absence. Up until Romeo's departure he speaks 120 lines and is onstage for 271 lines. While Romeo is offstage he speaks 132½ lines, about half of his lines and is onstage for 217 lines (35.6 per cent of his onstage life). We only get the full flavour of his character when Romeo has gone to Mantua, and Juliet is thrown back upon her family.

It is in this sequence that we have the full testing of the value of love as it confronts the demands of the feud and its deadly values, a test that Romeo failed when he killed Tybalt. It is in Romeo's absence that the importance of obedience, kinship, loyalty to the clan are heavily emphasized, and Juliet is pressed hard to conform to the mores of her society. We admire her because, under this pressure and in the absence of support from anyone save the friar and his hazardous plans, she resists the reflex actions of her society and remains true to the radical choice she has made. In the juxtaposition of masculine and feminine principles in Verona almost all the actions of the men, save for those of Benvolio and the friar, contribute directly to the gathering tragedy. The values that women can put against such dangerous forces often prevail in the comedies, but here in this tragedy they are centred solely on Juliet. Lady Capulet abandons her daughter to the whims of her father's temper. The Nurse temporizes and counsels a submission to patri- archal authority. Juliet is left alone to persist in her faith that the choice she has made can survive the deadly values of the hate-ridden society she lives in. The details of this emphasis and its focus on Juliet's struggle is Shakespeare's considerable modificatio~ of the proportions of the story as he found it in Arthur Brooke's poem. _ ~e more unbearable, therefore, that the audience, which is given such a concentrated and exclusive focus on the flickering hope she keeps alive in her desperate plight, is obliged to register the full impact of the tragedy with the realization that all of her sacrifices are in vain. Despite all of the evasions, the role-playing, the bravery in facing the terrors that the friar's plan entails, she is never given the reward for which she undertakes all of these sacrifices – the experience of Romeo alive again in her arms. It is one of the clearest signals of Shakespeare's shaping of the character of Juliet that, after all her trials, when she awakes in the charnel-house to find all of her hopes turned to ashes she does not give way to melodramatic laments, she does not blame the stumblings of Friar Laurence; she recognizes that she is now truly and finally bereft and determines immediately to resolve her predicament. Abandoned by the friar, she gazes on Romeo and, in fewer than a dozen lines, leaves the world she finds is not worth living in without him.

6

'I am dumb!': The absence and presence of Antonio in *The Merchant of Venice*

An important role to which the shaping of the audience's response is structured very deftly by the strategic use of stage absence is that of Antonio in *The Merchant of Venice*. By the end of I. iii the merchant has concluded his bargain with Shylock. He is then absent from the stage for a lengthy period – II. i, the introductory sequence with the caskets in Belmont (46); II. ii, the clowning of the Gobbos (192); II. iii, Jessica's farewell to Launcelot Gobbo and her anticipation of elopement (21); II. iv, the preparations of the Venetians to bear Jessica away (39); II. v, Shylock's departure for the feast at Bassanio's house (55); II. vi, the elopement of Jessica with her casket and Lorenzo, 1–59 (59). This sequence extends for 412 lines until Antonio re-enters to hurry Gratiano to the port to sail off with Bassanio, II. vi. 60–8, giving him a brief stage appearance of 9 lines before another lengthy absence ensues. This consists of Morocco's trial of the caskets in Belmont in II. vii (79); II. viii, Salerio and Solanio's exchange of news about Shylock's reaction to the loss of Jessica and a report of Antonio's reaction to the loss of Bassanio (53); II. ix, Arragon's trial of the caskets in Belmont (100); III. i, reports by Salerio and Solanio of Antonio's losses, their mockery of Shylock, and Shylock's reception of Tubal's report of Antonio's losses and Jessica's prodigality (115); III. ii, Bassanio's trial of the caskets is soon followed by news of Antonio's danger and Bassanio is sent off to offer money for his relief (326). This absence of 673 lines by Antonio is ended when he returns to the stage, in III. iii with Shylock, on his way to jail, with the Jew determined to have his bond. This whole sequence between the conclusion of the bargain in I. iii and the meeting again onstage of the merchant and Shylock in III. iii contains the central development of both plots and occupies 1094 lines (42.7 per cent of the play). During that period Antonio is onstage for only 9 lines (II. vi. 60–8) which is less than 1 per cent of the sequence. Shylock is onstage for 149 lines (13.6 per cent) in this period (II. v. 1–53 (53) and III. i. 20–115 (96)). So the two figures around whom the climactic trial scene is to develop are given comparatively little time onstage in the events leading up to it. In order to understand why Shakespeare made this choice in developing Antonio I will have to examine the way his part is shaped throughout the play and only then return to the necessary reasons for this long absence.

The absence of Antonio is not structured only to allow time for the development of the casket-sequence in Belmont and the elopement of Lorenzo and Jessica. Antonio's loss of fortune could not be presented onstage because it involves argosies wrecked in places such as the Goodwin sands. It is possible, however, that Antonio could have been brought onstage and his reaction to his sequence of losses shown. Shakespeare chooses not to do this and instead presents reactions to the loss in reports by Salerio and Solanio, figures who were established in the opening scene of the play as coping with Antonio's habitual melancholy and who speculated about the anxiety caused by having one's wealth at risk on the high seas.

The most practical explanation of Antonio's absence is the need for the actor to double another role. The actor of Antonio could certainly have doubled the role of Arragon in II. ix. By the time Arragon appears at II. ix. 4 Antonio has been offstage since his brief appearance at the close of II. vi for 135 lines. After Arragon's exit, in the only scene in which he appears, at II. ix. 77 there are 464 lines before Antonio re-emerges with Shylock in III. iii. This doubling seems to me quite probable and contains a subterranean theatrical irony for any audience which registers it. One actor plays two roles of characters who put themselves in danger for Bassanio in different ways. Antonio puts his life at risk to finance Bassanio's voyage to Belmont to win Portia. We have a good deal of evidence that the merchant is very much attached in friendship to the young man so that critics and directors have often implied that the melancholy in Antonio results from his anticipated loss of Bassanio. If the same actor performs Arragon he is in a role which involves the commitment that, should he fail the casket test, he will agree never to marry. Arragon's failure by choosing the silver casket paves the way for Bassanio to succeed with the one remaining lead casket. The role of Antonio, the modest, self-sacrificing, melancholy merchant is very far from the strutting, arrogant Arragon, and yet they both smooth the way to Bassanio's triumph. Arragon finds on the silver casket the motto 'Who chooseth me shall get as much as he deserves' and within it discovers the portrait of a blinking idiot and a verse which informs him 'Some there be that shadow kiss;/Such have but a shadow's bliss' (II. ix. 65–6). These apply in a different sense to Antonio also, for he has made his choice of Bassanio for friend, has risked everything for him, and comes very close to being a shadow. Even at the end of the play, and despite his recovered fortunes, he remains a lonely figure lingering in the shadow of the other three couples celebrating their unity.

If Shakespeare decided early in the writing of the play that it would be necessary for one actor to play Arragon as well as Antonio then it was possible to shape the character of Antonio in a way that would make his absence from the stage for such a long period, save for a brief 9-line appearance, plausible. Of the 1085 lines for which he is absent 38 per cent of them occur before this brief appearance and 62 per cent afterwards. His 9-line appearance seems to be inserted solely for the purposing of assuring the audience that he is still around. He comes on in II. vi merely to hurry Gratiano to the ship which is waiting to take him, along with Bassanio, to Belmont. It is a very brief appearance, and the function Antonio performs could just as easily have been undertaken by Solanio, or even Launcelot, or any messenger such as the Man from Antonio who appears at III. i. 65–9. The audience has had a number of reports about Antonio, and if we have been wondering where he has got to this serves to satisfy our curiosity. No audience, however, can be very surprised by Antonio's absence because Shakespeare has very carefully prepared us for it by his habitual method of making a virtue of necessity.

Shakespeare begins to shape the character of Antonio in the first scene of the play. It is a scene in which Antonio speaks more lines than in any other save the long trial scene. He speaks 24.9 per cent of all his lines in this first of the play's twenty scenes. Six characters appear in I. i, and though Antonio is the focus of much of the talk and is the only character who remains onstage throughout he speaks the least number of lines as a proportion of the lines he is onstage (with the exception of Lorenzo, who explains that he cannot talk because Gratiano gives him no chance to do so – 106–7). This first scene starts the Belmont plot in motion and establishes Bassanio's need for money but it also informs us of the great esteem in which Antonio is held even as it unfolds him as a reticent, enigmatic, melancholic figure set apart from his fellows. This is vividly caught in the proportions of the scene. At the outset Antonio says 'In sooth I know not why I am so sad' (I. i. 1), introducing an apparent mystery, a vacuum without explanation which the voluble Salerio and Solanio eagerly fill in a sequence of suggestions which have to do with possible anxieties about his merchandise upon the sea. This not only vividly establishes the mercantile atmosphere of Venice, it also prepares for the anxious speculation that will occur, especially from these two friends of Antonio, when his argosies put him in jeopardy because of his bond with Shylock. Antonio's initial 7-line speech, which expresses his inability to explain himself to himself, is followed by 33 lines of his companions' sympathetic explanations of why he may be sad, and how they would feel if they were in his position. All the evocative pictures of how everything would prompt the mind to anxiety about one's ventures at sea are, however, met by a brief and flat denial from Antonio (41–5), cancelling his friends' speculations as irrelevant. This leads to the suggestion that Antonio may be in love which he quickly rejects (46–7), and then to the idea that there may be no other cause for the sadness than the habitual temperament to which some men stubbornly cling (47–56). At this point Bassanio, in search of Antonio, enters in the company of Gratiano and Lorenzo, the cause of the merchant's sadness still unresolved. Though Lorenzo is ready to depart and leave Bassanio with Antonio, Gratiano is willing to fill the air with his speculations about Antonio's care-burdened features. Here Antonio manages to utter only 2½ lines (77–9), and in reply gets from Gratiano, who continues the pattern of Salerio and Solanio of filling the void created by Antonio's sad withdrawal, a speech of 25½ lines. Gratiano's suggestion is that Antonio may be seeking a reputation for grave wisdom by maintaining silence. Only when Bassanio is left alone with Antonio, and the issue of the merchant's melancholy is still left unresolved, does the conversation turn to other topics. As Antonio takes an interest in Bassanio's project for Belmont there is, for the first time, a little more balance in the conversation, though even here Antonio speaks only 26 lines to 47 by Bassanio. The pattern observable here establishes the relatively muted nature of Antonio's role throughout, for almost all of the first 118 lines of the scene (63.8 per cent) are devoted to speculations about and reactions to Antonio's sadness, and the rest of the scene is devoted to Bassanio's request for his financial aid in his pursuit of Portia.

Table 6.1 Act I, Scene i – 185 lines

Character	Onstage	Speaks	% of lines spoken of lines onstage
Antonio	185	45	24.3
Bassanio	129	50	38.7
Gratiano	56	33½	59.8
Salerio	68	29½	43.4
Solanio	68	21	30.9
Lorenzo	44	6	13.6

The scene establishes Antonio as a central figure and unfolds his great friendship for Bassanio. It also presents him as a withdrawn and not very voluble man who finds it difficult to explain himself and whom others find it difficult to explain, though there is no lack of willingness to talk about him at great length. Antonio appears to be a stoic, a man for whom, throughout the action, others express more apprehension about the jeopardy he is in than he ever expresses for himself. He is not a chatterbox or a gossip like Salerio and Solanio. He is not a man like Gratiano who 'speaks an infinite deal of nothing' (I. i. 114), nor is he a man like Bassanio, or even Lorenzo, who are full of their own plans and anticipations of happiness. He appears to be a man who, to a considerable degree, fulfils the kind of image Hamlet describes in Horatio, one who is no 'passion's slave' and behaves 'As one in suffering all that suffers nothing' (*Hamlet*, III. ii. 63). He is defined, to a large degree, in opposition to his nemesis Shylock who can be voluble, aggressive, triumphant, consumed by passion, so lacking in reticence that he can become a figure of public scorn as he laments the losses of his daughter and his ducats. Antonio is not a man we are going to miss keenly when he is offstage for such long periods. He is, in a sense, not very forcibly there when he is onstage. Thus he is a figure about whom we can accept various pieces of news from his concerned and more voluble friends, a figure who, as his losses accumulate, might be expected to go into seclusion enduring with sad and silent fortitude what increasingly threatens to be a tragic fate.

The pattern established in the first scene is repeated again and again. In. I. iii, where the bond is sealed with Shylock, it is Bassanio who establishes the terms with the money-lender for the first 35 lines of the scene to which Antonio will subscribe when he enters. When he continues the negotiations Bassanio subsides almost into silence, but Antonio does not become a dominant figure nor does he take a very large share of the conversation even though he is, in jest, wagering his life. Even when we acknowledge that this is Shylock's first scene in which his character is established his voluble chatter fills up the vacuum left by Antonio's terseness. When Shylock mocks him for begging money, asking how one who had so spurned him could have the nerve to borrow from him (102–25), Antonio does not give an inch, or temporize, or pretend that his principled rejection of money-lending will change thereafter (126–33). For his love of Bassanio Antonio is willing to compromise temporarily with his distaste for Jews and money-lending, but he boldly asserts, thinking he will never be called on to live up to it, that he will pay whatever penalty is required rather than submit to any suggestion that money-lending is acceptable or honourable. He issues his self-assured statement to brazen out his temporary embarrassment and loss of face, and this leads Shylock to propose 'in jest' the forfeiture of the pound of flesh.

Table 6.2 Act I, Scene iii, 36–177 – 142 lines

Character	Onstage	Speaks	% of lines spoken of lines onstage
Shylock	142	100½	70.8
Antonio	142	36½	25.7
Bassanio	142	5	3.5

The strategy of giving us more of Shylock and much more vivid and dramatic emotions from him than from Antonio is continued when the merchant's long exile from the stage ends in III. iii. Antonio on his way to gaol does, for the only time in the play, speak most lines in a scene, but after Shylock's entrance the Jew is so irascibly dominant that the merchant can scarcely get a word in edgewise.

Table 6.3 Act III, Scene iii – 36 lines

Character	Onstage	Speaks	% of lines spoklen of lines onstage
Antonio	36	17½	48.6
Solanio	36	3	8.3
Shylock	17	15½	91.2

Shylock foams and rages and identifies himself as something like the mad dog Antonio has accused him of being (6–7). The Jew is so obsessively insistent in his repetition of a phrase that he may seem to be growling like a dog: 'I'll have my bond! Speak not against my bond' (4). He emphasizes his reliance on his bond 6 times in 13 lines. Antonio manages to get in only 11 words as he fails to curb his snarling, self-righteous enemy. The only concessions we hear of are Antonio terming his oppressor 'good Shylock' (3), and his declaration, after the Jew's departure, 'I'll follow him no more with bootless prayer' (20), implying that he may have asked for sympathy. This seems unlikely given everything else we know of Antonio, and Shakespeare certainly does not present any abject pleas onstage. He uses this occasion again to emphasize the merchant's stoic defiance of the death he anticipates in contrast to the hopes his friends hold out. Salerio, in trying to cheer him up (25–6) by glimpsing a loophole, is confronted by Antonio's insistence that it would injure the state to deny the course of law. This almost seems to imply that the merchant is willing to accept his sacrifice for the good of Venice. Antonio does not go so far as to suggest that Shylock deserves his triumph in the bond, but he does acknowledge that Shylock has reasons and motives for his hatred (21–4). The only wish he is willing to voice is a prayer to see Bassanio before he dies (35–6). There may be in this, depending on the interpretation of the actor and director, some romantic wish in Antonio to have Bassanio witness the fact that his mentor loves him and is willing to hazard for him more than any wealthy woman could. In the trial scene, however, as I have noted, Antonio continues to be a remarkably shadowy, stoical, and unforceful figure, which leaves the stage to Portia who, by her ingenious wit, can confront Shylock in a more forceful way than any response we have seen from Antonio.

The trial scene is the most spectacular example of his reticence. He is onstage for the entire scene, and it is his life that is at stake during most of the 455 lines, and yet his part is quite small. Antonio embraces his fate philosophically (114–18), and urges that judgement be made rather than delayed by histrionics and forensic grandstanding. Of the eight speakers in the scene only Antonio and Bassanio are onstage throughout, and yet it is the other characters who conduct the merchant's defence against the obdurate and merciless Shylock. Antonio's taciturnity can be interpreted in a variety of ways. There is apparently no impediment for Christians to beg mercy of Jews

Table 6.4 Act IV, Scene i – 455 lines

Character	Onstage	Speaks	% of lines spoken of lines onstage
Portia	283	133½	47.2
Shylock	383	98½	25.7
Duke	405	68½	16.9
Antonio	455	64½	14.2
Bassanio	455	49½	10.9
Gratiano	452	33	7.3
Salerio	405	3	0.7
Nerissa	328	4½	1.3

since the Duke, Bassanio, and Portia do so at considerable length, nor is there any impediment to buying off a forfeit life since the same three characters offer considerable sums for ransom. But Antonio himself will not do so for reasons that appear to be enigmatically related to his restrained character. It may be that he resists pleas for mercy because of his pride, not deigning to lower himself to beg of the Jew he disdains. Maybe he refuses to do so on philosophic, stoic principles, caring so little for life as to be unwilling to be seen to sue for its continuance. Antonio remains a mystery, and Shakespeare can exploit it as an advantage through having shown so little of him onstage. We have heard a good deal about Antonio's fortunes, but we do not really know him. By the beginning of the trial scene the play has run 1783 lines (69.5 per cent of its 2564). Antonio has been onstage in four scenes for a total of 372 lines (20.9 per cent of the play to that point) and has spoken only 105 lines or 5.9 per cent of the play up to the point where he begins to face the possibility of public execution.

This shadowy character is shaped by Shakespeare for a specific purpose. Much of the focus of the trial scene is on the rabid nature of Shylock as he pursues revenge, on a variety of personal appeals for mercy which he rejects, and on the abstract legal arguments of Portia. What seems to be happening onstage is the trial of Antonio, but the audience gradually comes to realize that it is witnessing the trial of Shylock who, by his stubborn search for revenge exiles himself from community and forfeits the right to any mercy from those whose appeals he has denied. I am not asserting here that this is fair, that the Christians are blameless or Shylock's search for revenge baseless. The issues are not presented so unequivocally, but we are certainly made aware that Shylock digs a very deep hole for himself. Whatever losses of daughter and ducats he has suffered, and even though the Christians seem to have conspired against him in causing him those losses, such issues are eclipsed in the focus given to the legal technicality Portia employs and to the enigmatic character of Antonio. He is, at the outset of the trial scene, very clearly, in his own description, defined as the opposite of Shylock:

> I have heard
> Your Grace hath ta'en great pains to qualify
> His rigorous course; but since he stands obdurate,
> And that no lawful means can carry me
> Out of his envy's reach, I do oppose
> My patience to his fury, and am armed
> To suffer with a quietness of spirit
> The very tyranny and rage of his.
>
> (IV. i. 6–13)

The fact that Antonio is melancholic, that he seems, for never completely understood reasons, not to be very eagerly attached to life, and refuses to undertake any personal plea to Shylock, makes this trial appear to relate to more abstract and broader issues about mercy. Should any man's life be taken, even when, as in this case, the man seems resigned to death? Is the bond of community violated when a man such as Shylock takes matters so personally and seeks so relentlessly a revenge that is bizarre to the point of absurdity and which arises from an agreement whose terms seemed to be decided in jest?

All appeals for mercy come from others; from the Duke who is caught in a legal bind and wants Shylock to get him out of it; from Bassanio who, because of his personal sense of responsibility and backed up by Portia's wealth, wants to buy Antonio out of danger; from Gratiano who, as the most visible anti-semite, is given the task of pouring venomous contempt on the Jew; from Portia who seems to accede to the strictures of the law and makes a plea for mercy on broad humanitarian principles. Our judgement of Shylock's determination is not affected by any indications of craven fears in the victim in the face of death. Nor can it be affected by any strong personal attachment in members of the audience to Antonio since Shakespeare has not allowed us to get to know him very well. We are moved to side against Shylock not so much by any direct, personal response as by an almost abstract evaluation of the issue. There is something here akin to the Brechtian *verfremdungseffekt*. Because his friends exhibit such a personal concern and horror at the monstrous bond to whose letter Shylock clings we do not need to feel the issue as defining a great loss to the world, for Antonio is not an especially remarkable man. We are obliged to judge Shylock as a figure who sticks ruthlessly to technicalities, as a man who reinforces his narrow-minded animosity to the Christians because he has one of them on the hip and can feed his revenge by forcing them to pursue their own laws. We have a growing sense, even before the revelation of the saving loophole, that, in this juxtaposition of Christian and Jew, the Christian cedes up all the territory over which the Jew, with whooping confidence, advances, so that when the reversal occurs the Jew will not have a leg to stand on. He is lured forward like a ravening animal to a concealed trap which is sprung to drop him into a pit. The revenge taken on him is comprehensive and merciless – the most severe meted out to any character in the comedies (not excluding Malvolio). An audience is being induced not to be repelled by this, even when we reflect that Portia's strategy is very much like fattening up a lamb for slaughter. Antonio is so passive, so unresistant to the 'injustice' that it makes Shylock seem the more reprehensible because he preys on one who neither defies him nor rails against him.

This strategy is, to some degree, a deliberate sleight-of-hand. Shylock is a victim of the machinations of the Christians who connive to steal away his ducats and his daughter. Antonio is a victim of weather, the fortunes of the seas, and a confidence that he will never be called on to live up to the terms of a bond signed in jest. In the trial Shylock's losses are set completely aside and never made a significant issue by Shakespeare. Because the basis of Shylock's revenge is given no prominence at the trial his pursuit of Antonio's life seems even more malign.

We might expect Antonio to indicate his relief when Portia finds a loophole (IV. i. 303) through which to save his life, but 75 lines pass before he makes any comment at IV. i. 378 (which is 100 lines since he last spoke). As Portia not only closes her trap but makes it bite deeper and deeper Bassanio and the Duke make comments. In Gratiano's speeches we see relief turn to ironical sneering as he underlines how eagerly Shylock's insistence on the law has become a trap for himself rather than Antonio. There are 96 lines after the trap is sprung until Shylock's departure (IV. i. 303–98), and in that sequence Gratiano, a mere bystander, has eight speeches that add up to 15 of those lines, whereas Antonio, whose life it is that has been saved, has one speech of 11 lines defining his 'mercy' to Shylock in a sequence of stipulations which strip the Jew of his wealth and insist that he convert to Christianity. After all of Gratiano's taunting we may tend not to focus closely on the quiet but deadly savagery of Antonio's demands. No modern audience, nor perhaps even some in the Elizabethan audience, could find it easy to share in Gratiano's hooting, nastily reiterated mocking triumph when Portia turns the tables on Shylock: 'A second Daniel! a Daniel, Jew!/Now, infidel, I have you on the hip' (IV. i. 332–3). But this is only one of many examples of deflecting our attention from Antonio and exempting him from some of the worst excesses of the Christians. I can now turn to the techniques used in Antonio's long and almost continuous absence from the end of I. iii to III. iii to indicate how important it is in shaping our response to the play.

The key advantage of keeping Antonio offstage for so long is to detach him from those figures who seem to plot against Shylock when they engineer Jessica's elopement. We hear a great deal about Shylock's injuries, his specific motives, and his search for revenge. Antonio is dissociated from any entanglement in this plotting, but we are also aware that Shylock does not know of this and that it is plausible for the Jew to believe that the merchant is involved. We are able to see that Shylock's revenge is wrong and at the same time understand how, from his point of view, he feels justified in striking against the Christians and against Antonio, the one he has in his power. To get the best of both worlds Shakespeare indulges in a considerable amount of mystification.

It is necessary, therefore, to turn to the elopement of Lorenzo and Jessica and to see how very carefully Shakespeare handles it. Bassanio asks (I. iii. 29) that Shylock dine with him and Antonio to settle the final terms of the bond. Shylock rejects the idea of dining with the Christians (I. iii. 30–5), and when, later in the same scene, Antonio appears and the terms of the bond are settled it would appear that the invitation to dinner, which has already been refused, will not be pursued and no further mention is made of it in this exchange. All of this occurs before we have heard anything of the relationship of Lorenzo and Jessica and is, perhaps, innocent of any connection with the plans for elopement. In II. ii we hear that Bassanio is holding a feast this night for his 'best-esteemed acquaintance' (159) and that Gratiano (185–6) and other friends (187–9) will be provided with an evening of merriment. In II. iii we learn from Jessica that Lorenzo will be at the feast (5–6) as she asks Launcelot to deliver a letter to him and indicates (19–21) that plans have already been made to seal a marriage with Lorenzo. In II. iv we find some of the revellers (Gratiano, Lorenzo, Salerio and Solanio) preparing for the feast, and their exchange might seem teasingly to hint at collusion in a plot. Lorenzo declares 'we will slink away at supper time' (1) to put on a disguise, Gratiano feels that they have not made 'good preparation' (4), and Solanio seems to feel that if matters have not been carefully arranged they should not pursue their plans (6–7). Though these references could be to a plot in which they are to help in stealing Jessica, it seems more likely that the talk refers simply to the fact that, because of the hastily arranged feast, they may not be able to do themselves justice in adopting the disguises necessary for this kind of Venetian merriment. In any case Launcelot enters bearing Jessica's letter and he informs the revellers that he has been sent by Bassanio to invite Shylock to the feast (17–18). It would seem, however, that the invitation is not sent in careful calculation to lure Shylock from home to Lorenzo's advantage. Lorenzo does not reveal his plan here to Salerio and Solanio, and seems to be explaining it for the first time to Gratiano (29–33), so there is an implication that the plan has originated with Jessica. It is clear that Lorenzo intends to take advantage of the masque wherein Jessica, dressed as a page, will be able to pass with her father's gold and jewels undetected as Lorenzo's torchbearer (39). No mention is made by Lorenzo of how convenient it will be, in spiriting Jessica away from the house, that Shylock will be absent from it because he has been invited to the feast. We cannot, therefore, assert that this is more than fortuitous accident, and it seems to be Jessica who has recognized how to take advantage of it. If Bassanio is in collusion with Lorenzo to send an invitation to Shylock which the Jew once refused then Shakespeare does not make it clear to the audience.

In II. v we find that Shylock will go the to feast, though he is not eager to do so, and will leave his keys with Jessica so that she can keep his house safe. Shylock intends to go, in his thrifty, puritanical disdain, to waste the resources of 'the prodigal Christian' (11–18). We may not find this motive appealing but we may also wonder at Bassanio's conspicuous consumption. Here is a man willing to borrow money, and to allow his friend to sign a sinister bond which he mistrusts, who extravagantly decides to give himself and all his friends a send-off party on the eve of departure in the conquest of Portia. Launcelot's line 'they have conspired together' (22) might seem a hint at collusion in a masque that is, in part, designed to gull Shylock. It could equally well not be a Freudian slip but a malapropism of the kind he has just made, 'My young master doth expect your reproach' (II. v. 19–20), which will ironically become true in a way that Launcelot could never realize. It is clear, however, that Launcelot is aware of Lorenzo's intentions (39–41), and by II. vi it is evident that Salerio and Gratiano are aware of the plot.

In this sequence of scenes the knowledge of this plot seems to have spread from one man to another, and yet, apart from the lovers themselves, only Gratiano, Salerio, and Launcelot are aware of what is going on. Shakespeare has contrived to present the matter so that we do not see it as a carefully pre-planned conspiracy in which all the Christians share but rather as something unfolded to a few spontaneously at the last minute. It is indicated that other masquers enter in II. vi, but since they do not speak we cannot assert that they are part of the plot. We might ask, indeed, why Lorenzo informed anyone else, or what help he needed or received from his friends in stealing Jessica away from her home, and why Shakespeare chose to embroil others in this matter. The implication of Lorenzo's lines to the masquers, 'When you shall please to play the thieves for wives,/I'll watch as long for you then' (II. vi. 23–4), is that they have been keeping watch for him outside Shylock's house while he was involved in other preparations. The friends have witnessed Shylock's departure and are available to indicate the danger if the Jew were to abandon the feast and return home quickly, as he hinted to Jessica he might do (II. v. 49–50). It is possible, too, that Lorenzo may have needed help, and in productions he often receives it, to ensure that the booty Jessica throws down from the balcony is safely gathered in, but this is not essential. It seems possible that he has invited his friends along to provide safety in numbers so that Jessica, in her page-boy disguise, can pass undetected through the streets of Venice on their way to Bassanio's should they bump into Shylock returning from thence. But this seems hardly essential given the confusion of masques in real life and onstage and the convention of women in disguise as boys so common in Elizabethan comedies.

We have to conclude that Shakespeare embroils others in this plot to strengthen the basis of Shylock's motives for revenge later on. Lorenzo, perhaps, is not in himself a sufficient motive for revenge, in the eyes of the audience, because he is a lover, and we know that Jessica is a willing partner in the elopement. She is the one who indicates what wealth she will bring and, in the robbery, goes off to pick up more ducats for her flight (II. vi. 50). Others are involved in undertaking the theft as they will be involved later in mocking Shylock's agonized response to it. In his belief that the Christian community colluded in the theft Shylock is given, in general terms, a plausible motive for seeking revenge. He never says so specifically, but it would be natural for him to believe that a key to the plot was the invitation to supper which gets him out of the house. Yet Shakespeare develops the plot so that the audience cannot fasten with certainty on any deeply prepared collusion. Several Christians are embroiled but by no means all of them. We never see Solanio involved, though he may be one of the masquers in II. vi. If we suppose the invitation to supper is entirely innocent, then Shakespeare most pointedly does not involve Bassanio in the plot and above all he does not involve Antonio. One could argue that Gratiano, Salerio, and Solanio are included in the play precisely to appear as 'other Christians' to ensure that Antonio and Bassanio are not involved in duping Shylock nor in baiting and pouring scorn on him after his loss. These other Christians do help to dupe Shylock while Antonio is kept offstage in a lengthy absence in order to ensure, in the audience's eyes, that he is never implicated in the plot. Shakespeare can thus give Shylock some plausible motive for his savage search for revenge and yet ensure that Antonio is not an appropriate target but rather a sacrificial lamb for whatever sins the Christians have committed when he defaults on his bond.

It is true that Antonio does appear once during his extended absence (II. vi. 60–8) in the scene in which Jessica steals away. I have suggested that this appearance is simply to assure the audience that he is still in Venice without asking him to do anything particularly functional or an action that only he can perform. But we now see that this brief appearance is situated very exactly and in a way that makes it clear that he has nothing to do with the stealing of Jessica. Antonio does not come on while Jessica is making her escape. All but Gratiano, and some masquers perhaps, have left the stage before Antonio appears. One could speculate that Antonio may have known of the plot since he knows enough to come to Shylock's house to find the missing companion for whom Bassanio is waiting, but Shakespeare carefully squashes any such speculation when Antonio impatiently suggests that he has been searching in vain and seems merely to have happened on Gratiano:

> Fie, fie, Gratiano! where are all the rest?
> 'Tis nine o'clock; our friends all stay for you.
> No masque tonight. The wind is come about;

> Bassanio will presently go aboard.
> I have sent twenty out to seek for you.
>
> (II. vi. 62–6)

Antonio's ignorance of Gratiano's whereabouts and therefore of his involvement in Lorenzo's plot would seem to be confirmed here, for Antonio would hardly have sent out twenty to look for him if he had known what he was up to. Since Jessica has stolen away only seconds before Antonio's entrance we would expect, if he was in the plot, that he would inquire if matters had gone off successfully. Antonio makes no mention of the elopement nor does Gratiano. In fact the detail here would seem to exempt Bassanio also from collusion. We hear of his sudden change of plans because of the favourable wind, and this allows us to assume that Bassanio cannot be a conscious decoy of Shylock. His sudden decision to sail this very evening must have been made without any knowledge of and without any consideration of the plans for Jessica's escape, for it may have sent Shylock home from the feast earlier than intended thus endangering Lorenzo's plan.

Shakespeare goes to quite considerable lengths to dissociate Antonio from the stealing of Jessica. Antonio speaks to Shylock and to all the Christian Venetians in the play at some length, with the exception of Lorenzo. In the first scene of the play Lorenzo is clearly a close friend of Bassanio and the others who are trying to explain Antonio's melancholy. Lorenzo speaks 3 lines (I. i. 105–7) which may be addressed in farewell to both Bassanio and Antonio. Because Antonio is absent from the stage for so long he is not seen in the presence of any of the Venetians (save Gratiano briefly in II. vi) until the trial scene. In fact he is not seen in the company of Lorenzo again until the last scene, and in that final 181 lines of the play (V. i. 127–307) Antonio never addresses a word to Lorenzo or Jessica nor do they speak to him. So those 3 casual lines in the first scene are the entire substance of any relationship Antonio has with the two young lovers. Lorenzo is associated with all of the other Venetians but has virtually nothing to do with Antonio, and never shares the stage with Shylock, and yet his plot is the basis of Shylock's pursuit of Antonio.

Antonio is absent from the stage, save for the 9 lines required to get Gratiano to the ship for Belmont, for all the scenes in Venice which prepare and accomplish Lorenzo's escape with Jessica, for the scenes in which we witness Shylock's reactions, and the scenes which present the nasty mockery of those reaction by Christians. It is during this sequence that Bassanio departs for Belmont, and, given Antonio's affection for the young adventurer, we might have expected to see their farewell onstage. Shakespeare, however, prefers to give it in report and in some detail (II. viii. 36–49), again choosing not to associate Antonio with other Venetians who are enjoying the discomfort of the Jew. A further point is made in this scene of report (II. viii) which specifically underlines Antonio's lack of involvement in the Lorenzo-Jessica affair. It might have seemed possible to have the young lovers escape from Venice, and from the hue and cry raised by Shylock – in the available ship in which Bassanio is sailing to Belmont, especially since we will find them seeking refuge there later (III. ii). The report Salerio gives makes a variety of separate points which tend to exempt Bassanio and Antonio from the plot: (*a*) Bassanio is under sail and Lorenzo is not with him (II. viii. 1–3); (*b*) the Duke, aroused by Shylock, is told that the two runaways have been seen in a gondola (8–9), the implication being that they could have received no aid from Bassanio who has already sailed; (*c*) Antonio certifies that the fugitives are not in Bassanio's ship (10–11). This does not, I believe, imply that Antonio knows where they are. It suggests instead that neither he nor Bassanio knew of the plot and have not been applied to for help by the lovers. When the young lovers do arrive at Portia's house Lorenzo quite specifically makes the point that he had not intended to come thither (III. ii. 26–30), and this confirms the view that neither Bassanio nor Antonio could have been originally involved in the plans for elopement. Nor can it even be said that the arrival of the young lovers in Belmont serves the function of carrying news from the city. Jessica does testify to the seriousness with which Shylock's revenge should be regarded (III. ii. 284–90), but it is Salerio who reports on what is going on in Venice. Yet simply by the care with which this detailed information is supplied it becomes clear that no matter what Antonio certified, and no matter that he appears to be telling the truth, the circumstances could be interpreted by Shylock to lead him to the belief that he has been gulled by a conspiracy in which Antonio had a part. It could appear in Shylock's eyes that the insults and injuries are deliberate and that some of the money borrowed from him has been used to throw a party to which he was invited while Lorenzo stole his daughter and the wealth that went with her. The lovers, he could also believe, may have escaped in a ship which was hired by money borrowed from him, thus leaving him as a gull who has financed his own losses to become a figure of fun mocked in the streets by the Christians.

To many of the characters, and at times to the audience, Shylock is a figure of fun. But he is also a figure of pathos because of the delight some of the Christians take in his misery. There are several Christians in Venice who are uncharitable to the point of a savage nastiness. When we first hear of his distress in II. viii Shakespeare is careful not to involve Antonio in the ribald mockery. It would be incorrect, however, to exempt Antonio from the pervasive anti-semitism. His views have been clearly expressed in the only scene in which he holds an extensive conversation with Shylock (I. iii). His lines (37–48, 57–60, 66, 71, 87–91, 93–8, 102–9, and 126–33) make it clear what his current attitude is, what it has been in the past, and what it is certain to remain in the future. His objection seems to be partly a matter of principle and disdain for usury (38–40), and which Shylock later indicates Antonio refused to practise (III. i. 41–3). This injured Shylock's business by bringing lending-rates down; and Antonio also rescued those who became forfeit to him through their debts. This is also confirmed by Antonio who acknowledges this to be one of Shylock's motives in pursuing revenge (III. iii. 22–5). If we add up what Antonio says, and if half of what Shylock says about the merchant's attitudes towards himself and other Jews is correct, then we can see that Shylock has for long had a fixed animosity against him which their meeting (I. iii) only confirms.

In some sense the bond Shylock seals appears to be undertaken partly in mockery, for he claims that it is a jest and for once he will, like Antonio, lend money without interest. We may think that his motive for revenge grows only from the injuries he sustains at his daughter's departure, but Jessica's testimony denies that when she reports that Shylock has sworn 'he would rather have Antonio's flesh/Than twenty times the value of the sum' (III. ii. 286–7), which she could only have heard before she fled his house. Shylock's search for revenge is not motivated only by Lorenzo's flight with Jessica; rather, it is the immediate pretext of it, an opportunity long-awaited for and exploited because Antonio, he can believe, is connected to this latest and most serious of many injuries. Antonio's position of principle in the matter of usury is to some degree undermined by his need to borrow money for Bassanio, but it does not lead him to disguise his antipathy to Shylock. We might think that Shylock's assertions about the past signs of the merchant's contempt are rhetorical hyperbole ('You call me misbeliever, cutthroat dog,/And spit upon my Jewish gaberdine', I. iii. 107–8), but Antonio confirms it as no exaggeration ('I am as like to call thee so again,/To spit on thee again, to spurn thee too', I. iii. 126–7). Indeed, Antonio is proud and stubborn enough never to climb down from his haughty disdain, for even in his peril in the trial scene he unleashes his undisguised, anti-semitic contempt (IV. i. 70–80).

The conspiracy which injures Shylock is not something that the audience can lightly dismiss. He is wrong to believe Antonio implicated, but his grievances are serious enough to prevent the audience from seeing him simply as a comic figure of fun, which is the only reaction we see from the Christian Venetians. There is no doubt that Shakespeare makes us feel the Jew's anguish but he also shows his revenge as being irrationally vindictive (III. i. 44–7), as well as malignantly designed for his own ultimate profit (III. i. 111–13), and motivated by hatred rather than by any search for justice (IV. i. 40–69). The irrationality is the more emphasized not only by Antonio's absence, by choosing not to show the merchant, whatever he may have said and done in the past, stoking the fires of Shylock's hatred, but by Shylock's presence. We see him foaming in fury on the provocation of other Christians which locks him into a revenge on the absent Antonio.

This way of shaping the story seems to be Shakespeare's invention. The combination of plots, with the inclusion of a rebellious daughter of the Jew, is not in the probable source, *Il Pecorone*, nor in the other sources.

Shakespeare could have organized the elopement in a variety of ways: by involving all of the Venetian Christians in a conspiracy, including those who borrow money from the Jew; by involving none of them in the escape; or by including some of the Christians but not those involved in borrowing money – the choice he made. Some of the elements of the Lorenzo-Jessica plot could have been taken from *The Jew of Malta* and some from a story in Masuccio's *Novellino* but the bearing on and connection to the other plots was Shakespeare's. In the Masuccio story, it is true, the young girl, penned up at home by a miserly father, does steal much of his wealth. She effects her escape not with the help of others in the street but through a slave that her cavalier has cleverly inserted in the miser's house. Shakespeare retains some shadow of this in his use of Launcelot as a go-between for Lorenzo and Jessica as they make their plans. Launcelot knows only a little of the plot but is too stupid to be an agent of escape, for he almost gives the game away (III. v. 38–41). There seems to be no very urgent reason why Launcelot changes masters from Shylock to Bassanio, save to provide some comic interchanges. I would suggest that this is another trace of Shakespeare's general strategy. The audience can see that Launcelot is a messenger but that he has no part in the escape from Shylock's house. Yet because he is now Bassanio's servant and comes to invite Shylock to the feast is must seem to the Jew that Bassanio is part of the plot, using the servant who has defected from him to enable his daughter to defect from him. There is no hint in Masuccio which would lead Shakespeare to connect the eloping daughter to revenge through the forfeited bond because the old miser is not a Jew and the story therefore has no Christians celebrating the gulling of a usurer. The idea of having the young man celebrate his expedition to Belmont with a parting-feast and masque, thus providing an opportunity for the daughter to escape, also appears to be Shakespeare's. The idea of the Jew feeding his need for revenge because of the loss of his daughter and his ducats is also Shakespeare's since he ties together the separate plots from diverse sources. The animosity which exists between Shylock and Antonio because of past insults is not present in the tale Ser Giovanni tells in *Il Pecorone*, though complaints by a Jewish lender of long-standing injuries by Christians are present in some of the analogues, particularly Alexander Silvayn's *Orator* (Bullough, vol. 1, p. 483).

I have indicated the advantages Shakespeare gains by keeping Antonio offstage, and I turn now to the methods he uses to keep the audience informed about the merchant's fortunes. There are four major reports of offstage action: (*a*) II. viii. 1–49; (*b*) III. i. 1–16; (*c*) III. i. 87–110; and (*d*) III. ii. 243–83. As we learn of Antonio's and Shylock's losses we are also given an awareness of how much Shylock's search for revenge is being fuelled. These reports keep the various strands of plot in motion and give us a sequence of short-hand elisions which bring matters quickly to the climactic confrontation of the trial scene.

In II. viii we have a report not only of Antonio's actions offstage but a preliminary account of Shylock's distress which has made him a laughing-stock. We might think that the account is biased and exaggerated towards comedy by prejudice but in III. i we will find Shylock still alternating his lamentations for his ducats and his daughter. Salerio and Solanio cannot indulge themselves in amusement for long because they recognize what this humiliation of the Jew will mean for Antonio. The contrast between the two figures is made by the Christians very much to the advantage of Antonio. The decorum and reserve of the merchant is picked out as an admired standard: 'A kinder gentleman treads not the earth' (II. viii. 35). Antonio, though not onstage, is allowed, by a detailed report of his direct speech, to shine as a man totally dedicated to another's welfare. Antonio has encouraged Bassanio not to stint himself for time or money in pursuits of his aims. He values the young man's friendship so much that he is silenced and reduced to tears, but then insists that Bassanio have no concern for him, nor for the bond which hangs over him, even though he knows that, since Jessica's elopement, it must take on a more ominous significance (II. viii. 35–48). All of this heartfelt concern for a friend, so deep that it seems Antonio's sole reason for living (50), is clearly juxtaposed to the behaviour of a man ranting in the streets who cannot decide which is more important to him, the loss of his own daughter or the loss of his treasure. The admiring friends go off to cheer up Antonio, but the audience will not see them do so.

In III. i we have more news of Antonio moving steadily into Shylock's power still mingled with eulogies of the merchant (10–13). Shakespeare still denies us any onstage experience of 'the good Antonio, the honest Antonio' but he does not deny us the company of what the Christians call 'the devil . . . in the likeness of a Jew' (18–19). Shylock strikes immediately towards the source of his grievance, making it clear that he suspects the Christians of a conspiracy (21–2). He accuses both Salerio and Solanio, though the audience has only had clear evidence of the former's collusion. Far from denying it Salerio makes a joke about his knowledge of the flight, declaring that he even knew the tailor who made the page's suit in which Jessica effected her escape (23–4). Shakespeare shows the reflex nature of Venetian prejudice here (as he does in his other account of Venice, *Othello*). These Christian friends of Antonio have expressed apprehension about the danger the merchant is in, but they never even consider it might be politic to humour Shylock instead of baiting him. They even raise the issue of Antonio's losses (36–7), presumably to test Shylock's intentions, but cannot imagine that even a Jew would pursue such a barbarous revenge. They have no conception of how the world must look through the eyes of a Jew who has been continually mocked, recently duped and robbed, humiliated, stoned, and hooted at in the streets, and is even at this instant being called a devil and treated as less than human.

Shylock does not make any clear assertion that Antonio is directly involved in the plot that has gulled him, but he nurses a list of injuries he has endured from the merchant over a long period. It is possible that this general list of his grievances does, however, implicate Antonio in his most recent humiliating losses when he asserts of the merchant: 'He hath disgraced me and hind'red me half a million' (47–8). This central speech in which Shylock reminds his tormentors that he is human (46–64) often gains for him, and is aimed to gain, sympathy. It does so, however, in a specifically limited context in that the assertion of a plea of his common humanity is bracketed between opening and closing declarations of a savage and relentless revenge in which he will show that he can be even more ruthless than the most vengeful Christian (46–7, 60–4). The eloquent plea contains within it a detonating device which explodes and devalues the argument even as it is being made. Though Antonio's Man breaks off this plea when he comes for his friends we are not allowed to see the merchant yet. As the sequence with Tubal passes, Shylock's concern for Jessica seems to be occluded by his anguish at the prodigality of her spending ('Fourscore ducats at a sitting', 98) and the turquoise ring she exchanged for a monkey. Only the insertion by Tubal of news of Antonio's losses can deflect Shylock's attention from his immediate distress to the revenge that must placate him (88–115).

The fourth report in the sequence is delivered by Salerio in Belmont to Bassanio and confirms that Antonio is in Shylock's power. By this time we are so aware of the predictable end of Antonio's mercantile failures that the news can be delivered initially in a somewhat oblique manner. Bassanio receives Antonio's letter (III. ii. 232), and we are given various hints of the bad news it contains as clouds gradually cover the sunny happiness achieved in Bassanio's recent success with the leaden casket. First, Salerio indicates the contents of the letter are not good (242), then Portia records further bad signs gathered from Bassanio's reactions to the letter he is reading (243–50). Next, Bassanio, without revealing the contents of the letter, has to explain to Portia why Antonio is in danger (250–66) and then turns in a series of questions to Salerio about the failure of all the ventures that might have saved his friend (266–71). This may seem a very drawn-out way of dealing with the news but it is necessary as a transition from the earlier gay mood as the gravity of the situation sinks in. It is finally Salerio who indicates the extremity of the merchant's vulnerability to Shylock (271–83). Much of this will be rehearsed and repeated in more detail in the trial scene but the tension it will contain is being worked up long before we get there.

This elaborate method of reporting garners a particular benefit for Shakespeare in the 55 lines of its unfolding (242–96). It may seem very uneconomical especially when, after all the anguished reaction, the contents of the letter are read out anyway. It is, however, carefully designed to support the way Antonio's character is being shaped. The contents of the letter when we finally hear them are a radical contrast to the anguished reactions of his friends, unfolded in such detail, for they are entirely consistent

242

with Antonio's reticence from the very outset of the play on through to its final scene. We have heard already of his altruism in putting Bassanio's pleasure before his own danger (II. viii. 36–49). His reserve is emphasized here again especially in contrast to the emotional pain exhibited by Bassanio and Salerio about the tragically dangerous trap in which their friend is caught. Since Salerio is carrying the letter there is no necessity for brevity in its writing, but the letter reads almost like a kind of abbreviated recitation of facts that we might design nowadays to save money in sending a telegram (III. ii. 315–21). There is no expression of self-pity or shock. Antonio ascribes no blame to the impetuous adventurer who has put him in this situation. Instead, he absolves him of all debts if, he only tentatively suggests, the young man will do him the favour of returning to witness his execution, although he cannot bring himself to insist on it and still encourages his protégé to enjoy the freedom of pleasing himself. This underplaying of the dire straits he is in, the stoical endurance and modesty, is designed to make the audience concur again in Salerio's judgement 'A kinder gentleman treads not the earth' (II. viii. 35). He is a gentleman, a prince of a man, the more distinctly so in contrast to Shylock whom we have seen to be, and by report continues to behave, very much like a predatory animal – a contrast we will observe directly when Antonio returns to the stage to confront Shylock in III. iii.

During Antonio's long, almost continuous absence from the stage of 1094 lines we are kept in touch with his progress whenever it is necessary. No reference is made to him for a long time after his departure in I. iii. This is not surprising because Shakespeare occupies us with the concerns of other plots: the casket sequence in Belmont; Launcelot's transfer of service; Gratiano's request to accompany Bassanio to Belmont; and the Lorenzo-Jessica plot. We need to know nothing of Antonio as these events develop because his affairs are not yet critical and we assume he continues to conduct his own affairs in Venice. He is not only absent from the stage but no reference is made to him in the 412 lines before his brief appearance in II. vi. It is very rare in Shakespeare that such a prominent, central figure is offstage for so long without meriting any reference, but it serves, as I have suggested, to underline our sketchy knowledge of him and some of the mysterious reticence even his close friends find in him. The events which occur in his absence are not such that mention of him would seem probable but references to him in some of them would not be unexpected. In the feasting and anticipation of Bassanio's departure (II. iv, II. vi) reference to him might even be appropriate since it is quite possibly his money which furnishes the entertainment. Even in Shylock's anticipation of a feast with the Christians (II. v) some mention of the man who has mortgaged his body for these revels might be made. In none of these situations is Antonio's name even glanced at. It could, of course, be argued that during this long sequence Shylock is not particularly prominent either, but though he is onstage for only

149 lines they are some of the most expressive and revealing lines Shakespeare ever wrote in defining a character.

It is only after Shylock has been gulled that Antonio, as an available victim for revenge, becomes prominent in the reports of others. In the second and lengthier sequence of his absence, after his cameo role in II. vi, we might begin to wonder why he does not appear and this is when references to him begin to multiply. They are clustered in the reports I have already examined. In the 673 lines from II. vi. 69 to the beginning of III. iii there are, of course, sequences in the development of other plots where there would be no natural reason to mention Antonio, especially in Belmont – II. vii (79), II. ix (100), and much of III. ii up to at least line 219, since Portia knows nothing of the merchant or of Bassanio's relationship to him. In this 673-line absence there are 89 specific references to him which would indicate a frequency of once every 7.6 lines. But if we take out those scenes noted above (398 lines) to leave only those scenes in which we might expect reference to him then the frequency of reference is about once every 3 lines. [The references are Antonio (17), his (20), he (19), him (10), my/dear/dearest/good/true friend (11), and 1 each of my, me, they (with Bassanio), kinder gentleman, bankrupt, prodigal, beggar, Christian, one, best conditioned and unwearied spirit, kindest man, (Man from Antonio)]. Shakespeare, because of the exigencies of his multi-stranded plot, has a considerable variety of matter to present to an audience. He chooses to keep Antonio off the stage for long periods, but certainly in the main plot our attention is focused on him and his problems throughout the central section of the play. The frequent references to him, which are the only contact we are permitted, reinforce the idea that his friends are much more concerned for his life than he appears to be himself.

Table 6.5 Act V, Scene i, 127–307 – 181 lines

Character	Onstage	Speaks	% of lines spoken of lines onstage
Portia	181	73½	40.6
Bassanio	181	40½	22.4
Gratiano	181	33½	18.5
Nerissa	181	21	11.6
Antonio	181	11	6.1
Lorenzo	181	1½	0.8
Jessica	181	0	0

To complete and confirm this pattern of character-shaping by Shakespeare it is significant that being rescued from the jaws of death does not make Antonio any more prominent or voluble. In the final scene six characters share the stage, and Antonio is as shadowy as he has been throughout. Jessica, in another of Shakespeare's strategic silences, says nothing in response to her good fortune at the expense of her father. The important issue at the conclusion of the play is the resolution of the problem of the rings, but this is developed in such a way as to emphasize Antonio's position as a bystander. It is perhaps natural that the four principal lovers involved should be so prominent, but in taking up 93 per cent of the lines between them they push Antonio very much into the shadows. If we sum up his role we find that he is onstage in all for a total of 1008 lines (39.3 per cent of the play) and he speaks only 180½ lines (which is a mere 7.0 per cent of the play). This can be put in perspective to some degree by noting that in the trial which concerns his very life (IV. i) Portia, though she is onstage for only 283 lines, to the 455 lines Antonio is on, speaks over twice as many lines as the merchant himself. In fact, in this one scene Portia, on his behalf, speaks 74 per cent of the number of lines Antonio speaks in the entire play. Of all the plays that Shakespeare wrote which have characters mentioned in their titles Antonio, the Merchant of Venice, of the total of twenty-seven such plays, is given very nearly the fewest lines to speak, even though he is onstage at the outset and the conclusion of the play. Cymbeline is onstage for fewer lines, but speaks many more than Antonio. Julius Caesar is onstage for fewer lines but he speaks 142 lines, even though he is dead after 1160 lines (47.3 per cent of the play). Even Henry VI in the first part of the trilogy devoted to him, who appears for the first time in Act III and features in only five scenes, though he is onstage for only half as many lines speaks almost as many as Antonio. When the merchant receives news of his recovered fortunes at the close of the play (273–9) he replies 'I am dumb!' This response has more general relevance to his role throughout for, though he is not quite muted, he is one of the least voluble and most enigmatic central figures in all of Shakespeare, and for reasons which are related to the structure of the whole play. Three plots are entwined in the play, but the setting-up and consequences of Antonio's bond with Shylock takes up well over 50 per cent of the play's lines. Antonio is offstage for more than 60 per cent of the play, and of 1008 lines he is onstage he speaks fewer than 18 per cent of them. He is a figure whose absence offstage is as important to the effect and intention of the play as his presence onstage.

7

'O Julius Caesar, thou art mighty yet!': The potency of Caesar on and off the stage, alive and dead

In *Julius Caesar*, as clearly as anywhere in Shakespeare, we see the power that can emanate from the offstage world and from absent characters. Analysts of the play have frequently noted the pervasive influence of Caesar. I want to draw attention here to the deep preparation Shakespeare undertakes to develop Caesar as a consistently growing focus of interest in the play. This is achieved in a variety of segments of the play, in the Lupercalian ceremony, in the dramatic use of Caesar's corpse so effectively exploited by Antony, in the proportions of the major roles, in the conjuring references to the names of the characters, in the choices made about what to show onstage and what to report from offstage in battle. The emergence of Caesar's ghost in pursuit of revenge is simply the most obvious, culminating sequence of the pervasive power of Caesar that is being impressed on the audience by varied means throughout.

In I. ii we can see the considerable advantages Shakespeare could gain by keeping action offstage rather than in presenting it directly to the audience. It is the more effective in that the ceremony in which Caesar is offered a crown is only just offstage – so close, in fact, that shouts and flourishes from it have a very significant effect on the concurrent conversation between Brutus and Cassius which the audience is witnessing onstage. These sound effects are a kind of preliminary, enigmatic report of the ceremony which is only filled out in detail in Casca's account of it later in the scene. In Plutarch's *Life of Marcus Brutus* there are details and an extended conversation recorded between Brutus and Cassius (Bullough, vol. V, pp. 95–6) which could have provided Shakespeare with some of the material he dramatizes in I. ii. He used some of the details and ignored others, but much of the argument Cassius deploys in trying to seduce Brutus to join a conspiracy against Caesar, especially in its devious strategies and its rhetorical structures, is Shakespeare's invention. The crucial invention, however, is the timing, the coupling of the onstage conversation with the offstage ceremony as parallel events, which is Shakespeare's ingenious development of what one might term a portmanteau scene. In Plutarch's *Life of Caesar* Cassius draws Brutus into the conspiracy some time after the ceremony and without particular reference to it. In the *Life of Marcus Brutus* the seduction of Brutus into a conspiracy occurs before the offer of a crown to Caesar in the senate. Shakespeare radically pares down the time-scale of the events connected to the conspiracy and the assassination, and one of the elisions occurs in using the ceremony in tandem with the seduction of Brutus, thereby forcing on his attention in a vivid manner the urgent need for action.

I will suggest a number of artistic advantages Shakespeare gained in developing this portmanteau scene, but there may also have been practical reasons related to the doubling of roles for actors. We have been given some sense of the importance of the mob in the first scene of the play. To present the ceremony of the offer of the crown to Caesar onstage would have required the presence of the mob and a continuation of the crowded stage. Rather than over-expose the audience to the mob Shakespeare reserves them for III. ii and III. iii when they will play a central role in turning the tide, under Antony's spell-binding rhetoric, against the conspirators. So the mob goes offstage in I. ii accompanying Caesar to the ceremony, leaving Cassius to work on Brutus 'behind the scene'. If the ceremony had taken place onstage and involved the time it occupies as an offstage event (I. ii. 25–177) then the mob would have spent another 153 lines onstage. It seems likely that some of the members of the crowd were doubling roles, and among those roles may have been some of the conspirators who appear in II. i. For a considerable section of that scene (86–228) there are seven characters onstage where Cassius brings five fellow conspirators to visit Brutus. At times in II. ii there are almost a dozen characters onstage, and for most of the central sequence of the play (III. i – III. iii) the stage is very crowded. So for reasons of pacing and scenic variety, as well as the possible requirements of doubling, a way of cutting down the sequences when the stage is full of characters was desirable.

I have analysed elsewhere the advantages Shakespeare gains from keeping characters apart. It is significant how little onstage interaction he permits between Caesar and Brutus. To the point where Caesar is murdered and dies on his line 'Et tu Brute', Brutus and Caesar have shared the stage on four occasions for a total of 160 lines (13.8 per cent of the 1160 lines the play has run). Caesar speaks at most a total of 5 lines to Brutus, and Brutus speaks directly to Caesar 5 lines. In the sources, at the point where Shakespeare begins to dramatize events, there is a suggestion of some distance between Caesar and Brutus because of the latter's involvement in Pompey's challenge to Caesar. Shakespeare makes little use of this pretext provided by Plutarch to limit their interaction, but there are more obvious dramatic reasons why he develops the relationship thus. Shakespeare shapes Brutus very clearly as a man of principle, a somewhat removed, honourable, ascetic figure, purer in motive than Cassius. He has a genuine nobility which the conspirators wish to exploit to give their cause a veneer of respectability, as Casca and Cassius assert (I. iii. 157–64). Brutus is not as intemperate a figure as Hotspur but he values honour in much the same way and is not at ease with devious plotting, which Hotspur terms 'half-faced fellowship'. The purity of Brutus can more easily be maintained if he is not shown onstage as a close friend in frequent interaction with Caesar. If they were presented as close friends then, as the assassination plot matures, Brutus would inevitably appear as a devious, hypocritical role-player. Though a great deal of Brutus's talk throughout the play is about Caesar, his integrity is carefully maintained. It is emphasized by the contrast with Cassius who is clearly a devious politician inspired by rancorous envy. Many details are shaped to underline the fastidious nature of Brutus. He wants the assassination to be a sacrifice rather than an act of butchery (II. i. 166), and those responsible for the killing to be 'called purgers, not murderers' (II. i. 180). He can piously assert of himself to Antony 'I, that did love Caesar when I struck him', (III. i. 182), and strives to dignify the murder with euphemisms: 'And, gentle friend/Let's kill him boldly, but not wrathfully;/Let's carve him as a dish fit for the gods,/Not hew him as a carcass fit for hounds' (II. i. 171–4). This emphasis in the character of Brutus is stronger in Shakespeare than in Plutarch where he is won over more easily to join in a conspiracy.

The choice of not having Brutus witness the ceremony of the offering of the crown is consistent with Shakespeare's general aim. By keeping the ceremony offstage and using the time, and the effect of the nearby ceremony, to unfold the careful strategy Cassius has to employ to work on the high-minded anxieties of Brutus, Shakespeare was able to kill several birds with one stone. The handling of Antony during the first two acts of the play, in which he has only a small part, helps by contrast to delineate Brutus. On each appearance Antony is shown as being close to Caesar who has an indulgent and affectionate regard for the hedonist that he never shows for the more puritanical Brutus. Antony and Caesar are together onstage in I. ii. 1–24 (24), 178–214 (37), III. ii. 116-29 (14), III. i. 1–26 (26) – for 101 lines (8.7 per cent) before the death of Caesar. Caesar speaks to Antony 29 lines and Antony 6 lines to Caesar – so for one-third of the time they are together onstage they are speaking to each other. It is, of course, Antony who is offering the crown to Caesar offstage while onstage Cassius seeks to persuade Brutus to join a conspiracy. Brutus sails in the rarefied realms of high principle and seems to be above those around him and not skilled in engaging the hearts of the people. The more earthy Antony clearly understands the passions that can be aroused in men. For the mob, he is able to translate the claims Brutus makes of selfless sacrifice back into the savage butchery Brutus had wished to avoid and this leads the people to seize Rome from the conspirators.

The choice of keeping the crowning ceremony offstage gave Shakespeare several advantages and it avoided several problems that putting it onstage would have presented. If Brutus and Cassius had been present at an onstage ceremony it is possible that Shakespeare could have saved time. They could have indicated their reactions in conversational asides, and, since Casca would not be required to deliver a report of a ceremony they had witnessed, there would have been a saving of seventy lines (I. ii. 215–84) which could have been devoted to their reactions after the ceremony was over and Caesar, Antony, and the crowd had left the stage.

This kind of portmanteau scene, an action onstage commented on by others in 'asides' is very common throughout Shakespeare. In *Henry VI, Part 3*, Shakespeare was already working on such parallel structures. In III. ii. 11–108, Richard and Clarence comment on King Edward's speeches. In these 98 lines they have 22 lines between them in cynical comments 'aside'. *Richard III* has several 'asides' as a running commentary from Queen Margaret in I. iii. 109–56 (110–11, 117–19, 125, 133, 142–3, 154–6). They help to present her vividly as an isolated figure among the 'wrangling pirates' even before she comes forward to join issue with them. In *Troilus and Cressida* we have cynical commentary between Ulysses and Nestor behind the back of the posturing Ajax (II. iii. 156–218). Such an extended sequence of 'asides' does not pose any problems because Ajax is so wrapped up in himself and the emphasis is on the cynicism of the generals who so contemptuously mock the figure they are exploiting. In V. ii of the same play Thersites, Ulysses and Troilus, Diomed and Cressida form a spectacular triple-level sequence of commentary 'aside'. There are so many eavesdropping scenes and double-action scenes in plays such as *Love's Labour's Lost*, *Much Ado About Nothing*, *Twelfth Night*, and *The Tempest* that we can see that the crowning ceremony onstage with a parallel commentary of reactions from Brutus and Cassius was no insuperable problem for Shakespeare. A moment's reflection, however, indicates that such a scenic structure would not have served Shakespeare's purpose here.

The reactions of Brutus to the crowning ceremony which is just offstage do have something of the quality of 'asides' in his anxious exchanges with Cassius (I. ii. 79–82, 132–4). Such reactions cannot be developed at any length if there is a central action onstage to which they are a response. Nor can they be developed, as many of those I have referred to above in other plays are, as cynical, carping, or smart-alec observations. Such a limited tone might do for the reactions of Cassius but certainly not for those of Brutus. Shakespeare requires a scene in which he can, for the first time, fully unfold the quality of the minds of Brutus and Cassius to show the concentrated skill required of the latter in recruiting the former to a subversive plot. This kind of interchange could not be handled in two and three-line 'asides' interspersed among an ongoing action. Shakespeare places the ceremony offstage but close enough so that the shouts of the crowd from it can be heard as a catalyst in revealing the anxieties of Brutus and encouraging Cassius to ever bolder arguments. We can see how much emphasis Shakespeare needed to put on these arguments, and the reactions to them, by the length of the speeches involved which could not have been effectively presented as 'asides'. Between Caesar's departure from the stage and his return (I. ii. 25–177) – the duration of the ceremony – the exchange between Cassius and Brutus builds up from brief exchanges to longer, more complex speeches which I outline below (ignoring fragments of lines in the numbers).

Caesar departs (24)						Flourish and shout (78)		2nd Flourish and shout (131)		Caesar returns (177)		TOTAL
(Cassius) 1	1	5	4	9	13	1½	42		27	2½		106
(Brutus)	1	4	11	2	3	1½	8	3	13½			47

Shakespeare allows space for a careful build-up by Cassius of his views on Caesar. His persuasive speeches, which characterize Caesar as a flawed human being, who does not deserve the eminence that is being offered to him within earshot, grow longer and more elaborate. They are structured in three phases which allows for the unfolding of the very different characters of Cassius and Brutus. The reactions of these two men can be revealed in an accelerated fashion because of their anxiety about the threat to republican Rome that the ceremony nearby evidently poses.

In the following analysis I will outline in detail the complex process developed by Shakespeare to exhibit the cautious nature of Brutus and the skill that is required to draw him into the conspiracy. This can only be achieved in an extended and private conversation that uses some of the impact of the ceremony, the sound effects, without the distraction of any visual action which would interfere with the strategy of Cassius. This way of structuring events is one if the clearest examples of a method at work throughout the play. In the sources days, and often months, intervene in the various actions. Shakespeare diminishes or eliminates many of the time gaps to give the impression of continuous action. There is a rising tension in events, with scarcely any pause for three acts, providing a narrative drive that indicates 'a tide in the affairs of men' which are 'taken at the flood'.

Act I, Scene ii

Structure

(a)	1–24(24)	Caesar and his train on the way to the ceremony.
(b)	25–78 (54)	The first manœuvre of Cassius.
	i) 25–50 (26)	
	ii) 51–62 (12)	
	iii) 63–78 (16)	
.....................Stage direction 'Flourish and shout'		
(c)	79–131 (53)	The second manœuvre of Cassius.
	i) 79–92 (14)	
	ii) 93–118 (26)	
	iii) 119–31 (13)	
.....................Stage direction 'Flourish and shout'		
(d)	132–77 (46)	The third manœuvre of Cassius.
	i) 132–41 (10)	
	ii) 142–61 (20)	
	iii) 162–77 (16)	
(e)	178–214 (37)	Caesar and his train return from the
	i) 178–89 (12)	ceremony.
	ii) 190–214 (25)	
(f)	215–91 (77)	Casca's report of the ceremony.
(g)	292–304 (13)	Reactions to Casca's report and further plans.
(h)	305–19 (15)	Cassius summarizes his success with Brutus.

It is important in the whole sequence to notice the skilful unfolding of the strategy of Cassius. Brutus has to be approached with great care in a circuitous manner if he is not to be frightened off from any involvement in a conspiracy. Since he is a man of high principles there is no point in offering him power, the spoils of a *coup*. He will have to find a role, or be offered one, as a selfless figure undertaking a public service. The strategy Cassius employs, therefore, is to emphasize the way that Caesar, by putting himself above the other men, has abrogated the concept of freedom in the Roman republic, a concept very dear to Brutus. Cassius does not appeal directly to Brutus as a figure worthy to assume Caesar's power, but he subtly insinuates the idea in the most inoffensive way. He indicates in a comparison, first between himself and Caesar, that Caesar, far from being exceptional, is a feeble, ailing figure, and then, by pursuing the contrast in a comparison of Brutus with Caesar, that the latter is no better than Brutus and has no special claim to arrogate supreme power to himself. What is quite remarkable about the whole conspiracy is how little consideration is given to the practical consequences of removing Caesar from his powerful position. The assumption is, presumably, that the constitutional structure of Rome has been distorted by Caesar's ambitions and wrenched away from a republic towards a monarchy and that, if Caesar is removed, Rome will revert to the kind of structure that Brutus finds acceptable. To Brutus it is a piece of surgery to be handled rationally, clinically, and without any emotional excess, and presented to the public as a ritual sacrifice necessary for the public welfare. He has no concept whatsoever of how a political opportunist can work on a mob's emotions to make it believe that instead of losing a dangerous enemy it has lost a paternal benefactor and protector who had a special care for it. That kind of political misunderstanding, the lack of pragmatic skill in Brutus which will allow Antony to reverse his fortunes so swiftly, is first exhibited in his response to the manœuvres of Cassius.

(b) The first manœuvre of Cassius – 25–78 (54)

(i) 25–50 (26) Cassius and Brutus had, according to Plutarch, been in competition for a praetorship which Caesar granted to Brutus. Cassius must therefore clear the ground by claiming that he has not recently enjoyed the friendship of Brutus as he used to do in the past. Although it is not explicitly so stated, Cassius may be providing Brutus with an opportunity to indicate that the cooling in their relationship is a result of their political rivalry. Because outward observation suggests that Brutus is inwardly troubled an opportunity is offered to clear the air. The response Brutus makes is guarded, implying that the conflicting emotions troubling his mind are his own affair and have caused no diminution of his friendship for Cassius.

(ii) 51–62 (12) This encourages Cassius to suggest that the conflict in the mind of Brutus is not an entirely private matter and could benefit from the views of an objective observer. It is subtly implied that Brutus ought to be aware how many admire him and look to him for leadership because they are 'groaning underneath this age's yoke' (61). The tyranny that has produced this groaning is not directly stated though the connection is hard to miss since the only figure not included in this hope for leadership by Brutus is made clear in the sarcasm of Cassius, 'except immortal Caesar' (60).

(iii) 63–78 (16) Yet even this careful, periphrastic formulation is enough to flutter the sitting bird Cassius is trying to charm, for Brutus shies away from involvement: 'Into what dangers would you lead me, Cassius' (63). Cassius has introduced into his argument his major target, 'immortal Caesar', a man with pretensions to the status of a god. Brutus by contrast, Cassius suggests, has no such pretensions but must be made to see in a reflecting mirror in what high regard he is held by others. Brutus must accept the undistorted truth he is offered if he acknowledges that Cassius has no reputation as a crafty politician who flatters others only to slander them later. This reliance on a plain, blunt man's reputation to eliminate all suspicion of calculated duplicity has a touch of the method Iago uses to such devastating effect. The sequence is orchestrated with telling skill, for the timing of the ceremony offstage seems accidentally to reinforce the point Cassius is making. Cassius is asserting how little he is known as a flattering politician, how much as a friend he can be trusted, how little he is prone to curry favour with the mob: 'if you know/That I profess myself in banqueting/To all the rout, then hold me dangerous' (76–8). Precisely at that moment comes the noise from offstage, *Flourish and shout*, which indicates how that other close friend of Brutus, Caesar, may be behaving with 'the rout', and, by implication, how 'dangerous' he may be. The offstage sounds form a precise punctuation underlining the point Cassius has been circling towards, that Brutus must learn who his real friends are and how much they expect him to safeguard the welfare of Rome. This shouting, we will learn later from Casca, is the crowd's celebration of Caesar's refusal of the crown. But we, like Cassius, can see from his apprehensive reaction that Brutus fears Caesar may be being offered the crown and has no confidence that Caesar will refuse it. The misinterpretation by Brutus of the celebration offstage allows Cassius to proceed more confidently in his strategy. Brutus has been guarded and unwilling to share his private thoughts, but the noise from the ceremony catches him unawares and leads him to betray his disquiet that the state is in danger.

(c) *The second manœuvre of Cassius – 79–131 (53)*

(i) 79–92 (14) Cassius leaps on this chink in the reserved façade of Brutus. Brutus admits his fear but immediately tries to cover it over by insisting that he loves Caesar well (82). He indicates, perhaps, some irritation at the shadowy implications in the speech of Cassius, for he prefers things to be out in the open (83–9). He responds very much as Othello responds to the way Iago trails his cloak the better to draw his victim on (*Othello*, III. iii. 108–16, 130–3). Cassius is by no means as devious as Iago, yet he has managed to manœuvre Brutus into a position where, instead of secretively maintaining his own counsel, he is asking for a more open discussion of the issue Cassius has broached and provides him with the precise topic that is the next logical step in his argument. The nobility and honour of Brutus, in his concern for Rome, must ally itself to likeminded men, and he must be isolated from Caesar who is an enemy to the values they all share.

(ii) 93–118 (26) The story Cassius relates of Caesar's behaviour in the swimming-match in the Tiber is presented overtly as an illustration of the fact that Caesar has no right to any superior status because he is no better than Brutus or Cassius (93–9). The anecdote, however, presents a picture of a Caesar so enfeebled and so contemptible that the implication may be taken that he deserves his eminence rather less than those around him. This man who 'is now become a god' (116) owes his life to Cassius. Cassius does not assert that he ought to have supreme power himself but he does, in his carefully placed simile (112–15) about the very founder of Rome, characterize himself in the role of the heroic Aeneas saving in flaming Troy the life of his father, Anchises, a feeble old man, to whom Caesar corresponds.

(iii) 119–31 (13) This picture of a floundering Caesar is reinforced by another anecdote of his weakness in his vulnerability to epilepsy. If before he was compared to old man Anchises, he is now likened to 'a sick girl' (128). Cassius builds up his peroration into self-righteous anger about a man who is making himself the focus of all eyes, who manages to 'get the start of the majestic world/And bear the palm alone' (130–1). At that very moment, as though Cassius were a conjurer capable of drawing reality into filling out the picture he has imaginatively built up, there is again the sound of a flourish and the shouts of the crowd from offstage, from that ceremony to which all men have been drawn, leaving Brutus and Cassius alone here together to discuss the undeserved magnetic attraction of Caesar. Cassius has characterized Caesar with scathing satirical accounts. His contempt is so severe that we might, under normal circumstances, expect a close friend of Caesar's, such as Brutus, to take offence or at least protest against such extreme criticism. But the ceremony just offstage puts such pressure on the apprehensive Brutus and is organized in a way that prevents him from having to leap to the defence of his friend. Whatever defence he might feel called upon to make is replaced by more immediate fears, fuelled by the flourishes and shouts, that Caesar might be pursuing his ambitions, in accepting a kingship, to the extremes Cassius suggested when he asserted he might 'bear the palm alone'. The scene is organized to make the absence of any sustained defence by Brutus of Caesar's nature from the attacks of Cassius scarcely noticeable. This allows Cassius to develop his arguments to an extreme that would not otherwise be possible. The audience is persuaded that Brutus remains quite distinct from Cassius, retains his sense of honour and his integrity, and feels under such pressure that there is no time to confute the jaundiced smearing of Caesar's character by Cassius. Brutus asserts early in the scene (82) that he loves Caesar well and yet by the end of the scene himself proposes further meetings with Cassius which indicates he is considering joining the conspiracy. That is the harvest Shakespeare garnered in developing this portmanteau scene with its ceremony only just offstage.

(d) The third manœuvre of Cassius – 132–77 (46)

(i) 132–41 (10) The fears of Brutus of the 'new honours that are heaped on Caesar' (134) allow Cassius to sweep along in pressing his point against Caesar without any impediment. Now instead of presenting Caesar as a helpless old man or a figure trembling like a sick girl he changes perspective and pumps him up into a bloated, oversized statue like the Colossus of Rhodes. Caesar makes everyone seem pygmy-sized as they treat him like a god, and 'the rout' within their hearing seem to be ceding absolute power to him in their adulation. The remedy for this situation can only come from those who recognize that they are responsible for their own destiny and are willing to take hold of it.

(ii) 142–61 (20) Cassius has already compared himself to Caesar to the latter's disadvantage. He now compares Brutus to Caesar with the implication that he certainly deserves as much prominence as the man who might, even at this moment, be accepting a crown. His argument is designed to appeal to a man who believes that the freedom of Romans is based on equality and the denial of exceptional privilege to any man. Even though Cassius has focused much of his attack on Caesar's pride and ambition he is aware that a subtle appeal to the pride of Brutus may draw him into the conspiracy. It is the task of Brutus, he asserts, to maintain the principles espoused by his ancestor, Lucius Junius Brutus, on which the Roman republic was founded. The scarcely veiled implication is that an earlier Brutus got rid of the Tarquins, the tyrants who dominated Rome, and now that another tyrant rears his head it is the task of Brutus to repeat the act of salvation. This shrewd appeal to emulate his ancestors has the right heroic ring to it, the dependence of Rome on his family, and it seems to work to some degree because Brutus will later recall it (II. i. 52–4).

(iii) 162–77 (16) The response of Brutus is shaped with remarkable circumspection. We see how careful he is and yet how aware he is of the pressure of events demanding more of him than the reticent personal ruminations he hinted at earlier in this scene. The whole sequence has been contrived so that the central issue to which all the implications point has not yet been uttered. Cassius has still not announced that there is a conspiracy afoot, that Brutus is being looked to as a key figure to lead the conspiracy, that the aim of such a conspiracy is to kill Caesar. Shakespeare perfectly understands that politics is often a matter of nuance and innuendo. In dealing with someone like the honourable Brutus matters will have to proceed indirectly whereby one may be moving in a certain direction while seeming to look in another. Brutus is being encouraged to understand that swift, decisive action may be required while being allowed to maintain the illusion that he is acting with careful and deliberate calmness. Shakespeare telescopes the time frame presented in Plutarch but does so without making Brutus appear to act with intemperate rashness. He will counsel against the rash proposal of killing Antony, and it will come naturally and persuasively from him because he has been allowed to join the conspiracy as a prudent figure who counsels surgery not for spite or personal gain but for the health of the body politic of Rome. In his reply here to the suggestions of Cassius he speaks with the caution of a man who will not sully himself by clarifying exactly what it is they are talking about, who will not be rushed into dangerous admissions or ill-formulated plans. His phrasing has much of the tone of the communiqués of modern governments which never say anything specific but allow for a number of interpretations to be read into them, and a number of loopholes for the speaker to escape through to avoid irrevocable commitment. Brutus retains this manner of speech in planning the assassination and in explaining it afterwards. It makes clear that Brutus knows what Cassius is up to, 'What you would work me to' (163), acknowledges that he has his own view of the matter which stems from his principles. He explicitly warns Cassius off from pursuing the matter further at this time, but assures him that his efforts have not been wasted and that he will listen to further arguments and form his own independent response. He ends, however, with a statement of his own resolve which indicates how much he is aware that circumstances are developing rapidly enough that he can foresee he may have to act rather than allow his integrity to be compromised. It is a remarkable piece of coded-message transmission. Cassius takes the hint to underplay the effect of his own seductive method by acknowledging what Brutus wishes to have clearly recognized, that the source of any action by Brutus will come from within Brutus, based entirely on his own integrity and not from any devious manipulation from without. Shakespeare develops the whole sequence between these two men as complex, subtle, political manœuvring which requires a good deal of time to reveal fully the differences between them, the style of their political methods and the cast of their minds. This could not have been effectively accomplished in 'asides' watching the ceremony between Caesar and Antony among the mob. There would have had to be a private conversation of some length that could have been situated before or after the ceremony. In choosing to have their conversation concurrent with the ceremony offstage Shakespeare could increase the dramatic tension between the two men and within Brutus so that the fears he harbours and which Cassius fosters are not mere theory but an urgent, practical issue.

(e) Caesar and his train return from the ceremony – 178–214 (37)

(i) 178–89 (12) Shakespeare prepares for the report by Casca which will come after Caesar's departure. Brutus characterizes the mood of those returning by observing that they appear to be in a disturbed state.

(ii) 190–214 (25) We have already spent a good deal of time listening to savage portraits of Caesar delineated by Cassius who implies that his views are motivated by principles as high as those of Brutus. Caesar delivers to Antony his views on Cassius as a dangerous man motivated by envy and an unrelenting severity of judgement which never allows him to relax. Caesar's opinion here serves a number of purposes: (1) it may confirm some of the impressions Cassius has made on the audience; (2) it may give some substance to Cassius's malice, in that Caesar has never been at ease with him; (3) it may confirm some sense of Caesar's political shrewdness and, by comparison, a lack of it in Brutus who does not clearly state any suspicions of the motives of Cassius; (4) because Caesar judges Cassius in contrast to Antony a relative weighting of characters is advanced there also. The whole scene encourages us to make comparisons and to draw distinctions between the play's four major characters; (5) it helps to some degree to confirm the view Cassius has promoted of Caesar's debility. Caesar rather pompously asserts (211–12) that he is above the weakness of fear and acknowledges in the next line his deafness, the kind of frailty of which Cassius has made such a large issue. This section serves as a symmetrical bracket related to (*a*), surrounding the sequence which has juxtaposed the nearby ceremony with the manœuvres of Cassius. It provides a change of perspective and a bridge passage to the report by Casca of what exactly went on at that ceremony, the sounds of which have so tantalized Brutus and aided Cassius in his task.

(f) Casca's report of the ceremony – 215–91 (77)

In this fuller dilation on the details of the ceremony we find that the shouts and flourishes did not signify Caesar's acceptance of kingship, as Brutus feared, but the refusal of it. On the face of it this report might threaten to undo all the spadework Cassius has undertaken in drawing Brutus towards the conspiracy since Caesar has rejected the power Cassius has so vigorously asserted he seeks. Casca's report, however, is not simply of facts that are encouraging to cherishers of republican sentiments. The focus is not so much on the refusal as on the manner of the refusal. At no point in his talk with Cassius had Brutus indicated directly that he believes Caesar is himself ambitious for the crown. He fears that 'the people/Choose Caesar for their king' (79–80) and that 'new honors are heaped on Caesar' (134), which implies nothing more than submission to the will of the people. Brutus never fully submits to a belief in Caesar's unbridled ambition. Even in II. i he is not able to assert such a conviction (19–21), and he works on probability, on the way power usually works on human nature (21–34). In contrast to the rancorous envy of Cassius and his absolute certainty about Caesar's ambition Brutus can only bring himself to a subjunctive phrasing, 'So Caesar may;/Then, lest he may, prevent' (27–8). The slide from subjunctive to imperative is a determination by Brutus – better safe than sorry – of preventive surgery for Rome. In I. ii Cassius has harped a good deal on the human frailty of Caesar, and we sense the partial assent of Brutus at least to the possibility of ambition in Caesar from the fact that he makes no sharp rebukes to Cassius for the savage portraits he paints of his friend. This is why it is of crucial importance that it is Brutus who notes on the return from the ceremony that 'The angry spot doth glow on Caesar's brow,/And all the rest look like a chidden train' (183–4).

The essence of Casca's account is that in the rejection of supreme power Caesar was obviously reluctant. This way of presenting it does not confirm the picture Cassius has painted, but it does nothing to cancel it out either. Because it accords with the agitation Brutus has observed in Caesar it rather confirms the need to consider the issue further. Before Caesar returned Brutus indicated he was willing to talk more about the issue, and Casca's report indicates the danger may have abated only temporarily. Cassius is, as Caesar describes him, a subtle, driven politician, and his craft and rhetorical tricks cannot have remained entirely unnoticed by Brutus. Casca is a blunt man, noted for his 'sour fashion', who does not obviously have an axe to grind and does not set out to blacken Caesar's character for some obviously ulterior, political motive. He has to have his story dragged out of him, and seems not to shape it with subtlety, but to present it as though he were indifferent to it. There is an outspoken independence about Casca which indicates he is not a co-conspirator with Cassius or anyone that Brutus can suspect has been 'planted' to give a biased report to reinforce the seductive arguments Cassius has already made. Casca is not yet, of course, of the conspiracy, for Cassius only 'breaks' with him in the next scene (I. iii. 89–120). In Casca's role there are residual elements of the truth-speaker we find elsewhere in court-jesters, the kind of rough figure who cannot help but speak his mind, such as Kent, Enobarbus, Apemantus, or, more nastily, Thersites. Such figures are often trusted because they appear to speak their minds without fear of the consequences. It is Iago's supreme skill to pass himself off successfully as this kind of trustworthy diamond-in-the-rough. Casca temperamentally may be very different from Brutus, but the latter can appreciate in him a kind of integrity which speaks out fearlessly and has only contempt for sophisticated, political role-playing. In his account he displays precisely that contempt for what he sees as Caesar's role-playing. It can take others in but is transparent to a man such as Casca who despises such games. His brusque account of the three offerings of the crown is delivered, perhaps, with some impatience that one should have to endure such hypocritical behaviour. His posture as an uninvolved bystander is attested to by the fact that he could not laugh at the antics of Caesar, and the fools who were taken in by him, because he was more concerned to avoid breathing in the noisome air reeking from the rabble. Cassius manages, for the most part, to let Brutus absorb unhindered Casca's trustworthy account, but he cannot resist capitalizing on the observation Brutus makes that Caesar has the falling sickness. He asserts that he, Brutus, and 'honest Casca' have the falling sickness, reinforcing his earlier argument that they are all petty men peeping about between the legs of a pompous oppressor to find dishonourable graves. This allows Casca to establish his reliability even further by claiming not to understand this rhetorical trick and to insist only on the plain facts of his observation. (255–9). To Casca it is all a theatrical show plain folks should not take too seriously. This image of rustic ignorance is reinforced when he claims not to understand the Greek Cicero spoke. Yet though he is at the opposite extreme from sophisticated operators such as Cicero (and Cassius) he is not one to have the wool pulled over his eyes.

The effect of the report is for Brutus to look at the ceremony he has missed through Casca's eyes, which confirms his own observation of the anger with which Caesar returned. It is worth observing that there is some rough parallel between the experience described of Caesar offstage and that of Brutus, as we have observed it, onstage. Caesar was being offered a crown that he may have wanted but felt obliged to refuse it, resisting the proffered seduction with a portrayal of modest, virginal purity. Brutus has been offered seductive arguments which have encouraged him to submit, without any explicit statement ever being made, to a conspiracy that will ensure Caesar never accepts the crown he has feigned not to want. Brutus has resisted and put off those offers, just as Caesar has set aside the crown, but as the scene progresses we see that he is increasingly prone to accept them though he would like to maintain his virginal innocence. Nowhere in the scene is it made unequivocally clear that Caesar is as ambitious as Cassius and Casca, in different ways, assert him to be, and as Brutus is being persuaded to think he may be. Politics is demonstrated to be here, as elsewhere in Shakespeare, a process which has less to do with truth than with what men can be persuaded to believe, and bring themselves to believe, is true.

(g) Reactions to Casca's report and further plans – 292–304 (13)

After Casca's departure Brutus and Cassius discuss his nature for a moment. It is interesting that Cassius, himself such a dedicated political role-player, suggests that Casca puts on his blunt behaviour (294–9), which might seem to undermine his trustworthiness and the appeal his account has for Brutus as a kind of round, unvarnished tale. In fact, Cassius describes exactly how Casca has won credibility in delivering his account, and Brutus seems to acknowledge that this rudeness, which is a sauce to Casca's good wit, has indeed allowed him to digest his words with better appetite. Cassius with elaborate rhetorical strategies sought to shape an image of Caesar in the mind of Brutus. Casca artlessly gives a report of the man in action, a man so agitated by the ceremony that he fell down and filled out the picture of the helpless epileptic Cassius had described. Before Caesar's return Brutus has been vague about involvement in further discussions – 'I shall recount hereafter' (165), 'I will consider' (168), 'and find a time' (169). After Casca's report he engages himself in the urgency of the situation:

> For this time I will leave you.
> To-morrow, if you please to speak with me,
> I will come home to you; or if you will,
> Come home to me, and I will wait for you.
>
> (300–3)

By offering his own home for a meeting there is a tacit admission that he is no longer an outsider to whatever plans may go ahead but is willing to act as host and perhaps central figure in discussions. Brutus has not overtly admitted anything, nor yet himself spoken any words antagonistic to Caesar but he has been willing to listen to many hundreds of words from others who are antagonistic and contemptuous.

(h) Cassius summarizes his success with Brutus – 305–19 (15)

The position Brutus has shaped for himself is shrewdly and precisely defined by Cassius in a closing soliloquy. He is determined to augment the headway he has already made with further stratagems to recruit the noble Brutus. He is aware of the high regard Caesar has for Brutus and, considering how little motive, compared to himself, Brutus has for joining a conspiracy, Cassius takes him to be something of a fool (310–12). The high ideals espoused by Brutus, which he has pretended to share, are obviously not matters of great weight with him.

Shakespeare's method of structuring this scene secures advantages for him that could not easily have been achieved in other ways. The first movement of the play is shaped and sustained by the drive of consolidating the conspiracy, luring Brutus into it, and showing us enough of Caesar to indicate that there might be a basis for the alarm of Brutus as a potential threat to the republic. Much of this movement, which sets up the play, is based on the contrasts in the nature of the four or five principal characters, and Shakespeare needed to develop them in the revealing circumstances of a potential crisis where the cautious Brutus can commit himself to an assassination. The final step, which would undo the republic, has been proposed but not taken. There can be no guarantee that Caesar would not eventually be persuaded to accept the crown. The only conclusion to be drawn is that it is very late indeed but action might yet be taken.

There are other incidental benefits from keeping the crowning ceremony offstage. It keeps Antony in a minor position and allows him to emerge with astonishing force as the dominant figure in the events that follow the assassination. Antony is established as a close ally of Caesar, but we are not yet given much visible evidence of his skills. He is seen only in brief appearances as a playboy figure about whose political skills there is no consensus. If we saw him offering the crown to Caesar his character might have had to be unfolded more unambiguously. Presented as a potential kingmaker the audience might see more clearly the reasons for the fears of Cassius and his argument that he too should fall in the assassination. As it is we can consider Brutus to be imprudent even as we understand his queasiness about indulging in a bloodbath. By not presenting the crowning ceremony onstage Shakespeare not only mutes the threat of Antony, he avoids giving the audience any first-hand evidence that Caesar is as ambitious as Cassius suggests. We hear of his weaknesses and we see evidence of his self-regard each time he comes onstage but it is never clear that he is a dangerous and potent threat to republican Rome. The focus is kept on the conspirators and their plans. If the crowning ceremony had been staged with Caesar swooning in an epileptic fit then his debility would have been prominently featured. Shakespeare seems to be less interested in whether there is any plausible justification for the assassination than in how a figure like Brutus could come to lead the conspiracy. In reporting the events of the ceremony rather than in presenting them Shakespeare was able to take the opportunity to develop the figure of Casca, exactly the kind of figure who can plausibly confirm the fears Brutus already entertains. By using the time of the ceremony offstage to unfold the relationship of Brutus and Cassius Shakespeare can keep them apart from the sweaty mob. We hear of Casca's disdain for the mob. We will eventually see how little skill Brutus has in dealing with a crowd, and so, until the forum scene, he is seen only in relationship with the patricians, which helps to sustain our sense of him as a man apart who lacks some of the political skills required in the situation he is being drawn into.

Shakespeare often chose to present a hero as possessing devious, political skills. Prince Hal is a complex study of the kind of manipulative role-playing which is often associated with villainy in the drama of this period. Two of the major figures in *Julius Caesar*, Cassius and Antony, have extensive political abilities without being presented as deeply malicious villains. The central figure, Brutus, in his political instincts at least, is more like Hotspur. He is a noble figure seeking to sustain his honour even as he is involved in devious political stratagems. He can engage in duplicity and conspiracy without ever fully allowing himself to acknowledge that he is doing so. He can seek to justify the underhand means he pursues and dignify them with the high principles of the necessity of the ends they are used to achieve. This attitude destroys him because it inhibits him from following through with the ruthless political pragmatism required in securing the position he has taken. In this stance he is only a step along the way to the even more extreme and politically inept figure of Coriolanus who can be persuaded to adopt only reluctantly what he considers base means to achieve his ends. But Brutus is like him in that he cannot play any role that seems to infringe on the sense of integrity to which he is wedded. It is that central character trait that the complex structure of I. ii is designed to establish as clearly as possible.

The role of Julius Caesar is not very large, for he speaks only 144 lines (5.9 per cent of the 2454 lines of the play), and yet he has a potency out of all proportion to the lines he actually speaks. It is worth exploring how Shakespeare stretches his powerful impact across the play even though he dies after 1160 lines (47.3 per cent). He is present onstage as a corpse for another 440 lines (17.9 per cent) after his death (III. i. 178–297, III. ii. 40–259), and it can be argued that he is a much more potent figure dead than he is alive. Shakespeare had discovered the dramatic potential of a dead body onstage early in his career when he used the coffin containing Henry VI's corpse as a silent witness to Gloucester's extraordinary wooing of Lady Anne (*Richard III*, I. ii. 1–226). Later in his career he was to use the corpse of Cloten for another bizarre purpose (*Cymbeline*, IV. ii. 282–403). But Caesar's corpse is onstage for longer than these two sequences together, and it is there in scenes that are some of the most powerful in Shakespeare's work. The reappearance of Caesar as a ghost, in IV. iii. 275–86, serves to confirm the power that he exerts over the play.

The frail, vain, ailing, superstitious figure who appears before the audience in three of the eight scenes of the play up to and including the scene in which he dies (I. ii. 1–24 (24), 178–214 (37), II. ii. 1–129 (129), III. i. 1–77 (77)) is onstage alive, therefore, for 267 lines (10.9 per cent) which is 173 lines fewer than he is onstage as a corpse. In the whole play he is onstage alive, dead, and as a ghost for 719 lines (29.3 per cent).

After the assassination the conspirators stoop in the grisly ritual of bathing their hands in Caesar's blood (III. i. 105–18). Antony, on his arrival, speaks to the dead body (III. i. 148–50) and makes continued references and gestures to it. He shakes the hands of the conspirators so that he is smeared with Caesar's blood, which induces him yet again to address the corpse (III. i. 194–210). When the conspirators have gone he addresses the corpse and seems to use it as a source of power to unleash havoc on the murderers, conjuring, almost like an exorcist, the spirit that will turn the tide against Brutus and his allies (III. i. 254–75). In fact in III. i and III. ii Antony speaks directly to and about Caesar's body 132 lines (III. i. 148–50 (3), 161–3 (3), 194–210 (17), 219 (1), 227–30 (4), 254–75 (22), 291–2 (2), III. ii. 74–107 (34), 118–20 (3), 132–7 (6), 157–8 (2), 169–97 (29), 225–30 (6)) clearly demonstrating enough skill as an orator to 'put a tongue/In every

wound of Caesar that should move/The stones of Rome to rise and mutiny'
(III. ii. 228–30). Antony speaks nearly as many lines about the dead Caesar
as the live Caesar speaks in the play. It is this concentration over Caesar's
body, this theatrical exploitation of it, which gives Caesar such potency for
the rest of the play. Caesar may be dead but he is certainly not done with.

I have indicated the ingenious variety of effects Shakespeare can extract in
structuring a character's absence from the stage. Here we have effects which
help to shape the play from a figure who is not absent but who is not alive
either. We can gauge something of how this is achieved by counting the
references made to Caesar by various characters in the 479 lines of text
which follow his death onstage up to the point at which his corpse (which
is onstage, as I have noted, for 440 of these lines) is finally removed (III. i.
77 – III. ii. 259). The references are as follows: Caesar'/s (74), his (26),
thee/thou/thy/thine (21), he (17), him (17), friend (2) and 1 each of the
following: this little measure, the most noble blood, choice and master spirit
of this age, this, this hart, brave hart, thou bleeding piece of earth, this
corse, my best lover, Julius, the dead, the body, this costly blood. There are
thus 170 references to Caesar in these 479 lines, and for most of them the
body is there onstage to reinforce the potency of every reference. The
references thus average out at a little more than once every 3 lines, which,
with the exception of Coriolanus, is a frequency higher than to any other
absent or dead figure in Shakespeare. In this central section of the play only
once do more than 20 lines pass without a reference to Caesar (III. ii.
199–224).

After Caesar's body is taken off at III. ii. 259 there are 427 lines (17.4
per cent) before the ghost of Caesar appears to Brutus on the eve of Philippi.
The references to him radically diminish after Antony has used the corpse to
such potent effect. Though the conspirators sought to rid Rome of Caesar
they are not entirely able to rid their minds of him. There are only 10
references in these 427 lines (Caesar (5), him (2), Julius, his, the foremost
man – 1 each) but they keep the memory of Caesar alive until the ghost
makes its appearance before Brutus.

Shakespeare did not invent this after-life potency of Caesar or the
appearance of Caesar's ghost. A possible source, *Caesar's Revenge*
(Bullough, vol. V, pp. 196–211) had used similar emphases and has extensive appearances of a ghost on three occasions. In Plutarch the spectral visi-
tant is not named as Caesar's ghost but as the evil spirit of Brutus. But the
effect of exploiting Caesar's corpse with such power is largely Shakespeare's.
The events following the murder are found in the sources, though
Shakespeare makes changes in the timing and organization of the scenes, but
the content and detail of Antony's speeches to and about the corpse in III.
i and III. ii are almost entirely Shakespeare's invention. The emphasis on
Caesar achieving revenge acknowledged in the dying words of his murderers
is also Shakespeare's.

This, however, is part of a larger strategy in the play of juxtaposing the names of Caesar and Brutus. The relationship between them is obviously of central significance to the play, but it is worth noting how it is achieved. I have touched on these matters earlier in my analysis of I. ii but return to them here to give a fuller picture that is relevant to the structure of the whole play. Caesar and Brutus share the stage in I. ii. (1–24), but they exchange only a couple of lines, and the stage is left to Cassius's unfolding of his own views on Caesar and to his probing of the views of Brutus. One of the most telling segments of their conversation is the conjuring comparison Cassius makes of the names of Brutus and Caesar (I. ii. 142–61). In II. i we have a soliloquy by Brutus (10–24) in which he speculates about the need to kill Caesar. Brutus is one of the delegation in II. ii which comes to encourage Caesar to go the the Senate (108–29). Here they have only the second of their brief exchanges (114–15) before Caesar's death. They share the stage in the murder scene for the 77 lines that Caesar is alive and again have only a brief exchange (III. i. 52–5). This is a remarkable choice on Shakespeare's part if we consider that by the time of Caesar's death the play has run 1160 lines (47.3 per cent of its length), and to that point these two figures, whose different temperaments are a central part of the action, have spent onstage together only 160 lines, (13.8 per cent of this first movement of the play) and have, in direct exchange, spoken less than 1 per cent of it. Brutus speculates at length about Caesar and tries to make the assassination a matter of high principle and ritual sacrifice. But Antony can make this high-mindedness seem hypocrisy and such airy abstractions irrelevant when, with the vivid reality of the bloodied corpse as a theatrical prop to underline his rhetorical spell, he can reverse the tide of fortune. The heart of his method is caught in the two great speeches 'Friends, Romans, Countrymen' (III. ii. 73–107) and his recapitulation of the murder by reference to the bloodied mantle (III. ii. 169–97), and the essence of his method is to weave references to Brutus and Caesar hypnotically together.

Antony is onstage in III. ii for 232 lines (40–271) and he speaks 146 lines. If we look at the references only in Antony's speeches we can see the concentrated mesmeric power of the association he forges between the generous hearted Caesar and the trusted friend who destroyed him. The references are to Caesar and his possessions, and on a few occasions Brutus is referred to in more general terms denoting the conspirators. They are heavily weighted towards Caesar because the corpse is so valuable a prop for Antony, but the naming of Brutus is still remarkably frequent. Brutus is the figure and name the conspirators wanted to give their cause respectability, and Antony fastens on that respectability to destroy their aims. He whips the crowd to mutiny (226–31) until they determine to burn the house of Brutus, holds them on a leash a little longer as he reveals the terms of Caesar's will, and then lets them loose so that by the end of the scene we hear that 'Brutus and Cassius/Are rid like madmen through the gates of Rome' (268–9). His constant strategy is to wind the names of Caesar and Brutus together giving substance to the special relationship that Shakespeare has chosen not to show the audience onstage and which will only be completed at Philippi. In Antony's 146 lines of speech delivered to the plebeians we find the following interthreaded references; to Caesar – 59 [Caesar'/s (27), his (10), him (9), he (9), friend (2), the dead (1), himself (1)]; to Brutus – 27 [Brutus (15), they – Brutus as one of the conspirators (4), men (2), him (2), he (2), his (1), traitors (1)] – a combined total of 86 references in the 146 lines.

Ironically, the longest direct exchange between these two figures, whose names have been woven so deftly together by Cassius and Antony, occurs in IV. iii when the ghost of Caesar visits Brutus in his tent (275–86). These twelve lines are slightly more than the total they have exchanged before the murder completing their sharing of the stage at 172 lines (7 per cent) and their total interaction at 22 lines (0.9 per cent). After Caesar's ghost exists there are still 376 lines remaining in the play (IV. iii. 287 to the end). References to Caesar are not frequent but they are telling in that Cassius and Brutus both die with his name on their lips. It is clear that the relationship of Cassius and Caesar is given less stage time than that of Brutus and Caesar, but this is less surprising given Caesar's views of Cassius expressed to Antony (I. ii. 194–5, 198–210). Cassius and Caesar share the stage for 138 lines (I. ii. 1–24, 178–214, III. i. 1–77), but in all Cassius speaks only 2½ lines to Caesar (III. i. 55–7), and Caesar perhaps 2 in reply to him (58–9), before his speech, asserting his constancy, becomes a general statement to all the conspirators about to stab him. We hear towards the end of the play from Brutus that the ghost of Caesar has appeared to him on other occasions (V. v. 17–19) and that the spirit which haunts him signals his fate and in some sense induces him to submit to it. There are 17 references to Caesar in these final 376 lines [Caesar (11), thee/thou (5), the ghost of Caesar (1)] and they are testimony to his continuing potency. We have the sense of his spirit hovering over the battlefield until revenge is accomplished. Shakespeare here follows the practice he had established at Bosworth in *Richard III* and was to use in a more elaborate way in the various appearances of Banquo's ghost in *Macbeth*.

In terms of the four-part sequence usually exhibited in Shakespeare's battles, only a small part of *Julius Caesar* is devoted to the resolution of the issues developed in the first part of the play at the battle of Philippi. It could be argued that all of Antony's strategy in the Forum scene (III. ii) is designed to force the conspirators out of Rome in preparation for the confrontation at Philippi. In the structural rhythm of the action in the whole play, however, the Forum scene and the killing of Cinna the poet (III. iii), bring to a conclusion the sequence of events set out in the first three acts which present the development of the conspiracy, the assassination of Caesar, and its immediate consequences. In IV. i we begin with the new regime of the triumvirate pricking down its victims. The preparation for battle begins in this scene when Antony informs Octavius that Brutus and Cassius are levying powers and must be confronted on the battlefield.

(a) *The political build-up in events which occur before the action moves to the battlefield – IV. i. 40–51 (12), IV. ii (52), IV. iii (308)*
– 372 lines

The preparation among the triumvirate is brief, and the next time they appear onstage is on the plains of Philippi in battle-readiness (V. i). All of the remaining preparation is in the camp of Brutus at Sardis. Brutus and Cassius quarrel and then resolve their differences before advancing to Philippi. The scene does not focus completely on the disposition of forces for the coming battle until IV. iii. 163. The most ominous element of foreshadowing of the coming battle is the visit of the ghost of Caesar to the tent of Brutus (IV. iii. 275–86).

(b) *Preparation on the battlefield itself – V. i (125) – 125 lines*

(i)   Octavius and Antony consider their approaching enemies and arrange the disposition of their forces. 1–20 (20).
(ii) Brutus and Cassius enter with their army for a parley. Insults and words of defiance are traded back and forth until Octavius and Antony depart with their army. 21–66 (46).
(iii) Cassius considers foreboding omens of battle with Messala. 67–91 (25).
(iv) Cassius and Brutus bid each other farewell as they leave to command the different wings of their forces. 92–125 (34).

This play is extremely flexible in its use of actors, for there are 38 distinct speaking-roles and several scenes which require the augmentation of speaking-roles with Citizens, Senators, Attendants, and so forth. There must have been a large number of actors doubling roles and several taking on three or four minor roles. It is quite possible that only the four actors of Brutus, Cassius, Antony, and Caesar handled a single role, and the actor of Caesar, after his appearance in IV. iii as a ghost, would have been available if necessary to take part in battle. Many of the actors must have performed as conspirators in the opening movement of the play, returned as citizens in the Forum scene, and re-emerged either as named warriors or as unnamed soldiers in the army in the final act of the play. In the various episodes of the battle itself the stage is not heavily crowded although there is a general increase in numbers towards the end of it. Shakespeare does, however, provide an opportunity for the impression of numbers in the confrontation between the two armies in V. i before the battle begins. We may assume that the armies entered from each of the principal entrances and confronted each other across the stage. The numbers involved could have been the entire company. In addition to Brutus and Cassius and the 3 of their soldiers mentioned in V. i – Titinius, Lucilius, Messala – the actors of Pindarus, Young Cato, Strato, Volumnius, Flavius, Dardanius, and Clitus would be available since they appear later in the battle. In addition to Antony and Octavius only 2 other speakers are required in the ensuing battle on their side – the 2 soldiers who fight with Young Cato and Lucilius in V. iv. In the events at Philippi, before, during, and after battle, 16 speakers are required if we assume some of these roles were doubled. Although the majority of these actors play roles of figures who are on the side of Brutus and Cassius, since it is with those forces that most of the battle-episodes lie, they could, on a crowded stage and with the aid of helmets, have been divided into the two armies which confront each other in V. i, and several of them, disposed of in battle and whose speaking-roles were finished, could have returned in V. v as members of the army of Antony and Octavius. Shakespeare does not deny us the evidence of numbers and finds opportunity before and after battle to crowd the stage, but it is significant that in the battle itself, in its flow of brief episodes, he tries to avoid any interruption of the impression of speed and change by avoiding the problem of cumbersome entrances and exits. As can be seen in Table 7.1 there are several entrances and exits of 1 or 2 characters. On only one occasion are as many as 6 required to enter at once, and that number carrying the two dead bodies offstage with them is the most crowded exit.

To enact the battle 15 actors are required. Octavius never appears in the battle itself and comes onstage in V. v only after the retreat has been sounded. We never see any of the 4 principal figures engaged in combat, and had any hand-to-hand fighting between them been put onstage it could not have been conclusive. The sources and history demand that Cassius and Brutus kill themselves with the aid of their followers. Shakespeare, as elsewhere, could have engaged them in fights which were broken off, but chose not to do so. Brutus and Cassius are featured either as figures on their way to battle offstage or receiving news of engagements in other parts of the field. In the sixteen segments of battle there is only one (11) which requires hand-to-hand fighting when two soldiers enter to fight young Cato, who is killed, and Lucilius. There are, however, in the course of battle, three other deaths onstage, of those who take 'a Roman's part' – Cassius, Titinius, and Brutus. In structuring the action in this way it seems likely that Shakespeare may not have felt a need to present a complex sequence of combats as he had done for the battle of Shrewsbury. The rhythm of the play is quite different from that of *Henry IV, Part 1*. The build-up here is to a battle which resolves the issues broached in the central section of the play, but the stage is not as crowded with complex battle-action. This may be partly a result of the fact that in the middle of the play there are long scenes which

Table 7.1 (c) The battle of Phillippi. V. ii (6), V. iii (110), V. iv (32), V. v. 1–51 (51) – 199 lines

(Segment) Description	Category	Entrance	Exit	Number onstage	Lines about action offstage
V. ii					
(1) 1–6 (6) *Alarum*. Brutus, spying his advantage over Octavius sends Messala with messages to the other wing.	3/4	2	2	2	6
V. iii					
(2) 1–8 (8) *Alarums*. Cassius, with Titinius, recognizes the advantage Brutus has over Octavius but finds himself encircled by Antony's forces.	3/4	2		2	8
(3) 9–19 (11) Pindarus tells Cassius that Antony is in his tents. Cassius sends Titinius to find out if his forces have been routed by the enemy.	3	1	1	3	11
(4) 20–35 (16) Pindarus reports offstage action to Cassius about how Titinius is captured and the enemy shouts for joy.	3	1	1[a]	2	16
(5) 36–50 (15) The bondman Pindarus, on the orders of Cassius, kills his master, who dies remembering Caesar.	5		1	2	8
(6) 51–79 (29) Titinius, with Messala makes it clear that the report of Pindarus was incorrect. They realize Cassius must have killed himself after misinterpreting the meeting of Titinius and Brutus as defeat. Messala leaves to take the news to Brutus.	3/5	2	1	2 + 1[b] (3)	8
(7) 80–90 (11) Titinius laments the loss of Cassius and, after placing the garland sent by Brutus on him, kills himself.	3			1 + 1 (2)	9
(8) 91–110 (20) *Alarum*. Brutus with Messala and others finds the bodies of Cassius and Titinius. After elegiac comments he returns to the fray.	4/3/5	6	8	6 + 2 (8)	
V. iv					
(9) 1 (1) *Alarum*. Brutus rallies his troops and departs.	4/3	5	3	5	
(10) 2–6 (5) Cato asserts his determination to fight.	1			2	
(11) S.D. *Enter soldiers and fight* (with Cato and Lucilius).	2	2[c]		4	

Table 7.1 contd.

(Segment) Description	Category	Entrance	Exit	Number onstage	Lines about action offstage
(12) 7–15 (9) Lucilius observes Cato fall, declares himself to be Brutus, and is taken prisoner.	1/2			4	
(13) 16–32 (17) Antony enters and recognizes that Brutus has not been captured. He orders Lucilius be kept safe and news of Brutus brought to his tent.	3	1	5	4 + 1 (5)	3
V. v					
(14) 1–43 (43) The battle-weary Brutus whispers to his followers in turn begging them to kill him. *Alarums.* He refers to the ghost of Caesar which has appeared to him. *Alarums* and cries to fly continue. Brutus sends his followers off.	5/4	5	3	5	6
(15) 44–51 (8) Brutus asks Strato to hold his sword and running on it he kills himself.	5			2	
(16) *Alarum and retreat* is sounded signalling the end of battle.	4			1 + 1 (2)	
TOTALS		27	25		75

[a] I assume an exit and entrance here as Pindarus goes off to reappear above on the hill from which he makes his report.

[b] The dead body of Cassius remains on the stage until the end of the scene.

[c] I include only two soldiers here. The text requires the soldiers to speak. It is possible that the speakers were accompanied by other mute soldiers all of whom beset Young Cato and Lucilius.

have either an extensive series of entrances and exits or demand that the stage be filled with many actors for long periods. The assassination of Caesar (III. i) and the Forum scene (III. ii) are both lengthy, complex scenes which involve the choreography of large groups of actors, and Shakespeare seems to have felt that the battle of Philippi could, for much of its action, be reported as an offstage event. In the first 90 lines of battle, which is not quite half the lines devoted to it, 66 of those lines (73.3 per cent) are devoted in one way or another to events that have occurred offstage, and to reports by those onstage of action they can see taking place just off it. In the whole battle-sequence 75 of the 199 lines (37.7 per cent) are accounts of action offstage. The battle does have a rapid sequence of episodes, and of exits and entrances, a clash of swords, and even, in Lucilius impersonating Brutus, an episode of counterfeiting similar to that at Shrewsbury, but its focus is principally on the forces of one of the contending sides. Though we hear varying reports of opposition forces, in the whole battle the only evidence of them and of Antony himself occurs in V. iv. 7–32, 26 lines of the 199 lines of the battle. There is a fatalism about Cassius and Brutus as they speak of Caesar's revenge, so that they seem to be paying for the assassination as much as being defeated by the forces of Antony and Octavius. Cassius dies as a result of an error in a report of the action offstage. Brutus laments the mistake of Cassius and returns to battle, but his thoughts are only on plans for the battle for the 6 lines of V. ii, 4 lines at the close of V. iii, and for 1 line in V. iv rallying his troops. By the time he returns in V. v the tide of battle has already turned and his thoughts are only of death, 'Slaying is the word./It is a deed in fashion' (V. v. 4–5). The focus in the approach to battle and in the battle itself is on the continuing potency of Caesar which holds sway over his assassins almost to the conclusion of the play.

(d) Resolution of issues after battle – V. v. 52–81 – 30 lines

The tidying-up of the action can be brief because the accomplishment of Caesar's revenge is complete. All that remains is the report of the death of Brutus by Strato, Antony's elegy on Brutus, and the arrangements made by Octavius for his burial.

If we look at this final sequence of the play, the battle and its resolution (c and d) we can see how much of the 229 lines are devoted to the death of Brutus and Cassius and to the various responses to them and reports of them, which serves, instead of extensive clashes, to constitute the battle at Philippi.

Cassius
(1) Prepares for death and is killed by Pindarus: V. iii. 34–50. (17)
(2) Messala and Titinius discover his body and react to his death:
V. iii. 57–79. (23)
(3) Titinius sorrows over Cassius and kills himself: V. iii. 80–90. (11)
(4) Brutus comes to view the body of Cassius and mourns over it
and the consequent loss of Titinius: V. iii. 91–107. (17)

Brutus
(1) Brutus asks various followers to kill him and each refuses,
before Strato finally undertakes the deed: V. v. 4–51. (48)
(2) The followers of Brutus report his death and are promised
reward by Octavius for their loyalty to him: V. v. 52–67. (16)
(3) Antony's elegy on Brutus: V. v. 68–75. (8)
(4) Arrangements for his funeral by Octavius: V. v. 76–9. (4)

So of the final 229 lines there are 144 (62.9 per cent) devoted to the suicides of these two central figures.

When we look at these sections of the play we can also see what a preponderant emphasis is given to the forces of one side in this battle. In

Sections related to battle
(a) Preparations before the battlefield 372 lines (15.2 per cent)
(b) Preparations on the battlefield 125 (5.1)
(c) The battle of Philippi 199 (8.1)
(d) Resolution of issues after battle 30 (1.2)

726 lines 29.6 per cent of the
play's 2454 lines

Table 7.2 Stage appearances in the battle and to the end of the play – V. ii. 1–V. v. 81 – 229 lines

Character	Entrances	Exits	Lines onstage	Total lines onstage	Lines spoken
Forces of Brutus and Cassius					
Brutus	4	4	V. ii. 1–6 (6), V. iii. 91–110 (20), V. iv. (1), V. v. 1–81 (81)	108	60½
Cassius	1	1	V. iii. 1–110 (110)	110	31½
Messala	5	5	V. ii. 1–6 (6), V. iii. 51–79 (29), 91–110 (20), V. iv. 1 (1), V. v. 52–81 (30)	86	21½
Titinius	2	2	V. iii. 1–19 (19), 51–110 (50)	69	28
Pindarus	2	2	V. iii. 9–22 (14), 36–50 (15)	29	13
Young Cato	2	2	V. iii. 91–110 (20), V. iv. 1–32 (32)	52	7
Strato	2	2	V. iii. 91–110 (20), V. v. 1–81 (81)	101	7
Volumnius	2	2	V. iii. 91–110 (20), V. v. 1–43 (43)	63	2
Lucilius	3	3	V. iii. 91–110 (20), V. iv. 1–32 (32) V. v. 52–81 (30)	82	15½
Flavius	1	1	V. iv. 1 (1)	1	0
Dardanius	1	1	V. v. 1–43 (43)	43	2½
Clitus	1	1	V. v. 1–43 (43)	43	9
Forces of Antony and Octavius					
Antony	2	2	V. iv. 16–32 (17), V. v. 52–81 (30)	47	16
Octavius	1	1	V. v. 52–81 (30)	30	10
Soldier 1	1	1	V. iv. 7–32 (26), V. v. 52–81 (30)*	56	3½
Soldier 2	1	1	V. iv. 7–32 (26), V. v. 52–81 (30)*	56	1

* Assuming that the two soldiers return as part of the army at V. v. 52.

terms of the numbers of entrances and exits, lines onstage, and lines spoken it is clear Shakespeare shapes the events of the battle and its resolution to highlight the demise of the two conspirators. These details are summarized in Table 7.2.

This indicates that of the 31 exits and entrances only 6 of them are made from the forces of Antony and Octavius (and only 4 of them in the flow of battle). Of the speeches made in this section Brutus, Cassius, and their assorted supporters speak 198½ of the 229 lines (86.7 per cent). Of the 4 involved in sword-fighting none is a major character and 2 of them have no particular names. Shakespeare clearly felt that he had to show some physical combat but he manages with as little as possible, supplemented by reports of clashes offstage.

In summarizing the proportions of the play devoted to the various sections related to battle it is clear again that the time devoted to fighting itself is relatively small.

It is worth recording finally how predominantly masculine the action of this play is. Portia appears in only 2 of the play's 18 scenes. She is onstage for 123 lines and speaks 89 lines. Calphurnia appears in only 1 scene, is onstage for 122 lines, and speaks 24 lines. Between them they are onstage for only 245 lines (10 per cent) and speak 113 lines (4.6 per cent). Unless women appear as part of the crowd in the Forum scene no woman appears onstage after II. iv for the last 1371 lines (55.9 per cent). In those lines a woman, Portia, is referred to in reports of her death (IV. iii. 147–58, 181–95) only briefly, but it helps to heal the breach between Brutus and Cassius. This is a play dominated by men, and the figure who has the most persuasive influence on the action, among the main roles, is Caesar, the figure who spends the least time onstage.

8

'If that an eye may profit by a tongue': The functions of reporting and stage absence in *As You Like It*

A central speech in *As You Like It* is the report Jaques gives on the human condition as the seven ages of man (II. vii. 139–66) which contains vivid images of the repertory roles of folly we all carry within us. In this play, as elsewhere in Shakespeare, we are repeatedly confronted, to use Lear's phrase, with 'this great stage of fools'. In II. i we hear of an offstage encounter Jaques has with a wounded stag described as a 'hairy fool'. In II. vii Jaques gives us an uncharacteristically exuberant account of his meeting with the Fool, Touchstone, in the forest. Later, when Jaques stumbles upon Orlando in the forest, he says: 'I was seeking a fool when I found you' (III. ii. 272–3). In reply Orlando assures Jaques that he will find one if he looks at his reflection in the brook (274–5). The embroidering of foolish actions and their resolutions is achieved by a judicious mixture of actions on and off the stage. I want to examine stage absence and some reports of offstage action to indicate how they relate to each other. Though they all have a function in resolving a specific problem and providing dramatic economy some of them have less obvious underlying functions which are part of more extended structural strategies in the play.

The report which serves the most straightforward purposes is the one Le Beau delivers to Rosalind and Celia about the preliminary bouts which Charles the wrestler has fought (I. ii. 91–132). Some comedy is derived from the way the young women react to Le Beau's description of the 'sport' in which the wrestler has severely injured the three young men who have already challenged him. The sequence builds up tension for the audience which knows that Orlando intends to fight Charles and that Charles, with Oliver's encouragement, does not intend to show Orlando any mercy. This reporting of the prowess of Charles provides an excuse for Rosalind and Celia to meet Orlando before the bout in an attempt to dissuade him from taking on such a hazardous match. There is some slight awkwardness in the staging in that Le Beau indicates that Rosalind and Celia will see the next bout if they stay where they are because the combatants are coming to this very spot. This implies rather oddly that Charles is conducting a peripatetic sequence of bouts, three bouts elsewhere offstage before the bout here with Orlando onstage. Shakespeare needs to show only the match with Orlando, but the account of the ferocity of Charles in preliminary bouts enhances our appreciation of the reversal Orlando will achieve and the approbation he will receive from the young women whose apprehension on his behalf the report has aroused. The audience has already sided with Orlando because Charles, in the employment of the malign Fredrick, is so cocksure and has associated himself with the unattractive Oliver. The triumph of the underdog Orlando is the more acceptable to the audience and to Celia and Rosalind in that it is not only over the hulking, confident Charles but over a figure who has just maimed three other young men and brought them close to death. The nature of Fortune and its mercurial changes is one of the central topics of the play and is under discussion only a little before Le Beau enters to make his report (I. ii. 29–52). Rosalind has complained that the benefits of Fortune 'are mightily misplaced' (33–4), for she is one, like Orlando, brought low on its wheel. Even though circumstances threatened to bring Orlando lower it turns out that his fight with Charles heralds a swing upwards in his fortunes, along with those of Rosalind, because it brings them into contact and thus paves the way for their relationship in Arden where both have fled from their oppressors.

From the point where Rosalind enters Arden (II. iv), the same wood in which Duke Senior resides, Shakespeare assiduously postpones any onstage contact between the exiled daughter and her father. Rosalind, playing Ganymede, will not be ready for a long time to come out of her disguise. Shakespeare could not pretend that Arden was so extensive that there was little chance of running into Duke Senior. She meets with Orlando, who has contacted the duke, and interacts with Jaques, a member of his band, so their proximity cannot be doubted. There must obviously be a reunion between father and daughter at the conclusion, but Shakespeare saw no extended comic capital to be gained from having Rosalind as Ganymede performing before her father and his followers onstage. Since they have been separated for some time it might have seemed a little odd if they were presented together onstage without Rosalind revealing herself. The problem Shakespeare faced was that he could not have them meet effectively and to any purpose onstage too early and could not credibly pretend that they do not meet at all. Shakespeare handles the situation as discreetly, briefly, and lightly as possible. In III. iv Rosalind mentions an offstage encounter with her father but does not develop it save to indicate that she maintained her disguise and has more pressing things to deal with:

> I met the Duke yesterday and had much question with him. He asked me of what parentage I was. I told him, of as good as he; so he laughed and let me go. But what talk we of fathers when there is such a man as Orlando?
>
> (III. iv. 31–5)

The 'much question' she had with the duke might well have been a distraction had it been presented onstage. In reducing it to such a brief report as offstage action Shakespeare maintains a sense of priorities in making the relationship with Orlando Rosalind's central focus, in allowing her to foreground it as an attraction which causes her to postpone a reunion with her father. This allows her to maintain her mystery which will produce the *coup de théâtre* when she can surprise everyone at the conclusion simultaneously by revealing her real identity.

Shakespeare provides an unhindered focus on the confusion of the lovers by keeping the duke and his followers almost completely offstage between II. vii and the final scene, V. iv. Only in IV. ii do we have a brief sequence with the duke's party hunting, and the duke himself does not appear in it. The 18-line scene seems to have the purpose of reminding us of the duke's continuing presence in the woods. It does not add any detail to the plot and could come, one might think, at any point. If fact it comes about three-quarters of the way along in the 1300 or so lines that Duke Senior is absent between II. vii and V. iv. This brief hunting scene also occurs directly after the climactic scene of courtship (IV. i), which concludes with Rosalind's rapturous declaration to Celia of her love for Orlando (189–200), thus confirming that we are moving closer to marriage, the appropriate occasion for the re-emergence of Duke Senior to unite again with his daughter. There are still obstacles like a snake and a lioness to be negotiated, but by IV. ii the onstage courting has developed to a situation where confusion must begin to be resolved and the lovers re-integrated into a larger social world in which marriage will have its place.

After the last dark scene (III. i), where Frederick threatens Orlando, Shakespeare confines the action to the woodlands where the young lovers work out their various destinies. In the 1310 lines from the beginning of III. ii to the end of V. iii, which is very close to 50 per cent of the play's 2636 lines, the action is carried by 12 of the 22 named speakers in the play. Jaques is allowed to wander as a foil to youthful exuberance with his astringent commentary. Neither of the dukes is allowed to appear onstage nor are any of his followers, save for the brief appearance of the hunters in IV. ii. Even a benign, older figure such as Adam is given no role to play. To underline the sway the woodland world holds, when Oliver appears he is no longer the malign figure we knew in the dark, threatening opening movement of the play but a humble penitent quickly recruited to the troupe of lovers. The choice, therefore, of keeping a meeting between Rosalind and Duke Senior offstage and reducing it to a brief mention, is part of a much more extensive strategy at work in the way interactions are organized in the second half of the play.

The introduction of Jaques into the play is handled carefully. Before we see him onstage we are given, in the First Lord's vivid account to Duke Senior (II. i. 25–69), a detailed picture of his offstage confrontation with a wounded stag. In outlining Jaques's manner and in reporting his speeches it 'places' him among the duke's 'brothers in exile' as a melancholy, moralizing intellectual of a type the Elizabethan audience would easily recognize. As an outsider given to satirical criticism he obviously provides amusement for the duke though his co-mates are not inclined to share the gloomy view Jaques has of the world. Before he appears onstage this report provides us with almost everything we need to know about him. The only additional personal detail we are given about him to explain his disdain for love is the duke's comment that in the past Jaques has:

> been a libertine,
> As sensual as the brutish sting itself;
> And all th'embossed sores and headed evils
> That thou with license of free foot hast caught,
> Wouldst thou disgorge into the general world.
>
> (II. vii. 65–9)

The First Lord's report is of an offstage action that occurred 'today'. Shakespeare could not have presented Jaques and this observation of a wounded stag directly on the stage. Yet much of the material could have been presented more directly by Jaques himself in a report to the duke, perhaps in a moralizing account about the nature of hunting as a sport. Jaques later on will give a report of an offstage encounter with Touchstone, and, though I will turn to this matter soon, suffice to say here that Shakespeare's use of the First Lord eliminates an unnecessary duplication of reporting for Jaques. The painting of the picture of Jaques and the wounded stag before the melancholic appears primes our anticipation of him and defines him as an eccentric. This image of him in his sympathy for the wounded stag set apart from the rest of the herd, 'the fat and greasy citizens' (55) passing unconcernedly by, is related directly to the psychological state of Jaques. What Jaques says of the stag ('thus misery doth part/The flux of company' (51–2), meaning that the unhappy or wounded are left to themselves) is true of how he feels about himself, and of how the report presents him. Jaques does not acknowledge interruption and does not respond to his observers any more than the stag responds to him. The identification between the wounded and tormented subjects of the report is confirmed in its conclusion when Amiens and the First Lord indicate they left Jaques 'weeping and commenting/Upon the sobbing deer' (65–6). When, in subsequent scenes, we see Jaques wandering meditatively through the forest, overhearing others, sustaining fragmentary contacts, but invariably, in his satirical commentary, maintaining a gulf between himself and those he meets, we can always refer back to this initial report of him as emblematic of his situation in Arden. There is in his posture, as it is observed by his unseen co-mates, a touch of theatrical self-consciousness and absurd pomposity. We can guess that he is a man who takes himself too seriously from the fact that he cannot resist playing the role of dyspeptic critic of human folly, even when he considers himself to be alone. Until the very end of the play this figure, who is 'for other than for dancing measures' (V. iv. 187), will be remarkably like 'the hairy fool', the heaving, wounded stag dropping tears in the swift brook, as the herd of lovers around him frolic their way towards marriage.

One of the primary functions of this report is to provide scene-setting, or what in film would be described as an establishing shot. We are used to the fact that Shakespeare's stage was adaptable to any setting – street, forum, court-room, dungeon, brothel, battlefield, forest. Shakespeare can tell us we are at Elsinore, or the Senate in Venice, and costumes and the imposing façade of the tiring-house wall will serve as setting. There are many situations in which the tiring-house wall has to be ignored, especially on battlefields (though it can often be effectively pressed into service as battlements) and in the green-forest sections of plays such as *The Two Gentlemen of Verona*, *The Merry Wives of Windsor*, *A Midsummer Night's Dream*, and *Cymbeline*. Nowhere is this more true than in *As You Like It* where the scenes in the forest of Arden amount to 2034 lines, or 77.2 per cent of the play. Shakespeare's theatre may have brought on a tree as a stage prop or a sign to indicate the setting, but, as usual, his major resource is his poetic skill to invoke the benign ambiance of the woodland that is so important to this play and set in such distant contrast to the court of Duke Frederick in which the play opened. Something of the atmosphere of the pastoral world is, in productions nowadays and probably in Shakespeare's day, signified by the use of rural accents for the shepherds, but only 6 of the 17 named characters we meet in Arden are not exiles from the court we observed at the outset of the play. The first scene in Arden is II. i, and it opens with Duke Senior's celebration of the simple life and the sweet uses of adversity (1–17). There are references to the winter's wind and to the ugly and venomous toad for purposes of pointing out how precious things can be found in unpromising places. This is a place where man 'exempt from public haunt,/Finds tongues in trees, books in running brooks,/Sermons in stones, and good in everything' (II. i. 15–17). This is a promising start in creating the image of Arden as a world very different from the court we have left and where adversity was, in any case, the primary mode of experience. It provides not simply an evocation of the physical detail of the forest, but sees it through the eyes of an educated man given to philosophical speculation. Shakespeare had already exploited a habit of philosophical speculation to find the silver lining of clouds in dark circumstances in characters such as Friar Laurence, and he was to continue to do so with others such as Duke Vicentio, Edgar, and Gonzalo.

The First Lord's report on the encounter of Jaques with the wounded stag provides another example of the extraction of intellectual commentary from the observation of nature. Jaques, of course, does not find 'good in everything', but by report, we get a taste of the posture that will become habitual with him, that of a man so jaded that he can 'suck melancholy out of a song as a weasel sucks eggs' (II. v. 10–11). The report takes us into the woodland world and its wild animals (eventually to be improbably augmented with a lioness) and creates a picture of Arden that the resources and style of Shakespeare's theatre could not have produced onstage. We are told of Jaques lying under an oak-tree with antique roots, and a nearby brook brawling in the woods, a poor sequested, wounded stag panting and dropping tears into the brook, and of a herd of deer passing carelessly by (II. i. 29–43, 52–7). Shakespeare establishes the character of Jaques at the same time that he is providing a necessary image of Arden. Duke Senior and his followers are intent upon hunting and are presumably dressed appropriately and carrying bows and arrows. Even though we cannot see the hunting onstage we can hear of a wounded victim of their activity. This report provides an appropriate prologue for the six among the human herd wandering through Arden who are wounded by Cupid's darts.

There may, of course, be a much more practical explanation for presenting Jaques initially in report and delaying his appearance onstage until II. v when only one brief scene (III. i) at Duke Frederick's court remains. It may be that the actor portraying Jaques was not involved in doubling but he was certainly available to take a role in the court scenes of the first two acts. The doubling, if it was required, could not have been of Duke Frederick, for Jaques exits at the end of II. vii just before the humorous duke's last appearance in III. i. The actor of Jaques could, however, have doubled the role of Le Beau. Le Beau makes his final exit at I. ii. 267. If the actor were to reappear as Jaques, and Shakespeare had thought about bringing the character onstage in II. i instead of providing a report of him there would be, from I. ii. 267 to the opening of II. i, 137 lines in which the actor could change costume and affect any necessary alteration of appearance. That, no doubt, is sufficient time for an accomplished actor to achieve a transformation, and so the possible doubling can not have dictated the report and the delay of the onstage appearance of Jaques, though it could have had some influence in prompting the strategy. We have to remember the fact that a loyal audience who may have seen many of the actors in this company week-in and week-out over many years in many plays, and often in two or more parts in some of them, are not likely to have been deceived by costumes and beards or to forget who the familiar actors are in any of their doubled roles. There are elements involved in the aesthetics of doubling which are never formally acknowledged, and it is probable that a dramatist such as Shakespeare, who worked for one company and was a sharer in it, would be able to work always with specific actors in mind for major roles, and for any doubling that they could, by foresighted arrangement in a script, be allowed to perform. It seems likely that, wherever possible, he would prefer to leave some time between an actor's exit as one character and his reappearance as another, not only for the convenience of costuming but for purposes of credibility. I am not suggesting that a long gap of time helps the actor to take in the audience completely so that the doubling is not even registered, but I would argue that an extended gap does help the *character* if an actor is not asked to exit in one role and to reappear in another one after only the hundred or so lines it takes to modify his appearance. If the actor playing the role of Le Beau did double it with Jaques then, by providing a report of Jaques in II. i instead of an onstage appearance, 261 lines (II. i. 1 to II. v. 1) are added to the 137 lines Le Beau has already been absent, and thus a gap of almost 400 lines is provided between the roles. The actor performing Le Beau could, of course, have doubled several other roles such as Corin, Silvius, William, Sir Oliver Martext, or Hymen. If, however, Le Beau and Jaques were doubled it would simply provide another example of Shakespeare's skill in making a virtue of necessity and of the way that, in establishing our first contact with a character, he outlines a trait in him that is significant throughout.

I noted earlier that one explanation of why Jaques is presented in a report by the First Lord instead of being allowed to make his own report of his encounter with the wounded stag to the duke may have to do with the fact that when Jaques first comes before the duke he is engaged in delivering another report. We first heard of Jaques in juxtaposition to a 'hairy fool', the stag. His own report is concerned with his first encounter, offstage, with another fool, Touchstone (II. vii. 12–42). This report is of an exchange that Shakespeare could have presented onstage had he wished to do so. In the second half of this play, which is given over to the lovers, Jaques is allowed to wander as a commentator, but his impact is tightly controlled. He is allowed to interact with Touchstone, Rosalind, and Orlando, but his direct interaction with each of them lasts no more than 30 to 40 or so lines. Before the final scene we know that Jaques meets Touchstone twice, but only one encounter is presented directly onstage. The report establishes the melancholic's introduction to and enjoyment of the jester in 29 lines so that, in III. iii, Jaques can stand apart to observe the courting of Touchstone and Audrey and step forward to take part in the marriage after the arrival of Sir Oliver Martext.

The report Jaques makes on Touchstone relates the two as commentators on the mutability of life. We are given an even clearer picture of the melancholic's perversity when he comes before Duke Senior exultant at having his grim views of mankind's folly confirmed by a fool so that he 'did laugh sans intermission/An hour by his dial' (II. vii. 32–3). He had found something to celebrate in this fellow spirit who sees man as subject to time and decay in a world where 'we ripe and ripe' and then 'rot and rot'. This view allows Shakespeare to introduce the idea that Jaques will dilate on in the seven ages of man speech later in this scene (II. vii. 139–66). This report on Touchstone railing on Lady Fortune and on the inevitable process of decay is connected to the report of the comments Jaques made on the stag out of fortune weeping about its own animal frailty as it confronts death. Jaques declares himself to be 'ambitious for a motley coat' (42–3), and the encounter provides him with an opportunity to underline his self-defined role as a scourger of folly (47–50). When he meets Touchstone again, this time onstage (III. iii), the jester, because he has fallen in love, has lost his privileged position as independent commentator on the folly of the world, and so Jaques can take it upon himself to counsel him. As the play progresses Jaques, though he is not as scabrous, develops a touch of a quality we find in Thersites. He looks to the world as a kind of theatre that puts on performances which reinforce his own view of human folly. He prides himself on his independence as an observer, invulnerable to the attractions of pairing which go on around him. Each of his appearances is an echo of that initial encounter with the stag. He looks on Orlando as a wounded figure (III. ii. 239–81), a fool as Signior Love. When he appears to observe the courting of Touchstone and Audrey in III. iii he again assumes the position of theatre critic at a comedy. With Rosalind (IV. i. 1–34) he tries to assert the uniqueness of the melancholy he has so carefully cultivated and receives only a mocking appraisal of his vain self-regard. He will eventually take it upon himself to render his independent judgement on the marriages that are knit up in the final scene (V. iv. 178–86).

Shakespeare develops two reports, one about and one by Jaques, of his offstage action to establish the character trait that defines him – his apartness. The play is full of odd encounters, the mix of human and animal worlds – stag and man, snake and man, lioness and man, and of rustics and courtiers. Arden is a kind of democratic crossing-place where Touchstone can love Audrey, and Phebe can yearn for Ganymede. Orlando can court, as he thinks, a man and a shepherd who can yet turn out to be a duke's daughter. In this world Jaques is a shadowy will-o-the-wisp figure who hovers on the margins as an observer and is scarcely ever at the centre of things. Our first experience of him is in report in the midst of other things, a description of a solitary figure talked about among the community of the co-mates in exile within the flow of a scene. Jaques appears in seven of the play's scenes and makes seven entrances and seven exits. He seems to join ongoing action rather than directing it. Two of his entrances (II. vii, III. ii) are within the flow of a scene, and though he enters at the opening of III. iii he stands aside to observe the interaction of Audrey and Touchstone and does not make his presence known to them until 62 lines have passed. Four of his exits occur before the conclusion of the scene (III. ii, III. iii, IV. i, V. iv), again confirming our sense that events flow around and beyond him. This is particularly underlined in his exit before the celebratory dance of those united and reunited at the conclusion. We first hear about him musing alone in the woods by a wounded stag. He departs at the end to muse alone in Duke Senior's 'abandoned cave'. In a world of radical change he persists as a remote, unattached figure committed to nothing save his own sense of alienation.

One of the most extensive sequences reporting offstage action occurs when Oliver returns to the stage (IV. iii. 84–157). Francis Berry, in *The Shakespeare Inset* (pp. 64–8), noted the difficult nature of Oliver's part because of the radical changes in his character in his widely spaced appearances, and characterized this report as an interior plot-required inset. He does not, however, consider why Shakespeare chose to present the reconciliation of Orlando and Oliver in report as an offstage event. The report avoids the practical difficulty of bringing a snake or a lioness onto the stage even as it embroiders the idea of the forest as a wild and almost magical place by reconciling brothers the audience has hitherto experienced only as deadly enemies. Oliver has not only demeaned and neglected Orlando; he has also plotted against his life. Our first experience of their relationship in I. i is of physical combat as well as verbal argument. On his last appearance at court Oliver declares that he has never loved his brother in his life (III. i. 14), and at that point all of his lands are impounded until he can return Orlando to the danger of Frederick's custody. Given such circumstances it is difficult to think of a way that Shakespeare could have presented onstage a resolution of their fractious relationship as quickly as it is accomplished in report. If Oliver is to be converted from hatred to love it has to be caused by something as radical as having his life saved by his brother, so snake and lion are made agents of a swift metamorphosis. There is considerable dramatic economy in bringing on an Oliver who has already had a life-changing experience.

The report is presented in such a way as to provide other advantages that serve the play's purposes. The audience has not seen any onstage discussion of Oliver's character between Orlando, Celia, and Rosalind, but when Oliver, without having yet revealed his identity, refers to him, it is evident the women know all about him and his 'most unnatural' (IV. iii. 123) behaviour. In this elision, which shows the women to be biased against him, Shakespeare provides occasion for them to give his report a partisan reception which allows Oliver to display his transformation the more fully by acknowledging how little he has deserved to have his wretched life saved. The report can thus be broken into three phases (84–98, 98–133, 134–57) in a sequence of interactions instead of being delivered as an unbroken narrative. It is possible, of course, that the dramatic impact is augmented if the narrative is given not only as a surprising revelation to the women but to the audience also. The audience has not seen Oliver for almost a thousand lines, and his description of himself indicates that he may be transformed and not easily recognized, save by a brother, for he is 'A wretched ragged man, o'ergrown with hair' (107). An audience might be more inclined to accept this transformation if he is initially as unrecognizable physically as he soon is in temperament and behaviour. Even though we are accustomed to miracles in comedy, it will help if this dastardly brother is so completely changed that we can believe that someone as delightful as Celia, who knows of his past crimes, can fall in love with him more or less immediately.

The report also helps in revealing an admirable side of Orlando's character. He was a courageous wrestler early in the play. We know, too, how willing he was to risk danger, as he thought, in searching out succour for the loyal and weary Adam. But in his 'courtship' of Rosalind he has been subservient to her tutoring and the subject of her mockery. Rosalind has trapped herself in the masculine role of Ganymede and has begun to chafe against it in her eagerness to resume her feminine identity. Oliver's report presents Orlando in a way that could not have been easily achieved onstage. He has almost killed Charles, the wrestler, onstage, so he must go one better than that. He becomes, therefore, a lion-killer offstage. The news of the injury he has sustained provides Rosalind with an opportunity to signal her movement back to her feminine identity when, at the sight of the bloody napkin, she swoons.

In its third section (134–57) the report indicates that not only is the reconciliation between the brothers complete but that Oliver has already been introduced to Duke Senior and so will not be treated as a stranger in Arden. In other words all the problems, that could have taken up considerable time had they all been worked out in conversations onstage, attendant upon Oliver's reintroduction into the action, are all resolved in about 80 lines (76–157). All that is required of him henceforth is to fall in love with Celia, propose to her, and marry her. Shakespeare interposes only about 60 lines of V. i before announcing that the marriage has been arranged for the morrow. Shakespeare can move matters along at a brisk pace because of the beneficent effect of Arden on those who stray within her confines. The improbable speed with which that offstage wooing is conducted is registered with wry humour in the near incredulity of the questions Orlando asks Oliver (V. ii. 1–4). Any audience member still inclining to scepticism has to be won over by the way Shakespeare meets it head-on in giving Rosalind a comic catalogue of the energetic frog-march of the lovers' progress through the stages of love (V. ii. 28–39). The variety of love is wondrous, and there is a deliberately comic contrast in relationships which is related to the onstage and offstage worlds in this play. The movement to marriage of Orlando and Rosalind is accomplished almost entirely onstage in a meandering process which stretches well over two thousand lines and across almost the entire play. Oliver and Celia meet and are onstage for barely a hundred lines, and of their wooing we see virtually nothing. We hear of their rocket-speed trajectory toward marriage, but we see them married without having heard a single word devoted to love and wooing between them.

Shakespeare did not invent all of the details included in Oliver's account of the incident that saved his life; he adapted them from Lodge's source story, but he did so in a way which tells us something about his practice of dramatic economy. The problems involved in a radical transformation of character are very different for a fiction writer and for a dramatist. In the first place the narrator, at least until quite recently, can usually be relied on to speak with authority about his characters. Because he is an omniscient mediator the reader is inclined to accept assertions he may make about a change in character. The fact that the fiction writer is not usually subjected to severe limitations in time and space means that he can devote as much narrative detail as he wishes to unfolding a change within character so that it may carry conviction with the reader. The dramatist is not usually involved directly in the kind of mediation available in narrative commentary. The audience is confronted by the characters themselves, and any changes they have to make are accomplished usually within the particular time-span that is appropriate to the performance-length commonly accepted by the age in which it was written. If a character seems to make a change that is improbable and unacceptable to an audience we can, if we choose, explain away the matter by indicating that it is a result of theatrical convention not designed for those habituated only to a realist style of drama, or we can blame the writer, or the actor, or the director.

In Oliver we have a character who is needed onstage for a romantic pairing with Celia, and so the audience cannot simply be presented with a report of his transformation by a third party in a strategy which keeps him entirely offstage. That, of course, is the strategy Shakespeare adopted in dealing with Frederick because he has no significant function to perform at the end of the play that demands his onstage presence, and I will return to the report which handles that matter later. The best and most authoritative way to convince the audience of a change in character is to have the character himself report the miraculous transformation. The audience's acceptance of the new Oliver is very considerably aided by his willingness to chastize himself for his past unnatural behaviour. In Shakespeare's comedies we are in any case disposed to accept the notion that nature has a wisdom of its own and will, in the end, reassert its sway to overcome deviancy. Shakespeare cannot resort to narrative authority but he can use the authority of the physical presence of the actor to induce acceptance of his change. By outlining how the sequence of events is handled by Lodge I can indicate how Shakespeare dispensed with all of the extensive details that are appropriate to narrative fiction and exploited those which can be economically adapted to drama in the selected elisions tied together in Oliver's report. Shakespeare has to have a transformed Oliver but he does not wish to expend much time on it, for the audience is already involved in pursuing several other relationships which will not benefit from any lengthy digression devoted to the establishment of a new one. In Lodge Shakespeare found hints that prompted him to present this crucial change as an offstage event, a *fait accompli*, which does not impede the ongoing flow of action but instead speeds it up. Lodge divides up the transformation into several phases:

(a) Saladyne (Oliver) is arrested and banished, events which Shakespeare uses in a modified form in III. i. Saladyne's guilt and the repentance of the evil he has done his brother come immediately after he has run foul of the erratic and greedy Torismond (Frederick). Had Shakespeare followed this sequence then Oliver's repentance would have come in III. i, or immediately following, and would not have been caused, as it was not in Lodge, by the saving of his life. The repentance in Lodge occupies 30 lines in Geoffrey Bullough's *Narrative and Dramatic Sources in Shakespeare*, vol. II, p. 198–9, but Shakespeare does not develop it as a separate scene and delays it until after the wooing of Orlando and Rosalind. He allows the magic of Arden to establish itself in the eyes of the audience before bringing Oliver under its influence.

(b) The incident in which Rosader (Orlando) saves Saladyne occurs in Lodge (Bullough, vol. II, pp. 215–20) and is divided into two sections.

(i) When Rosader comes upon his sleeping brother there is a narrative account of him contemplating and then rejecting revenge which occupies 44 lines of the text. Shakespeare reduces this conflict within Orlando to 3 lines (IV. iii. 128–30), a detail which must have been subsequently reported to Oliver after his reconciliation with his brother.

(ii) The battle with the lion occupies 15 lines in Lodge (Bullough, vol. II, p. 217), and leads to the awakening of Saladyne. Shakespeare records this in 3 lines (IV. iii. 131–3).

(c) There is an extended conversation as Saladyne first thanks his saviour and, without realizing he is speaking to his brother, unfolds his story and his offences against Rosader, until at last he recognizes his saviour. He then makes a full confession of guilt to achieve reconciliation in a sequence that occupies 100 lines (Bullough, vol. II, pp. 217–20). Lodge chose not to deal with the way a meeting between the brothers could result in a conflict which might only slowly be resolved as the injured brother provoked repentance in his former tormentor. There is no confrontation because Saladyne fails to recognize his brother and reveals all of his guilt which can proceed directly to reconciliation when he does recognize Rosader. In handling it this way Lodge dispenses with narrative economy, for Saladyne repeats the history of his relationship, which the reader has already been taken through at considerable length earlier in the book. Shakespeare does not use Lodge's idea of having the saved figure fail to recognize his saviour or record any elaborate confession of guilt. He assumes that if Orlando risked his life to kill a lioness in saving his brother then he must have already forgiven Oliver, and that Oliver, recognizing that his brother has saved his life, must know that he is forgiven. The elaborate process of recognition and reconciliation recorded in Lodge is reduced by Shakespeare to 3 lines (IV. iii. 140–2).

(*d*) The brothers go to Duke Gerismond (Bullough, vol. II, p. 220) in a sequence which occupies 18 lines, handled by Shakespeare in 3 (IV. iii. 143–5). In Lodge, Saladyne is reconciled with the servant Adam, a detail omitted by Shakespeare.

(*e*) Rosader reveals the reconciliation he has made with his brother Saladyne to Ganimede and Aliena in 5 lines (Bullough, vol. II, p. 221). Shakespeare ignored this and borrowed a detail from the next sequence, conflating elements of the story to kill two birds with one stone in making Oliver report the reconciliation.

(*f*) Ganimede, Aliena, and Rosader are set upon by outlaws, Rosader is wounded and the women in danger of capture, when Saladyne arrives to rescue them in a sequence which occupies 41 lines (Bullough, vol. II, p. 222). Lodge uses this incident to bring Saladyne and Aliena together and to confirm the bond of brotherhood by having the elder brother perform the role of saviour in which the young brother featured earlier. Shakespeare devotes considerably less space to the elder brother than Lodge, and, since he must meet Celia as quickly as possible, it is Oliver who gives the account to the women of the slaying of the lioness that saved his life and brings the news of Orlando's temporary incapacity. Shakespeare, therefore, invented the bloody napkin to telescope events that are, in Lodge, separated out into several incidents. The napkin becomes a pretext to bring Oliver onstage, to reveal his repentance and reconciliation with Orlando, his meeting with the Duke, to provide Rosalind occasion to faint as she prepares to reveal her feminine nature, and to introduce him in an attractive light to Celia. The brigands are eliminated, but the wound Rosader received from them is transferred to Orlando's battle with the lioness.

(*g*) After the battle with the brigands Aliena admires her rescuer, learns that he is Rosader's brother, and Ganimede tends to Rosader's wound in a sequence of 16 lines (Bullough, vol. II, pp. 223–4).

It is possible to see how Shakespeare tailored this sequence to his own needs and especially to the time-limitations of drama which provided no constraints for Lodge. In Lodge the saving of a brother from a lioness by the brother he has estranged is not the trigger for a transformation of character. It is rather the occasion whereby Rosader comes to know of Saladyne's change of heart recorded earlier in the story in response to a different incident. Saladyne plays a major role in Lodge, but Oliver is only of minor interest compared to the focus Shakespeare places on Orlando and Rosalind. Shakespeare took the risk of telescoping events so that Oliver's conversion is an instant response to his salvation, and though he courts melodrama he protects himself by making it an offstage event. There is plenty of material in Lodge to provide a more fully developed Oliver involved in a more elaborate process of repentance. Shakespeare chose to ignore it because he needed Oliver at the ending of the play more for symmetry of design, the multiplication of harmonious couples, and the swift course of love's infection, rather than for any intrinsic interest in his character. One can see how Shakespeare came to his radical elision in the report Oliver gives, for Lodge provides examples of two key meetings in which the teller of a story is unaware that his listener is a subject in it – the delay in Saladyne's recognition of Rosader after his rescue, and the delay in Aliena's recognition of Saladyne after he rescues her from the brigands. Shakespeare turns this into Oliver's delay in revealing his identity to Celia and Rosalind which helps to convince them, and therefore the audience, that he is indeed a changed man. Shakespeare thus found a way of selecting, among a variety of discrete episodes in Lodge, those details that could be tied into one sequence. In Bullough, the action Lodge presents occurs in several episodes in a variety of locations. It begins on page 198 and is not fully concluded until page 223 and the incidents altogether are covered in some 270 lines of dense prose. The essence of Oliver's report in Shakespeare, altered and streamlined from the discursive leisure of narrative fiction to the leaner efficiency which drama demands, is transmitted in some 80 lines of verse (IV. iii. 76–157).

Shakespeare was not yet finished with exploiting the magical potential of the offstage world. Out of that mysterious world emerges the brother of Orlando and Oliver to report on the religious conversion of Duke Frederick in 'the skirts of this wild wood' (V. iv. 145–60). Shakespeare seems to be counting on the idea that it is easier for an audience to accept improbable transformations and astonishing developments if, instead of being isolated incidents, they are part of a pattern. In creating the dark atmosphere of the first part of the play Duke Frederick featured as a splenetic, humorous monster. In his rapid changes of mood he was an erratic, unpredictable figure, and it is not entirely surprising that within the magic world of Arden such a volatile figure might make another radical change, for in his behaviour to Orlando, Rosalind, and Oliver he could veer from tolerance to tyranny in quick succession. Yet Shakespeare shows his discretion in ensuring that we only hear about the change in him out there in Arden. We do not need to see Frederick onstage as a penitent begging forgiveness of his brother. His conversion can be made even more dramatic confined as it is to report. He had been leading a force to Arden to capture and execute his brother but as soon as he entered the forest he was diverted towards another way of life. We are more inclined to accept this not only because comedies have a habit of producing this kind of event, but because we have accepted the change in Oliver, witnessed the acceptance of Silvius by Phebe, the reuniting of Rosalind with Duke Senior, and, above all, because the forest has just produced the most visible manifestation of its beneficent atmosphere in the appearance of Hymen who advised the mortals to feed themselves 'with questioning,/That reason wonder may diminish/How thus we met, and these things finish' (V. iv. 132–4). Frederick has not only abandoned his rancorous enterprise, he has abandoned the court world. His choice of the solitary, contemplative life which eschews society means that he does not have to be integrated back into community and thus can be kept offstage. Shakespeare has enough business to handle in the pairing-off of the couples. He does not need another solitary, contemplative figure set apart from these nuptial celebrations. He already has one there in Jaques and by keeping Frederick offstage he can provide an excuse to get the melancholy commentator off to join the new convert.

Another advantage in keeping Frederick offstage is the avoidance of repetition. We have heard and seen something of the reconciliation of one pair of brothers. We do not need to experience the reconciliation of another pair. We are not left with a sense of incompleteness because a relationship is not brought to a resolution onstage. Duke Senior suffered usurpation and exile before the action of the play began, and we have seen no interaction between the dukes onstage. In the mellow, philosophical humour of Duke Senior we have not even detected resentment of his usurping brother. The play is resolved in the completion of the process of substitution. At the outset we had Duke Frederick, in the court world, taking the place of the absent Duke Senior who, in the woodland world, was experiencing the philosophical consolations of a simpler life. At the conclusion we have Duke Senior returning to court to take the place of Frederick who now replaces his brother in Arden in the pursuit of wisdom in a simpler world without the seductive exercise of power to distract him.

In Lodge, the resolution is achieved by quite different means. In Bullough, (vol. II, pp. 255–6) we have 40 lines devoted to the description of violent battle in which Torismond (Frederick) is slain thus leaving Gerismond (Duke Senior) to reclaim his realm. Shakespeare obviously felt that a battle would involve unnecessary complications and create an atmosphere inimical to the serene air of harmony which has been created in Arden. He retains, therefore, only Frederick's intention to wage battle but then dismisses the impulse to battle as inappropriate by inventing a fortuitous encounter with 'an old religious man'. In restoring all the exiled figures to their land he confirms our sense of Arden as a charmed world where anything can happen. A part of the evidence of that potent charm is the fact that Shakespeare can unfold the final astonishing transformation, which revolves Fortune's wheel to allow those who have hitherto been landless exiles to recover what they have lost, in a report that occupies only 16 lines (V. iv. 145–60). This may not be quite the Land of Cockayne, but we can see why there is no hurry to return to the court world and why the Duke can suggest the celebration be continued in the place that has supplied so many benefits:

> Meantime forget this new-fall'n dignity
> And fall into our rustic revelry.
> Play, music, and you brides and bridegrooms all,
> With measure heaped in joy, to th' measures fall.
>
> (V. iv. 170–4)

Here in *As You Like It*, as in the other plays I have examined, it is evident that reports serve varied and vital functions. Many of them take us from 'here' to 'there'; they provoke our imaginations in providing an essential supplement to the action. They may change our perception of events we have experienced onstage, they may prepare us for events or characters that we will see, or they may recount events which cannot be presented onstage. What we see is always being augmented by what we hear. When Oliver comes onstage to deliver his account of his rescue from the lioness, he has already received, offstage, a report from Orlando which allows him to recognize Ganymede and Aliena though he had never seen them before. The lines which make this clear speak also for the audience's response to drama and the importance reports have for the playwright in helping him to shape our reception of a play's characters and events:

> If that an eye may profit by a tongue,
> Then should I know you by description.
>
> (IV. iii. 84–5)

9

'He is himself alone': The use of battle, report, and stage absence in *Coriolanus*

None of the other major tragedies that Shakespeare wrote has such a singular and almost obsessive focus on the central figure as *Coriolanus* does. In noting the singular character of Coriolanus I am again travelling over familiar ground extensively analysed by many critics. What I want to draw attention to is the comprehensive nature of the varied techniques used to create this man apart. When he is offstage he is being criticized, praised, defined, discussed. When he is onstage he is, by the singularity of his manner of address or by his actions, defining himself in ways that compel attention. He situates himself in opposition to his country's enemies outside of Rome and to many of the citizens within Rome. Even his friends, the patricians, constantly define him as an exceptional figure, at times almost as inhuman, 'a thing of blood', 'a planet'. He wants to be a nonpareil and acts almost as the sole survivor of an uncompromising aristocratic code which he finds crumbling around him. He is an army of one against all, and everything at the outset of the play is designed to highlight him definitively in that role in his assault on Corioles. He will eventually abandon Rome and 'go alone,/Like to a lonely dragon' (IV. i. 29–30), but that is only a formal statement of the posture he takes from the moment we first see him at the task of defining his oppositional stance to the plebeians – 'Who deserves greatness/Deserves your hate' (I. i. 171–2). The character is created not only by what he says of himself and what others say of him but by Shakespeare's decision not to develop any alternative focus of interest. The actions in battle and in politics are developed in such a way that consideration of his contributions and responses to them are the only significant issues.

At the outset of *Coriolanus* a form of political unrest is established which threatens to develop into a civil disturbance pitting the plebeians against the patricians in general and Caius Marcius in particular. The threat of war from forces outside Rome is not mentioned for some time. Shakespeare's habitual method of a gradual, lengthy build-up through particular phases to battle is not fully in operation here because battle in this play is not the culmination in Act V of a rising action but is instead the focus of much of the action of Act I. The threat of battle will be reported as it returns in Acts IV and V, but no battle-action is presented onstage at that time. Coriolanus is then the attacker of Rome and allied with the man he defends the city against in Act I.

Shakespeare could have chosen, had he so wished, to begin the action of his play with the political candidacy of Coriolanus after he had returned crowned with battle-honours from Corioles. That would have involved presenting his hero in circumstances to which he was completely unsuited. Shakespeare usually gives us an initial picture of the grandeur and status of his hero before the movement towards tragedy begins. We do not see any of Macbeth's sterling feats of battle in defending Scotland but we hear about them and see him receiving honours for them from Duncan. We see Othello in calm control in the streets of Venice and in the Senate before Iago begins to work on him directly to encompass his destruction. We see Lear in complete control of his court before he throws his power away. It is true that we come upon a melancholy Hamlet but even though we see him at odds with the world around him we do have some sense of his character before the complication of the Ghost's demand for revenge are laid upon him. Caius Marcius is not a reflective figure. The distinguishing mark which sets him apart from almost all of the other characters in the play is his prowess in battle and if we are to get a clear sense of his exceptional nature we have to see him in his proper sphere. His claims, or the claims made on his behalf, to political office are based entirely on his service as a warrior. If Shakespeare had not shown him dominating the action in battle it is difficult to see how he could have been presented as a hero at all. By opening his play before the triumph at Corioles Shakespeare is able to define the nature of his hero before battle, during the battle, and after the battle, as a man apart, not only lacking the common touch but fundamentally opposed to that most basic of political skills. His bravery in battle and the eulogies poured on him mask for a while from his patrician friends and the citizens, though not from the tribunes or the audience, his total incapacity for political office. The battle here is, therefore, not designed to complete our sense of character and action, as it is of Prince Hal or Falstaff, or, as in *Troilus and Cressida*, to confirm our understanding of the decayed values exhibited in the first four acts, or, as in *Henry V*, to deploy a variety of responses to a patriotic crusade. This battle is used to unfold quickly and vividly the nature of the central figure before he moves into arenas where his particular qualities are liabilities rather than advantages.

(a) *The political build-up in events which occur before the action moves to the battlefield – I. i. 218 – I. iii. 108 – 203 lines*

(i) The initial threat of civil unrest arising from the clash of Caius

Marcius with the citizens and their tribunes is set aside when news arrives that 'the Volsces are in arms' (219). Marcius welcomes the news, and after his departure the tribunes indicate their resentment of him and speculate about how he will turn the apparent disadvantage of serving as second-in-command to Cominius to his own advantage (247–74).

(ii) In I. ii we are shown the preparation in the camp of the Volsces and hear of the attitudes of Tullus Aufidius to Caius Marcius.

(iii) In the domestic scene, I. iii, more views of Caius Marcius are sketched in as Volumnia recalls her son's battle-deeds, and anticipated further triumphs. Valeria's report on the son of Caius Marcius defines another aspect of this family. Despite its domestic setting the scene, in a variety of ways, fills out a picture of the hero which is to be confirmed in the ensuing battle and the siege of Corioles referred to towards the end of the scene (86–98). The battle is, in some significant aspects, not quite like any other battle in Shakespeare. In *Macbeth* I indicated how the central figure was isolated and overwhelmed, how Macbeth is, in a sense, his army and his defeat inevitable. In *Coriolanus* something like an opposite effect is achieved. There are other figures onstage in the fighting, but the figure on whom the action focuses is Caius Marcius and his triumph against overwhelming odds. Since the battle itself will give him remarkable prominence the phases leading up to it do the same. This may nominally be a battle of Romans against Volscians but in the way it is approached and carried out it is Caius Marcius against all-comers (not excluding those Roman soldiers, whom he contemptuously calls 'geese'). When he says to his enthusiastic supporters on the battlefield 'O, me alone! Make you a sword of me' (I. vi. 76), he is simply verbalizing the method Shakespeare has adopted since the threat of battle was first broached. Corioles is his battle and it gives him the identity Coriolanus and everything before, during, and after battle registers that fact for the audience.

(b) *Preparation on the battlefield – I. iv. 1–18 – 18 lines*

A wager between Marcius and Lartius indicates that the forces have not met, but, in a parley with the Senators on the walls of Corioles, drums and alarums from the other wing of the army on the battlefield indicate the commencement of the action which leads at once to the siege of the city.

By this point in the play virtually all of the characters with significant speaking-parts have already appeared onstage. Around 14 actors would be required to perform the name parts, the citizens, Roman Senators, Senators of Corioles, and the gentlewoman who speaks in I. ii, though some of these subsidiary roles could be doubled. But on the stage in the first scene there must have been several citizens, and there are mute senators and attendants in other early scenes also indicated onstage. This play has an unusual number of scenes in which unnamed citizens, senators, soldiers, watchmen, serv-ingmen have prominent speaking-parts (II. ii, II. iii, IV. iii, IV. v, V. ii, V. vi), as well as many scenes in which significant numbers of mute bystanders are required. It is possible that several actors each played 3 or 4 of these generic roles, but the action even so seems to require an unusual number of actors to dress the stage. Most of the actors who have appeared in the opening three scenes are available to fill the stage in battle. The domestic scene, I. iii, with the 3 women allows all the actors who performed as citizens in the opening scenes to dress as soldiers for battle. Even the 3 boy actors playing the women in that scene could, if required, have appeared in some parts of the battle for they are not required onstage again until 90 lines into II. i, well after the battle is concluded and the victory celebrated. In terms of distinguishable named parts only four – Caius Marcius, Cominius, Lartius, and Aufidius – appear in battle. There are, in fact, only a dozen such distinguishable parts in the whole play, and the action is other-wise sustained by the large collection of citizens, soldiers, senators, etc. Several of such characters appear in the battle scenes – soldiers, scouts, a lieutenant, a messenger, and there were plenty of actors available to fill out the various skirmishes indicated in the text. I am assuming in the outline in Table 9.1 that there were 8 actors available as mute supers – 4 Romans and 4 Volscians – in addition to those minor roles individually indicated. They could have handled the various speaking-roles if required but it seems likely that at least that number were available simply to dress the stage.

The battle takes place at a variety of locales – before the gates of Corioles, in the streets of Corioles (in the view of some editors), and at places near Cominius's camp where part of the Roman army copes with Aufidius in the open field. The battle focuses little on speeches of defiance hurled back and forth among the generals, and this is understandable since the play has not yet been going long enough to give us a fuller range of characters which often confront each other in those plays which have battles in Act V. Aufidius is the only general ever distinguished among the Volsces, and his competitive relation with Marcius, which is to develop to the end of the play, is built up here. The battle does not focus only on single combats for there are a number of sequences in which skirmishes and a general mêlée of combat of advance and retreat with several actors are indicated.

All of this action serves only as the backdrop against which the sterling prowess of Marcius can be isolated and highlighted. We see Roman soldiers beaten to their trenches, gloating over their loot, and being harangued by Marcius. The battle depends so much on his skill that he is the only figure we see surviving in both of the principal fights against overwhelming odds. He is the key figure not only in the taking of Corioles but also on the other

Table 9.1 (c) The battle – I. iv. 19 to 'retreat' sounded in I. ix – 181 lines

(Segment) Description	Category	Entrance	Exit	Number onstage	Lines about action offstage
I. iv					
(1) 19–29 (11) The Roman army, with Marcius and Lartius, is onstage in parley with the senators on the walls of Corioles when an alarum sounds from elsewhere on the battlefield indicating the commencement of fighting. When the Volscian army enters Marcius encourages his troops to fight bravely.	3/4	4		9 13	
(2) *Alarum*. The Romans are beaten back to their trenches.	2/4		3	10	
(3) 30–46 (17) Marcius pours scorn on the Roman soldiers for their cowardice and encourages them to follow him through the gates of Corioles. He follows the Volsces, enters the gates, and is shut in alone.	3/2		5	5	
(4) 47–61 (14½) the soldiers consider Marcius doomed now that he fights within the city alone. *Alarum*. They explain his fate to Lartius when he returns and praises the courage of Marcius.	3/4	1		6	
(5) Marcius enters bleeding, assaulted by the enemy.	2	5		11	
(6) 61–2 (1½) Lartius and the Roman soldiers come to his aid and fight the Volscian soldiers back into the city.	2			11	
I. v					
(7) 1–3 (3) Roman soldiers enter, discussing the spoils they have gained in Corioles. *Alarum*.	3/4	3		3	
(8) 4–25 (22) Marcius indicates to Lartius his contempt for these base slaves and, as he leaves to help Cominius fight Aufidius, he receives the praise of Lartius.	3	2	1	5	
(9) 26–8 (3) Lartius orders a trumpet-call to summon the officers of the town so they can hear of his intentions.	3		4	4	
I. vi					
(10) 1–9 (9) Cominius, in a pause in action in another part of battle, anticipates further fighting.	3	5		5	5
(11) 10–20 (11) A messenger brings news of the initial repulse of the forces of Marcius and indicates the delay in the news results from his avoidance of Volscian spies.	3	1		6	7[a]

Table 9.1 contd.

(Segment) Description	Category	Entrance	Exit	Number onstage	Lines about action offstage
(12) 21–46 (26) Marcius brings news of his triumph in Corioles and expresses his scorn for the cowardice of 'the common file'.	3	1		7	9
(13) 47–87 (41) He enquires about the battle against Aufidius and begs to be set in action against him. Cominius tells him to pick his best men to accompany him, and the soldiers celebrate his enthusiasm by lifting him up as he promises to lead them against Aufidius.	3			7	9a
			7		
I. vi					
(14) 1–7 (7) In Corioles Lartius gives instructions about guarding the city and then sets off to join his fellow generals on the field of battle.		6		6	
			6		
I. viii					
(15) 1–13 (13) Marcius and Aufidius hurl defiance at each other in preparation for combat.	1	2		2	
(16) Marcius and Aufidius fight.	2			2	
(17) 14–15 (2) Volscian soldiers come to the aid of Aufidius, and he declares his shame at this unsolicited aid.	2	3		5	
Marcius drives off the enemy.			5		
I. ix					
(18) *Flourish. Alarum* and the battle ends as the retreat is sounded.	4				
TOTALS		33	42		30

a Some of these lines to Cominius about action offstage are reports of action the audience witnessed in I. iv.

wing of battle out in the open plain in confronting Aufidius. The other generals involved in battle are comparatively passive. Lartius is offstage when Marcius assaults Corioles alone. After he has settled matters in Corioles he hurries out to lend aid against Aufidius but arrives only in time to celebrate Marcius's victory. Cominius has engaged with Aufidius but has not been successful. That part of the battle only goes in favour of the Romans when the bloodied Marcius arrives and confronts Aufidius. Aufidius is not onstage in battle for long but he too features principally to exhibit the exceptional qualities of his opponent, since he not only fails to prevail but is even driven offstage with his soldiers when Marcius single-handedly copes with them. Marcius is a one-man show, and the other figures are there to receive his contempt or to marvel at his singular prowess.

It is important for the subsequent development of the play that Marcius is displayed as an isolated figure not only in his battle-feats undertaken on Rome's behalf but in his spleen against 'the common file' of Romans. It is not clear, when the Romans are beaten to their trenches, where, on the stage, those trenches might be. Some soldiers along with Lartius may be beaten through the exits in the tiring-house wall, though that appears to be featured as the walls of Corioles with gates in the middle of that wall. It is possible that the soldiers escaped down trapdoors or were beaten off the sides and front of the stage into the yard, but it is clear that they are somewhere about the stage when he harangues them (I. iv. 30–40), for they come forward after he has entered the gates of Corioles. Marcius continues here in the posture he established in the opening scene and anticipates the eventual path he will take when he threatens that he will 'leave the foe/And make my wars on you' (39–40). In his extravagant invective he invokes 'All the contagion of the south' (30), calls them a 'herd' which deserves 'boils and plagues' (31), asserts they have 'souls of geese' and less bravery and skill than 'apes' (36). The effect of this is that we come to view the battle not as a Roman victory but as a personal triumph for Marcius achieved, at least in part, in spite of his soldiers. His behaviour indicates that he wishes to be defined as if he alone were author of himself, and he already has the potentiality which will lead him to declare 'I banish you'. Irritated by the concessions made to the plebeians he already believes that he is fighting for a country that is not worthy of him. His language is full of images of infectious diseases as he considers himself to be surrounded by the plague which has corrupted the body politic. His identity is increasingly defined in opposition to those around him. When the soldiers fall to pillage before the battle is over, he immediately rushes out to risk his life again by searching out Aufidius.

The battle is 181 lines long, and almost every aspect of it sharpens the definition of Caius Marcius. There are five separate segments in which physical combat is required, and Marcius is featured in all of them. He is onstage for 129 lines (71.3 per cent) of the battle. He speaks 90 lines – half of all the lines. Of the other speakers none comes close to his prominence – Cominius speaks 35 lines, Lartius 27, Aufidius 8. The speeches of Marcius break into a few prominent strands: (i) lines urging his soldiers to battle (31); (ii) lines scorning them for cowardice (20); (iii) lines of defiance to Aufidius (8). The other speakers in the battle are used to define his courage and exceptional nature. In this task there are another 47 lines concentrating on him – Lartius (17), Cominius (14), Aufidius (6), Messenger and Soldiers (10). When we look over the lines spoken in the battle surrounding the fighting in which he is so prominently featured we find that only 26 of the 181 (I. iv. 19–21, 22, I. v. 1–3, 26–8, I. vi. 1–9, I. vii. 1–7) are not devoted to his speech, or speech in praise of him, or about his actions. It is here that he is most potent, a figure of here, there, and everywhere, a man in his very element. Never again in the play will he be as free to define himself by his own actions. We see him at Corioles as a man who rejoices at the task of searching out enemies, the more the merrier, and who needs no allies, and we recognize these qualities as inappropriate and destructive in the political arena.

(d) *Resolutions of issues after battle – I. ix. 1 – II. ii. 132 – 517 lines*

In most of Shakespeare's plays that involve battles they occur in Act V as the culmination of the action, and the consequences usually involve a brief celebration of victory, the decisions on the fate of the vanquished, and an assertion of a commitment to continuing order. In *Coriolanus* the battle is concluded in Act I, leaving the rest of the play to work out the consequences of the victory. Marcius receives the eulogies of his fellow generals and the gratitude of the patricians and, in the heady atmosphere of victory, temporarily wins the support of the commoners who overlook their earlier grievances against him sufficiently to accept him as a candidate for the consulship. Throughout the celebrations Shakespeare develops more deeply the aspects of Marcius – his pride, his individualism, his disdain – which will prove fatal to his political success. His disdain for 'the common file' before and during battle have made it clear that he will find it difficult to sustain a broad-based popularity. In the attitudes of the patrician women in I. iii and in the admiration of his fellow generals we can see how his skill as a defender of Rome dazzles the patricians and makes them incapable of recognizing his unsuitability for political office.

In I. ix there is initiated a struggle between those, such as Cominius and Lartius, who wish to broadcast his heroic deeds in various parts of the battlefield and the distaste of Marcius himself for such public display of his endeavours. Such wooing of a reluctant candidate occasionally works effec- tively in politics, but it cannot be sustained for long because politics is a public art which depends not on hiding your light under a bushel but in allowing your deeds and skills to be promoted widely. This need to play up to the public, to polish up reputation, is not peculiar to politics, as Ulysses insists to Achilles in *Troilus and Cressida*; it is an attribute which all men, soldiers included, must cultivate if they are to win the favour of their fellows. The behaviour of Marcius after battle is that of a man who acts to please himself and his own internal standards unrelated to public opinion. He does not hunger for a public validation of his worth but instead disdains it. The focus in this scene on Marcius is total. Of the 93 lines only 4 (74–7) are not concerned with him or his responses to praise. The closing sequence of the scene (78–90) in which he begs freedom for the poor man who used him kindly presses home the point which the whole scene makes. It is a momen- tary flash of magnanimity in the great hero, and perhaps surprises us that he can show concern for the lowly. It is a moment which might remind us of Sir Philip Sidney at Zutphen begging succour for a fellow soldier, or of Shakespeare's Antony sending his treasure after the deserter Enobarbus. It is out of such gestures – Churchill or George VI mingling with the victims of the London blitz – that a politician, with appropriate publicity, can build up his career. It seems likely that Coriolanus is not calculating a deliberate gesture to set a flourish on his reputation. A politician must ensure that his gestures do not misfire, and, in the exhibition of the personal touch, the ability to remember names is a valuable asset because it asserts the bond which ties the public figure to his obscure supporters. It can serve as the mortar of democracy, even at times seem like the touch of the healer, since it reinforces the idea of unity in tying the polity together. That Coriolanus has forgotten the name of his benefactor who became a prisoner is only a passing incident, but it is expressive in the way that it distinguishes him as a square peg who will never fit into the round hole of political candidacy, which will be offered to him on his return to Rome.

Politics requires that a man turn himself into a commodity and sell himself, or allow himself to be sold, in the market-place of public opinion. When the generals here begin the task of packaging him for public consumption, we can see how deeply antipathetic the method is to Coriolanus. In the urging of the patricians in Rome and in the ceremony of the voices where he must expose his flesh to buy votes, we will see how resistant he is to playing the role required. But already we can see that he regards this process of transformation as a devaluation of his essential being, a self-betrayal. His disdain of tangible rewards may win him the cheers of the soldiers, but politics is not predicated on such ascetic independence. The politician is given power in the form of a reciprocal contract, and he exercises it, based on the votes he has received on the fundamental understanding of his obligations in a commodity-exchange. It is precisely this basic tenet of the democratic system, which is here in Rome not yet fully-fledged, to which Coriolanus is opposed. Because he maintains himself as a man alone he resists praise and reward as the obligation of debts he cannot accept because he cannot admit the authority of others to judge and evaluate his deeds. The ethics of the market-place would undermine his conviction that he is unlike other men and is not to be weighed with them in the same scale. He rejects all of the conventional rewards but does accept the mark of recognition which singles him out as unique in the history of Rome from other men – the name of Coriolanus. We can recognize that his reactions to praise are more than modesty and border on the pathological from the remark of Cominius that his rejection of eulogy is so rigid that he may have to be treated like a madman (I. ix. 52–7).

In I. x we see the effect of defeat on Aufidius, but here too 21 of the 33 lines are devoted to Coriolanus and to the Volscian general's sense of shame and his determination to seek revenge on his enemy. In II. i we get the reactions of the citizens of Rome to the news of success, and much of it focuses, in Menenius's bandying of words with the tribunes, on the nature of the character of Coriolanus (1–31, 82–6). When the patrician women enter, the talk is of the hero's imminent return and the celebration of his success (90–

151). At his entrance he is welcomed by his friends and relatives (152–93). Only at the end of this sequence is the next significant development in the action broached when Volumnia hints at the political office which would crown her son's achievement (189–91), and Coriolanus indicates he is not willing to compromise his own standards to achieve advantage (191–3). The tribunes reflect on his popularity and anticipate his success (194–211) but consider that he will lack the political skill to remain consul long and devise strategies to provoke him. In this 259-line scene, therefore, all but 55 lines (32–82, 86–9) are concerned with Coriolanus.

In II. ii we have the juxtaposed reactions of two officers before the action proceeds to further eulogies which Coriolanus finds so unbearable that he refuses to stay onstage to listen to them. At 130–2 the declaration is made that the Senate are 'well pleased' to make him consul. It is at this point that I would assert that all of the immediate consequences of battle have been worked out. Something of the ensuing phase of the action has already been anticipated in the talk of the tribunes, but the next significant event, moving the plot forwards toward the crisis, is only fully unfolded in the anticipation of the ceremony of the voices. This phase is completed when Coriolanus is celebrated in public for his battle-deeds and offered the reward of the consulship for his services. This division may seem a little arbitrary, and I am aware that Shakespeare's plays do not work in self-contained blocks, for there are always transitions paving the way for the next phase of the action. We are aware in all of the behaviour of Coriolanus and in the foreshadowing of the tribunes' plans that his candidacy for the consulship will be fraught with difficulty, but only in the ceremony of the voices does the action turn away from the celebration of his performance in battle to confront him with another major challenge.

In summarizing this section in Table 9.2 we can again see the remarkable emphasis on the character of the hero. The only sequence of any length which does not highlight his attitudes or reactions to him is II. i. 32–82 (51), when Menenius teasingly defines his own character to the tribunes. This post-battle sequence exhibits the development of the various political factions sketched in the opening scene and developed in Coriolanus's attitudes to the common soldiers in battle. The tide of praise, which is at the flood in this sequence, is juxtaposed to the unfolding of opposition to him which will form the dialectic of the central movement of the play. Marcius was not only the dominant actor but the dominant speaker in the battle-sequence itself speaking 50 per cent of the lines. In the aftermath of battle he is as prominent neither in presence nor in speech onstage. In this sequence of 517 lines he is onstage for 34.6 per cent of them. Of the lines when he is on he speaks 63 (35.2 per cent) or only 12.2 per cent of the entire sequence. He is still overwhelmingly the centre of interest for, as Table 9.2 indicates, 83.8 per cent of these 517 lines are in one way or another about him. It is now more fully evident, in the careful juxtaposition of these two sections, that he can only fully

Table 9.2 (d) Summary of the action

Scene	Not about Coriolanus	Praise of Coriolanus and enhancement of his reputation	Criticism of Coriolanus	Coriolanus resisting praise	Coriolanus onstage	Coriolanus speaks
I. ix (93)	72–7 (5½)	1–13 (12½) 19–27 (8½) 29–36 (7) 52–66 (14½) 78–93 (16)		13–19 (6) 28–9 (1½) 36–52 (16) 67–72 (5½)	93	39½
I. x (33)	1–7 (6½) 27–33 (6½)	7–27 (20)			0	0
II. i (259)	19–29 (11) 32–82 (51) 86–9 (3½)	1–4, 6, 8, 9, 11–12, 14–15, 30 (12) 83–6 (3½) 90–157 (68) 159–91 (32) 193 (½) 194–211 (17½) 247–57 (9)	5, 7, 10, 13, 16–18, 31 (8) 211–47 (37) 257–9 (2½)	158–9 (11½) 191–3 (2)	42	15
II. ii. 1–132 (132)		1–4 (4) 7–14 (8) 23–34 (12) 35–55 (20½) 58–60 (2) 62–6 (4) 75–132 (57½)	5–6 (2) 15–22 (8) 55–8 (3) 60–2 (2) 68–9 (1)	66–8 (2) 69–75 (6)	44	8½
517	84 (16.2%)	329 (63.7%)	63½ (12.3%)	40½ (7.8%)	179 (34.6%)	63 (12.2%)

become himself on the battlefield. That arena allows him to demonstrate his physical superiority to all those around him and it allows him to unload his profoundly rooted spleen against the commoners in ways which pose no threat to him or to Rome. In the world of peace there is no outlet for these central aspects of his personality without undermining his bid for the political role which others want him to take. Politics is not an area for the unrestrained, unconsidered, reflex activities which constitute his battle-skills. Of the 63 lines he speaks in this section 40 of them demonstrate his irritable resistance to praise. It is evident that someone who can barely tolerate the praise that is freely given is going to have considerable problems soliciting approbation from those of whom he had said in his first lengthy tirade in the play 'He that will give good words to thee, will flatter/Beneath abhorring' (I. i. 162–3) and 'He that depends/Upon your favours swims with fins of lead/And hews down oaks with rushes' (I. i. 174–6). At the conclusion of all of these sequences connected with battle we are fully aware that it is that kind of impossible task upon which Coriolanus is launched.

In summary: of the various sections analysed above we thus have (in this play of 3293 lines)

(a)	The build-up to battle	203 lines	6.2% of the play
(b)	Preparation on the battlefield itself	18	0.5
(c)	The battle of Corioles	181	5.5
(d)	Resolution of issues after battle	517	15.7
		919	27.9

When Shakespeare presents a report by characters who have taken part in an event the audience has witnessed onstage to others who happened to be offstage at the time he usually does so as quickly as possible. There are occasions when such reports are not merely part of the practical mechanism of keeping everyone onstage in the picture but have a more complex significance in the larger structural patterns of the play. In Act II, Scene iii, of *Coriolanus* we observe the ceremony of the voices which the play's hero undergoes with the citizens, and then we hear their confused reactions to it as they report to the tribunes their varying views on whether the ceremony was properly performed.

Most of Shakespeare's tragic heroes change quite radically before our eyes in the developing process of the play. Coriolanus, however, is revealed as being more and more himself, ever more inflexibly monolithic despite, or indeed because of, the inappropriate roles being thrust upon him. On the face of it Shakespeare would seem to be confronted with a problem of how to maintain interest in or develop tension around a central character who is so predictable and resistant to change. One of the ways of doing this is to suggest that the forces against Coriolanus are not monolithic. The ceremony of the voices, altered from the way it is presented in Plutarch and given much more significance, is shaped to help the audience come to grips with the volatile nature and uncertain judgement of the citizens. In order to indicate why this ceremony is such an important step in the structure of the play I will have to show how Shakespeare prepared for it and used it as a springboard to get to the climactic moment of the exiling of Coriolanus.

The citizens start out in the play in a state of uproar in which they assert that Caius Marcius is chief enemy of the people and must be killed. Yet even in this tide of animosity the mob is not monolithic. The Second Citizen is not so cowed by the violent mood of the mob that he fears to speak in opposition. He reminds the mob of the services Caius Marcius has done the state and excuses him on the ground that he is only being true to his nature (I. i. 27–8, 38–9). These are attitudes which recur and are all that can ever be said in the defence of Coriolanus. They serve to interrupt the initial determination to proceed violently long enough to allow Menenius to come in to calm the situation. The idea of having the citizens in the first scene single out Caius Marcius as their enemy in seeking redress of their grievances is Shakespeare's. Plutarch mentions no enmity to him in this situation though he does provide a reason for it because it is Caius Marcius who speaks out to the senators urging them to make no concessions. In Plutarch the first rebellion of the people has to do with their weariness with battle. Only after the battle of Corioles does the grievance focus particularly on the scarcity of corn. In Plutarch Menenius alone deals with the mob. Shakespeare reorders events to lay the groundwork for the eventual rejection of Coriolanus by making the initial rebellion focus on the price of corn and by having Caius Marcius interrupt the peace-making strategy of Menenius to harangue the commons with an unambiguous demonstration of his contempt.

Shakespeare interprets Rome as being in a situation where the sense of a common goal is beginning to fail and some of the varied forces, though still in embryo, are capable of breaking the society into splinters if the delicate balance is disturbed. Menenius, in the first scene, is aware that the situation is serious enough to try to seal over the fissures in society with his fable about the organic interdependence of the members of the state. Caius Marcius, however, is not willing to give up any of his certitude about patrician privilege and the necessity of keeping the rabble in its place. He does not have to pay a price for enflaming the mob with his disdain because of the threat of war with the Volsces in which he is the indispensable instrument. We only return to the disdainful nature of Coriolanus and attempts to obstruct his political candidacy when Sicinius and Brutus voice their fears about his popularity and begin to speculate about how to destroy him (II. i. 194–259). What we hear from the tribunes is that they do not have a constituency ready to take their lead in denying Coriolanus his political reward. The commons will have to be reminded of their 'ancient malice'. Their chief ally in achieving his defeat will be Coriolanus himself. They calculate that if they can force on him 'the napless vesture of humility' he will undo himself. But in the messenger's speech at the end of the scene we hear that the whole of Rome, nobles and commons, are united in their praise of the hero (II. i. 249–57).

Shakespeare has to handle the problem of how to develop, through various phases, cross-cutting opinions about and a convincing conflict with a man who is an expert at alienating those he is supposed to woo. To achieve some balance in the play Shakespeare develops throughout a sense of uncertainty and disagreement about the nature of Coriolanus. In many plays such juxtaposed versions and opinions create a genuine sense of the richness and complexity of the central figure. We become aware of how difficult it is to get to the truth about a character or to the essence of a situation. We recognize that a character is a complex weave of the way others look at him and the way he looks at himself, and that a situation is an amalgam of people's actions in it and reactions to it. But in Coriolanus the audience is dealing with a character whose behaviour is not difficult to interpret. The complexity can only come from the fact that the opposition to him has not hardened into unquestioned hatred because, despite his patrician disdain and his political ineptitude, he is Rome's saviour. The citizens are not politically sophisticated: they have not yet developed, despite their grievances, a sense of themselves as a unit, nor can they easily make a distinction between a man's military reputation and his political abilities. The tribunes never waver in their rooted opposition to him as a danger to the rights of the plebeians and to their own recently won power. Their constituents, however, have to be goaded and tutored into forming an effective opposition. To some degree the events of the play support the uncertainty of the citizens and hold in question the unfaltering conviction of the tribunes. For a while it seems that it might have been better to have Coriolanus as a bad consul rather than rejecting him and driving him into the camp of their enemies where he could wreak revenge in the destruction of Rome.

To emphasize the fact that there is continuing diversity about Coriolanus's fitness for the consulship Shakespeare introduces in II. ii juxtaposed opinions about his character among the officers. The First Officer considers that he is proud and not a lover of the common people. The Second Officer sees that as no fault, in that Coriolanus does not act like those politicians who can hide their disdain behind flattering speeches. The First Officer strikes a deeper note in observing (17–22) that Coriolanus seems actively to antagonize the populace on principle. The Second Officer thrusts this aside by harping on his service to the state and insisting that his deeds speak for themselves. Coriolanus does not have to behave like the politician who must be careful to woo the people because he has no deeds to speak for him. The First Officer seems to be won over by this judgement. Shakespeare, I believe, is providing compensation for the fact that, to the audience, there can be scarcely any ambiguity about his central, very singular character. In many plays Shakespeare had presented the subtle deceptions and complex role-playing of a great variety of political figures. We are often given the impression that there is something deeply disturbing about the ascendancy of such sophisticated duplicity. Shakespeare, in this play, was interested in portraying a society that was aware of political duplicity and yet not weary and cynical enough to distrust all seekers after office. There are those who value and respect Coriolanus precisely because he has so little political skill. At least you know where you are with such a man. Coriolanus seems to be a survivor from an older and simpler age. When he returns from the battlefield he is badgered by the advice of the patricians and confronted with the political agitation of the tribunes. Like a lumbering, unwieldy bear with dogs barking and biting at it, Coriolanus is driven into exile and death.

The scene of ritual humiliation (II. iii) that Coriolanus has to undergo is, therefore, a key event in the development of the play, in our understanding both of the nature of the hero and of the plebeians. Coriolanus can only bring himself to the point where he can barely go through the motions. His performance cannot be so overtly disdainful that the citizens recoil instantly and reject him but it must be played with enough negligence and irritability that we can see it will soon be called into question. What allows him to get by initially in this test is the habit of behaviour he has exhibited since his return from battle. He has refused on earlier occasions to sit still to hear public praise of his deeds. In his dedicated isolation he disdains the hero's meed, the social process of sharing the glory of his deeds with the members of the community in whose name he did battle, because he was fighting for himself and his own singular conception of Rome. His seeming humility stems from a fundamental pride because he cannot tolerate the idea that anyone should think there is base alloy in his motives, that he would turn the emblems of his battle-prowess into the cheap coin of seeking political advantage.

The ritual of the voices seems to be part of that familiar mechanism of initiation rites whereby a candidate for high office has to undergo a separation from his caste before he is reintegrated as a leader. Anthropologists have examined such rituals extensively as examples of *communitas* which involves a movement away from the rankings of a structured society into a temporary system of status-levelling. By showing his wounds Coriolanus will share the signs of his suffering in the common cause of Rome and in taking upon himself 'the napless vesture of humility' he will acknowledge his common humanity. Coriolanus is, of course, a specialist in raising himself above the general level. A man who cannot stand to hear his wounds talked about by patricians is certainly not going to display them publicly to plebeians. But Shakespeare has developed the situation so that Coriolanus can go through the form of the ritual without acting out its substance and without very seriously compromising his fierce sense of integrity. Even though, as we learn later, the tribunes have carefully tutored the citizens to provoke a situation in which they can reject Coriolanus, they are in a mood where they can give him the benefit of the doubt. Although the behaviour of Coriolanus may seem arrogant enough to the audience we can see how it can be taken as shyness by the citizens, a reticence in hearing his 'nothings monstered', and a refusal to practise the typical glibness of a politician.

The scene is divided into three distinct sections which themselves have clear divisions within them:

(a)	Preparation for the ritual request for voices	(i) 1–45 (45)	
		(ii) 46–59 (14)	59
(b)	The ceremony of requesting voices	(i) 60–106 (47)	
		(ii) 107–19 (13)	
		(iii) 120–32 (13)	73
(c)	After the ceremony – reactions and plans	(i) 133–45 (13)	
		(ii) 146–203 (58)	
		(iii) 204–58 (55)	126

At the outset of the scene we find the citizens discussing quite amiably the formal aspects of the ritual and their legal obligations to it. No matter what the tribunes have told them, they still have enough respect for Coriolanus to agree that if he fulfils his part they will have to assent to his induction as consul. In spite of their fiery and belligerent words on some occasions we can see that the citizens are not ready to be incensed easily to a rejection of Coriolanus. They are uncertain, cowed by patrician authority, prone to submit to the kind of soft-soaping of which Menenius is capable. They are not yet eager to be the immovable obstacles the tribunes would like them to be. Some of them are willing to believe that they may, in the past, have gone too far in their rebellious behaviour and that the censure Coriolanus poured on them (I. i) may have been justified (13–16). The Third Citizen indicates that they are far from operating as a unified force with a block vote: 'I think if all our wits were to issue out of one skull, they would fly east, west, north, south, and their consent of one direct way should be at once to all points o' th' compass' (19–22). The citizens are not approaching the ritual with any bitter prejudices, as we can see when the Third Citizen seems to voice the general mood: 'if he would incline to the people, there was never a worthier man' (35–7). The tribunes have designed a strategy of having the citizens build up a cumulative pressure by reiterated demands on Coriolanus in the hope that he will explode in anger, but the citizens themselves do not seem to be actively seeking such a result.

We discover in the exchange Coriolanus has with Menenius (46–59) that he is very much in a frame of mind to utter insults that would certainly lose him the voices of the citizens and fulfil the aim of the tribunes with little difficulty. Even though he steels himself to the task of controlling his tongue the audience is left in no doubt about his distaste for the ritual and his contempt for the plebeians. We are able to see in the ensuing sequence what the citizens fail to recognize, his seething and barely controlled hatred of them.

In the first round of the ceremony of the voices with three citizens he is told that the price of the consulship is to ask it kindly (72). He manages to mouth the required words but indicates that he will show his wounds in private, relying on his assumption that the plebeians will not have the temerity to demand that of him. He seems to believe that his donning of the gown of humility, as an almost unbearable concession, is as far as he can be expected to go. Two of the citizens have immediate second thoughts about whether the ceremony is being correctly performed. In the second trial Coriolanus makes a request for voices without being prompted for he begins to see that there may be a way of getting through this trial without having to perform seriously the humiliating prescribed duties. The Fourth Citizen, while praising his battle-prowess, indicates that he has 'not indeed loved the common people' (89). It is potentially a moment where he might break out in rash, splenetic contempt, but he manages to get around the accusation in an elaborate speech (90–9) which is really an insult but does not register as such with the citizens. He seems to reject the role of flattering politician and asserts he prefers to be known for his blunt sincerity which fits in with the views of him expressed earlier in admiration (II. ii. 7–15, 23–6). Again he avoids revealing his wounds and does not even promise a private viewing. The citizens yield their voices without revealing any second thoughts. In a soliloquy before the third trial (107–19) Coriolanus reveals how irksome he finds the process, almost brings himself to the point of calling it off, but decides that since he is already half-way through he will stick it out. It seems probable that the speech of appeal he makes in the third trial, though it sounds adequate to the occasion, is delivered with a touch of parody, tongue-in-cheek, which nevertheless satisfies the citizens.

At the beginning of the third phase of the scene the tribunes are obliged to admit that the ceremony seems to have been performed adequately. Only after the departure of Coriolanus, when the citizens compare notes in reporting on the ceremony to the tribunes, is there a growing realization that they have been taken in by a hollow show. The audience has had the benefit of the private side of Coriolanus in his talk with Menenius and in his soliloquy. But, of course, the public side of this proud patrician is not very far from the private, and it takes only a few moments for the citizens to discuss the nature of his performance. The Second and Third Citizens who were the least taken in during the first trial, when Coriolanus performed with least assurance, are convinced they have been mocked. The First Citizen, who did not indicate any objections initially, is still willing to give Coriolanus the benefit of the doubt by taking his behaviour to be merely a reflection of his 'kind of speech' (156). The Third Citizen's report of the exchange that the audience witnessed is considerably embellished. He puts a number of sentences in the mouth of Coriolanus which were never spoken (163–8), though we may take these words as a translation of the impression that Coriolanus made on him. The tribunes can only indicate their chagrin at the way the citizens have ignored the approach they advised them to take in the ritual. Brutus, in fact, reiterates the lines and the arguments they had fed the citizens and hoped they would use to make Coriolanus angry and disqualify him for the role of consul (171–85). The frustration of the tribunes in playing out the roles of needling Coriolanus, roles in which they are so expert and the citizens so inept, verges on the comic. This, however, serves as anticipation of the technique they will use in their hastily improvised plan of trying one last-ditch confrontation to draw out the real Coriolanus and destroy him.

I have gone to considerable lengths in outlining the detailed political development of this scene, and the time expended on reviewing a sequence that the audience has witnessed onstage, because it seems to me one of the key scenes in the delineation of Rome and of the place of Coriolanus in it. It is also developed in a manner quite different to the way it is presented in Plutarch. The dramatic exploitation of the ceremony of the voices as a tension-filled sequence in which we can observe Coriolanus barely able to hold himself in check and surviving the test largely because of the lack of sophistication of the citizens, their divided opinions, and their uncertainty about the power of their unity, is almost entirely Shakespeare's invention. In Plutarch (Bullough, vol. V, p. 518), the account of the ceremony of the voices gives no indication that Coriolanus resists the ceremony as an imposition or tries only to go through the motions. He seems to be a Roman who accepts the form of the ceremony which in Plutarch, takes 'certen dayes' rather than the cursory quarter-hour Shakespeare's Coriolanus is willing to give it. Plutarch records the patrician's showing of his wounds with no evident distaste. By thinking his way into the character Shakespeare uses the ceremony as a stepping-stone in a sequence of events which are designed to reveal the extreme nature of his hero's pride. In Plutarch the rejection of Coriolanus for consul comes out of a general history of dissatisfaction with him. By fastening on a detailed development of this ceremony Shakespeare can give us a vivid example of how unsuited Coriolanus is to the sphere of politics. The scene also emphasizes the relentless agency of the tribunes in trying to find some way of using the plebeians to trip up Coriolanus. Shakespeare focuses our interest on the complex manœuvring among the patricians, the tribunes, and the plebeians, forces which demonstrate considerable flexibility, as they advise, tutor, attack, defend, confront, manipulate the central inflexible figure. The ceremony of the voices is the last in a sequence of events in which Coriolanus indicates how unwilling he is to have the purity of his singular actions sullied by the evaluation of others. That he manages to survive the ceremony at all is surprising, but we can see that he has had about as much as he can take of compromising his integrity. He is at a point where a mere word will trigger the volcanic temper that can scarcely be held in check. The success of the play depends largely on creating in the audience an awareness that Coriolanus is a dangerous explosive device. The tribunes, after the ceremony, again instruct the citizens on how to light the fuse.

Plutarch was concerned simply to record a sequence of events whereas Shakespeare had to order them and shape them to provide vivid dramatic impact. In the events in Plutarch following the ceremony and leading to the expulsion of Coriolanus there are elements which Shakespeare could not use. The ceremony I have analysed was part of a structured sequence, an essential building-block leading to a climax, which Shakespeare was able to develop by expanding some details, cutting others, and editing the timing that he found in Plutarch. In Plutarch there is no record of the rejection of Coriolanus as consul in a vivid confrontation in which he is baited and driven to fury. Plutarch gives a homily on the pride and passion of Coriolanus. When Coriolanus goes home in high dudgeon at the loss of the consulship, he is followed by many young patricians who are his supporters and incensed at the treatment he has received. He gives a long speech against the rights of the commoners which wins him such support among the senators that there 'were only a few olde men that spake against him' (Bullough, vol. V, p. 521). When the tribunes send officers to arrest him they are fought off and the senators help to keep him free. On the following day the senators try to calm the commons and offer corn at reasonable prices. When Marcius is summoned by the tribunes to answer the charges against him he puts himself beyond the pale by his haughty answers. The attempt to cast him off the rock Tarpeian fails because he is defended by the senators. When there is continued insistence that he be brought to trial there is a lengthy debate among the senators about how the crisis should be handled. In Plutarch, Coriolanus has many defenders and he is carried along within a complex and extensive political process. Shakespeare radically compresses this protracted political process and turns it into a compact, irreconcilable conflict resulting from the violence of Coriolanus's temper in which he becomes isolated and his patrician allies can do nothing to save him. The baiting of Coriolanus, his furious outburst, his rejection as consul, and his exile are shaped into one tumultuous sequence of continuous public action. Shakespeare dispenses with the political factions among the patricians, with the various defences of Coriolanus, with the debates in the senate, and with the trial, to produce a figure who is so self-willed that he resolves the issue by leaving Rome because he finds the thought of a continuing life there unbearable. The trajectory to that departure from Rome is initiated in the first scene of the play but is subjected to a series of temporary halts and digressions. The battle at Corioles postpones the showdown, the rapturous response to the hero's return delays it again, the ceremony of the voices provides one last deviation. But in each situation we can see, in the progressive unfolding of the disdainful behaviour of Coriolanus, that the consequences of such obsessive and isolating pride are inevitable.

Coriolanus has an extended absence from the stage which is exploited in a manner that is rather different from such sequences that I have examined in other plays and which is dictated by the particular nature of this tragic hero.

Of all Shakespeare's plays only *Richard III* and *Timon of Athens* have the kind of singular focus we find in *Coriolanus* where all of the actions and reactions are organized in relationship to the central character. Whenever Coriolanus is offstage (which, save for the extended sequence in Act IV and V under examination here, is never for very long), almost all of the conversation is about him. Whenever we are with Aufidius his concerns are with Coriolanus. When we have the only fully domestic scene early in the play (I. iii) with the three women the talk is about Caius Marcius, his upbringing, his battle-feats, and how much his son is like him. Menenius is developed as a canny political character, but for most of the play he is involved in the thankless task of trying to advise Coriolanus on how to repair the damage he has done to himself and his political fortunes, or trying to persuade him to have mercy on Rome. The tribunes never talk of anything save how to destroy the political candidacy of Coriolanus or to celebrate their success when they have done so. Even in the major tragedies, which deal with individual careers, this singular, almost obsessive focus is unusual.

In *Hamlet* we have two major figures in conflict, and the plot developed around the members of Polonius's family occupies a good deal of our attention. The fate of Hamlet is certainly our central concern, and many reactions are organized to the mystery of his antic disposition, but the plots and stratagems developed by Claudius and Polonius give us a sense of complex forces at work. In *Othello* we have a clear understanding of Iago's controlling power, and yet we are interested in the separate fates of Cassio, Desdemona, and Emilia not merely as reactors but as figures who initiate actions independently even though Iago takes advantage of them for his own purposes. We are aware also that Iago becomes caught up in the mechanism of his own plotting as Othello presses relentlessly on in his pursuit of justice. In *King Lear* we have a fully developed sub-plot and the fates of the characters involved in it to follow. Many of the actions in the play stem initially from Lear, but then other figures, who inherit his power, attract our separate attention. Much the same is true in *Antony and Cleopatra* as we are transported back and forth between the camps vying for Antony's allegiance. In *Macbeth* there is a great deal of focus devoted to the actions of the tyrant to the exclusion of any sub-plot activity, but we are concerned also with the power of Lady Macbeth in urging on her husband and then with the decline of her influence and its consequences as he isolates himself from her. None of these plays is organized with the same tight focus on one central figure as *Coriolanus*, and it can be argued that this is one of the play's limitations.

Shakespeare had developed techniques in almost all of his tragedies for unfolding change in the central character. One of the most useful devices for effecting that change is the use of an extended absence offstage. I have indicated how such transformation could be achieved even in a short absence as when Angelo, during II. iii, spends a night ravaged by his desire for Isabella between his two interviews with her. I have noted also the change when Hamlet returns to Denmark. There is a similar change during Macbeth's absence in Act IV and V when he returns, beset by enemies, wearied, and even more sickened by contemplation of his crimes. During Lear's absence in Acts III and IV we are also aware that he has penetrated more deeply into madness which has allowed him to formulate the uncompromising nihilism he tries to reveal to Gloucester and Edgar in IV. vi. Coriolanus presents, however, quite a different problem, for he is a rigid and inflexible figure who is virtually incapable of any fundamental change. At the end he is scarcely changed from the man we met haranguing the plebeians in the first scene of the play. To develop a tragedy around such a man Shakespeare produced a flexibility in virtually all of the other characters which, by their combined efforts, drive him to disaster. Shakespeare had presented inflexible figures in other plays – Hotspur, Jaques, Bertram, Angelo – but Coriolanus is a monolithic tragic figure who, in his own words to his mother, can only 'play/The man I am' (III. ii. 15–16) and who, unusually for such a major character, seems incapable of learning from his experiences.

His extended absence from the stage certainly provides a pause for the actor in a very heavy role. Coriolanus is onstage for 1606 of the play's 3293 lines (48.8 per cent) and he speaks 791 lines (24.0 per cent). The pacing of this play has some unusual qualities because of its placing of a long battle-sequence so early in the action. After Caius Marcius harangues the plebeians in the opening scene he has a 174-line break (I. i. 247 to the end of I. iii). The battle scenes from I. iv to I. ix occupy 292 lines of the play, and Caius Marcius is onstage for 244 of them (83.6 per cent), a heavy commitment involving a good deal of physical activity early in the play. After the battle there is another offstage break of 184 lines (I. x – II. i. 151). Because of the long sequence of tumultuous political scenes concerned with his candidacy for the consulship an actor certainly needs this break for, until the extended break in Acts IV and V, he is onstage almost constantly without any lengthy pause. From the moment when he returns from battle (II. i. 152) to the time when he is accepted by Aufidius in Antium (IV. v. 148) there are 1480 lines (44.9 per cent) – the very heart of the play – and during that sequence Coriolanus is onstage for 948 (64 per cent) of these lines. On only two occasions in this period is he off for as much as 100 lines or more (II. iii. 146–258 (113), IV. ii. – IV. iii. 47 (100)), and he speaks 442 lines (29.9 per cent of this section) which is 55.9 per cent of the lines in his role. The load he carries at the heart of the play is, therefore, considerable, which may be why he is given two significant breaks early in the action and an extended break when his failed political candidacy drives him into exile. The significant factor, however, is that, unlike his practice elsewhere, Shakespeare does not use this break to turn to other matters, to develop other characters in depth, to produce a transition in the character of the tragic hero. He gives the actor a rest but he does not give the audience any variety of material to switch the focus away from Coriolanus; rather, he intensifies our awareness that concern with this haughty warrior, his whereabouts, his intentions, is a topic which excludes all other interests.

Coriolanus, accepted by Aufidius in his exile from Rome, leaves the stage at IV. v. 148 and reappears onstage at V. ii. 57, which constitutes an absence of 438 lines. In IV. v after his departure almost all of the talk of the servingmen in the camp of Aufidius is of their master's reception of this exiled warrior (149–215), and only at the close of the scene does the talk turn to a more general discussion of war and peace. In IV. vi we are shown an effective chain of reactions to the absence of Coriolanus from Rome. Because the audience already knows that Coriolanus intends to fight with Aufidius against Rome the initial complacency of the tribunes at how much better things are going now that Coriolanus is banished becomes comic. Even Menenius is not critical of the new-found harmony in Rome (16–17), and the citizens congratulate the tribunes for the peaceful atmosphere which prevails. All of this mutual congratulation paves the way for the 180-degree swing in reactions to terrified apprehension when news arrives that Rome is under threat from Aufidius and the Volsces, their usual opponents, and from Coriolanus, their usual defender. Everyone rapidly changes tune about the wisdom of banishing Coriolanus. In the 161 lines of the scene there are 52 references to this absent but potent figure. In IV. vii, where Aufidius discusses with one of his officers the impact Coriolanus has already made on his camp and his authority, references to him flow even more frequently – 37 in 57 lines. The potency of Coriolanus in his absence continues in V. i, where all talk is of whether Menenius will go to him and appeal for his mercy, after Cominius has already failed in an embassy to him. We are so used, by this time, to all talk referring to Coriolanus that we have no problem in figuring out who 'he' and 'him' refer to before his name is used at line 11 of the scene. This whole scene is compacted with references to *him*, what *he* can be expected to do, what *his* attitudes have been – and 53 references to this looming threat to Rome accumulate in the 74 lines of the scene. In V. ii we observe Menenius preparing to make another plea for mercy but uncertain about the reception he will receive from the man to whom he has acted as mentor.

In the 438 lines of his absence there are 415 lines (94.7 per cent) that are devoted to conversation relating to Coriolanus, 170 lines (38.8 per cent) that contain specific references to him, and he is mentioned by name, by pronouns, and by other appellations an astonishing 204 times. If these references were spread evenly across this absence he would be mentioned specifically once almost every 2 lines. [The references are: Caius Marcius (12), Coriolanus (7), he (71), his (50), him/himself (49), my/thou/our/your general (8), their/them/(of Coriolanus and Aufidius together) (3), thou (Coriolanus addressed by Aufidius in imagination) (1), the Roman (1), our countryman (1), thy Captain (1)]. This is simply another way of noting how much he is in everyone's thoughts and on everyone's lips in the half-hour or so that he is offstage. The only time in the whole sequence when he is not the prominent topic of conversation is in the final 23 lines of IV. v when the servingmen discuss their preferences of war over peace, but they only talk in this way because Coriolanus has come to lead the Volsces. For the rest of the sequence on only a couple of occasions do as many as a dozen lines pass without direct reference to him.

Shakespeare has not stored up any considerable amount of new material to be uncovered during his absence. We learn more about Tullus, but all of the other characters who appear in this sequence have already been effectively developed. What we hear during his absence about his behaviour indicates that there is no modification of his monolithic nature, and that he is as haughty among the Volsces as he was among the Romans. In the various reports we receive of him we recognize how difficult it is for him to fit in anywhere. We observed him lay the seeds of his own destruction in Rome, and it is evident that outside Rome his self-destructive nature persists. He is fundamental to the plans of the Romans, those who support him and those who oppose him, and he is a key figure for the enemies of Rome, and yet he is not able to make the significance of this centrality count in his favour. He may perform the feats of a superman but is incapable of acting effectively as a politician. The focus on him is so heavy because there is no convincing opposition to him. Neither Tullus nor the tribunes can defeat him outright; they can only prevail by providing the opportunity for him to destroy himself. Tullus relies on his power as a soldier at the same time that he is preparing for his downfall. The tension of the play, therefore, does not develop around a balance of conflicting forces within Rome or between Rome and its enemies. The central issue is a conflict between the strengths and weaknesses within Coriolanus, or rather how, in certain circumstances, his strengths become his weaknesses. The play focuses on the destruction not of a nation but of one man who is both idol and pariah because he can only be, as he was at Corioles, 'himself alone' (I. iv. 51).

Throughout the absence of Coriolanus offstage we are constantly being reminded of his potency as a soldier as he advances on Rome. The play is unusual not only in its early battle scenes but also in the amount of fighting onstage at Corioles. We see him at the outset, as I have noted, in his very element. This serves Shakespeare's purposes when Coriolanus unsuccessfully endeavours to move from casque to cushion and also allows for dramatic economy when this exiled warrior returns in arms against Rome. When we hear of the terror he strikes into the hearts of the Romans we are not obliged to relate it simply to his reputation as soldier but can draw on our direct experience of his near-miraculous single-handed invasion of Corioles. We can easily understand why the Volsces talk in terms of delight and fascinated awe about him and why the Romans scramble to send a sequence of begging ambassadors to avert what they anticipate as sure catastrophe. It may be necessary to give Coriolanus a period offstage, but the play has been shaped in such a way that even during his absence of 438 lines it will seem inevitable that 94.7 per cent of those lines will be devoted to discussion of him.

For most of the play there seems to be no one who is a match for Coriolanus or who can defeat him without the warrior's personality being the chief contributing factor. It turns out, however, at the climax of the play that Volumnia is not merely his match but a figure capable of controlling him. The role of Volumnia is not large, but Shakespeare reserves most of her potency for her one major scene (V. iii). We see her pride in her son and her attempts to tutor him earlier in the play, but the full force of her character comes in her appeal for mercy as we can see in the proportions of the scene. Shakespeare gives her the predominant share of the audience's attention. She is onstage with Coriolanus for 188 lines (V. iii. 22–209). Her son is about to overwhelm Rome, and she is making a last-ditch effort to avoid disaster. For several hundred lines, mostly in the absence of Coriolanus, we have heard of the mounting terror of the Romans and of the failure of appeals for mercy. The tide is turned by Volumnia who is given considerable space by Shakespeare to argue, confront, hector, pull out all the stops in handling what had seemed to be her unstoppable juggernaut of a son. Of the 188 lines she is onstage she speaks almost 100 of them and Coriolanus speaks nearly all of the rest. It is her extended speeches (94–125 (32), 131–82 (51)) which focus her power. They are two of the longest speeches in the play. There are only half a dozen or so other speeches in the play longer than 20 lines (II. ii. 80–120, III. i. 90–112, III. i. 140–61, IV. v. 66–102, IV. v. 102–36, IV. vii. 28–57, V. iii. 8–37). Volumnia is given, in two speeches, over 80 lines to frame her eloquent appeal which produces the stunning reversal of the play's climax. Only now is it possible to see the importance of the way Shakespeare develops the sequence during the absence of Coriolanus in producing this climax. For 438 lines no one could speak of anything else save the overwhelming force of Coriolanus to produce imminent destruction in Rome. Shakespeare uses almost every element in his play – plebeians, patricians, soldiers, servants, tribunes, enemies, friends – to bear witness to this warrior as a thunderbolt about to land in revenge. He reserves, however, Volumnia as Rome's secret weapon. She makes no appearance onstage during her son's absence and she is only referred to three times (V. i. 29, 71–3, V. ii. 78), once indicating a possible appeal from her. In fact, when Volumnia eventually appears before Coriolanus in V. iii she has been offstage since the conclusion of IV. ii for a total of 729 lines (22.1 per cent of the play). Her victory is a swift reversal of everything the audience has been led to expect for hundreds of lines and is accomplished in a matter of minutes from the moment she first speaks to him to his indication that she has prevailed (V. iii. 52–189 (138)). She appears in only 6 of the 29 scenes of the play. She speaks a total of 280 lines, and 98 of them

(35 per cent) are in her final and, to Coriolanus, fatal appearance. The scenes of his absence have built him up as an impregnable fortress, and yet Volumnia single-handedly breaches the fortress and emerges triumphant just as her son at the outset of the play had taken Corioles. Again and again the play demonstrates that he is a combination of overwhelming masculine force and child-like temper-tantrums alternating with submissive respect for his mother. On the three occasions he is defeated in the play, when the tribunes and (later) Aufidius arouse his irascible temper, and when Volumnia scolds him, the child within him is aroused and exploited at the expense of the man.

In his portrayal of politicians Shakespeare often makes a distinction between the public and private aspects of a man which relate to onstage and offstage versions of the self he manipulates. There is the heroic figure shaped for public consumption and the shrewd manipulator of that image working 'behind the scenes'. Prince Hal is the supreme exemplar of that skill in Shakespeare. At the opposite pole is Coriolanus. He has little capacity to distinguish between the onstage and offstage worlds of politics – what to show to the public and what to keep to himself. He can with difficulty bring himself to submit to the ceremony of the voices and to the mercy his mother demands of him. But his recoil in consequent self-disgust from his own or other's criticisms of the compromises he has made leads on one occasion to the fury which triggers his exile from Rome and on the other occasion to his death. He is incapable of concealing behaviour that is suitable only to the private 'offstage' indulgence of his friends. Lacking a private side he must stage himself to the view for, as Menenius puts it, 'His heart's his mouth./What his breast forges, that his tongue must vent' (III. i. 257–8). So for the audience, as for the characters, what we see of him onstage and what we hear about him offstage confirms that he is blessed and cursed in always being inescapably himself.

Index